DATE			

© THE BAKER & TAYLOR CO.

Auto Slavery

Class and Culture
A series edited by Milton Cantor and Bruce Laurie

Auto Slavery

The Labor Process in the American Automobile Industry, 1897-1950

David Gartman

Rutgers University Press
New Brunswick and London

Grateful acknowledgement is made to the following for permission to use previously published material:

Industrial Workers of the World: "Auto Slavery" by Louis Burcar, from the *Industrial Worker*, July 18, 1933. Copyright 1933 by the Industrial Workers of the World. Reprinted by permission of the Industrial Workers of the World, 3435 North Sheffield, Chicago IL 60657.

Antioch University: "Harmony?" by an anonymous poet, from Stanley B. Mathewson, *Restriction of Output Among Unorganized Workers*, Southern Illinois University Press, 1969. Copyright 1931 (renewed 1959) by Antioch University. Reprinted by permission of Antioch University.

Monthly Review Press: Material included in chapter 5 that originally appeared in a different form in the author's "Origins of the Assembly Line and Capitalist Control of Work at Ford," in *Case Studies on the Labor Process*, edited by Andrew Zimbalist, Monthly Review Press, 1979. Copyright 1979 by Andrew Zimbalist. Used by permission of Monthly Review Press.

JAI Press Inc.: Material included in chapter 6 that originally appeared in different form in the author's "Basic and Surplus Control in Capitalist Machinery: The Case of Mechanization in the Auto Industry," in *Research in Political Economy*, vol. 5, edited by Paul Zarembka, JAI Press, 1982. Copyright 1982 by JAI Press Inc. Used by permission of JAI Press Inc.

Library of Congress Cataloging-in-Publication Data

Gartman, David, 1950–
    Auto slavery.

    (Class and culture)
    Bibliography: p.
    Includes index.
    1. Automobile industry workers—United States—
History. 2. Automobile industry and trade—United
States—Automation—History. I. Title. II. Series.
HD8039.A82U645 1986   331.7'6292'0973   86-3798
ISBN 0-8135-1181-X
ISBN 0-8135-1104-6 (pbk.)

British Cataloging in Publication Information Available.

*For working people everywhere,
that they may dream of new, liberated ways
to organize their labor.*

*And for my mother and the memory of my father,
two working people who shaped
my own dreams of liberation more than
they will ever know.*

Auto Slaves
(Graveyard Shift—Stamping Plant)
By Louis Burcar

With the automatic movements timed to great
Machines, these metal-workers seem to reel
In some weird dance. Like marionettes they wheel
With insane music at a maddening rate.

Automatons . . . What if they learn to hate
Machines whose hungry maws demand a meal
Of metal—piece upon piece of sweat-stained steel?
They work. Monotony and madness wait . . . .

For these are human beings racked with pain,
Grotesquely hued by blue-green mercury lights . . .
Monotony within this noisy hell
Will breed maggots of madness in the brain—
Stop the tongue so it can never tell
Of torturing through these unending nights.

Contents

Contents

List of Tables

Preface

All intellectual work is a product of a specific time and place. This is no exception. This analysis of the automotive labor process is a product of my graduate studies at the University of California at San Diego during the mid and late 1970s. Compared to the euphoric campus days of the 1960s, these were sobering times, even for those of us working-class students who had been too busy trying to secure our mobility out of factories and refineries to be actively involved in the earlier movements. "The system" had not come crashing down with a few gleeful shoves. It was much stronger and more resilient than it appeared; it possessed deeply rooted social, cultural, and economic defenses that we had not anticipated. During the 1970s, many student radicals abandoned superficial slogans and facile rhetoric for in-depth analysis of the supports of the social system that we still hoped to change fundamentally.

The University of California at San Diego provided an intellectual atmosphere in which such serious critical analysis thrived. The presence on this young campus of such luminaries of the intellectual left as Herbert Marcuse, Frederic Jameson, and Herbert Schiller had a profound influence even on those of us who were not their formal students. They taught us that the capitalist system had entrenched itself not only in our economic and political institutions, but also in our art, literature, philosophy, communications, technology, science, and psyches. To root it out required, among other things, politically committed yet serious, thorough-going scholarly analysis. In the Sociology Department, where I studied formally, there were no luminaries of the left, but there were innovative and critical scholars, who were fundamentally challenging tired, encrusted sociological traditions. People like Aaron Cicourel, Joseph Gusfield, and Randall Collins created a lively, open, tolerant intellectual atmosphere within which a wide range of work flourished.

My work on the automotive labor process germinated in this fertile environment as my Ph.D. dissertation. The idea of analyzing the structure of work and technology as a socially biased artifact was inspired by Herbert Marcuse's work on technological rationality. But this basic idea was fundamentally molded by Harry Braverman's seminal work, *Labor and Monopoly Capital*. The flood of literature that followed in its wake exerted a profound influence on the project's development. Also instrumental in shaping my thinking in its formative stages was an unpublished paper by Norbert Wiley, whose concept of surplus power alerted me to the existence within organizations of repressive-control measures that have little to do with technical efficiency.

Numerous individuals are responsible for nurturing the nascent project through its slow, steady growth to maturity. To my teachers I owe an incalculable debt. Perhaps more than anyone, Randall Collins molded the project with his brilliant synthesis of conflict sociology as well as his relentless critique of my first stumbling formulations. I only hope that he can recognize his hand in the finished product. Joseph Gusfield provided exemplary guidance and support. The patience and freedom he afforded my work are rare commodities in the hustle of today's academic marketplace. And Bruce Johnson subjected my work to an untiring, incisive, selfless examination at every stage. Whatever precision and clarity I have achieved is undoubtedly due to his advice. Equally responsible for support and stimulation was a group of fellow students and close friends. Gregg Robinson, Ira Studin, Rick Nadeau, and Judy McIlwee created the atmosphere of intellectual challenge, personal support, and political commitment in which the project flourished. In addition to these, the following individuals generously provided helpful commentary on and encouragement for this work during its long journey to fruition: Richard Arneson, Stanely Aronowitz, David Brody, Andrew Feenberg, Paul Goldman, David Noble, Will Wright, Paul Zarembka, and Andrew Zimbalist.

The appearance of my original study in book form is due mainly to the generous assistance and efforts of Milton Cantor and Bruce Laurie. They recognized the value of this work long ago, submitted it to a penetrating critique, and worked tirelessly to bring it into print. My editor at Rutgers University Press, Kenneth Arnold, also provided invaluable assistance in steering the manuscript through the perilous publishing process relatively unscathed.

The personal debt I incurred with my family in the completion of this project is perhaps greater than the intellectual and professional ones. What this work owes to my wife, Betty Barnett Gartman, is impossible to calculate or express. Unlike many wives of academics, she did not write, type, edit, or even read in its entirety her spouse's book. She was much too busy with her own professional and political work. Yet her unflagging support—financial and personal—is written between every line on every page. More than any other single person, she is responsible for this book. And Greta Marie, who was born during the later stages of this project, helped in her own inimitable way. Her demanding presence was a continuous reminder of the indissoluble link between the personal and the political.

Finally, I extend ironic thanks to all those who raised obstacles to the realization of this project. The struggle to overcome them increased my determination and made my work stronger.

The errors and failings of this work are due in no small part to my stubborn resistance to the best advice of all these people. They are all mine.

Auto Slavery

CHAPTER 1
A Theory of the Capitalist Labor Process

For too long the critique and analysis of modern capitalist society has been infused and defused by technological fatalism. This ideology sees modern social development driven by an inexorable logic of technique. Our choices about production, government, even culture are said to be dictated by the neutral calculus of the most efficient means to shared ends. So if our work is fragmented and alienated, our government bureaucratic and demagogic, and our culture monotonous and meaningless, these are only the unintended results of our well-intentioned quest for efficiency and productivity in the service of all. Unless we are willing to trade our autos for horses and our impersonal bureaucrats for personal despots, there is little that can be done about these accompanying evils of efficiency.

This technological fatalism has formed the unspoken basis of most social-scientific analysis of industrial work. Social scientists have documented well the effects of our system of production: alienation, social isolation, powerlessness, anomie. But few have analyzed its causes. It is generally assumed, by "experts" and lay public alike, that work is organized in accordance with some universal technical imperatives that lie beyond the realm of social research.

The major aim of this study is to dispel the myth of technological fatalism and replace it with a model of social choice. The social maladies created by work organization in advanced capitalist society are not the unintended results of the application of some neutral techno-logic to public ends. Rather, they are in large part the intended results of industrial means chosen to further private inter-

1

ests. The choice of industrial techniques—both the mechanical hardware and the organizational software—is never a neutral, technical process. It is a social process, shaped by the social relations of the society in which production takes place.

A new conceptualization of the actual process of capitalist production has recently emerged that emphasizes this social determination of technique. Arising within a variety of disciplines, this theory is generally based upon an analysis of social classes drawn from Marxism. The mode of production of capitalism divides society into two principal classes that are necessarily conflictual and antagonistic. And these class antagonisms profoundly influence the technical choices in the labor process. The class of wage workers labors not for its own purposes and benefits, but for the enrichment of a small class of capitalist owners and managers. Therefore, workers generally resist attempts by capitalists and their managers to produce greater profits. In order to overcome this resistance, capitalists choose techniques that strip workers of their power. The alienation, isolation, and powerlessness of modern capitalist industrial organization are thus seen in this theory as intended effects, produced by the unequal social relations of capitalist society.

Although this new theory of the capitalist labor process adopts the general outlines of Marx's class analysis of capitalism, it self-consciously rejects much of orthodox Marxism's specific analysis of the labor process, which has a great deal in common with technological fatalism. This orthodox analysis interprets Marx's social theory as a brand of technological determinism that sees the technical forces of production as the driving force of history. Productive forces develop autonomously, according to a scientific rationality, and directly determine the rest of society and its historical development. The class or property relations of society are directly determined by technology—"the hand-mill gives you a society with the feudal lord; the steam-mill, society with the industrial capitalist." But because there is a lag in this determination, the newly developed productive forces come into conflict with surviving property relations. This contradiction between the forces and relations of production engenders class conflict, which ushers in new property relations adjusted to the new technology. The political implication of this orthodox interpretation of Marx has been a focus on changing the ownership of capitalist productive forces rather than the forces themselves, which are uncritically accepted as inevitable and efficient. Capitalism has built a wonderful productive apparatus, contend the defenders of orthodoxy, but it is used for the enrichment of the few. We intend to wrench it from the hands of these exploiters and put it to the service of the masses.[1]

The neo-Marxist analysis of the capitalist labor process refutes this orthodox interpretation of Marx. Although his writings contain definite strands of technological determinism, the corpus of his work reveals a more complex, dialectical theory of technology and production. In reality, Marx held that the labor process does not develop autonomously, but within a social framework of class relations. It is conflictual class relations, not some neutral technical rationality, that provides the impetus for the development of the techniques and organization of production. Therefore, the productive forces of capitalism embody in themselves a repressive social logic. Building a truly liberated society requires changing not only the ownership, but the very nature of these forces. Although threads of this interpretation of Marx have existed for years, they were first woven together into a coherent garment by Harry Braverman's seminal *Labor and Monopoly Capital*. Blending a warp of textual exegesis with a woof of empirical proof, Braverman weaves a powerful neo-Marxist analysis of the capitalist labor process.

BRAVERMAN'S NEO-MARXIST THEORY OF THE CAPITALIST LABOR PROCESS

Braverman builds his analysis on the assumptions of Marx's political economy. Human labor, in all societies, is the ultimate source of all value. With this unique resource, people alter the materials of nature to create products that meet their needs. The capitalist mode of production is distinguished from all other social organizations of production by the purchase and sale of the human ability to work, labor power, as a commodity. The actual workers are separated from the means of production, which are centralized in the hands of private owners, the capitalists. In order to gain a livelihood, workers must sell their only possession, labor power, to the capitalists, who then utilize it to produce commodities that may be sold for a profit.

Capitalists' achievement of this goal of producing profit or surplus value, however, is made problematic by the social relation of wage labor. Having sold their labor power to others, workers have no interest in the process of production. It is the capitalists' responsibility to turn the productive potential of purchased labor power into actual labor embodied in commodities. They must ensure that work

3

proceeds so as to produce a quantity and quality of commodities that yield a profit when thrown onto the market. Because wage workers do not share in the profits of production, they generally oppose capitalist attempts to wring the most work possible out of their labor power. The opposing interests of workers and capitalists turn the workplace into an arena of class conflict. In order to maximize surplus value, therefore, it becomes imperative for capitalists to seize absolute control of the labor process from workers.[2]

Braverman explains the development of the capitalist labor process as a progressive centralization of control by capitalists, driven by the imperative of maximizing surplus value under the social conditions of antagonistic class relations. He shows that virtually every aspect of the organization of production is tainted by this inherent social logic of capitalism. Even the rise of the factory is seen as a step toward capitalist control. Prior to this development, early capitalists attempted to avoid the problem of control with putting-out and subcontracting systems, which left the actual control of the labor process in workers' hands. But these production systems failed to realize the full potential of labor power because of irregular hours, slow pace, embezzlement, and resistance to innovation. The centralization of employment under one roof, that is, factory production, was an attempt by capitalists to achieve greater control. The concentration of all workers in one location made it easy for capitalists to impose long hours, a fast pace, and harsh discipline.[3]

Factory production also facilitated capitalist innovations in production techniques, one of the first of which was the division of labor. Braverman argues that the subdivision of unitary crafts into detailed tasks was not dictated by technical efficiency, but by the necessity of producing surplus value under antagonistic class relations. The detailed division of labor allowed capitalists to employ low-wage workers for the unskilled tasks of the craft, reserving for high-wage craft workers only skilled tasks. The overall cost of labor power was thereby lowered and the rate of surplus value increased. The division of labor also increased surplus value by enhancing capitalist control of work. Because it destroyed the skill and knowledge used by craft workers to control their work, minutely subdivided labor shifted control of the unskilled fragments of work into the hands of capitalists.[4]

Braverman argues that capitalists' attempts to transfer the skill and knowledge and thus the control of work from workers to themselves was also the main motive behind the scientific management movement. The sweeping changes introduced into the capitalist labor process by Frederick Taylor and his followers were not neutral attempts to improve work efficiency, but socially conditioned attempts to control a refractory working class under antagonistic capitalist relations. Prior to Taylor, managers sought merely to control the general setting of tasks, leaving their performance to workers. Taylor's scientific management introduced the notion of managerial control of the precise manner of task performance. Engineers and technicians gathered the detailed knowledge of work, its methods, and timing, that was traditionally in the sole possession of workers. This knowledge was then centralized in a planning department, where personnel close to management determined the exact timing and motions for each job in the shop. In this way, capitalists rendered workers powerless to control their work and hence to resist exploitation. Capital was thus better able to exploit the full potential of labor power, extracting greater and greater amounts of surplus value.[5]

The very tools of production are not exempt from contamination by the conflictual class relations of capitalism, according to Braverman. The machinery developed by capitalist industry is deployed within the labor process so as to favor capital in its battle against labor. In and of itself, machine development increases the productivity of labor and the potential for human control over work. But within the context of antagonistic class relations engendered by capitalism, machinery is used to divest the mass of workers of their control of work and to place it in the hands of capitalists. Because automatic machines build control of tool action into an inanimate mechanism, capitalists may use them to separate the mental from the manual tasks of work and to centralize the former in their hands. Workers are thus further stripped of the knowledge and skills with which they can struggle against the relentless capitalist drive for more work and more profit.[6]

DISTINGUISHING NEUTRAL AND BIASED TECHNIQUES

Harry Braverman's path-breaking analysis extricates the threads of technological determinism from Marxism by revealing the capitalist labor process to be the product of the social logic of conflictual class relations, not a neutral logic of technical efficiency. Yet despite its power and cogency, his work is plagued by gaps and ambiguities that subsequent writers in the Marxist tradition have pointed out. One of Braverman's ambiguities concerns the exact extent of the contamination of the labor process by capitalist social relations. Are all aspects of production in this mode of production influenced by the imperative of capital's domination of labor? Or do there exist some production techniques that are indeed neutral, determined solely by a technical logic of efficiency? Braverman does not give a clear answer. At some points he seems to claim that the entirety of capitalist production is infested with the social logic of domination. At others, he proclaims the neutrality of some techniques in and of themselves, holding that it is only their use that is determined by capitalist social relations. The latter position is particularly evident in Braverman's analysis of machinery. While arguing convincingly that the development of increasingly automatic machinery is a key weapon in capital's class struggle for control of work, he holds that the major motive behind mechanization is not class control, but the socially neutral attempt to increase the productivity of labor. It is only the capitalist use of this machinery after it comes into existence that is perverted: "it is not the productive strength of machinery that weakens the human race, but the manner in which it is employed in capitalist social relations."[7]

Subsequent neo-Marxist analysts have sought to clarify this ambiguity by distinguishing two different imperatives that are intertwined within the capitalist labor process—one neutral, the other socially biased. David Gordon, for example, separates the socially conditioned quest for class control of work from the neutral aim of maximizing physical output from a given input. The latter aim he labels quantitative efficiency and postulates that organizing productive resources so that they yield as many physical products as possible is desirable in any society. Within capitalism, however, this aim of increasing output per unit of input is used to further the accumulation of capital under the pressure of competition from other capitalists. Gordon labels the aim of increasing class control within the labor process qualitative efficiency and sees it operating only in class societies. A class society can continue to exist only if its production process reproduces the relations of class domination. In capitalism, this aim demands that capitalists seize complete control over the labor process under the pressure of class conflict with workers. The development of the capitalist labor process is the result of a combination of these two ends. Capitalists have available to them numerous quantitatively efficient production methods and choose from among these the ones that maximize qualitative efficiency, that is, their class control of the labor process.[8]

Gordon thus conceives of class control as a separate end of the capitalist labor process, distinct from the end of producing goods that yield surplus value. But this conception is inconsistent with the basically Marxist framework he employs, which holds that the sole motive of capitalist production is a drive for profit enforced by competition. Braverman's analysis is more consistent with this view, for it recognizes the capitalist control of the labor process as a means to the end of producing surplus value, not an end in itself. In order to maximize profit as demanded by competitive pressures, capitalists must seize control of the details of production from the workers, whose divergent interests ensure that they will not voluntarily work as fast and efficiently as possible. As Richard Edwards states in his analysis of class conflict and control of work, "the capitalist need not be motivated to control things by an obsession for power; a simple desire for profit will do."[9]

What distinguishes the neutral production techniques from those biased by the class relations of capitalism is not their intended purpose, but the means by which this purpose is accomplished. All production methods introduced by capital increase the production of surplus value by bringing the processes of work increasingly under human control. However, some forms of control increase surplus value merely by enhancing the productivity of labor; others, by repressing the antagonistic class relations of production. Marx himself recognized this twofold nature of capitalist control of the labor process.

> The driving motive and determining purpose of capitalist production is the self-valorization of capital to the greatest possible extent, i.e. the greatest possible production of surplus-value, hence the greatest possible exploitation of labour-power by the capitalist. As the number of the co-operating workers increases, so too does their resistance to the domination of capital, and, necessarily, the pressure put on by capital to overcome this resistance. The control exercised by the capitalist is not only a special function arising from the nature of the social labour process, and peculiar to that process, but it is at the same time a function of the exploitation of a social labour process, and is consequently conditioned by the unavoidable antagonism between the exploiter and the raw material of his exploitation. . . . If capitalist direction is thus twofold in content, owing to the twofold nature of the process of production which has to be directed—on the one hand a social labour process for the creation of a product, and on the other hand capital's process of valorization—in form it is purely despotic.[10]

Various scholars in the Marxist tradition have recognized this distinction between types of direction or control. Dan Clawson develops an argument in Marx's own words. Richard Edwards distinguishes between coordination and control; Andrew Friedman, between coordination and authority. Synthesizing and elaborating upon this work, I will use the terms repressive and nonrepressive control to refer to the same distinction. A certain amount of control is necessary in any large-scale production process, regardless of the relations of production, in order to coordinate and direct the actions of work and workers. I will label this nonrepressive control. Such control is a neutral instrument, which, under any social organization of production, increases the productivity of labor, that is, the quantity of products yielded by the same amount of labor in a given time. However, an additional amount of control is made necessary by the antagonistic relations of production of class societies. I call this repressive control. In the class society of capitalism, workers resist capitalist authority in the factory because production is also their exploitation—it is capitalists who reap the main benefits in the form of surplus value extracted from workers' labor. Workers thus struggle to curtail the extent of their exploitation. They resist attempts to intensify their labor (make them work harder) or extend the working day, for both mean more work for the same pay. And they may even resist capitalist attempts to increase the productivity of their labor, for even though doing so involves no more work, it may mean displacement and disqualification of human labor by mechanization. The greater the workers' control over the actual production process, the greater is their power to resist attempts to increase their exploitation. Thus, in order to expand the production of surplus value and meet their competition, capitalists must repress this class resistance by establishing a level of control over the labor process beyond that necessitated by mere productivity.[11]

The end of both types of control within capitalism is an increase in the production of surplus value. The distinction rests on the means through which this end is achieved. Nonrepressive control increases surplus value by increasing the productivity of labor, without affecting the social relations of production. Through the coordination and regulation of work and workers, it reduces the quantity of labor time required to produce a product, and would do so under any social organization of production. Repressive control increases surplus value solely by repressing the inherent tendency of workers to resist exploitation. It takes control of the labor process out of the hands of recalcitrant workers, thus allowing capitalists to extract from them more labor than they would voluntarily give up. Although this repressive control may in some instances further productivity by overcoming worker resistance to more productive methods, it increases the production of surplus value mainly by intensifying labor. With it, capitalists force workers to expend more effort in

8

the same time by speeding up the work pace and eliminating breaks and interruptions.[12]

The distinction between the two forms of control is analytic, not physical or organizational. In most cases it is impossible to say that this production technique—mechanical or organizational—is purely repressive, and that one, purely nonrepressive. Most techniques are a complex combination of both. And because it makes little difference to capitalists how their end of surplus value is achieved, they generally do not recognize this distinction. However, for those concerned with objectively determining the specific impact of social relations on the organization of the labor process and separating it from the effects of more universal, technical causes, this analytic distinction is crucial. It identifies class conflict as a crucial variable in determining the shape of the capitalist labor process. Marxist theory assumes an underlying tendency to conflict between labor and capital built into the very structure of capitalist production—workers and capitalists have opposing, structurally determined interests. But the realization of this tendency depends upon a number of other factors affecting the power of the opposing classes: product and labor markets, political relations, existing production techniques, class organization and consciousness. The theory thus explains changes in the capitalist labor process as due in large part to the level of class conflict, which in turn is explained by these other political and economic factors.

The degradation of work is thus the largely intended result, the conscious end, of changes in the labor process introduced by capital to repress class conflict. This does not mean, however, that capitalists always clearly anticipate this specific result of their production innovations. Their general, system-imposed motive is the production of more and more surplus value, and they seek to accomplish this end through whatever means possible. A particular alteration of the labor process may not originally be intended to deskill work and shift its control to capital. But, because of the antagonistic relations of production, once capitalists discover measures that have these effects, they will diffuse and utilize them consciously to repress worker resistance.

POLITICAL AND IDEOLOGICAL STRUCTURES

Another weakness that subsequent analysts have revealed in Braverman's seminal work is his exclusive concentration on the technical and economic aspects of the capitalist labor process. He focuses on changes in the technical organization of immediate work tasks: division of labor, Taylorization, mechanization. By changing work operations in this way, capital is able to deskill work and thus seize complete control over the labor process. Workers are cajoled into submitting to this degraded, mindless labor, he argues, by "powerful economic forces," namely, high wages and the destruction of other forms of labor organization.[13]

Braverman's exclusive focus on technical and economic aspects of class control has drawn fire from other analysts in the Marxist tradition. Transforming the technical relations of workers to physical production is not sufficient to achieve capitalist control of the labor process, they contend. Changes in the structures of power and ideology within the capitalist firm are also necessary. Capitalists use not merely economic inducements but also political coercion and ideological manipulation to secure the subordination of workers. Although these political and ideological structures of the factory may be based upon and bolstered by larger societal structures, they have their origin and impetus in the capitalist production process itself and its conflictual class relations.[14]

Neo-Marxists have therefore come to focus greater attention upon the organizational structures of command and compliance and the structures of subjective relations among and between workers and capitalists. One of the common findings of much of this research is that, in addition to centralizing the technical control of work, capitalists centralized and bureaucratized the political structure of the firm. Within large firms, the structure of issuing commands and enforcing compliance with them was historically transformed from a decentralized, personal, and brutal organization to a centralized, impersonal, rule-governed hierarchy. I follow the recent work of David Gordon, Richard Edwards, and Michael Reich in labeling the former power structure the drive system and the latter the bureaucratic system. However, Michael Burawoy's distinction between the despotic and hegemonic organization of the capitalist labor process seems to capture the same transformation. Under the drive system, the power to issue commands governing work and to enforce compliance with them was almost totally controlled by foremen on the shop floor. Due to their technical knowledge, they completely controlled the immediate work process. And their commands were enforced by their often brutal and arbitrary administration of sanctions under their control: hiring, firing, fines, layoffs, wages, and promotions. However, this power structure became increasingly problematic for big capital, largely because it created a unified worker resistance against the brutal regime. Shop-floor conflict, high labor turnover, and the industrial union movement all forced capital to seek alternative ways of exercising power over labor. Through a gradual process of trial and error, a new political structure was slowly created and consolidated, the bureaucratic system. Within this structure, control over work and workers was centralized away from the shop floor and into the hands of specialized rule-making departments. The immediate work process was controlled by specialized engineering or production departments, which set impersonal standards and rules to be enforced on the shop floor. Worker discipline was similarly centralized into personnel departments, which set policies governing hiring, firing, sanctions, wages, and promotions.[15]

Not only did the bureaucratic system give top management the power it needed to counter increasing worker resistance. It also served to defuse and deflect this resistance by altering the consciousness of workers. The bureaucratic power structure had the ideological effect of undermining the growing level of class consciousness. Richard Edwards observes that by depersonalizing the exercise of power—investing it in a structure rather than a person—bureaucratic control caused the basic capitalist-worker relation to fade from sight. The brutal, driving boss served as a dramatic focus of conflict and class consciousness. The diffuse structure refractioned conflict and consciousness. Michael Burawoy similarly argues that the system of rules generated consent to capitalist exploitation by causing workers to think of themselves, not as member of a class, but as individuals. The bureaucratic system constituted workers as "industrial citizens," as individuals with specific rights and obligations within a state-like legal structure. As a result of this altered worker consciousness, conflict was displaced from a general battle over capitalist relations as such to specific skirmishes over particular "laws" and standards.[16]

The divisive, individuating effect of the bureaucratic power structure was exacerbated by the creation of job ladders or internal labor markets. In large firms, capitalists artificially divided technically similar jobs and arranged them in a hierarchy differentiated by wages and status. Then rules were established to control the passage from lower to higher jobs. In this way, capital was able to overcome the growing class consciousness engendered by the leveling of skill differentials between workers. As neo-Marxist analysts like Edwards, Burawoy, Katherine Stone, and Howard Wachtel have documented, such job ladders undermined worker unity and generated competitive individualism by pitting workers against one another for promotion. These divisive effects of job hierarchies were further emphasized by superimposing upon them important status distinctions, namely, sex, race, and ethnicity. As Stanley Aronowitz and others have noted, the discriminatory confinement of minority groups to the lowest jobs created resentments and divisions within the working class that capital often manipulated to break a united class front.[17]

Recent analyses further reveal that wage and benefit policies cannot be treated simplistically in isolation from these emergent political and ideological structures, as Braverman tries to do. Wage measures instituted by capital are not mere quantitative increases in workers' consumption to buy off their resistance. Capitalists also use levels and forms of compensation to effect a qualitative change in workers' consciousnesses and personalities in order to get them to adapt to the new political and technical organization of work. The influential Italian Marxist thinker and partisan, Antonio Gramsci, wrote in the early 1930s that wage increases by Ford and other capitalists were aimed at creating a "new type of man suited to the new type of work and production process." He revealed that capitalists tied the new wages to the stabilization and rationalization of workers' consumption and work habits, which were required by the mechanized and bureaucratized labor process. Elaborating on this theme, Stone, Edwards, and Stuart Brandes have demonstrated the intentional use of profit-sharing and stock-subscription programs to shape worker habits and create the "true capitalist man." Capital also used incentive wages to stimulate individual ambitions and to break down workers' collective identity. Critical reinterpretations of industrial welfare work have also demonstrated a degree of conscious capitalist manipulation aimed at creating ideological ties between labor and capital. As Brandes' historical analysis shows, employers offered improved services, benefits, and working conditions largely in order to cultivate an identification between workers and the firm, thus breaking down antagonistic class identities.[18]

Even unions became part of this monolithic structure of capitalist control of the labor process, according to many neo-Marxist analysts. Burawoy, Aronowitz, Michel Aglietta and others have argued that after offering an initial challenge to capital, the industrial unions accomodated themselves to the bureaucratic system of industrial power—they became another tool of capitalist control. In return for organizational recognition and higher wages for their members, the unions assisted in enforcing employer policies on work standards, discipline, and job structure. Labor contracts guaranteed absolute capitalist control over technology, work standards, products, etc.

And union agreements reinforced the divisive job ladders by negotiating job classification and promotion procedures. In order to
accomplish this accommodation, union leaders and capitalists cooperated in bureaucratizing the structure of labor relations. The grievance and bargaining procedures were formalized and centralized in
order to defuse rank-and-file militancy and thus stabilize the accumulation of capital. The entire corporatist system of labor relations
was consolidated at the level of the state by a legal structure and a
bureaucratic enforcement machinery. An earlier generation of Marxist thinkers generally attributed this union accommodation to the
misleadership and opportunist ambitions of top labor leaders. However, the neo-Marxists have emphasized the structural constraints
upon the unions. The basic strength of the capitalist political economy after the Second World War and the overwhelming dominance
of corporate capital within it foreclosed any opening for organized
labor radicalism. If unions wanted to survive, they had to play the
only role open to them—that of stabilizer and controller of the commodity of labor power.[19]

DIALECTICAL DEVELOPMENT OF THE LABOR PROCESS

Most neo-Marxists agree upon this basic outline of the structure and
functioning of capitalist control over the labor process. However,
there has arisen a disagreement over the origins and development of
this control structure. One school argues that the development of
the capitalist-controlled labor process is the determinate realization
of the functional requirements of capitalism, while another stresses
a contingent, dialectical development driven by class conflict.

Harry Braverman's analysis of the capitalist labor process falls into
the functionalist school. He offers a picture of an inexorable and
unstoppable expansion of capitalist control—a creeping juggernaut
that gradually destroys all independent worker control and resistance. The force driving the juggernaut is capital accumulation.
The laws of producing surplus value engrained within capitalism
themselves dictate a divestment of all discretion and thought—all
subjectivity—from recalcitrant workers. And these workers are
powerless to stop the capitalist juggernaut. In Braverman's analysis,
workers are the passive, powerless objects of manipulation, ci-
phers in the equations of accumulation. They never fight back
or resist their domination and exploitation. We are given a history without contradictions, a structure without openings, in which

all are inevitably subsumed under the domination and exploitation. We are given a history without contradictions, a structure without openings, in which all are inevitably subsumed under the domination of the system.

Recent works on the capitalist labor process by Michael Burawoy and Michel Aglietta similarly depict its development as a gradual, noncontradictory realization of the laws inherent to the mode of production, although the laws they identify are different from Braverman's. For Burawoy, capitalist production requires not merely accumulation, but also legitimation. The capitalist labor process must secure surplus value by exploiting workers and simultaneously obscure this exploitation from workers' vision. This dual structural imperative of securing and obscuring surplus value drives the development of the labor process. In the early, competitive stage, capitalists adopted a despotic organization of work, securing surplus value through such coercive measures as firing, speed-up, and wage cutting. However, this despotic labor process made visible the exploitative relation between labor and capital and thus generated tensions and conflicts. In order to better obscure exploitation, capitalists in the monopoly stage developed a hegemonic organization of work, which produced consent by offering workers limited autonomy within the limits of capitalist control. This transition was not driven by class struggle or resistance, but by the requirements of the system. Burawoy does take class struggle into account, but merely as a secondary factor that facilitates rather than contradicts the immanent development of the labor process.

Michel Aglietta's structuralist study of the labor process shares the same functionalist logic—the laws of capitalism require a specific type of labor process, so it emerges. Aglietta, however, takes into account the requirements of capitalist consumption as well as production. Capitalism requires that workers be separated not only from the means of production, but also from the means of consumption. In the first stage of capitalism, the regime of extensive accumulation, workers were separated from the control of the means of production through the Taylorist labor process. But they remained united with their traditional means of consumption, which continued to be produced at home. This state led to an imbalance between the producer-goods and consumer-goods departments, whose rectification required that workers' means of subsistence be transformed into commodities. To accomplish this and to usher in the regime of intensive accumulation, a new Fordist labor process emerged, whose intensified assembly-line methods made workers' purchases

14

of commodities both more possible and necessary. Missing once again from the analysis is any major role for class struggle and resistance in the development of the labor process.[20]

This functionalist approach has come under strong criticism from those who view the development of the capitalist labor process as a dialectical process. Labeling this approach "capital-logic theory," Stanley Aronowitz argues that it completely ignores the subjective and cultural factors influencing this development. Braverman, Burawoy, Aglietta, and others depict the abolition of the historical subject under the crushing weight of the laws of capital accumulation. The working class is relegated to the status of a mere object within a labor process totally controlled by capital. To capital-logic theory, Aronowitz opposes a complex, dialectical theory, which recognizes the continued importance of class struggle. The subordination of all work and workers to capitalist control within the labor process is no more than a tendency. There are important forces countering this tendency, emerging from the subjective struggle of people. Workers are able to create a culture that sustains struggle and resistance against absolute capitalist domination. And this culture is often strengthened by the very development of the capitalist labor process that is supposed to completely crush such resistance. The capitalist labor process is contradictory. At the same time that it degrades and deskills individual workers, it also reorganizes workers into large, homogeneous, interdependent groups with a greater awareness of their class interests.[21]

This dialectical approach, which recognizes the importance of the interaction of capitalist laws and class struggle, seems superior to the functionalist approach. The laws of accumulation of capitalism exercise an important influence upon the development of the labor process, but this influence is mediated by class struggle. At any particular historical juncture, capitalists institute a specific form of accumulation, within which the labor process is the key element. This form gives rise to a particular structure of classes and resulting forms of class struggle, which often threatens continued accumulation. In order to continue to produce and realize surplus value under the laws of capitalism, capitalists attempt to overcome this struggle by introducing changes in the form of accumulation, the most important of which alter the labor process. These changes give rise to new forms of accumulation and class structure, which reconstitute class struggle and lead once again to changes in order to overcome it. Therefore, the development of the labor process under capitalism is not a gradual emergence of functional requirements, but a dialectical development in which capitalists are forced to constantly revolutionize production methods in order to overcome the struggle of workers generated by the contradictory class structure.

Such a dialectical approach is followed by Gordon, Edwards, and Reich in their recent analysis of the historical transformation of labor in the United States. They analyze the history of U.S. capitalism into three overlapping stages, each of which is characterized by a particular structure of accumulation, the key element of which is the labor process. Each structure of accumulation has a dialectical life cycle. After an initial period of successful accumulation, the institutions begin to generate contradictions that exacerbate class struggle. This struggle causes capitalists to introduce new forms of labor organization to overcome it and renew the upward cycle of accumulation. The first stage was that of initial proletarianization, during which a supply of wage workers was first created from a previously nonproletarian population. Lasting from the 1820s to the 1890s, it was marked by a wide variety of labor processes, many of which left considerable control to workers. However, this worker control stood in the way of accumulation in an increasingly competitive economy, leading capitalists to search for new forms of labor control. This search resulted in the consolidation of a new structure of accumulation in the stage of the homogenization of labor, lasting from the 1870s until World War Two. Workers were controlled through the drive system, whose principal components were mechanized and deskilled work and powerful foremen. But this labor process generated greater resistance among a unified and homogeneous work force, leading capitalists to introduce changes giving rise to the new stage of labor segmentation. In this contemporary period, which began around 1920, the drive system was replaced by a bureaucratic system of structured rules and incentives, which segmented the working class both within and between firms.[22]

APPLICATION

Neo-Marxists have developed a powerful theory for the analysis of the capitalist labor process. It holds that the methods of organizing capitalist production are profoundly influenced by the conflictual class relations of this society. Although some methods are nonrepressive, increasing surplus value by enhancing productivity, many others are clearly repressive, increasing surplus value by repressing the resistance of an exploited working class. However, despite their best efforts, capitalists cannot totally repress the conflictual class relations of capitalism. In fact, many of the measures introduced to quell conflict have the contradictory effect of organizing and exacerbating it.

The following study of the labor process of the American automobile industry attempts to apply these theoretical insights to the industry that laid the foundation for modern mass production. Over the course of half a century, automotive capitalists and managers gradually transformed the production of autos from a process in which skilled, knowledgeable craft workers exercised considerable independence and autonomy into one in which unskilled, detail workers were enslaved to mechanical and organizational masters. I seek to prove that this transformation of auto work was motivated in large part by conscious attempts to overcome the resistance of an exploited and recalcitrant work force.

Although my analysis thus takes the conflict of labor and capital as a major variable in explaining the development of the production process, the empirical focus is mainly on capital. I concentrate on the actions and motives of automotive capitalists and managers in shaping the labor process—specifically, the ways they perceived worker resistance and took steps to overcome it. My justification for this focus is both practical and theoretical. Practically, I could not do justice to both sides of the conflict in one study. Recent labor scholarship has begun to fill out the historical record of American auto workers. But a similarly detailed account of industry capitalists and managers is missing. Theoretically, this focus is justified by the assumption that within capitalist systems, capital is generally the initiator of economic action. The institutional distribution of power in such societies makes capitalists and managers the initiators of policies that shape the labor process. Labor is generally the reactive party, responding to capital's production policies. These reactions, however, then shape and modify subsequent capitalist measures.

Further, my study focuses primarily at the micro-level of the capitalist firm. At this level, the systematic imperative to maximize surplus value is brought to bear on capitalists, who make intentional decisions that shape the labor process. And it is also at this level that capitalists first encounter the struggle of workers against their exploitation. Therefore, the principal dialectic shaping the development of the capitalist labor process is located at this micro-level of the capitalist firm. Other macro-level forces like the state and culture also influence this development. But their influence is secondary and generally limited within a framework of problems and possibilities defined by the capitalist firm.

The following chapters thus concentrate on how automotive capitalists and managers, in their attempts to produce a profit in a social
environment of conflictual class relations, shaped the labor process
in the formative years of the industry, from its beginning until 1950.
An initial examination of the origins of the industry in chapter 2 reveals the predominance of a craft method of production that left
considerable control over work in the hands of skilled workers. This
worker control became an obstacle to production for a new mass
market. Auto capitalists were thus motivated to seize control over
the process through the division and mechanization of work, a process detailed in chapters 3 through 7. However, as chapter 8 makes
clear, this technically reorganized labor process contained various
contradictions that actually exacerbated class conflict. Auto capitalists were thus forced to institute new bureaucratic control measures,
which are described in chapters 9 through 11. The unionization
drive, which represented the culmination of the contradictions of
the labor process, briefly challenged capitalist control of work. But,
as is argued in chapter 12, the union was gradually forced to accommodate itself to the system of bureaucratic control.

Taken together, these chapters tell a story not of technological inevitability but of social repression—of degradation, dehumanization, domination, and alienation of workers. This is the story of
auto slavery.

CHAPTER 2
Work, Workers, and Workers' Control in the Early Auto Industry

The rough engine casting is loaded by two workers onto the end of a track that winds its way back and forth across the vast, sparsely populated floor of the shop. Isolated at intervals along the track stand workers, monitoring the invisible forces that manufacture engines from behind panels of switches and telltale lights, whose strange red glow turns human faces into monstrous caricatures. The loaded casting mysteriously comes to life, advancing slowly down the track and jerking to a halt at the first station. Here a set of whirling millers reach out, shave off a precise amount of metal, and retract, leaving brilliant surfaces where dull gray had just been. This job finished, the engine block jerks to life, advances to the next station, turns itself on its side, and receives another set of reaching cutters. Having advanced through several such stations, the engine again jerks to a halt, turns itself over, shaking out a flood of bright metal chips, and is bathed in a cloud of steam. Satisfied with its cleanliness, it moves on to a drilling station, where an army of spinning fingers reaches out from all directions and pokes precise holes at carefully spaced intervals. Relentlessly forward the engine winds, jerk by jerk, as if controlled by some rough god. Through millers, drillers, borers, grinders, reamers, washers, taps, and broaches it moves, until it emerges as a completely machined engine block at the end of the line. During it all the few workers passively stand, watch, monitor, wait, and only rarely assist the mechanical master that performs the work.

This is the scene that would greet us if we walked onto the floor

19

of a modern factory for the manufacture of automobile engines. The machine described is an automatic transfer line, and it performs all of the machine work upon engine blocks with almost no direct human intervention. Such a high degree of automation in manufacturing is not, of course, unique to the contemporary automobile industry. Similar and higher levels of automation can be found in steel, petrochemicals, food, electronics, and other industries. What is unique about the auto industry is not its current level of automation, but the innovative role it has played in automatic manufacturing processes. The auto industry of the United States has been at the forefront of technological innovation in manufacturing since its beginning. In fact, more than any other single industry, automobiles have been responsible for that unique, modern system of manufacturing that is the basis for contemporary automation— mass production.

Mass production is the manufacture of large quantities of standardized products through the precise mechanical production and assembly of interchangeable parts. In such a system, the responsibility for the integrity of the final product is removed from the skilled hands of craft workers, where it had previously resided, and vested in an intricately interrelated system of simplified, mechanical operations performed by unskilled workers. The American automobile industry was not, of course, singularly responsible for this modern system of production. It was preceded by hundreds of years of experimentation with standardized, divided, mechanical production. The immediate precursors of mass production, who began to assemble the separate principles into a system, are familiar names in American history. Eli Whitney, producing muskets for the army by assembling interchangeable parts manufactured on specialized machinery; Samuel Colt, turning out thousands of revolvers a year with minutely divided labor and highly specialized machines; Cyrus McCormick, manufacturing farm equipment on a continuous production line—these were the innovators who laid the foundations for this revolution in production. But the industry most responsible for erecting the actual structure of mass production upon this solid foundation was automobiles, which, standing at the culmination of a long period of gestation, synthesized isolated, preexisting elements into a systematic method of production.[1]

Due to its innovative role, the American automobile industry is thus the key case to examine in deciphering the hows and whys of this revolution in the labor process. Was mass production the inevitable development of a neutral, universal techno-logic, which ensures the most efficient production of goods? Or was this monumental change in production at least partly the result of a historically specific socio-logic? Did the antagonistic class relations inherent in capitalism leave their indelible mark upon the deepest foundation of this method of organizing society's labor? A careful examination of the industry at the vanguard of this revolutionary change should help to answer these questions.

ORIGINS OF THE AMERICAN AUTO INDUSTRY

Although preceded by many years of laborious invention and experimentation with motor vehicles, the origin of the manufacture of vehicles for sale on the market is generally dated a few years prior to the beginning of the twentieth century.[2] Before 1897, a few American firms had been established for the commercial production and sale of motor vehicles. Their products, however, were not actually manufactured in any volume, but continued to be the unique products of individual mechanics and tinkerers, built one by one upon no systematic basis. The year 1897 saw the beginnings of the first firms truly to manufacture motor vehicles. In this year Alexander Winton launched the Winton Motor Carriage Company as a spin-off from his successful bicycle company of Cleveland. The Pope Manufacturing Company of Hartford, Connecticut, the largest bicycle manufacturer in the U.S., also entered the industry with the production of an electric-powered vehicle. But perhaps the most important event of this year was the founding of the Olds Motor Vehicle Company of Detroit by Ransom E. Olds as a spin-off from his father's machine shop.

These pioneer firms well illustrate a characteristic common to nearly all firms in the early auto industry—their construction on a preexisting base of capital and manufacturing facilities. Because of the conservatism and skepticism of traditional investment sources, completely new auto manufacturing firms were rare. The more common pattern was the addition of an automobile line to an existing manufacturing operation as an attempt at product diversification. Businesses predominating in this process were machine shops, bicycle manufacturers, and carriage and wagon manufacturers. All had products and manufacturing processes similar to automobiles and could thus undertake their production conveniently with existing capital, plant facilities, and labor. But the most important of these industries was clearly bicycles. The decline of the bicycle boom in the last years of the nineteenth century left large amounts of capital, equipment, and skilled labor searching for profitable use. Automobiles were a natural choice. Not only were the two vehicles very similar mechanically, but they also required similar work processes for their manufacture—the production of metal parts by skilled machinists on machine tools and their assembly by skilled mechanics. As a result, the American automobile industry was built largely with the technical, mechanical, financial, and labor resources of bicycle manufacture.

The early auto industry could not, however, utilize many of the valuable production innovations of the bicycle industry because of the limited market for its product. The large demand for relatively cheap bicycles had provided the basis for steps toward mass production. But the early automobiles were extremely expensive, and their market was confined to the wealthy, in whose hands they became objects of sport and conspicuous consumption rather than practical transportation. With prices ranging from one thousand dollars to twelve thousand dollars, the products of the infant industry were well beyond the financial reach of the great majority of Americans. And this limited market clearly inhibited the imitation of the steps toward mass production that had been taken by other industries. Specialized machinery, large plant facilities, a large work force—all of these requirements of mass production were expensive, and few early automobile manufacturers were willing or able to risk such a large investment on a small and uncertain market.[3]

WORK IN THE EARLY SHOPS

Due to these market limitations, the early automobile firms generally produced on a very small scale. And while firms associated with an established bicycle or machine shop had sufficient capital and facilities to undertake the complete manufacture of an automobile, the common practice among the less-endowed infant companies was merely to assemble vehicles out of purchased parts. These firms purchased, often on credit, a chassis and body from a carriage maker, an engine and transmission from a machine shop, tires from a rubber company, wheels from a manufacturer of bicycle or carriage wheels, and so on. Then they merely assembled these parts into the vehicle. This method of production had the advantage of requiring little capital investment in expensive machine tools, shop space, and skilled labor. Henry Ford, for example, founded his Ford Motor Company in 1903 with a work force of only eight, composed of himself, a shop assistant, three skilled mechanics, a pattern-maker, a draftsman, and a blacksmith. They worked in a tiny shop equipped with only a few universal machines: two lathes, two drill presses, a milling machine, a wood planer, a grinding wheel, and a forge.[4]

Final Assembly

The main work process in these tiny shops of the infant auto industry was that of assembly. A small work force used a few crude machines and much handwork to assemble a myriad of often incompatible parts produced by dozens of separate firms into some semblance of a functioning motor vehicle. Such work was not suited to fumbling, second-rate mechanics. Only craftsmen[5] of the highest skills could turn the heap of parts into a running machine.

> The early automobile was essentially a hand-made mechanism. Personal craftsmanship entered into it to a great degree. When first built, it was made up of a variety of parts drawn from a dozen different sources. Because of errors in specification and because of further inaccuracies in fabrication the percentage of misfits was enormous; hence the extensive use of craftsmanship in order to obtain a working machine from a collection of dissimilar and inaccurate parts.[6]

As a writer for *Machinery* magazine stated upon visiting the Chalmers-Detroit Motor Company in 1909, "the highest class of skilled mechanics must be employed" in assembly.[7]

The usual assembly practice was to place the metal frame of the car, once it had been assembled, upon several wooden horses or metal stands that held it two to three feet off the ground. To each frame was assigned a gang of two to five workers, who labored together to build up the car on the spot from a pile of parts to a running mechanism. Henry Ford stated of this early assembly process that "we simply started to put a car together at a spot on the floor and workmen brought to it the parts as they were needed in exactly the same way that one builds a house."[8] The parts were generally placed in a central storeroom after having been received and inspected. And various members of the assembly gang journeyed back and forth to the storeroom to pick up the parts as they were needed. Heavier parts, such as the motor and transmission, were transported by small hand-pushed trucks. Near the assembly location there was usually a workbench, where workers kept their standard tools and performed various necessary operations. Perhaps the most frequently used tool—and one that aptly symbolizes this early labor process—was the file. With it, workers slowly and laboriously shaped the metal parts so they would fit together properly. For special tools and equipment necessary for their work, workers made frequent trips to the central toolroom of the shop, set up to keep tabs on the expensive equipment.[9]

An immense amount of detailed and intricate handwork was required in this early assembly, involving much alteration or repair of parts that did not fit, and much drilling, riveting, and bolting to fasten the parts together. Numerous items had to be separately adjusted: exhaust, muffler, tail pipes, brakes, brake rods, wheels, tires, levers, dashboard, windshield, fenders, etc. Therefore, work proceeded very slowly. One auto worker who had been employed assembling cars in the early days of the Packard Company reported that it took two workers three-and-a-half days to turn out a complete car.[10]

It is evident from the description of this early labor process of automobile assembly that the skilled workers were themselves largely in control of their own work. Because of their knowledge and skills, the successful completion of the assembly depended entirely on them. It was impossible at this stage to dispense with such skilled workers by the division and specialization of labor. As long as the imperfect parts required fitting and adjustment, work had to remain unitary. The workers had necessarily to keep in mind the peculiarities of each part and to adjust subsequent parts and operations accordingly as they proceeded. If labor had been divided, workers on subsequent operations would have had no knowledge of what had been done previously, and consequently they would scarcely have been able to make allowances. The result would have been a worthless conglomeration of parts.

Parts Manufacture and Assembly

The early auto manufacturing firms did not rest content with a labor process that involved merely the assembly of parts manufactured by others. A trend toward more integrated production became evident as early as 1903. The trend was the result of several pressures. While the system of assembling purchased parts required a small investment and was easy to manage, it left the firm little control over its supplies. The failure or delay of a consignment could slow or completely halt the entire operation right in the middle of the rush season, which could spell disaster for the small, struggling firm. Further, the assembly of purchased parts usually produced a car of questionable quality. Despite the best efforts of the skilled crafts- men, the widely variant natures of the design, material, and ma- chining of parts purchased from outside suppliers made the early cars highly unpredictable and unreliable. A trip of any distance over a few blocks that did not require at least some minor repairs was un- heard of. Driving these cars was better suited to the adventuresome than those in search of reliable transportation. In order to expand the market for automobiles, as well as to compete better with rival firms, it was necessary to improve their quality, which required tighter control over the design, material composition, and manufac- ture of parts. Thus, auto producers were driven by the uncertainties of supply and the sagging quality of their products to undertake the production of their own parts.[11]

The early manufacture of parts by auto firms was generally con- fined to the various metal parts making up the motor, transmission, and frame of the automobile. The manufacture of bodies, as well as various accessories like tires, wheels, and electrical parts, was as yet left to outside suppliers. In effect, then, the early venture into parts manufacture usually meant the addition of a foundry, a forge shop, a machine shop, and, only later, body and trim shops to the rudi- mentary assembly and inspection rooms of the early auto shops. In the foundry and forge shop, metal parts were roughly formed, by casting molten metal into sand molds in the former, by hammering metal into die forms in the latter. From there, both castings and forgings went to the machine shop, where various machine tools were used to cut the metal parts into finished forms, suitable for assembly. In the body and trim shops, wood, leather, paint, and cloth were worked into an attractive outer shell for the mechan- ism. These shop additions did not, however, alter the basic nature of the labor process. In all of these additional processes, highly skilled workers were required to ensure the successful completion of parts production.

Forge shop and foundry. Most of the early shops that merely as- sembled autos had a blacksmith to hammer recalcitrant parts into shapes more accommodating to assembly. But for the later purpose of large-scale manufacture of metal auto parts, the blacksmith's hammer, muscle, and anvil were replaced by the forging machine. This was a steam-powered mechanism with a huge, heavy, solid- metal ram or hammer, which dropped onto a base holding a die, a metal block with the desired form sunken into it. The forge operator usually heated the metal part to be formed—although cold forging was also done—held it with metal tongs upon the die, and pushed the trip switch, causing the ram to fall and force the part into the die.

Although the machine and the die replaced some of the blacksmith's skill in forming the metal, the early forge operator remained a highly skilled worker. Because the low volume of production prevented the specialization of forges for specific parts, the operator had to change and adjust the die for each different part forged. This required great skill. Further, the proper heating of the metal between forging operations to relieve internal stress was determined solely by the operator's skill. Over the course of years of training and experience, he became able to judge the temperature of the metal by its color, and knew what temperature was necessary to attain a certain strength and tensility for each type of metal. Finally, the proper placement of the part on the die was due solely to the worker's skill. One slip and the part was rendered worthless.[12]

The degree of worker skill and discretion over work was similar in the early foundries. Here the metal of numerous parts was given its initial rough shape by being cast in molds. The work process here was complex and mainly skilled. First, the patternmaker hand-carved a wooden or metal replica of the part to be cast, following a blueprint or drawing. This was probably the most highly skilled craft in the early auto shops, requiring an extensive apprenticeship. Using only a few simple hand tools, numerous measuring instruments, and the blueprints, the patternmaker turned a block of wood or metal into a three-dimensional reproduction of the part, exactly to specification. More of an art than a manufacturing trade, this delicate process was completely controlled by the skill of the craftsman.

In the next step of producing a casting, a molder used the pattern to make a sand mold of the part. To do so, he took the pattern, placed it in a casting box or flask, and packed sand around it to make a perfect impression. This work was very complex and highly skilled. The molder first mixed the sand, attaining a properly proportioned mixture of new sand, old sand (previously used in molding), and a gluey material. Next, he carefully placed the pattern in the flask and rammed or packed the sand in around it. The ramming had to be done uniformly in all directions or the casting would be irregular in shape. The molder then took out the pattern, repaired the mold if it was damaged in the process, and cut the air vents and gates. Next, he properly located the cores, solid forms made of sand that were placed inside the mold to make hollow areas in the casting. The cores were formed in molds by separate workers, coremakers, and baked in ovens. After the molder had securely wired the cores into position, he fitted the top of the flask (the cope) over the bottom (the drag) and secured the two pieces together. This complex process had to be repeated for every part cast, for a mold could be used but once.

Only the most highly skilled workers, with years of apprenticeship training and experience, could successfully complete a mold. This was especially true of the all-important mold for the engine cylinder, which formed the very heart of the automobile. Thus, one early writer warned manufacturers against trying to cut costs by replacing skilled molders with cheap help, or by underpaying the skilled workers.

> The matters of the tempering of the sand, venting, placing of the cores, gates and accurate matching of the flask parts are "up to" the molder. If cheap help is employed, and these important parts of the work slighted, the results will be such as to show the cause plainly. Tempering the sand, which means no more than mixing the proper quantity of old and new, and keeping the whole properly wetted, is directly "up to" him, and if lazy or underpaid, he will shirk it. If this is slighted the castings will show it.[13]

The message is clear. Molding is skilled work, and the accuracy of the casting lies within the discretion of the molder. He controls the work, so do not mistreat him or try to replace him with unskilled labor. The results will be disastrous.

Preparing the molten metal to pour into the molds was also a highly skilled task. The chief founder was given this responsibility. He charged the furnace with scrap or pig iron, smelted the iron, refined and dephosphorized the charge, added carbon, manganese, nickel, removed the slag, brought the metal up to a given temperature, and tapped the furnace into pouring buckets. All of these tasks depended largely on empirical skills developed through watching and doing and little on scientific instruments and measurements. Other jobs in the early foundries necessary for completing the casting process were pouring the metal into the molds, shaking the castings out of the molds, and various rough finishing processes on the castings. Most of these were performed by semiskilled or unskilled laborers.[14]

Machine shop. In the expanded parts-producing automobile firms, undoubtedly the addition most responsible for the accuracy and reliability of the finished product was the machine shop. Here the rough castings and forgings were finished to precision parts with the use of metal-cutting machine tools. And nowhere was highly skilled labor more important. For even though there were machines that to a certain extent aided the human eye and hand in their tasks, skilled machinists were necessary to operate these machine tools of the early shops and ensure their proper and accurate functioning. This was due both to the state of the art of machine tools at this time and the volume of production of the auto firms.

In the early years of the twentieth century, machine tools were far from the massive, precision, electrically driven, automatic instruments that they would become just three decades later. These early machines were generally much smaller, lighter, and much less rigid, resembling more a table with a mechanism on top than a massive, solid block of steel. They were driven not by individual electric motors, but by a central power source, to which each machine in the shop was connected by a web of shafting and belting. In terms of precision, numerous weaknesses prevented the mechanism itself from ensuring precise tool guidance: inaccurate chain or screw feed, imprecise gearings and cams, unstable cross-slides and carriages, and weak tool steels. Because these early machine tools left much to be desired from the standpoint of precision, accurate production depended upon the skill of their operators.

Furthermore, although there were available at this time certain specialized machine tools, which were inalterably constructed to do one specific metal-cutting job and could hence be operated by less skilled workers, the small auto firms could not make use of them. Small volume of production militated against the use of these specialized machines, which would have had to stand idle much of the time for lack of work. Thus, early auto manufacturers were forced to use universal or general-purpose machine tools, which could be adapted to do a wide variety of different work, but required skilled operators.[15]

These universal machine tools of the early auto shops were basically power tools with hand controls. To the simple tool had been added a physical framework that limited and guided its motion. For example, the simple drill was mounted in a drill press, a metal frame that limited its movement to a defined vertical path. However, the application of the tool to the work piece within these mechanical limits was directed by the operator. He controlled the amount of action, its duration, and its direction relative to the work piece. For example, the drill-press operator had to properly clamp the piece to be drilled on the work table, lower the drill by the hand wheel, and hand-feed the drill into the work, determining the speed at which the metal was cut. Too rapid a feed could cause burning of the metal by excess friction, distortion of the hole, or breakage or premature dulling of the drill.[16]

These universal machines required not only skilled guidance during operation, but also skilled set-up before work began. Setting up the machine tool was the process whereby the machinist adjusted the machine to do a specific type of work. These machine tools had a broad range of capabilities, and it was up to the machinist to select from this range the proper setting for each type of work. Among other things, setting up the work involved selecting the tool, mounting it, selecting the tool speed, adjusting the angles of tool rests and slides, and setting the flow of lubricants to the tool. To accomplish these complex tasks, it was necessary for machinists to be able to read blueprints of the parts they were to produce. Besides operation and set-up, skilled machinists were also assigned the tasks of routine maintenance of their machines: cleaning, oiling, tool sharpening. These workers also inspected their output to make sure it conformed to specifications.

All of these tasks required machinists of the highest skill. They had to be thoroughly familiar with the machinery with which they worked, its capabilities and limitations. The same was true of the materials they worked on. These machinists had to know the proper tools, speeds, and feeds for the various types of metal, and be able to change these variables quickly due to the variant and unreliable nature of the materials. And these skills were not theoretical, not formulated into a precise body of written rules and laws. They were largely empirical, gained mainly through long apprenticeship training and experience in watching and doing work itself. Machinists' skills were a series of a thousand little knacks, jealously guarded and transmitted from generation to generation. Workers learned intuitively to "feel" if the tool was getting dull, if the tool speed was too fast, if the casting was of poor quality. Thus, in the early auto machine shops, the workers remained the masters of the machine. The accuracy and precision of the work they turned out was entirely within their discretion.[17]

Not only the nature of the machines, but also their placement in the shop, made for worker discretion within the machine shop. At first, all the different types of machine tools were simply placed in a largely random fashion in a single room. But as the early auto factories expanded and added more and more machines, manufacturers faced the problem of their proper grouping or arrangement. The generally accepted practice in the smaller machine shops, like those of the auto industry, was grouping machinery by the function or process it performed, which was called functional or process layout. Thus, all grinding machines were grouped into a separate department, as were milling, boring, lathe operations, etc. The alternative method of layout was by purpose or product, that is, all machines devoted to the production of the same product were grouped together. But this method was feasible only when the volume of production on that particular product or part was sufficient to keep machines solely devoted to its production continuously occupied. At this early stage, the relatively low volume of the auto industry prevented the use of this type of layout.

The functional layout of the early machine shops gave auto workers a great deal of discretion and control over their own work. In some early shops, the production of an entire part was assigned to a specific worker. It was his task to perform all the various machining operations necessary to produce a finished part ready for assembly. Such workers were necessarily free to move about the shop floor, visiting the various functional departments as they deemed necessary in the course of their work. Later, it became common practice to confine workers to one machine department, where they performed only operations on its machines, and to move the parts from one department to another. But this arrangement still left a great deal of discretion to workers, for they worked at a number of different machines and production tasks largely as they saw fit.[18]

Subassembly work. The assembly of these parts produced in the machine shop into subassemblies to form the components of the final assembly process was also a unitary, skilled labor process over which the workers themselves asserted considerable control. Smaller parts were assembled at workbenches, to which all the necessary parts and tools were delivered. Larger subassemblies like the engine were usually assembled on stands constructed to accommodate them. However, in both instances these subassembly jobs were like their counterparts in final assembly, performed by first-class mechanics. Even the parts manufactured by the auto firms themselves left much to be desired in terms of precision and accuracy. They still required much hand-fitting to be assembled into accurate products. Take, for example, the assembly of the motor, in which the closest tolerances in the shop were required. The motor assembler had to lap (polish with a fine abrasive) each cylinder by hand to match the variable pistons. Valves were hand-ground and seated. And each crankshaft bearing was hand-scraped to ensure a close fit with its corresponding crankshaft pin. Such variant and skilled processes could not be divided and standardized. Work had to remain unitary so the assembler could take into account and adjust for earlier variations and discrepancies in later work.[19]

Body and trim shops. Among the last additions made to the more integrated automobile manufacturing firms were the body and trim shops. Manufacturers delayed production of their own auto bodies because of the high overhead costs and the large number of skilled workers required. Originally, the auto industry inherited its body-building methods from the carriage industry. Thus, the construction of early all-wood automobile bodies was a woodworking art. Carpenters used hand tools and a few woodworking machines to shape rough wood stock into parts for the body. Then carriage workers carefully hand-fitted these parts together into a body frame, which they then covered with wooden panels. Each of these jobs required the highest of woodworking skills.

After these workers had completed the basic wooden body, it was turned over to the paint department. Here, skilled workers using slow-drying varnish paints took an entire month to complete one body. They sanded the body and then hand-applied as many as fifteen coats of finish with brushes. After each separate coat, the body was meticulously sanded and/or rubbed and touched up. After the next-to-the-last coat of clear varnish had been rubbed and polished, a handsome striping job was applied by the highest-paid workers in the shops. Then the body was finish-varnished, dried, and sent off to the upholstery shop. Here, skilled upholsterers and leather workers applied their great skills to handcrafting and fitting seats and panels to finish the interior. Trim workers also busied themselves fitting the body with incidental accessories: dust pans, tool boxes, running board shields, head lamps, and luggage racks.

In 1909 some of the skills of the woodworkers in the body shops were eliminated when the Fisher Body Corporation of Detroit replaced the wooden body panels with pressed sheets of aluminum and steel as a covering for the wooden frame. These sheets could be stamped out in dies on huge presses, similar to the forging machines. But workers of considerable skill were required to operate them. And considerable handwork—snipping, filing, welding—was still necessary to fit the pressed metal sheets together over the frame. On the whole, the body and trim shops remained for many years the sanctuary of skilled workers who were in virtually complete control of their own work.[20]

WORKERS' CONTROL OF THE EARLY LABOR PROCESS

The highly skilled nature of work in these early shops of the automobile industry left a great deal of control over the immediate pro-

31

duction process in the hands of the workers. It was they, not the capitalists or their managers, who determined the details of auto work—what was done, when, and how fast. Because of the highly variant and unstandardized nature of this early labor process, it was impossible for owners or their agents to issue detailed production commands. The uncertain elements of work necessarily remained within the discretion of workers, who employed their skills and knowledge to make important production decisions. In the words of the early auto capitalists themselves, auto work was dependent upon the "human element" or the "personal equation."

This is not to say, of course, that workers ruled the early auto shops. Although capitalists did not directly control the immediate labor process, they exerted considerable power over the process of production as a whole. As owners of the means of production, they made decisions about general investments and resource allocation. They determined the location and scale of production, production technology, product type and design, and the marketing of products. And they exerted general control over workers by determining the conditions of the purchase of their labor power: wages, hours of work, hiring, firing. This power of early auto capitalists was sufficient to allow them to subordinate work and workers to their aim of producing a profit. Yet, as long as workers exerted virtual control of the immediate labor process, they had the power to defend themselves against capitalist attempts to arbitrarily increase their exploitation.[21]

The obstacle to complete capitalist control over exploitation and accumulation erected by workers' control of immediate production became manifest when auto entrepreneurs began to envision the mass production of low-priced cars. Workers' control was not particularly problematic for capital as long as auto production remained on a relatively small scale. Craft workers producing at their own pace and discretion could turn out a sufficient number of high-priced cars to supply the small luxury market. However, auto visionaries like Henry Ford and Ransom Olds were not content to make luxury cars for the rich. They aspired to tap the potentially large American market for cheap transportation through the volume production of simple, low-priced autos. But workers' control embodied in the craft method of production was a major obstacle on the road to the cheap, mass-produced car. Auto capitalists found that the "human element" was often recalcitrant and refused to produce in a manner and pace necessary to lower production costs.

The resistance that auto capitalists aspiring to mass production encountered from skilled workers was not, as some have postulated, the cultural resistance of a group of workers with preindustrial backgrounds against the strange demands of industrial capitalism. Employees of the early auto shops were generally second- and third-generation industrial workers, who were perfectly at home in their industrial environment. They had a well-developed sense of industrial time, were largely organized into craft unions, were highly disciplined both individually and collectively, and regarded factory production as natural. Rather, this was the class resistance of workers who had developed a sense of class warfare. As David Montgomery has documented, the industrial craft workers of this period were engaged in a collective and deliberate struggle with their bosses to establish and maintain control of their own production.[22] Under these antagonistic production relations inherent in capitalism, workers' control over production, its pace and accuracy, was one weapon that they used to struggle against their own exploitation. As long as they possessed this power, mass production of autos under capitalism was impaired.

Often this class struggle in the early auto shops erupted into overt, organized, conscious struggle, as when union machinists struck Olds in 1897 and again in 1901 over wages and working conditions. But more often, early auto workers' struggle against capital was covert, clandestine, and only partly conscious. Because they were aware at some level that it was the owners and not themselves who reaped the main benefits from production, workers were not particularly concerned with working very intensively, or sometimes very accurately either, for that matter. Evidence of this clandestine struggle is found in a series of reports by a labor spy hired by the Ford Motor Company in 1906 to "keep an eye on" the workers in the shop. The spy reported that "many of the men neglected their work, malingered, put imperfect parts into cars, and cheated the timekeeper." In one reported incident, two machinists made a bet on the workings of a motor, and, to settle it, stopped work for half an hour to take off the side plates of the motor. In another incident, five car testers stood around from 6:45 A.M. until noon waiting for cars, but refused to help get any ready for testing. When asked by the foreman to help with the cars, one tester replied defiantly that he was getting paid for testing and not for working on cars. The power over the labor process that the skills of these workers afforded them was largely responsible for this sort of behavior on the shop floor. It allowed them to resist with impunity the demands of their bosses for faster and more accurate production.[23]

The writings of early auto capitalists and those who spoke for them clearly revealed that they perceived workers' control over the labor process as an obstacle in the path of increased production and profit. In trade papers, biographies, and autobiographies, they complained about a generally recalcitrant shop culture. Workers were described with such disparaging phrases as "fluctuating temperaments," "tending toward error," "varying in effort," "wasteful of time," and "inattentive, negligent, and inexperienced." A series of maxims labeled "Profit Chokers" that appeared in Ford's employee magazine demonstrated similar resentment by capital of workers' power to thwart attempts to intensify production. The series included the following: "Chronic strollers and time killers," "Killing time under day-work pay," "Sulkers, grunters, back-talkers, mumblers, knockers," "Employees not doing what they are told," "Antagonism to improved methods," "Employees working 'their' way instead of the 'Company's,'" and "Padded pay rolls through tardiness and shirking."[24]

In addition to complaining generally about a recalcitrant shop culture, auto capitalists and managers also resentfully pointed to specific gaps in the labor process through which workers asserted their power to slow the rush for greater production. They recognized, for example, that the layout of the shops left workers considerable discretionary movement, which they used to slow work intensity. In the final assembly process, workers were not tied to their work positions and thus subject to the constant visual supervision of foremen, but made frequent trips to the toolroom and stockroom. The sight of this precious commodity of skilled labor power wandering leisurely about the shop instead of diligently devoting itself to production was intolerable to its purchasers. "The practice of the time was to assemble a car in one spot on the floor of the factory. Tools and parts were elsewhere. This meant that the workman wasted a lot of time and effort going to different departments in search of tools and materials." The functional layout of the machine shops also required a great deal of discretionary worker movement, which made close supervision very difficult. When workers moved about from machine to machine and department to department, noted one trade journalist, "time is lost and it is impossible for the department heads to keep in accurate touch with the location of the men and at the same time to check the progress of the work." Henry Ford summed up the situation with a note of wry humor: "The undirected worker spends more of his time walking about for materials and tools than he does in production; he gets small pay because pedestrianism is not a highly paid line."[25]

Employers complained not only about the layout of work, but about the inherent nature of work as well. They realized that the skilled, variable work gave workers a power that they used to thwart the drive for greater and more accurate production. This realization is evident in the following advertisement from a trade journal, which lists the dangers to employers of leaving control of precision gaging in the hands of workers.

> "To err is human" . . . and costly! Inexperience, ineptness, fatigue, ill-health, inattention, indifference—all are possible bugaboos when using fixed gages [operated with the skill and discretion of workers] on extremely close tolerance work (i.e., checking to "tenths" [ten thousandths of an inch]).
>
> Scrap, wasted time, production slow-downs, faulty products— these are the high costs of rejecting good parts or passing incorrect parts as being good.
>
> "Hangovers"—physical or mental—make no difference when using a Visual Gage, Multichek, Precisionaire, Electricchek, or other Sheffield precision gaging instruments. Mechanical skill built into these gages eliminates the need for "top performance" individual skill to precisely and accurately inspect to "tenths."
>
> Sheffield precision gaging equipment eliminates "human" error.[26]

The message is clear. Auto capitalists aspiring to tap the potentially large market for cheap cars could ill afford to leave the control of the labor process to the discretion and skills of a class of basically recalcitrant workers. Within the context of the antagonistic relations of production of capitalism, to leave control of the pace and accuracy of work in the hands of labor inevitably meant to settle for less than maximum output and accuracy.

Workers of the Early Auto Industry

In order to fully understand the labor process of the early auto industry in the United States, we must examine not only the nature and control of work, but also the people who did this work. For just as the jobs shaped the workers, the workers also shaped the jobs.

The early auto industry grew up in two specific areas of the United States, largely because of the availability of a skilled labor force in these localities. In the New England area, mainly in Massachusetts and Connecticut, the auto industry grew up around the declining bicycle industry, drawing its skilled labor force from this as well as from a few other machine-building industries. In the Detroit area, the other center of early production, the auto shops

35

drew their skilled workers from a number of industries. From the carriage and furniture industries came skilled carpenters, woodworkers, painters, and upholsterers; from the stove manufacturers came patternmakers, molders, and sheet-metal workers; and from the railroad and machine shops came skilled machinists, molders, and blacksmiths. This concentration of skilled labor around Detroit combined with the area's generally lower wages to cause the rapid concentration of the industry there as opposed to New England.[27]

Early auto workers were thus not fresh recruits to industrial labor. Most had had experience with similar work in other industries. They were usually second- or third-generation industrial workers, thoroughly imbued with the requirements and culture of the factory.

Ethnically, the early auto workers were predominantly native-born descendants of early English colonists or recent immigrants from northern European countries. In New England, the reputed Yankee mechanics dominated the early shops. But in the Detroit area, the skilled auto work force was a bit more heterogeneous. As the city's industries grew in the last half of the nineteenth century, they began to attract immigrant groups to supplement the basically American and English working population. The Irish predominated among the early immigrants, but the Germans soon outnumbered them and all other nationality groups. Also among the ethnic groups making up Detroit's early working class were large contingents of Canadians and Poles. All of these groups were represented in Detroit's early auto shops, but American, English, and German workers seem to have predominated.[28]

Most of Detroit's early auto workers were organized into strong craft unions. In the last two decades of the nineteenth century, the skilled workers of Detroit, like their counterparts throughout industrial America, had formed numerous and vigorous labor organizations. The largest and strongest of these were organized by the metal-trade workers: iron molders, machinery molders, patternmakers, metal polishers, and machinists. Of the approximately forty-six thousand wage earners in Detroit at the turn of the century, perhaps twelve thousand belonged to craft unions. Judging from the reports of labor strife in the early shops, these unions were active in the auto industry.[29]

In Detroit, as in the rest of industrial America, an initial period of accommodation between employers and the trade unions around the turn of the century soon degenerated into bitter hostility. Employers everywhere began to see union efforts to regulate output and production methods as a major obstacle to their quest to cut costs and increase profits, which went into high gear after 1900. So under the favorable conditions of the depression, employer associations launched a nationwide open-shop drive around 1903 to break the unions. The local drive of Detroit's capitalists, organized into the Employers' Association of Detroit (EAD), was typical of this movement. In its attempt to crush the unions and make Detroit a bastion of the open shop, EAD employed a variety of methods: lockouts, refusing to meet union representatives, discharging and blacklisting union workers. But its most effective weapon was its Labor Bureau. With its extensive records on Detroit workers, the bureau helped employers break strikes by supplying them with nonunion labor. It also helped to prevent competitive bidding among employers for scarce skilled labor by negotiating wage-fixing agreements and actively recruiting labor from other areas. By 1907, EAD had won a total victory for the open shop in Detroit. The craft unions were crushed, leaving the workers of the budding auto industry largely unorganized for thirty years. This victory was itself a major factor in attracting auto capital to Detroit and making it the center of the new industry.[30]

There were other factors, however, besides the open-shop drive that contributed to the decline of unions in the early auto shops. One was the highly favorable labor market and employment conditions for skilled auto workers. In the years after 1904, when the industry began its rapid growth, skilled labor was in extremely short supply. In the busiest months of this highly seasonal manufacturing enterprise, even ordinary unskilled laborers were in keen demand. Despite the best efforts of the Employers' Association, this tight labor market led to competition among capitalists for workers. Every Sunday the advertising columns of the Detroit newspapers were full of appeals for help. As a result, wages were bid up substantially.

This labor market situation also caused high rates of labor mobility and turnover and created a certain spirit of independence among auto workers. They moved around from job to job, enticed by the high-wage offers of auto capitalists. The tight labor market further enhanced the power of skilled workers on the shop floor. They could not be forced to tolerate overbearing foremen pushing for production, for they could easily pack their tools and get a similar if not better job elsewhere. Describing worker behavior under such labor market conditions, one scholar of the history of American production wrote that "a highly skilled craftsman could command his own price and was likely to pack his tools at the slightest provocation." The same sense of power and independence is evidenced by Walter Chrysler's account of his early days as a skilled mechanic. "I lacked patience then; I wasn't willing to stick around a shop to prove that I was good. If they did not appreciate me, if any foreman dressed me down, I'd get my time, pack my bag, forward my tuba [!] and head for the next shop town."[31]

Not only their great skills, but also the severe shortage of workers with such skills created conditions under which workers could defy capitalists' attempts to assert their authority over the labor process. This shortage, as well as high wages, good working conditions, and power on the shop floor, accounted for the absence of many of the traditional impulses that could sustain strong unions in the auto industry.[32]

But this balance of power between labor and capital in the auto shops was soon to be tipped drastically in favor of capital. The market for automobiles was growing rapidly in the later years of the first decade of the century, but manufacturers were saddled with a labor process that restricted production by leaving control in the hands of workers. So they went to work, slowly at first but soon feverishly, to create a process for the production of cars that they could completely control and dominate.

CHAPTER 3
First Steps Toward a Capitalist-Controlled Labor Process

The rapid growth in the market for automobiles toward the end of the first decade of the century was largely the result of a change in the product of the industry. A few American capitalist visionaries saw that there was little future for an industry producing large, luxurious, coach-like vehicles for the rich. They envisioned a small, cheap, buggy-type auto affordable by the masses. The narcotic inducing their visions was, of course, the desire for huge profits reaped from such a mass-marketed product.

The first entrepreneur to turn this vision into reality was Ransom Olds, one of the pioneers in auto manufacturing. Although he had launched his company by producing several high-priced models, in the fall of 1900 Olds began to manufacture a small, low-priced runabout in hopes of cashing in on a mass market. The crude horseless buggy had a curved dash, a single two-passenger seat, a rear-mounted, one-cylinder engine, and was open to the weather. But its retail price of six hundred and fifty dollars was far below any other American car. Olds' runabout was such a hit with American buyers that he was soon producing this model alone, and his biggest problem became producing enough to meet the demand.[1]

The second capitalist visionary of the low-priced car was, of course, Henry Ford. From the beginning he had desired to produce a car for the masses, but pressure from investors forced the early Ford Motor Company to concentrate on high-priced models. In 1906, however, with Ford exercising greater control, the company introduced the six hundred dollar four-cylindered Model N runabout. Ford's vision was approaching realization. A burst of enthusiasm and demand greeted the low-priced car, and in 1907 Ford made the decision to dispense with the high-priced models and manufacture the Model N alone.[2]

The low-priced cars of Ford and Olds generated the consumer demand that fueled the drive for changes in the labor process. Auto capitalists could not possibly meet this demand with a labor process that left the quality and quantity of production in the hands of an exploited and recalcitrant work force. They had to wrest control over every aspect of work out of these unwilling hands. The motive behind this transformation of the labor process was clearly stated by Henry Ford in an attempt to apologize for its effects upon workers.

> Factory organization is not a device to prevent the expansion of ability, but a device to reduce the waste and losses due to mediocrity. It is not a device to hinder the ambitious, clear-headed man from doing his best, but a device to prevent the don't-care sort of individual from doing his worst. That is to say, when laziness, carelessness, slothfulness, and lack-interest are allowed to have their own way, everybody suffers. The factory cannot prosper and therefore cannot pay living wages. When an organization makes it necessary for the don't-care class to do better than they naturally would, it is for their benefit— they are better physically, mentally, and financially. What wages should we be able to pay if we trusted a large don't-care class to their own methods and gait of production?[3]

What Ford failed to understand, or was unwilling to admit, was that the "laziness and carelessness" of the "don't-care class" was the result, not of some inherent characteristic of human nature, but of a social system in which the fruits of production are appropriated mainly for the benefit of a privileged few.

INTERCHANGEABILITY AND STANDARDIZATION

One of the first steps that auto capitalists took in the creation of a labor process controlled by themselves, not workers, was the achievement of interchangeability of parts. The production of parts so uniform that no fitting was required in their assembly was pioneered in small arms manufacture in the 1840s and spread gradually to other industries, like sewing machines and clocks. But the techniques of armory practice were brought to perfection by the bicycle industry, from which many early auto manufacturers inherited them. The automobile industry was also fortunate enough to undertake the making of interchangeable parts during a period when rapid improvements in machine tools were making their quantity production more feasible. Among the most important of the improvements introduced in the early years of this century was the increase in the massiveness of the base of the machine, which greatly aided in securing rigidity for the whole mechanism. In the area of power, the centrally driven shaft-and-belt system was gradually replaced by individual, variable-speed electric motor drive. Transmissions and clutches for quick speed changes were introduced and improved. And the speeds of the tool spindles and the tool feed were made independent. Hard, high-speed-steel cutting tools made for greater precision and faster tool speeds and feeds. Other improvements included longer and wider carriages, greater use of anti-friction bearings, larger spindle diameters, rod feeds, more accuracy in regard to flatness and squareness in general, truer pitch of screws, power feeds, more accurately calibrated adjustments, quick spindle-returning devices, and better lubrication systems for both the mechanism and the work in process. All of these general improvements greatly increased the precision of the parts turned out by skilled machinists on the machine tools. Parts that were virtually identical could be produced, one being so much like the others that they were interchangeable.[4]

But the single most important factor facilitating the interchangeability of auto parts was the introduction of an entirely new machine tool—the production grinding machine. In order for steel auto parts to be made durable, they had to be hardened by heat treating. This produced a distortion of the part that had to be corrected after hardening. But conventional machine tools—lathes, millers, planers—could not cut the hardened steel, their operations being confined to the soft, pre-heat-treated steel. The accuracy and interchangeability of auto parts depended upon finding a machining process to remove the distortion from the hardened steel parts. The grinding machine was the answer. In 1900, Charles Norton introduced his heavy production grinding machine. The machine's precise application of a rapidly turning abrasive wheel to hardened steel parts achieved standards of precision previously unknown with metal cutters. Its application to auto work beginning around 1903 was the crucial factor facilitating the quantity production of precise, interchangeable parts.[5]

The achievement of interchangeability did not substantially affect the skill of machinists. The improved machine tools and the grinding machine still required skilled and knowledgeable operators in order to turn out precision parts. However, interchangeable parts did create the possibility of reducing the skill requirements of assembly workers. Because parts were precise and fit together exactly, the large amount of skilled handwork previously required to ensure accurate assembly of imprecise parts was no longer necessary. Ordinary semiskilled mechanics could quickly and simply put together interchangeable parts. The immediate result of this reduction in the skill of assembly work was the reduction of workers' control. The removal of uncertainty from this work meant that decisions about its accuracy and pace were no longer necessarily made by workers. Interchangeable parts made it possible for capital to standardize and dictate the time for each assembly operation and thus control the pace of labor. As one automotive engineer stated, interchangeability made assembly "a matter of timed operations rather than of individual ingenuity in getting mismatched pieces together."[6]

The potential of interchangeability to reduce the skill and thus the control of assembly workers was clearly perceived by automotive capitalists, and it consequently formed an important motive behind this innovation. If any had overlooked these advantages, the manufacturers of machine tools that made interchangeable parts called their fellow capitalists attention to them as selling points in their advertisements. One particularly interesting appeal was contained in an ad of the Heald Machine Company, a manufacturer of the all-important grinding machine.

> Cut down your assembly costs. Cylinders, piston rings, gears and other automobile parts—of absolutely uniform diameters—perfectly interchangeable—accurate to quarter-thousandths of an inch if necessary—are being produced easily, quickly and cheaply day after day on Heald Grinding Machines. Think of the savings in assembling costs—no uncertainty—no delay—no hunting around for parts that fit.[7]

This ad strikes to the heart of the auto capitalists' problem. As long as parts were not precise, there was uncertainty in assembly work, and skilled workers consequently exercised great discretion. These workers controlled their own pace of work and took advantage of pores in the working day. But as the ad stated, interchangeability did away with the uncertainty and hence reduced the skill of work. The result was better capitalist control over the pace of labor—"no delay—no hunting around for parts that fit."

The same advantage followed from the achievement of a related component of mass production pioneered by earlier firms—standardization. This principle involved the adoption of standard designs and dimensions for a product and its component parts, thus eliminating variety and variation. In the automobile industry, standardization might mean, for example, that instead of producing four types of motors, one for each model, a company produced only one standard motor and used it in each model. Or at a higher level of standardization, a company abandoned production of all models save one. Both Olds and Ford took this latter step early (1901 and 1907, respectively).

Standardization had an effect similar to that of interchangeability on the struggle for control over the labor process. With the great variety of parts and models eliminated, the skills of assemblers were no longer essential. The essence of skill is discretion, control over a choice of alternative methods. When there was no longer any variety in parts to be assembled, no such discretion on the part of assemblers was required.

This elimination of skilled assembly labor was only a potential, not a necessary consequence of interchangeability and standardization. Skilled workers feasibly could have continued to assemble interchangeable and standardized auto parts and probably would have done a better job than semiskilled workers. It was the antagonistic class relations of capitalist production that motivated capitalists to develop this potential. These class antagonisms caused skilled workers to use their control over the labor process to resist increased exploitation. Thus, auto capitalists, seeking to cut costs and increase production under these social conditions, were motivated to seize this deskilling potential in order to repress worker resistance. Clearly, then, there was a strong element of repressive control embodied in the introduction of interchangeability and standardization into the automotive labor process. These innovations increased production and decreased costs to a certain extent because they repressed the resistance of a class of exploited workers by decreasing their control of work.

Repressive control was not, however, the sole capitalist motive for these two innovations. Both interchangeability and standardization had numerous nonrepressive-control advantages, which enhanced the production and serviceability of automobiles without affecting the class relations between labor and capital. Precise, interchangeable parts increased the productivity of assembly labor, regardless of who controlled it. Workers turned out more products without working more intensively, because the arduous, time-consuming tasks of filing and fitting parts were eliminated. Interchangeability also made repair of automobiles faster and cheaper, for spare parts produced by manufacturers fit disabled vehicles without scraping or filing. Standardization of automobiles and auto parts increased the productivity of parts-producing labor by eliminating the necessity for constant adjustment of machinery to accommodate the variety. It also eliminated the waste of productive resources on superficial and useless model differentiation. These nonrepressive advantages certainly were partially responsible for the introduction of interchangeability and standardization. However, intertwined with and inseparable in results from these neutral advantages was the distinctly social advantage of deskilling assembly labor, which capitalists developed solely to repress the antagonistic social relations of production.

Division of Labor and Progressive Layout

The introduction of interchangeability and standardization was only the opening salvo in a capitalist seige on the fortress of workers' control. It weakened worker battlements and prepared the ground for a devastating assault on worker skills—the detailed division of labor. Like the two earlier innovations, this splintering of the skilled crafts of auto work into a plethora of unskilled and semiskilled fragments embodied certain neutral advantages that increased productivity without affecting social relations. But it is clear that auto manufacturers undertook this fragmentation of work in large part to destroy skilled workers' control of the labor process, which, under the system of antagonistic class relations, stood in the way of increased exploitation and profits. Coupled with the progressive layout of the resulting detail tasks, the division of labor severely crippled the ability of auto workers to defend themselves from further capitalist onslaughts.

In the assembly shops of the auto factories, the first assault on the unitary work process was the division of the labor of actually assembling parts from that of transporting them. The first assemblers did their own "stock chasing" as well as assembly work itself. This arrangement made for great discretion of workers over the pace of their own labor and for very difficult supervision. To overcome these problems and assert a greater control over the workers, auto capitalists began dividing the craft of assembly around the middle of the first decade of this century. Adopting a practice standard in most high-volume shops, they hired groups of unskilled workers exclusively to transport parts from the stockroom to the assembly floor. At first haphazard, the handling of parts became very systematic by the later years of the decade. Several companies reported the use of trucks especially constructed to carry all the parts of an entire chassis or engine assembly. Consequently, only one trip to the stockroom had to be made for each assembly.[8]

The next step taken by auto manufacturers was the division of the actual labor of assembling parts, which was dependent upon the earlier introduction of interchangeability and standardization. As long as parts were imperfect and had to be hand-fitted, it was impossible to divide the work of assembling them between different workers. The different operations were necessarily interdependent. The worker had to keep in mind the peculiarity of each part and adjust subsequent parts and operations accordingly as he proceeded. However, the precision of standardized and interchangeable parts rendered assembly operations invariant and independent, thus making possible their division between separate workers. Thus, in the years between 1905 and 1907, shortly after the introduction of standardized and interchangeable parts, some of the larger-volume companies began to assign specialized tasks to the members of the small assembly team. In the final assembly at the Ford Motor Company, "in the place of the jack-of-all-trades who formerly 'did it all,' there were now several assemblers who worked over a particular car side by side, each one responsible for a somewhat limited set of operations."[9] While one small group mounted and secured the engine to the chassis, another was working on the rear system, and still another worked on the transmission and center portion of the frame.

This early method of dividing assembly labor was limited by the number of workers who could crowd around one assembly station. In the years between 1907 and 1910, however, auto capitalists solved this problem by devising a system of linear layout and rotating assembly gangs. Describing such an assembly system in operation at Ford's Piquette Avenue plant around 1907, one worker recalled: "The cars were all lined up on a row to be assembled. You went up one side and down the other. We had about forty-five cars lined up in this circle." Only one highly specialized assembly gang worked on a car at a time. When its task was completed, it moved on to the next car in the line, and the gang behind it moved in to take its place and perform its specialized task. "These assemblers would move from car to car. By the time the man got to the last car the first car would be all done." There were gangs specialized in frame assembly, motor mounting, wheel mounting, fender assembly, body assembly, and so on. And stock handling as well as assembly labor was divided and specialized. One worker did nothing but haul fenders from the body shop to the assembly floor; another hauled dashboards exclusively; still another, axles; and so on.[10]

A similar division and specialization was introduced into the machine shops, subassembly operations, and the foundries of the early auto factories. The skilled crafts of each of these manufacturing processes were shattered into a myriad of specialized and relatively unskilled fragments, which could be filled by workers with a minimum of knowledge and training. And the specialization and deskilling of these crafts was accompanied by an even greater alteration of shop layout than in assembly work. Previously, auto shops had been laid out functionally, in departments of similar work processes. Functionally similar machine operations had been grouped into separate departments, as were other work processes like assembly, inspection, foundry, testing, and heat treating. This layout had been adapted to the craft labor process, for each worker in a department was able to perform the great variety of different activities handled in it. As we have seen, functional layout created problems of control for capital: excessive transportation, work delays, general confusion, discretionary worker movement, difficult supervision. Some of these problems were alleviated by the progressive arrangement of the functional departments in the order of their usual place in the manufacturing process. In the new Packard plant of 1903, for example, departments were arranged so that the materials flowed progressively around a central storehouse. But many problems persisted. Yet as long as work was based upon functional crafts, no other arrangement was feasible.[11]

But as capitalists began to splinter the auto crafts into specialized detail jobs, a different arrangement became possible that allowed them greater control of work and workers. This was the progressive layout. Functional departments were destroyed and new product departments formed. All the different processes devoted to one part or product were grouped together and arranged in order of their work on it. In machine shops, for example, all machine tools used on one part were arranged in one progressive, heterogeneous line. Henry Ford seems to have achieved such a progressive layout in the engine-machining department of his new Bellevue Avenue factory in 1906. The plant superintendent, Max Wollering, recalled: "We didn't group our machines by type at all. They were pretty much grouped to accommodate the article they were working on. They were beginning to set up progressive flow."[12] Each machine tool and its operator performed one and only one operation on the engine block, after which it was passed to the adjacent machine and its operator, who did likewise.

The division of the craft of machinists and the progressive layout of the resulting specialized tasks struck at the heart of workers' skills and knowledge. No longer was the machinist engaged in a variety of operations on a number of different machines in a functional department. He was confined to one specific operation on one specific machine in the progressive line. For example, instead of performing a wide variety of drilling operations sent to the drilling department, one worker stood at the same drill press all day drilling the hole in the left stub-axle as this part progressed in the axle department. Because he performed the same operation time and time again, day in and day out, the skill and discretion required of him were minimal.

As labor in the machine shops became more and more divided, many of the previous operations that had required knowledge and skill were split off from the ordinary machine operator and concentrated into specialized, privileged occupations close to management. The first step in this process was the creation of a position called the "speed boss," a supervisor whose job it was to determine the exact speed, feed, and set-up of machines and enforce these specifications upon workers. Describing the speed boss in the Maxwell-Briscoe shops in 1912, one trade journalist wrote: "This man is a practical mechanic, born and grown up in the shop, so to speak. By many years' experience he knows exactly what each machine may do and not do, and it is his business to see that each tool is used most efficiently. He is in the shop at all times, watching the work of the men on the machines and working on them himself to positively determine maximum capacity of the equipment."[13] Gradually, however, the tasks of the speed boss were divided among an entire crew of "machine setters" or "tool setters." These skilled supervisory workers not only set up the machines and determined speeds and feeds; they also took over from the machinists the skilled task of sharpening tools. Various other skilled parts of the machinist's craft—oiling, repair, maintenance—were also divided off from machine operators and turned over to specialized, skilled occupations closely responsible to capital.

The division of labor and progressive layout were also introduced into the subassembly shops of the auto industry, resulting in a similar fragmentation of the previous unity of skilled crafts. As early as 1903, Ransom Olds had introduced minutely divided and progressively arranged work into the engine-assembly department of his Olds Motor Works. Describing this process, one trade journalist wrote that "the motors are passed, step by step, down the assembling bench toward the testing department, which is in the next room, a new piece being added at every move with clock-like regularity."[14] By 1908, other large auto manufacturers were employing this process in most subassembly operations. Each worker performed a minute fraction of the total job and passed the part rapidly to the next worker along the assembly bench. By 1914, Henry Ford had refined this division and progressive layout of work with impressive results. The once unitary job of assembling motors, for example, had been shattered into eighty-four fragments, each meticulously timed down to the second and laid out progressively in a line. While it had previously taken the solitary craft worker 9.9 worker-hours to assemble a motor, the eighty-four detail workers required only 3.8, a savings of over 60 percent. "Dividing and subdividing operations," Ford said of this and similar jobs, "keeping the work in motion—those are the keynotes of production." "The net result of the application of these principles," he continued, "is the reduction of the necessity for thought on the part of the worker and the reduction of his movements to a minimum. He does as nearly as possible only one thing with only one movement."[15]

Auto capitalists and managers also introduced the minute division of labor and the accompanying progressive layout into the foundry, basically changing the early labor process. The integrated craft of molding became fragmented, and the discretionary portions were centralized by capital. Instead of employing all-around molders assigned a variety of work, auto manufacturers divided and specialized molding tasks. The foundry at Ford, for example, became divided into product units, each specialized in the molding for one particular part. The molders in each unit, therefore, became specialists in a very narrow molding task. Henry Ford boasted of this arrangement that it rendered 95 percent of the foundry workers unskilled, "or to put it more accurately, [they] must be skilled in exactly one operation which the most stupid man can learn in two days."[16]

Labor within each specialized foundry unit was divided more and more minutely. By 1914 the previously highly skilled job of cylinder molding had been divided into eight specialized operations, each performed by a different worker. A cylinder molding gang included a cope rammer, a cope rammer's helper, a drag rammer, a drag rammer's helper, a drag finisher, a cope finisher, a barrel-core setter, and two bankers. These operations were arranged progressively along the foundry floor. A similar division and specializtion was imposed on the once-skilled labor of core making. The skilled craft of preparing the molten metal for pouring was also divided among a number of unskilled, detail laborers: one who prepared the charge, another who dumped the charge in the furnace, another who tapped the furnace, and so on. Even the relatively unskilled foundry jobs were fragmented and deskilled further. The job of pouring the metal into the mold, for example, was divided among several specialized workers in a pouring gang.[17]

Repressive and Nonrepressive Control in the Division of Labor

As with the introduction of interchangeability and standardization, the decision of automobile capitalists and managers to minutely divide unitary crafts and progressively arrange the resulting fragments was motivated in large part in order to establish repressive control. Both measures shifted control of work away from workers and centralized it into the hands of capitalists, who then used it to repress the resistance of these recalcitrant workers and thus increase their exploitation.

By allowing auto manufacturers to replace skilled workers with semiskilled and unskilled workers, the division of labor had a great impact on the class struggle for control of the labor process. Because the unitary craft labor process required workers to use their knowledge to determine the precise nature of work, they had a wide range of discretion with respect to its productivity, intensity, and accuracy. Auto managers realized that this exercise of discretion lowered the intensity of labor in their shops. Recalcitrant workers could use this power to slow down operations to a human pace and take breaks between tasks. The division of automotive labor centralized the skill and intelligence of work into the hands of capital. As Henry Ford stated: "we made it unnecessary for the highest types of mental ability to be engaged in every operation in the factory. The better brains are in the mental power-plant."[18] With this concentrated dynamo of mental power in their hands, managers reduced the workers' need to think and, along with it, the pores in the working day. Thus, as two engineering journalists wrote of the minute division of labor in bench assembly work at Ford: "Where a worker can perform absolutely similar successions of movement, he soon gains great skill combined with great rapidity of muscular action; but if the routine of the workman's movements is broken, he must inevitably call his brain into action to find the best means of bridging his troubles, and must lose some time in devising and executing his unusual line of procedure." The minute division of labor "allowed" the worker "to perform his unvaried operation with the least possible expenditure of will-power and hence with the least brain fatigue."[19] In reality, capitalists and managers were less concerned about workers getting tired brains than about their using discretionary time to decrease the intensity of labor.

The division of automotive labor destroyed another pocket of workers' discretionary time by eliminating the necessity of movement about the shop. With specialized stock chasers to bring parts to assembly locations, workers no longer had an excuse to take long and leisurely trips to the stockroom. Assembly could now proceed "without there being any need for the mechanics to walk more than a yard between the stand and the supply." Similarly, Ford attributed a large part of labor saved by dividing subassembly operations to the fact that specializtion eliminated the time spent by the solitary assembler walking around at the workbench. And in the machine shop, with workers tied to one position and one machine: "No time is lost by the operator. The parts come to his machine and are removed to the next automatically. His attention is only on his job." His foreman was sure to see to that. With workers confined to specific work stations, their foremen could maintain constant surveillance of their work and thus exercise stricter supervision.[20]

The division of labor further reduced worker discretion and enhanced capitalist control of work by making time study possible. Once labor became divided and no longer unified by the individual craft worker, managers imposed themselves as the unifying and coordinating force of the fragmented labor process. They began to study the detail jobs in order to determine the pace and manner of work that ensured greatest production. Through such time study, the knowledge of production that had previously rested with the workers was transferred to capital. Time study was, of course, part of Frederick Taylor's scientific management program for the reorganization of industry. However, the first managerial efforts in the auto industry to time and study minutely divided jobs do not seem to have been directly inspired by Taylor. Auto managers independently discovered and applied time study without knowledge of Taylor's work. Thus, in 1907, before Taylor's ideas were widely known, Ford's production superintendent, Max Wollering, began elementary time studies. "We would get a man whom we had confidence in and who knew what he was doing as to whether it was a lathe or a screw machine or a grinder. He knew the fundamentals of it and he would take a stop watch and operate this machine to get a fair idea of what could be done, and then he would put a man on there to test it out."[21] After these initial efforts, time study spread quickly within the auto industry, due both to the imitation of innovative auto shops and the proselytizing of Taylor, who visited Detroit twice in search of converts.

Like other capitalists, automobile manufacturers used time study to intensify labor by eliminating workers' discretionary time. Standard times for jobs were set so as to allow workers little or no time between operations. Usually the more rapid workers were timed when setting standards. And when the time-study personnel got wise to workers' tactic of deliberately slowing down when being studied, they routinely subtracted an arbitrary percentage from the recorded time. The results of such time study are well recorded from the auto workers' point of view in a letter to the Industrial Workers of the World's organ, *Industrial Worker*.

> For several weeks we have an agent of the scientific department on the floor where I'm working. With watch in hand he was timing every operation performed. Machines were put on first speed. Calculations made by the pushers are based upon what a man could turn out by working the lathe, drill press, milling machine, gear cutters, etc., at top speed; cut out the too frequent sharpening of tools, bumming a chew from a fellow worker on the other end of the floor, going after a drink too often, etc., and not content with this they added from 5 to 10 pieces required to the total amount of pieces turned out by the men. Example: We say 150 pieces was considered a day's work before this "manager" came. Machines ran at 3rd speed, time was taken in adjusting work, etc. Now by working machines at top speed 200 pieces can be turned out and by working the men at top speed 225 pieces will be considered a day's work. (When the men ran their (?) [editorially inserted question mark] machines at slow speed, they had a chance to sit down and watch while resting, but now the dirt is flying). . . . No more loafing 'round the grindstone to sharpen drills and tools, no more excursions to the tool crib or stock room and many more scientific schemes of working while a fellow is resting. As a matter of fact, those seeming little time killing tricks are absolutely necessary, for no man can work steadily at top speed and not get bughouse and worn out in short order. A little relaxation must take place every once in a while.[22]

The drastic reduction in skilled workers effected by the division of labor also strengthened managerial control of the labor process by eliminating the inhibiting traditions of these workers. They had acquired, through long experience, certain notions about how work should be done. The speed and feed of machine-tool cuts, the set-up of machines, a normal day's work, the specific manner to accomplish a certain result, the quality of output—all of these aspects of work were regulated by long-established, traditional norms. These traditions quickly proved to be a major obstacle in the path of complete managerial control of labor. It was difficult to speed up and generally to control the labor of workers embued with such traditions. By dividing labor into relatively unskilled fragments, these skilled workers, with their inhibiting traditions, could be dispensed with and replaced with semiskilled and unskilled workers. Having no remembrance of the standards and traditions that governed work when workers exerted greater control, these workers put up little resistance to the absolute control of capitalists and their managers over the labor process.

One academic spokesman captured this capitalist preference for the relatively unskilled when he wrote: "The unskilled or semiskilled worker is more apt to be content with the simple and repetitive task. He will perform the work for which he is trained and is not so likely to question the method of doing the job or to fuss over unnecessarily good quality."[23] A concrete example of this advantage of eliminating skilled workers through the division of labor was given by one engineer who studied Ford's River Rouge plant. Noting the extreme crowding of machine tools on the shop floor, he observed:

> An old time machinist might feel himself decidedly cramped if confined to the space allotted him in this machine shop. Inasmuch as the majority of operators at River Rouge, however, are specialists who perhaps have never seen a machine tool before their employment by the Ford Company, they have no precedents or ingrained habits with respect to tool operation and they soon become accustomed to carrying on their operations in the space provided, which in all cases is carefully figured to avoid the drawback of actual crowding.[24]

Perhaps engineering journalists Horace Arnold and Fay Faurote best captured this reason for auto managers' disdain for the skilled and their preference for the relatively unskilled when they wrote: "As to machinists, old-time, all-round men, perish the thought! The Ford Company has no use for experience, in the working ranks, anyway. It desires and prefers machine-tool operators who have nothing to unlearn, who have no theories of correct surface speeds for metal finishing, and will simply do what they are told to do, over and over again, from bell-time to bell-time."[25]

The replacement of skilled workers with semiskilled and unskilled detail workers allowed by the division of labor strengthened capital in the struggle for control by altering the supply as well as the skills of labor. The supply of skilled workers available to the burgeoning auto industry was not large enough to meet the growing demand. This skilled labor shortage added market power to the considerable production power workers wielded in their struggle for control of the labor process. Tight labor market conditions severely weakened the effectiveness of the major sanction used by auto manufacturers to control workers—firing. Realizing that their bosses were reluctant to fire them because of the difficulty of finding replacements, skilled auto workers were able to exert even greater control over their own work. This relationship between worker power and labor shortages was obvious to capitalists and managers, as evidenced by an *Automotive Industries* editorial published during the First World War, when the industry again suffered tight labor market conditions. "High wages coupled with extraordinary demand [for labor] create a situation where workers may be independent, not only of their jobs, but also of the employer, with a result that includes costly labor turnover, increased accidents, extravagant time demands, exorbitant accident compensation and other evils."[26]

The minute division of labor helped capital to undermine the market power of skilled workers and thus enforce stricter discipline on the shop floor. As Henry Ford observed, "the subdivision of industry opens places that can be filled by practically any one." With a minimal amount of training, an immigrant or farm migrant could perform one fragment of the previously skilled labor process efficiently. The minutely divided work of Ford's foundry allowed its superintendent to boast that "if an immigrant, who has never seen the inside of a foundry before, cannot be made a first-class molder of one piece in only three days, he can never be any use on the floor; and two days is held ample time to make a first-class core maker of a man who has never before seen a core-molding bench in his life."[27] Although unskilled industrial labor was also relatively scarce in the United States in this period, at least it was more abundant than skilled labor. By drawing on this more abundant labor supply, capitalists were able to put the fear of unemployment back into workers, who were more reluctant to defy their bosses knowing that a line of immigrants and "farm boys" stood at the factory gates ready and able to replace them. Capitalists manipulated this fear in order to intensify labor.

Not willing merely to create the potential for a greater labor supply by dividing labor, automobile employers actively sought to expand this supply of unskilled workers with control motives in mind. As one critic of the industry observed: "The charge is often made that individually, if not concertedly, the big plants stimulate the coming of workers to Detroit in order to have a sizable labor pool to pick from, to spread the fear of losing your job, and to keep control in their hands."[28] In Detroit, the vehicle of labor market manipulation was the Employers' Association of Detroit. This association worked in a number of ways to control the competition for labor and to expand the labor supply. The EAD sought to persuade U.S. immigration authorities to divert a large part of the incoming stream of immigrants to Detroit. And the association financed a nation-wide advertising campaign to draw on the internal labor resources of the United States. The EAD's *Labor Barometer*, a weekly bulletin on the Detroit labor market, was also used to manipulate labor supply. Instead of reporting factually, Detroit employers used inflated reports of employment opportunities in this publication to stimulate the flow of workers to the city. Individual auto companies used similarly erroneous newspaper reports about increased employment to attract the labor supply to their factories.[29]

That this stimulation of labor supply was a conscious capitalist strategy aimed at greater control of workers on the shop floor is made evident by an editorial in *Automotive Industries*. The author stated that an "over-supply of labor is far from furnishing the ultimate answer to the labor question," but observed that:

> During the recent labor shortage, some manufacturers looked to the importation of unskilled labor from Europe as the solution to our labor problem. They believed that the solution consisted chiefly in getting so many men for every job that each individual would work harder because he feared losing his job. That situation has come about to some extent at present. . . . Recent reports, which indicate that production per man is rising, seem to bear out the theory that perhaps nothing more was needed than a little fear of joblessness in the minds of workmen.[30]

Some recent neo-Marxist analysts have argued that the minute division of labor was introduced by capitalists not only to better control the labor process but also to lower wages. Harry Braverman, for example, argues that dividing a craft cheapens its parts by allowing employers to hire low-wage labor to perform unskilled tasks and to use highly paid skilled labor solely on skilled tasks. Although lowering the wage bill in this way may have been a major motive for the division of labor in other industries, it does not seem to have been important in the American auto industry. The general shortage of labor, both skilled and unskilled, in the industry prevented capitalists from using the division of labor to force wages down. These conditions enhanced the market power of workers, forcing auto manufacturers to maintain relatively high wage rates in order to attract and hold employees. Under these circumstances, capitalists focused their cost-cutting efforts not on cutting wage rates, but on lowering the labor time spent on any one unit. The real object of the capitalist reorganization of the labor process was low unit labor costs, not low wage rates *per se*. By increasing the intensity and productivity of labor, auto manufacturers could lower the costs of labor expended on each car, while retaining the high wages necessary to attract and hold workers. As one trade journalist wrote, "management is not concerned so much with increases in pay as it is in obtaining an honest day's work for a day's pay."[31] The division of labor allowed managers to extract more labor for wages paid largely by increasing their power to repress the resistance of recalcitrant workers.

Not all the benefits motivating capitalists to divide automotive labor, however, were the result of greater repressive control. Intertwined with the socially biased advantages of the division of labor were certain neutral, nonrepressive advantages, which increased production and enhanced efficiency without affecting the conflictual class relations. One such aspect of nonrepressive control was the increased productivity of labor. As Adam Smith argued in *The Wealth of Nations*, the detail worker, engaged in the same task day in and day out, developed a certain dexterity through repetition and learned all of the tricks and shortcuts to do the work with a minimum of effort. In this, he held an advantage over the more versatile worker, whose switching from task to task prevented him from doing one job long enough to get really good at it. So this concentration of the detail worker on one task raised the productivity of his labor by reducing the labor time necessary to perform it.[32]

Auto capitalists recognized this advantage, and they cited it as one of the motives behind their push toward a greater division of labor. For example, Henry Ford was fond of stating that the minute division of labor so increased the productivity of unskilled workers that they too could earn high wages. Upon examining the division of labor in the Ford shops of 1914, engineering journalists Arnold and Faurote concluded: "Minute division of operations is effective in labor-cost reducing . . . by making the workman extremely skillful, so that he does his part with no needless motions. . . . " "Where a workman can perform absolutely similar successions of movement, he very soon gains great skill combined with great rapidity of muscular action. . . . "[33]

There may also be a nonrepressive aspect involved in the capitalist use of the division of labor to increase the available supply of labor. The shortages of skilled labor not only affected the balance of class forces on the shop floor, but they also placed a severe limitation on the growth of the industry. To a certain extent, the division of automotive crafts into detail tasks capable of being done by unskilled and semiskilled workers was an attempt by capitalists to secure the labor they needed to expand as much as an effort to dilute the market power of craft workers. As Henry Ford stated: "As the necessity for production increased it became apparent not only that enough machinists were not to be had, but also that skilled men were not necessary in production. . . . If every job in our place required skill the place would never have existed. Sufficiently skilled men to the number needed could not have been trained in a hundred years."[34]

Within capitalist America, of course, the benefits of these nonrepressive-control advantages of the division of labor accrued mainly to the owners of auto firms. The increased productivity of labor raised the rate of surplus value. And the rapid growth of firms on the foundation of a larger labor supply increased the mass of surplus value or profits at the disposal of auto capitalists. But the lopsided appropriation of these benefits should not obscure the different manner of their achievement—through the more efficient use of society's productive resources. By contrast, the repressive-control advantages achieved greater production solely by allowing capital to intensify labor over the resistance of workers. It was the class conflict between labor and capital rather than some neutral efficiency that motivated auto manufacturers to deploy the division of labor in a way that weakened the control of workers over the labor process.

Repressive and Nonrepressive Control in Progressive Layout

A similar intertwining of repressive- and nonrepressive-control advantages motivated capitalists to lay out the newly divided tasks in progressive lines. The main repressive-control advantage inherent in progressive layout was the increased capitalist control over the intensity of labor, which allowed managers to speed up work against the resistance of workers. Progressive layout increased capitalist control of work pace in several ways. First, it made supervision of work closer and easier. With workers crowded together in a small area, foremen could maintain a large force under constant surveillance. Further, as one engineering professor noted, "the steady flow of work through the line automatically leads to the quick detection of delays. It also holds operators at their work; on certain lines each worker must be on the job constantly."[35]

Second, progressive layout gave managers greater control over work intensity by allowing "stretch-out," the operation of more than one machine by a worker. Because machines were grouped close together, it was possible for the first time for a worker to cover the short distance between them. The stretch-out that often accompanied progressive layout was illustrated at the Cadillac plant, where a change in the layout of connecting-rod production forced half the previous workers to operate the same number of machines.[36]

The main way, however, that progressive layout enhanced capitalist control of work intensity was by insuring a rapid, continuous flow of work past operators. Even though work at this time was simply passed by hand between operations, this movement exerted a certain "pull" on workers and forced them to work rapidly so as not to fall behind. As Arnold and Faurote noted of progressive layout in the Ford shops of 1914, "it succeeds in maintaining speed without obtrusive foremanship." Another engineer noted generally that progressive line production produced a "tautness in operating sequence."

> One of the psychological advantages of the line production is the tendency to draw closely upon the work ahead. In most cases there will be but a few parts between operations. Employees will make a constant effort to keep this material from building up ahead of them and to pass the work along promptly to the other workers on succeeding operations. This results in a steady pull from operations down the line which tends to increase production.[37]

Automobile capitalists and managers were not content, however, to allow the natural "pull" of the line to speed up work. They used a couple of methods to actively seize control of the pace of line work. One was time study. By setting and enforcing job times that allowed no discretionary actions by workers, manufacturers could control work intensity. For example, a Bureau of Labor Statistics researcher reported of one auto body factory that had recently instituted progressive layout and applied time study: "Much of the slack between operations was obliterated, and a steady flow of work was secured throughout the establishment, so that an operation on one body would be finished just in time to make way for the next body."[38] The other method of controlling the pace of progressive line production was the use of pacesetters. Also called lead men and straw bosses, these were particularly fast and loyal workers who were placed in strategic points along the line to maintain a rapid work pace. Of one such pacesetter on a progressive milling operation at Ford, a researcher wrote that "when he worked very rapidly he passed the materials on to the others at the same rate, and the others had to either keep up or pile up an excess of parts and thus call the attention of the boss to their delay."[39]

An MIT expert on progressive line production summed up its effects on control of work intensity in this way.

> The operator in a production line has less control over his working speed than the job-shop employee. Each worker has certain work assigned to him which must be completed in the time allotted. Otherwise, the line beyond his station, as well as other dependent lines, may be delayed. Where there is no slack in the float [material in process between work stations], the worker's pace is precisely determined when the speed of the line is established and the operations assigned. He is required to work at the same rate continuously. . . . the fact that the pace of work is more directly under management's control in line production is an important one. The power which management is thus given to set the speed of the line is not to be taken lightly. Used wisely, it may maintain production at a high level.[40]

However, as with the division of labor, there were also nonrepressive advantages to progressive layout that made production more efficient without affecting the class struggle for control of the labor process. For example, placing successive work operations close to one another cut down on the amount of back-breaking labor necessary in hauling heavy parts from place to place. This relieved workers of a great burden and cut down on fatigue, allowing them to be more productive in their labor. Further, progressive layout reduced substantially the amount of resources tied up in stock and inventory. Because it cut down on delays and ensured a smooth flow of work, stockpiles of parts between stations previously necessary to ensure continuity were virtually eliminated, releasing these resources for productive utilization. Finally, progressive layout saved floor space, because there was less need for aisles for handling and storing materials.[41]

Thus, these first steps toward a capitalist-controlled automotive labor process—interchangeability and standardization, division of labor and progressive layout—were motivated by a complex combination of neutral and socially biased advantages, or repressive and nonrepressive control. In public forums, auto manufacturers liked to focus on the neutral, nonrepressive advantages as their main motivations. But their more private communications clearly revealed, as we have seen, that they were also motivated to wrest control of the labor process out of the hands of skilled craft workers. The resulting mindlessness of work was thus in large part a result of a conscious class struggle in the auto shops. These new production methods resulted in higher levels of production and higher profits, not mainly because they made work more productive or efficient, but because they overcame the resistance of a class of recalcitrant workers to increased exploitation.

CHAPTER 4
Early Mechanization

C losely following and often overlapping with these first changes in auto work was another giant step along the road to a labor process controlled and dominated by capital—mechanization. By this I do not mean the mere introduction of machines to replace handwork. Machines of various sorts were present from the beginning of automobile production. Rather, I understand mechanization as the gradual, evolutionary process whereby the control of work is removed from direct producers and incorporated into an autonomous mechanism. The most pertinent social fact about machinery is that the control over the motion of tools comes to be exercised by an inanimate mechanism, rather than by the skill and intelligence of human laborers. This ultimately shifts control of work to those purchasing and making decisions about productive equipment, who are, under capitalism, the capitalists and their managers. Therefore, the gradual, ongoing process of mechanization was another weapon used by capitalists in their class struggle with workers over the control of the labor process.[1]

FROM UNIVERSAL TO SPECIALIZED MACHINES

The automobile industry of the United States began its journey along the road of mechanization not at the beginning but in the middle. It drew on the mechanical heritage of several centuries of

European and American civilization, beginning production with the use of fairly sophisticated machines: lathes, planers, millers, borers, drill presses, drop forges, etc. But these machines were generally of the universal type, constructed to perform not one specific task, but a wide variety of work. They offered a broad range of mechanical possibilities. And the limitation of that range to accomplish a specific task was not inherent in the mechanism itself, but was the job of the skilled operator. Because universal machines only minimally constrained the tool motion, they represented a relatively low level of mechanization.

A step toward a higher level of mechanization was taken with the introduction of specialized machines. Instead of providing a broad range of mechanical possibilities ultimately limited by the operator, these machines were constructed to perform one specific work task only. For example, a milling machine was constructed solely to mill the bearings on the motor crankcase. Instead of having a range of adjustments allowing for different spindle speeds, feed angles, and cutter positions, as did the universal milling machine, the specialized miller was built so that each of these variables was rigidly and inalterably fixed in the manner appropriate for the crankcase job. The level of mechanization was significantly advanced because the constraint or limitation of tool motion was built into the mechanism itself. The personal action, initiative, and intelligence of the worker were in large part appropriated by the specialized machine.[2]

This step from universal to specialized machinery was not, of course, the innovation of the American automobile industry. The concept of the specialized machine is very old indeed and had received extensive application in numerous mass-production industries of England and the U.S. This big step on the scale of mechanization was, however, delayed in the auto industry until three necessary preconditions for it had emerged. First, standardization of parts and overall design of the automobile model by firms was necessary before machines could be specialized. The wide variety of parts and models produced by early firms prevented them from achieving the volume necessary to use specialized machines. However, when innovative auto entrepreneurs like Ford and Olds began to concentrate on the production of one or two standard models and a small range of standard parts, they achieved sufficient volume to make specialized machines economically feasible. The second precondition for specialized machines was the division of labor in auto shops. As long as work remained unitary and encompassed by the skilled operators, their machines and tools had to be universal, encompassing the broad range of tasks they performed. However, when auto capitalists reached sufficient volume, they began to divide and specialize labor. With complex machine operations thus broken down into simple parts, it became possible to construct machines to perform one task only.[3] Third, a high volume of production was a precondition for the operation of specialized machines in an economically feasible manner.

EARLY MECHANIZATION OF AUTO WORK

When the large auto firms met these preconditions during the first decade of the twentieth century, they began to introduce specialized machinery into their shops. As with the earlier changes in the labor process, this mechanization process was motivated by a complex combination of repressive and nonrepressive control. Auto capitalists and managers replaced universal with specialized machines, partially because the latter improved the productivity and precision of machine work. However, they also undertook this change because the new machines allowed them to wrest greater control of work precision and intensity out of the hands of workers, as a detailed examination of capitalist motivations will reveal. But before turning to this examination, let us first survey the large auto factories of this period and describe the changes wrought by mechanization.

Foundry

The division of labor in the foundry had already deskilled and degraded the previously skilled work of making metal castings. Mechanization furthered this process. The first step was the introduction of molding machines, which replaced the hand-ramming of the sand with pneumatically driven rammers or vibrating devices. Much of the skill required of the molder in order to achieve a uniform packing of sand was thus eliminated. Molding machines had been in use in other American industries since the 1880s, but only with high-volume production did their use become feasible in the auto industry. After their introduction, they became gradually more specialized to handle the making of one type of mold alone. Skilled hand-molding became confined to the fabrication of tools or special orders.

The delicate and skilled job of mixing sand for the molds was taken from the molders and centralized into a mechanical system

62

that automatically produced a specific and unvarying sand mixture for each different type of work. At Ford, such a system was installed in 1912. The various machine mixers were located in a gallery above the foundry floor and delivered sand to the molding machines through chutes. When the castings were shaken out of the casting boxes over a grate, the system carried the sand back to the machine mixers, which reprocessed it and again delivered it to the molding machines.

Mechanized ovens installed in foundries took much of the skill out of making the sand cores. Previously, coremakers had had to know the exact time to bake a particular type of core to attain the desired characteristics for a casting. However, in 1912 Ford introduced an endless-chain core oven, consisting of a chain-driven conveyor that moved the cores continuously through an oven at the precise speed required to bake them the proper time. Another foundry skill was thus eliminated.

What did more to eliminate foundry skills than the mechanization of the old casting process was the invention of new processes to perform the same work. For some parts, like pistons, mechanized die-casting replaced casting in sand molds. In the die-casting machines, parts were cast in specially treated, reusable metal dies instead of sand molds, which could be used but once. And many parts that had once been cast began to be produced by metal-stamping machines. Both processes eliminated the need for making sand molds for every part produced and, consequently, reduced greatly the skills involved.[4]

Forge Shop

In the labor of forging, the drop-forging machine early on replaced the blacksmith's hammer and anvil. But the small volume of production of the early shops dictated that forging machines remain general purpose, with skilled workers changing the dies and generally adjusting the mechanism for each type of part. However, increased volumes of production made it feasible to specialize machines in the forging of one part. Dies were permanently set, and other machine variables—power, length of stroke, size of ram—were fixed to accommodate one job alone. As a result, the skill of setting and operating drop-forging machines was substantially reduced.

Mechanization also brought different types of forging machines into use to replace drop forgers. One secured multiple die sets inside a heavy metal cylinder. Once the parts were loaded, the cylinder was rotated rapidly, causing rollers within it to force the dies together at a rate of three thousand five hundred times per minute (over twenty times the rate of any drop forger). This not only increased productivity, but it also removed considerable discretion from the operator.

The heat-treating process associated with forging also underwent mechanization. In the early days of the industry, the worker judged the temperature of the metal from its color. But towards the end of the 1910s, pyrometers were installed on furnaces to give precise readings of treating temperatures. Another skill of the forge worker was thus appropriated by machinery.[5]

The extent to which these special machines had eliminated much of the skill of forging is illustrated by the labor of making auto springs. Prior to the introduction of special machines, spring production was a handicraft in which quality depended upon the skill of the workers who forged and bent the "leaves" (metal plates) of the spring. The workers heated the leaves in a furnace until, by their judgment, they were ready to be worked upon. Two workers then gripped a plate with tongs and bent it by hand to a curved template, judging the accuracy of the curve by eye. Then the hot metal was quenched in oil and afterwards hammered by hand to remove imperfections. But around 1915, special spring-making machines and pyrometers removed much of the skill from the job. The pyrometer showed the exact temperature of the heat-treating furnace, eliminating the necessity of judgments by workers. And the skills of bending, quenching, and forging the metal plates were eliminated by a specialized forging machine. A pair of dies on the machine automatically squeezed the plate to absolutely true form and then, in the same motion, plunged it into the oil bath. The workers were left the tasks merely of placing the plate on the machine's dies and pulling a lever. Only the "smallest modicum of common sense suffices to operate a good machine," wrote one trade journalist of the specialized spring-maker.[6]

Paint and Body Shops

The paint and body shops of the automobile factories also took steps toward higher levels of mechanization that reduced their heavy complement of skilled labor. In the woodworking shop, where rough wood stock was shaped into parts for the wood body, universal woodworking machines were gradually replaced by specialized machines, rigidly constructed to do one specific task. Power saws were constructed with stops that determined the precise length and depth of the cut. Drilling machines with multiple spindles drilled all the holes in one part in the proper alignment. Surfacers were built with multiple cutters rigidly positioned to finish all sides of a body part at one pass. Similarly, other woodworking machines—band saws, gainers, jointers, miter saws, planers, ripsaws, routers, tenoners, mortisers—became specialized and arranged in progressive lines.

In the body shop, the assembly of the pliable wooden parts into a rigid and exacting body frame remained a relatively skilled job, but some of the skill was eliminated by the use of framing jigs or bucks. These were rigid and precisely built metal structures within which the frame was built. The buck held the wooden parts in precise alignment while they were secured together, thus ensuring exacting work with minimal worker skills. The same type of bucks or jigs were also introduced into the job of assembling the metal panels to the frame. The final-assembly jig allowed the panels to be attached to the frame and welded together only in the precise way, eliminating much of the hand-fitting involved.

The process of welding in the body shop also underwent substantial mechanization. When pressed-metal panels and parts first replaced wooden ones *circa* 1909, welding was done by acetylene torches. Highly skilled workers fused parts by melting a metal rod at the joint with hand-held gas torches. However, some of this skill was displaced by the introduction of electric welding machines. These machines secured electrodes to each of the parts, which were then brought together, completing the electric circuit and fusing them. Special electric welding machines were constructed to hold the parts in exact alignment, as they were "upset" (thrust together) to make the weld. However, these machines still required skilled operators in their early stage. The workers had to set the proper voltage and amperage, time the current, determine the length of preheating contact, and properly time the upset.[7]

In the paint shop, the long, tedious, skilled process of brush-painting bodies underwent substantial mechanization in order to simplify and speed it up. Around 1914, two machine processes were discovered. One was the flow technique, by which a stream of paint was squirted on and allowed to drip off, leaving a smooth finish. William Knudsen, one of Ford's production geniuses, is said to have invented this process. A second method, which Walter Chrysler claimed to have applied first, was air-brush or spray painting. This involved spraying the paint from a nozzled gun by air pressure. Drying ovens began to be used in conjunction with both of these new painting techniques to speed up the process of drying paint between applications. Probably first used at Ford, these ovens were similar to the core ovens used in foundries. They were long, gas-heated tunnels through which auto bodies and parts were slowly moved by conveyors.

Special machines were also invented to handle the painting and enameling of smaller parts. At Ford, for example, wheels were painted on a machine that dipped them in a vat of paint and spun them dry. A machine was also devised to paint the decorative striping on the bodies, an operation previously done by highly skilled artists. Enameling machines were invented that automatically carried fenders, windshield frames, and other parts through the cleansing, dipping, and drying stages. The skilled method of hand-dipping was thus eliminated.[8]

Machine Shops

By far the most important and greatest advances in the mechanization of auto work took place in the machine shops. The industry had begun with a few universal machine tools, which were nursed in their operations by highly skilled machinists. However, high production volumes, the minute division of labor, and progressive layout made possible the devotion of a machine tool to one specific operation. This motivated auto production experts to search for ways to make these machines more efficient in their sole tasks. The result of this process was the specialized machine tool, a mechanism adapted specifically for and capable of performing one machining task only.

The first step toward specialized machine tools was the use of jigs and fixtures in conjunction with universal machines. (See table 4.1 for a summary of the steps of mechanization.) These devices were not part of the machine proper, but rather were appliances that were attached either to the work being machined or to the machine itself in order to guide tool movement. The jig was generally attached to the work itself and guided the tool in a prescribed manner. The simplest such device was the drill jig, a pattern with pre-drilled holes that fit over the part to be drilled. In order to drill exacting and properly aligned holes, the drill-press operator had only to guide the drill through the holes in the jig, then on through the part. The fixture, on the other hand, was a work-holding device that was fastened to the machine itself. It held one or more pieces of work in a position that ensured that the tool contacted them

TABLE 4.1. Steps in the Mechanization of Machine Tools in the U.S. Automobile Industry

Steps in mechanization	Year of introduction	Distinguishing machine operations	Operator's intervention
1. Universal machine tools		Broad range of mechanical possibilities limited by human skill	Set up, load/unload, start/stop, feed, inspection, machine maintenance
2. Jigs and fixtures on universal machine tools	c. 1903	Temporary limitation of tool movement to prescribed path	Load/unload, start/stop, feed
3. Specialized machine tools	c. 1905	Permanent limitation of tool movement, spindle speed, feed, fixture for one part	Load/unload, start/stop, feed
a. Compound machines	c. 1905	Simultaneous performance of multiple operations of same type	Load/unload, start/stop, feed
b. Complex machines	c. 1905	Simultaneous performance of multiple operations of different type	Load/unload, start/stop, feed
c. Revolving fixtures	c. 1905	Simultaneous performance of multiple operations or simultaneous machining and loading	Load/unload, start/stop, feed
d. Ganging of work	c. 1905	Simultaneous loading, feeding, machining of multiple parts	Load/unload, start/stop, feed
4. Semiautomatic machine tools	c. 1905	Automatic feed of work	Load/unload, start/stop
5. Fully automatic machine tools	c. 1912	Automatic feed of work, continuous operation, simultaneous machining and loading	Load/unload
6. Automation	c. 1935	Automatic loading and transfer of work, mechanically controlled	Surveillance, reporting of trouble

in the prescribed way. The larger auto firms with relatively high volumes—Olds, Cadillac, Ford—began to use jigs and fixtures in a variety of machine tasks around the middle of the first decade of this century.[9]

The use of jigs and fixtures was a step upward on the scale of mechanization, for they limited the possible paths the tool might take to one. These appliances, not the skill of the machinists, specified the proper limitations within the machine's range of mechanical possibilities to accomplish work in the prescribed manner. However, this step fell short of specialized machinery as such. Jigs and fixtures were merely applied to universal machine tools; the constraint they provided was temporary and reversible. The machines could be converted to other production tasks once these appliances were removed.

Soon, however, higher and higher volumes of production of standardized models and parts gave auto capitalists the incentive to begin to specialize the machine tools themselves. Work tables were designed to hold one type of part only. Cutting tools were rigidly fixed in one position. Spindles were inalterably set at one speed. Feed paths were determined by ways and stops, doing away with numerous adjustments and settings. The transition from universal to rigidly specialized machinery was gradual. At first, the range of universal machine tools was merely narrowed to accommodate one general type of operation—for example, crankpin grinding. But higher volumes and greater standardization gradually brought more and more specialized machine tools, until many were rigidly constructed to take one cut on one specific part of a specific model, and nothing else. Thus, by 1927, the machinery of the Ford Company had become so rigidly specialized for the production of one car, the Model T, that it took Ford six frantic months and $18 million to tool up for production of the new Model A. He had to completely rebuild over half of his existing stock of forty-three thousand machine tools and purchase four thousand five hundred new ones.[10]

One way in which machine tools were specialized for work on a specific part was by combining in one machine several previously separate operations. That is, multiple-operation machines were constructed to perform several metal-cutting operations with only one set-up and loading. There were generally two broad types of such multiple-operation machine tools. First, compound machines simply combined and coordinated identical operations. The simplest compound machine tool, and one of the first to appear (1859), was the multispindled drill press. Instead of one drill spindle, this machine had several, all driven by the same motor and fed simultaneously by the same mechanism. Thus, instead of loading and clamping the work to be drilled into a series of machines, or instead of adjusting and changing one machine to drill several holes, the operator could completely drill the part with one loading, set-up, and pass of the machine. The auto industry adopted the multispindled drill press around the middle of the first decade of this century for drilling the numerous holes in the cylinder block and cylinder heads. The same principle of compounding operations into one machine tool was soon applied to other operations in auto machine shops: turning, milling, boring, and grinding.[11]

The second type of multiple-operation machine tool was the complex machine, which grouped together several different machine tasks that might be performed simultaneously or successively. One of the first complex machine tools was the turret lathe. On a regular lathe was mounted a rotating tool carriage, the turret. This carried a number of different cutting tools—turning tools, drills, borers, reamers—that could be brought successively into contact with the turning part without removing it from the lathe. The operator simply backed the tool carriage off the part, revolved the turret until the desired tool was in working position, and fed it back into the work. The turret lathe was adopted by the auto industry as soon as the preconditions for specialized machinery were met. And during this same period, innovative auto entrepreneurs and production managers began to build other complex machine tools designed for the specific needs of the mass production of automobiles.[12]

Another specialized machine feature, which was often used in conjuction with multiple-operation machines, was the revolving fixture. This feature was often incorporated into complex machine tools so as to allow the simultaneous performance of two different operations on the same machine. The fixture held two sets of parts, and the machine had two different types of tools on opposite sides of the fixture. The operator simultaneously performed the two different machine operations on the two parts, and then revolved the fixture to perform the opposite operation on each. The revolving fixture was also used in conjunction with compound machinery. Instead of having two work stations, one on either side, the machine's fixture had one idle station—the loading station—and one work station. This allowed the operator to unload the finished parts and load rough stock while the machine tool was in operation. When machining at the work station was complete, the operator merely revolved the fixture, bringing the finished parts into the loading position and the rough stock into the work position. This arrangement allowed for the constant and uninterrupted work by both machine and operator.[13]

Another specialized machine feature was the ganging fixture, which allowed not one but numerous parts to be loaded, set up, and worked on at once. This fixture was particularly applicable to milling machines. By 1909 it was common practice in auto machine shops to equip millers with long flat ganging fixtures called tables, on which were provisions for clamping many parts in a row. Table millers that could accommodate sixteen cylinder blocks were not uncommon. Dozens of smaller parts, like piston rods, were lined up to be milled on such machines. Once properly loaded and set up, the parts were successively fed past the millers by simply moving the table, either by hand or power feed. Ganging fixtures were also applied to grinding and drilling machines.[14]

Although these specialized machine tools began appearing around 1903, a qualitative turning point in their use came in 1907 and 1908. There was a competitive shake-out of the industry during and following the financial panic and depression of these years. Cutting costs required new economies in production, and specialized machine tools were introduced in order to provide a substantial proportion of these.[15]

Repressive and Nonrepressive Control in Early Mechanization

This early mechanization of various types of auto work was motivated by a combination of repressive and nonrepressive control. Auto capitalists and managers found the new machines preferable in part because they increased the accuracy and productivity of work. But it is also clear from their own statements that they undertook mechanization in order to weaken the opposition of workers and shift the control of work to themselves. Manufacturers of this period generally cited two advantages of mechanization as their motives: (1) increased precision of the finished work, and (2) decreased unit labor costs of production. A close examination, however, reveals that both of these seemingly neutral advantages were achieved partly by repressive control.

Increased Precision

There were competing opinions within the American automobile industry on the relationship between precision and mechanization. There were many who claimed that mechanization was undertaken primarily to improve precision in machine work and, consequently, to make parts interchangeable. Thus, one early commentator wrote in *The Automobile*: "We hear so much of the labor saving idea that most of us fail to remember that there is a second and stronger reason for using special machinery in a shop. . . . it is of far greater importance to be able to duplicate parts [make them interchangeable] than it is to save a little labor. . . ."[16] These capitalists and their commentators asserted that the limitations placed on tool movements by jigs, fixtures, and various other specialized features ensured that work was done in exactly the same manner, day in and day out. Prior to the use of these mechanical strictures, when the range of variation of tool movement was left within the hands of workers, such precision could not be attained, they claimed.

Others in the industry, however, disputed this alleged relationship between specialized machinery and precise, interchangeable work. Typical of this opinion was the following statement in *The Automobile*: "Expensive special machine tools in many shops account for the quality of the work done, but it is not absolutely necessary to use them, nor will the quality of the work done fall below a desirable standard in the absence of them—in fact, in the shop it is true that 'fine feathers do not necessarily make fine birds,' so to speak, referring to machining processes."[17]

There is good evidence to substantiate the contention that specialized machinery was *not* necessary to achieve precision in machining, and that universal machines could produce accurate work. As was documented in chapter 3, the mechanical improvements in universal machine tools and the introduction of the grinding machine were mainly responsible for the increased precision that made possible the quantity production of interchangeable parts. The fact that such universal machines could ensure precision work is substantiated by their predominance in Henry Leland's Cadillac shops, the precision of whose output was validated by an independent test, and in shops producing trucks and luxury cars, where levels of precision higher than normal were required. This evidence casts serious doubt on the claim by many that precision work could be attained only with the use of special mechanical devices that inalterably fixed tool movement beyond the control of workers' hands.[18]

But auto capitalists' claims that they were motivated to specialize machinery by the greater resulting precision should not be lightly dismissed as simple apologetics meant to obscure their real motivations. If examined closely, their statements reveal a basic truth about attaining precision under the social condition of the antagonistic relations of production characteristic of capitalism. The preceding evidence shows only that precision work was technically possible on universal machines operated by skilled machinists. But we have not yet taken the social relations of production into account in this equation. Under the antagonistic relations of production characteristic of capitalism, workers resisted being exploited in their labor. This resistance often took the form of a general shop atmoshpere of indifference toward work, not only its intensity, but also its accuracy. Such indifference could prove disastrous in a labor process that left the accuracy of work in the hands of these recalcitrant workers, as did the early auto shops. Hence although precision in this labor process was technically possible, the relations of capitalist production often rendered it socially impossible, or at least uncertain. As long as indifferent, recalcitrant workers were responsible for the precision of machine work, its attainment was sporadic and intermittent at best, fluctuating with wages, working conditions, the labor market, and other social factors. Auto capitalists aspiring to mass production could not operate profitably under such uncertain conditions. The solution was the introduction of specialized machinery, which reduced the control over accuracy by the unpredictable, recalcitrant "human element." Therefore, these machines increased precision largely through increasing the repressive control of capital over work.

Auto capitalists were well aware of the danger to precision constituted by the recalcitrant workers in control of the labor process. As one trade journalist wrote, "the very fact that American labor will take the initiative when it is left to its own devices constitutes a danger, and the personal equation represents a serious situation, which, like the inaccuracies of process must be subdued and controlled." And the solution was clearly formulated. "Special machinery, special jigs and special fixtures, supplemented by the especially designed gages, leave no room for the human element which is the foe to interchangeability in manufactured products."[19]

In the introduction of specific machines, this general capitalist motive toward reducing workers' control over accuracy was also clear. For example, when comparing a new spring-making machine to the previous craft method of production, a writer for *The Automobile* candidly admitted that the craft method

> produces excellent work *so long as the men are utterly reliable*, but it is easy for one lacking in skill or in care to bend a little wobble in the plate or to twist it a little. . . . The new way is to pull a lever, which brings down another die on top of the other; so squeezing the plate to absolutely true form, and then, in the same motion, sousing plate and

dies beneath the surface of oil in a great tank. Not only is the new process quicker, but *the human element is eliminated.*[20]

The social relations of production, not any technical considerations, prevented skilled wage workers from producing accurate parts. These relations ensured that many workers would be lacking in care toward their work, and that precision could be guaranteed only by removing workers' control over production.

Jigs and fixtures were another method of reducing workers' control over machine-tool accuracy, "so that the workman need exercise no care or scrutiny in operating and working them," as engineering journalists Arnold and Faurote wrote of Ford's machines.[21] The possibility of workers who were consciously or subconsciously resisting capitalist exploitation through careless work; or workers who were simply fatigued from capitalist-imposed overwork; or workers who were hungover from an attempt to find escape from their work—the possibility of such workers making errors was reduced by using jigs and fixtures. These so constrained tool movements that work could be done in only one way, no matter how resistant, fatigued, or hungover workers were. Thus, of a specialized milling machine, a trade journalist wrote in *The Automobile* that "the cylinders are held in a fixture, the object of which is to eliminate the personal equation, preventing the workman from setting up the cylinders excepting in a way to afford the desired results."[22]

The claim by this and other capitalist interests that specialized machines totally eliminated the effect of workers on accuracy is surely an exaggeration, a product of wishful thinking. Although the operators of such machines were no longer in complete control of work, they were still responsible for loading and clamping parts, as well as tool feed, all of which had an impact on work precision. But these quotations do establish that the elimination of workers' control of accuracy was an important capitalist motivation behind and a partial accomplishment of early mechanization.

It is clear, then, that specialized machinery ensured greater precision in auto production partially by increasing repressive control. By transferring responsibility for accuracy from workers to mechanical devices, capitalists and managers were able to repress the effects of antagonistic social relations upon accuracy. However, it is also clear that the increased precision of specialized machines was partially the result of increased nonrepressive control, which had nothing to do with the social relations of production. Some of the specialized machines were able to work at levels of precision of which skilled workers with hand tools or universal machines were simply incapable, no matter how willingly and diligently they worked. Take, for example, the specialized mulitple-operation machine tools. Prior to their introduction into the auto shops, the work had to be loaded, located, and set up for each cut taken on it. Because it was impossible to locate the part in the machine precisely each time, no matter how careful workers were, the possible deviation from the desired accruacy was greatly multiplied by the large number of separate operations. However, with the use of compound and complex machines, there was only one loading, location, and set-up for a large number of cuts. Although the work might deviate from the prescribed measurement due to imprecise location and set-up, at least all of the cuts taken with one machine deviated in the same direction and amount, thus ensuring the proper alignment of the cuts. Other specialized machine tools, with their special clamps, work heads, and work supports, similarly ensured precision without affecting the relations of production under which they were used. Therefore, both motivations toward repressive and nonrepressive control were behind the auto manufacturers' attempts to increase precision through greater mechanization.[23]

Decreased Unit Labor Costs

Increased precision seems, however, to have been of only secondary importance in motivating auto capitalists to mechanize work. As the trade literature reveals, they were motivated to introduce specialized machinery in their shops primarily by the necessity of lowering unit labor costs. The early auto industry was highly competitive, with over two hundred and fifty firms competing for customers in 1908. Lowering prices was a prime means of competing, and in order to do so and remain profitable, production costs had to be cut. Because labor costs comprised such a large proportion of overall production costs—as much as 25 percent—they were a prime target for cuts. But, as we saw earlier, the shortages of labor for the burgeoning shops prevented capitalists from cutting labor costs by lowering wages. Even though mechanization and the earlier changes in the labor process allowed the increasing replacement of skilled with semiskilled and unskilled workers, the scarce supply of even the latter strengthened workers' market power and forced auto capitalists to keep wages relatively high in order to attract and hold these workers. As a result, real wages in the industry rose steadily in this period, despite the deskilling of work. So capitalists sought to cut labor costs in the only other way possible—by lowering the labor time expended on any unit of production, thus lowering unit labor costs. This goal was achieved in large part through the introduction of specialized machinery.[24]

Capitalist use of machinery reduced the amount of labor time expended on an automobile in two ways: (1) by increasing the productivity of labor, and (2) by increasing the intensity of labor. Increasing productivity means increasing the quantity of products yielded by the the same quantity of labor in a given time—that is, workers do not have to work any harder. Increasing intensity means increasing the quantity of products yielded in a given time by increasing the quantity of labor expended in that time—that is, workers have to work harder.[25]

It is clear from the evidence that increased productivity was an important motive behind mechanization, and that this reduced labor time and consequently cut labor costs. Many of the special jigs, fixtures, and machines allowed workers to turn out more work in the same time without working any harder. Jigs and fixtures enabled workers to load and set up machines quickly. They did not have to spend time adjusting and aligning each piece to ensure accurate machining, for the jigs and fixtures took care of that. The same was true of specialized machinery of various sorts. Because these machines were constructed to perform only one task, the workers did not have to spend time in setting up and adjusting them.

In addition to reducing set-up time, specialized machines also increased the productivity of labor in many cases simply because they were capable of performing operations much more rapidly than machines or work processes that required extensive worker intervention. Spray- and flow-painting machines, for example, were able to apply paint much faster than a worker with a brush, regardless of how hard he tried. It was estimated that enameling machines cut 30 percent of the labor time required by hand-dipping. In one body plant, an electric welding machine allowed a worker to produce sixty welds an hour, as against the average of about thirteen for a welder using a torch. Multiple-operation machine tools greatly reduced the time required to machine a part; in about the same time required previously to take one cut, numerous cuts were just as easily made. The ganging of work on machines similarly increased the productivity of auto labor. Parts loaded into such ganging fixtures could be cut quickly in succession, without the necessity to stop the machine and reload. An example of the labor savings that could be achieved by combining the multiple-operation and ganging features is provided by the Velie Motor Company. This manufacturer reported in 1912 that the replacement of a universal miller with a specialized miller, which took five simultaneous cuts on a succession of four cylinder blocks, reduced machining time per block from sixty-five to twenty-five minutes. The machine saved twenty hours of labor time on a day's output of blocks.[26]

The increased productivity achieved in these ways by mechanization was clearly a nonrepressive-control measure. The mechanical innovations increased workers' output without affecting the social relations of production by making more efficient use of human labor. Such a use of machinery was certainly socially neutral. However, capitalists used the new machines to cut unit labor costs in another way that was not neutral, but repressive, rooted in the antagonistic relations of production of capitalism. Machines were used repressively to increase the intensity of labor. Like increased productivity, intensification of labor increased workers' output in a given time, but did so by forcing workers to expend more energy in that time, that is, to work harder. Specialized machinery allowed capitalists to intensify labor by taking control of the work pace away from workers and thus insulating it from their resistance. Auto manufacturers and their spokesmen were fond of emphasizing the nonrepressive aspects of mechanization—that it "lightened the burden of labor" and allowed workers to produce more with the same or less effort. But they were also well aware that machinery could be used to intensify labor, and this formed a major motive force behind their drive to mechanize auto work.

Machinery was used by auto capitalists and managers to intensify labor in several ways. First, it took the skill and judgment out of work, and hence it eliminated the discretionary time during which workers exercised these. As long as the tasks performed were not uniform and specialized but uncertain, workers had to be relied upon to determine exactly what to do and how. Work was at their discretion. And so was its timing. It was impossible to determine precisely how long jobs should take, because they were varied. Thus, workers were largely in control of the pace of their own labor. And they could use this control to resist capitalist pressure to intensify labor.

Mechanization, however, limited the range of human skill and discretion required in auto work. This was particularly true of the specialized machines that were appearing during this period. Only one type of unvaried, specialized work was done on these. And work tasks were fixed so that they could only be performed in one way. Workers were not required to exercise much skill in setting up, loading, or running these machines. This reduction of skill decreased worker control over work pace. Because tasks were standard and uniform, it was easy to determine how long they should take. Machines thus limited the impact of the uncontrollable "personal equation" on work intensity as well as accuracy. Auto capitalists were aware of this, and it formed a major motivation for mechanization. Thus, one industry spokesman wrote approvingly of some new specialized machines that "the accuracy and speed of production is dependent upon the process and the machinery equipment, rather than upon the skill of the workmen and other like considerations. . . . " Another wrote of specialized machinery that: "The theory of establishing a single speed and single feed was to *eliminate the judgment of the operator and to predetermine the day's output*. If this was not obtained, the cause was readily detected and almost as readily remedied."[27]

Once again, these capitalist claims that specialized machinery had completely eliminated workers' control of labor intensity were surely exaggerations. Auto manufacturers probably used the trade journals to engage in a boastful rivalry with their competitors over production methods. And machine-tool manufacturers were inclined to exaggerate the acomplishments of their products in their statements to and advertisements in these journals in order to stimulate sales. The specialized machines of this early period still required considerable human intervention: loading, clamping, tool feed. Although these operations did not involve the range of discretion exercised by skilled machinists on universal machines, they nonetheless required workers to exercise decision-making abilities that required some experience and training. For example, feeding tools to the work often required operators to make discretionary adjustments for tool wear and material quality. The operators of these machines are best described, then, as semiskilled workers. These remaining pockets of discretion prevented capitalists from seizing total control of the work pace. But despite these exaggerated claims, it is not to be doubted that eliminating workers' control of labor intensity was an important capitalist reason for early mechanization, even if that was not the result.

A development that illustrates this motive for increasing labor intensity through reducing workers' skills was the invention of the flow-painting technique by William Knudsen of the Ford Company. Around 1914 spray guns were coming into use in some painting jobs, but to apply the finishing coat of varnish still required highly skilled workers, who were in scarce supply. Knudsen was experiencing difficulties with the skilled finisher in the Ford paint shop.

Every Monday morning he was very slow beginning work, complaining of the brushes, varnish, or room temperature. Knudsen was frustrated and stymied by the delays, until one Monday morning he noticed that the finisher's hands were shaking.

> "So," he said, "that's it."
> "What's that Bill?" asked the finisher.
> "You've been lifting too many drinks over the week end."
> "That's my business," returned the finisher, feeling secure in his job.
> "Go and get your pay," ordered Knudsen. The paint foreman, standing by, heard the dismissal and came over to Knudsen. "Now you've done it," he cried. "What are we going to do? You've fired the only finisher we've got."
> "Go down the street and get a sprinkling can," said Knudsen. "Bring it back here and I'll show you what to do."[28]

With that sprinkling can, Knudsen sprinkled the varnish on the car and thus devised the first crude flow-paint system.

Now as long as applying the varnish coat was a highly skilled job, demanding great knowledge and dexterity, Knudsen could do nothing about the slowness of the worker on Monday mornings. It was the finisher who determined how fast the job was done. And as long as he possessed these vital, scarce skills, his drinking was his business. But as soon as Knudsen had replaced this skill and discretion of the worker with the mechanized flow-paint system, it was capital that determined the pace at which cars were painted. Mechanization allowed capital to control the intensity of labor by deskilling workers and hence reducing their discretionary time.

A second way that auto manufacturers used machinery to intensify work was by making it more continuous, with no idle moments for workers. As they often admitted, capitalists designed their machines "so that the operator must keep moving" or to "keep an operator busy."[29] Special fixtures were the main way of ensuring continuity on the early machines and hence filling up the unproductive pores of the working day. Previous to their introduction, the auto worker had set up and loaded the machine and then engaged the mechanism. Many of these machines had power feed, so that the worker was idle during the actual machining process, merely watching the progress of the work. Of course, seeing this precious commodity of labor power idle was more than capital could bear. Special fixtures were designed so that the operator was forced to set up and load one set of parts while another was being machined. The compound machine with the revolving fixture is an example of this work-intensifying feature. Clearly such machines did not increase the productivity of work, but rather its intensity. Workers had to work harder, for capital had expropriated, through the design of machines, the idle, unproductive pores of the working day and crammed them full of continuous, unrelenting work.

A third way that auto manufacturers used machinery to intensify labor was by drastically reducing the number of handlings of work. Previous to the introduction of specialized, multiple-operation machines, capitalists had divided labor in the shops into a large number of detail operations. Each worker performed one small task on one machine. Although this minute division of labor had the desired effects of increasing productivity and deskilling labor, it had the pronounced disadvantage of wasting time in the passage of work between the numerous workers and machines. Such numerous handlings of work would waste labor time under any system of production relations. But this was especially so under the antagonistic relations of production of capitalism, for these handlings provided workers with opportunities to slow down the pace of work by being slow in passing it on.

As long as the level of mechanization was low, and, consequently, the control of machines was in the hands of workers, the advantages of increased productivity and decreased skill requirements outweighed this disadvantage. However, with the increased mechanization and specialization of machines, the control of work was increasingly transferred from workers to machines, and the advantages of the minute division of labor diminished. Productivity became more dependent on the machine than on the proficiency of the detail worker. And the deskilling of work became increasingly ensured by the machinery itself, rather than the division of labor. The disadvantage of this division—wasted time in work handling—came to weigh heavily on the managerial mind. The solution to this problem was found in reversing the trend toward an ever more minute division of labor and beginning to recombine machining operations in multiple-operation machines. By reducing the handling of work, these machines increased work intensity by depriving workers of the opportunity to slow down the flow of work. But at the same time, the higher level of mechanization ensured that this renewed unity of work would not provide the basis for a resurgence of powerful skilled workers.[30]

Auto capitalists were well aware of the great waste of labor time in human work handling. One engineering journalist wrote of the Ford Company that "they have learned that the greatest machine shop waste occurs in the handling of the part being machined rather than in the cutting operations themselves."[31] And capitalists were equally aware of the solution. As Ford wrote:

> The best that we can do is to combine as many operations as possible, using to a very considerable extent the principle of the turret lathe—which is one of the most important principles in modern manufacturing. For example, if a part had to be drilled, reamed, turned, and faced under the old system it would pass through eight or nine single-purpose machines each managed by a man and there would be a great deal of handling and of opportunity for error. Now most of these operations are performed on a single machine with a single operator who just clamps the part into a turret. . . . Thus there is no lost time or motion; the parts are handled but twice—once in loading as a rough forging and again in removing as a finished part.[32]

A fourth way that auto capitalists and managers used machinery to intensify labor was simply by increasing the operating speed. On the universal machines operated by skilled machinists, the speed of the tool was of necessity left at the discretion of workers. Because work was varied and irregular, machinists had to adjust tool speed to the peculiarities of the job and materials in order to produce accurate work. However, as parts and tasks became increasingly standardized and labor increasingly divided, it became more feasible for capital to dictate the speeds of machines so as to intensify work. Speed bosses were introduced into the shops to determine precisely, with the help of time study, the highest possible machine speed at which a particular job could be done. The result of such capitalist control of machine speed is illustrated by the letter of the auto worker quoted in chapter 3. When workers set their own machine speeds, they allowed themselves plenty of time to relax—"to sit down and watch while resting." However, capital and its supervisors set speeds that forced workers to "keep busy."

Specialized machinery gave capitalists and managers even greater control of machine speed and thus facilitated the intensification of labor. Machines were constructed with rigidly determined high spindle and feed speeds, thus making it impossible for workers to operate them at a slower speed.

That machine speed-up was a conscious policy of auto manufacturers is beyond doubt. A trade journalist reported of one auto company that: "In accordance with its policy of increasing the speed of production as greatly as is consistent with the best workmanship, the company has had all the machines in its shop speeded up from 25 to 50 per cent."[33] One critical Ford biographer reported: "Ford's factory bosses, driven from the top and fired by the potentialities of line-production, had come to accept as a matter of course the act of speeding up a new machine on an experimetal assembly line 100 to 200 per cent at a single lick. In pushing his machines, Ford of necessity pushed his men."[34]

Finally, it should be noted that mechanization was used like the division of labor to intensify labor by increasing the supply of labor and eliminating the traditions of skilled workers. Because specialized machines progressively did away with the necessity of employing skilled labor, they helped capital to alleviate the shortages of this crucial commodity. Realizing this advantage, one of Ford's production supervisors called the jigs and fixtures he installed "farmer tools." "Bring in the farmer and put him on the machine," he boasted, "and he can do just as good a job as a first-class mechanic."[35] These devices allowed capitalists to draw upon the more plentiful supply of unskilled labor from the farms of the midwest and southern United States and from southeastern Europe. And this larger labor supply, which was often manipulated, created pressure on the shop floor for workers to submit to intensified labor. Further, auto manufacturers preferred to employ semiskilled and unskilled workers not only because they were more plentiful, but also because they had none of the traditions and standards that blocked the capitalist control of work. All of the evidence given in chapter 3 to substantiate these points with respect to the division of labor is equally applicable to mechanization, which was a part of the larger strategy of deskilling work in order to increase capitalist control of the labor process.

In all of these ways, then, auto capitalists aspiring to mass production used machinery repressively to seize from workers control over the intensity of work. As a result, production increased and unit labor costs of automobiles decreased. But unlike the nonrepressive aspects, these repressive aspects of machinery achieved these results solely by repressing the resistance of workers to capitalist exploitation.

In the process of mechanization, as in other changes in the labor process, repressive control was found alongside of and intertwined in complex ways with nonrepressive control, which was based on the socially neutral logic of economization of productive resources. The difficulty with seeking to separate conceptually the repressive from the nonrepressive aspects of productive technology is that often both aspects were combined in the same physical features. For example, the same fixtures that reduced the labor time necessary to set up and operate a machine also stripped workers of control over their work and allowed capital to intensify labor. However, other aspects of machinery can be characterized as predominantly one or the other type of control. The revolving fixture used on many machines had the sole purpose of intensifying labor and thus was a pure form of repressive control. On the other hand, many of the special work heads, clamping devices, and work supports on machine tools ensured more precise and productive work without affecting social relations, and were therefore pure forms of nonrepressive control.[36]

As with other aspects of the automotive labor process, the development of machinery was not a neutral process dictated by universal imperatives of efficiency. Technological development took place within a social context that to a certain extent determined the direction and form of innovation. Within capitalist America, this context was one of conflictual social relations between classes, which dictated development of machinery that transferred control of work away from workers as well as increased efficiency. It was not merely the use of machinery that was socially determined, as Braverman seems to argue, but the very form of machines themselves.

This conclusion should not be interpreted as a romantic attack against machinery and technology *per se*. I am not advocating a wholesale return to handicraft production. Mechanization in and of itself is progressive, for it contains the potential to relieve human beings of toil and drudgery, to develop human abilities and capacities, and to increase the material wealth available to all. But this potential is perverted by the social system of capitalism, which steers technological development into specific forms that often increase rather than relieve drudgery, stifle rather than develop human capacities, and impoverish rather than enrich society as a whole.

CHAPTER 5
Birth of the Moving Line

n the short span of time from its rudimentary beginnings around 1897 until the mid-1930s, the process of manufacturing automobiles in the United States had greatly changed under the whip of capital. From a skilled process of unitary craft production, the auto labor process had been transformed into a minutely divided, closely timed, mechanized process of mass manufacture performed largely by unskilled workers.. As a result, control and domination over the labor process had to a large extent been won by capital.

Yet, auto manufacturers could not rest content with their accomplishments. They had yet to solve one great production problem—continuity. They had already crammed workers and machines so closely together that making one's way through the maze of speeding muscle and metal was a major hazard. This ensured that only the shortest possible distance was travelled by any part in its process of completion. And as many work processes as possible had been crowded into one machine to cut down on human handling. But the progress of work between machines and assembly stations was still dependent on that irrepressible "human element." Human hands still largely controlled the pace of work flow, although they were beginning to feel the pressure of the progressive line. In an attempt to wrest the control of work flow away from workers, auto manufacturers began to transfer the handling of materials from human hands to mechanical devices. This mechanization of materials handling culminated in a device that revolutionized mass production throughout the world and became a symbol of the dehumanized and meaningless work of contemporary capitalism—the moving assembly line.

Work Slides, Rollways, and Slideways

The first step in the process of mechanizing work handling consisted simply of bridging the space between work stations on progressive lines with devices over which materials could be conveyed by hand or gravity. One such device was the work slide, a sheet-metal trough spanning the distance between line stations. As one worker completed his or her operation on a particular part, he or she placed it on the slide and gave it a shove, thereby propelling it along to the next worker. The first record of the use of work slides comes from the Ford shops. Recalling the engine-block-machining line in operation at Ford's Bellevue plant in 1906, Max Wollering, the production superintendent, stated: "We put short conveyors to push it [the block] along to the next operation. It was not automatic. It had to be hand conveyed. When the man finished the milling operation he'd take the block, put it on the slide, and push it over to the next station. They would pick it up and put it on the drills and then they'd push it on. There wasn't any hand carrying in the plant from one station to another."[1] Other sources question this early date for work slides, but most agree that before the close of the first decade of the century, Ford production men began to use such devices to speed up and ensure the continuity of work.

This basic work-slide principle was applied in different forms in auto shops. One was the gravity slide, which was generally used on bench work. An inclined trough of sheet metal was placed on the bench, thus connecting the various operations along it. As one worker completed his or her operation, he or she placed the part on the gravity slide, on which it slid down to the next worker, who took it off, did his or her operation, and did likewise. This device had the added advantage of not depending on the workers to push parts along. Once the part was placed on the slide and released, gravity carried it rapidly to the next work station.[2]

Similar work-handling devices called rollways and slideways were installed to handle the larger, heavier parts. The former consisted of long tracks of rollers held off the ground at a convenient working height. When placed on the track and given a push, even the heaviest parts were moved along with ease. If one end of the track was slightly elevated, gravity carried the parts along with no human effort. Slideways worked on the same principle, except that they had no rollers. Parts were simply suspended between the two sides of the track and pushed along between work stations by workers.

These slideways and rollways were introduced in the motor-machining shops of many American auto companies around 1913, and their use spread until most machining lines were connected by these devices. An example of the labor time that they could save was provided by the installation of a gravity rollway in the flywheel-machining line at Ford around 1913. Previously, two truckers had been kept busy full-time transporting the flywheels between the twenty-seven separate machine tools operated by eighteen workers in the production line. It took about thirty-one minutes to complete one flywheel. However, when the gravity rollway was installed between the machines, the truckers were eliminated, and the average completion time was cut to less than twenty minutes. This materials-handling device thus reduced labor time by over one third.[3]

Stimulated by such labor savings, auto manufacturers introduced rollways and slideways into the subassembly processes on heavy parts. For example, the eighty-four separate operations on the Ford motor-assembly line were connected by rollways.[4]

Beginnings of Power Conveyance

At the same time that these work slides and rollways were being tested and installed in several innovative auto shops, an innovation in materials handling was being developed that would shortly revolutionize automobile production—autonomous, power-driven conveyance. Work slides, rollways, and slideways had not yet rendered materials handling completely independent of the workers themselves, for they depended on the workers' energy to push parts along, or at least to place them on the track or slide to be carried away by gravity. This proved unsatisfactory for capital, which sought to remove any worker control whatsoever over the intensity of labor. The power-driven conveyor would go a long way toward accomplishing this goal.

Power conveyance of materials in process had an extensive history of use in such industries as brewing, milling, canning, and meatpacking, which influenced the thinking of auto production men. The first use of power conveyance in the auto industry seems to have come in the Ford foundry late in 1912. Previously, the heavy work had been transported by human muscle, assisted by a few simple trucks and carts. Then a foundry mechanic named Gregory, who had worked in a brewery that had used conveyors to transport grain, suggested that a line of moving hoppers be employed to carry mixed core sand to chutes above the molders' benches. A system was installed that not only delivered sand to the molding machines but also recovered it from the shake-out grates and reprocessed it. This was the first power-driven conveyor in the auto industry. Soon the principle was applied in the Ford core ovens, which were fitted with chain-driven conveyors to slowly push cores through and properly bake them.

These first power conveyors merely transported materials to work stations. The first use of power conveyance to move parts while workers simultaneously worked on them came in the mold-producing process in the Ford foundry. Previously, the molds had been placed in a stationary position on the floor and the molten metal transported to them for pouring in ladles. But in February of 1913, Ford introduced several elliptical, overhead conveyors driven by an endless chain. From the conveyors hung "pendulums" upon which the molds were carried. One side of the elliptical conveyor passed a row of molding machines, where completed molds were loaded onto it. The conveyor then carried the molds a short distance to an area where the molten metal was poured in them as they moved continuously. From there the molds rounded the corner and passed slowly down the other side of the conveyor, until they reached the shake-out grate, where the hardened castings were shaken out of the molds. By late in 1914, the Ford foundry was equipped with ten of these conveyors, which greatly increased output.[5]

The great success of these first power-driven conveyors in cutting labor costs caused Ford production managers to begin experimentation with them in other parts of the shops. The first application of the moving conveyor to assembly work came in the flywheel magneto, a part of the electrical generation system. Previously, the whole assembly operation had been performed by one worker, who took about twenty minutes (.33 worker-hours) to complete the job. In April 1913, Ford production managers went to work and split the job into twenty-nine separate operations, laid out along a moving belt. The assemblers worked on the flywheel magneto as it moved past them, without removing it from the line. The results were startling. Assembly time immediately dropped to thirteen minutes and ten seconds of one worker's time (approximately .22 worker-hours). After some experimentation and adjustments, assembly time was further reduced to five minutes of one worker's time (.083 worker-hours), a labor saving of 75 percent over the original labor process! The moving assembly line was thus born.[6]

THE FINAL ASSEMBLY LINE

The truly monumental event was yet to come, however—the introduction of the moving line in final assembly. This occurred in August of 1913 at Ford, but the groundwork for it had been laid years
before. Ford did not originate the principle of putting cars together
"on the move." Ransom Olds had actually conceived and applied
this idea over a decade before Ford. When the sales of his curved-
dash runabout began to outrun his capacity to produce them, Olds
searched for ways to expedite production. In 1901 he devised
an assembly method that had all the traits of Ford's chain-driven
final assembly line except continuous motion. The auto frames
were placed on wooden stands fitted with casters and hand-pushed
down a line of work stations, where all the parts necessary to complete the car were assembled. Henry Ford is said to have paid frequent visits to Ransom Olds' factory, which undoubtedly influenced
his later methods.[7]

Ford's production managers began experimentation with a moving final assembly line considerably earlier than 1913. Charles Sorensen, one of Ford's top production executives, claimed that he and
others were experimenting with a moving assembly line as early as
July 1908. They placed parts needed in the assembly in a line along
the floor, in order of their assembly. The frame was put on skids
and pulled along with a towrope past the piles of parts. As soon as
the axles and wheels were on, the chassis was rolled along. However, this method was not really developed into a workable production process until some five years later. As late as September 1913,
Ford continued to assemble cars at stationary locations by the rotating-gang system described in chapter 3. At this time, the final-
assembly department employed six hundred workers—five hundred assemblers and one hundred component carriers—who
worked to turn out about four hundred and seventy-five cars in a
nine-hour day. The best time attained by this rotating-gang system
was twelve hours and twenty-eight minutes of one worker's time
(approximately 12.5 worker-hours) required for the assembly of
one car.[8]

Experiments with a moving line resumed in August 1913. Ford,
P. E. Martin, C. W. Avery, and Charles Sorensen tested a line pulled
by a rope and windlass. The chassis was placed on wheels and
slowly pulled past successive piles of parts placed in a line on the
shop floor. Six assemblers followed each chassis the entire length of
the 250-foot line, picking up parts from the successive piles and

assembling them. This crude line reduced the average number of worker-hours required for chassis assembly to five hours and fifty minutes, a savings of about 53 percent over the stationary method.

Constant experimentation rapidly changed the shape of this first final assembly line. In October 1913, Ford managers divided assembly tasks between one hundred and forty stationary workers, who remained in one spot and performed their minute tasks as the chassis were pulled down the 150-foot line. By the end of December, a 300-foot line was in operation, along which one hundred ninety-one assemblers pushed the cars along by hand, at the command of the foreman's whistle. In January 1914, Ford managers introduced an electrically driven endless-chain conveyor, which moved the chassis constantly down the line. By April, further improvements had reduced assembly time on such lines to one hour and thirty-three minutes of one worker's time (about 1.5 worker-hours), allowing Ford to turn out one thousand two hundred and twelve assemblies in an eight-hour day. In this short time, the moving assembly line had nearly tripled production and slashed 88 percent off the original labor time![9]

With such a rapid rate of assembly, the old method of hand-trucking parts to assembly stations proved woefully inadequate. Thus, Ford's production engineers began installing power-driven supply lines to satisfy the huge appetite of the speeding final assembly lines. Eventually subassembly lines were laid out to feed immediately into the final assembly lines at right angles, so that their parts did not have to be transported at all. By the time Ford had completed his famous River Rouge plant in 1920, the entire manufacturing process was so closely coordinated and interrelated that production was one continuously moving process; from the holds of iron-ore ships to the loading of completed Model T's onto railroad cars, the flow of production never stopped.

The use of Ford's revolutionary moving production lines spread rapidly to other manufacturers and to other manufacturing processes. By early 1916, about three years after Ford's first moving line, most of the big auto producers—Maxwell, Paige, Hudson, Packard, Studebaker, Dodge, Reo, Overland, Chevrolet, Buick, Saxon—had installed moving final assembly lines. And the moving conveyor lines were also applied to subassembly jobs, such as body assembly. In some work processes, however, the straight conveyor line did not prove adaptable, so circular or elliptical devices were introduced to ensure the same continuous motion of work. Many small, simple subassembly jobs were done on moving turntables, or merry-go-rounds. One manufacturer placed wheel assembly, for example, on a turntable that held four wheels and occupied four workers, one at each of the four work stations. Each worker performed his or her assembly task, after which the turntable revolved and brought another wheel to be worked on. The labor of constructing a mold was placed on similar merry-go-rounds in some auto foundries.[10]

It is probably no exaggeration to say that American industry in general went somewhat "conveyor crazy" after the news of the auto industry's phenomenal successes got out. Any and every process that could be divided into a series of simple work tasks performed without removing the work off the line was conveyorized. The Westinghouse Electric Company went so far as to install an assembly-line cafeteria! A moving conveyor was installed that carried employees' trays past the food selections, thereby speeding them along and allowing thirty-four workers per minute to be served at each counter! Although certainly less efficient than the feeding machine in Charlie Chaplin's "Modern Times," which fed workers as they labored, the assembly-line cafeteria was based upon the same principle that underlay most attempts at mechanization—cutting unproductive labor time to an absolute minimum and cramming every second of the working day full of productive activity.[11]

Repressive and Nonrepressive Control in Mechanized Materials Handling

As with the other changes introduced into the auto labor process by capitalists, mechanized materials handling was motivated by a complex, imbricated combination of socially neutral attempts to ensure efficient use of productive resources and socially biased attempts to seize control from a resistant class of workers. Mechanization of parts transport, unlike that of parts production, seems to have had little effect upon the precision of finished work. The main capitalist goal of this change in the labor process was the reduction of unit labor costs through reducing the labor time expended in the production of an automobile. But shifting responsibility for materials transport from workers to machines reduced unit labor time in several ways, some repressive and others nonrepressive.

The original motive of auto manufacturers in introducing mechanized materials handling into auto factories seems to have been a socially neutral attempt to reduce the amount of labor time and the costs devoted to transportation. Traditionally, manufacturers defined transportation as unproductive labor, not contributing to the value of the product, but merely forming a portion of the overhead costs. They therefore sought to reduce these costs to a minimum, and one way to do so was to replace the human labor involved in transportation with machines. Thus, for example, when Ford introduced the gravity slide on a subassembly job, he claimed that it was to save the time assemblers previously had devoted to walking about for parts and tools. Similarly, in communications among themselves, auto manufacturers pointed to the elimination of those jobs devoted exclusively to transportation as a major advantage motivating the introduction of other mechanical devices for handling materials.[12]

Under the capitalist economy of the United States, of course, reducing the labor costs of transportation was intended to and actually did benefit mainly auto capitalists by increasing surplus value or profits. However, this should not obscure the nonrepressive character of this advantage. Mechanization of materials handling increased the productivity of labor without affecting the social relations of production by eliminating the necessity of humans transporting heavy parts and thus more efficiently using society's labor power. Workers thus relieved of this back-breaking toil could devote their energies more fully to automobile production.

These work-handling devices resulted in more efficient use of other productive resources as well, in ways that were not originally anticipated by manufacturers. One journalist stated in *Automotive Industries* that, although such devices were originally installed to reduce the labor costs of transportation, subsequent "investigations have shown, however, that the decrease in indirect labor costs may and usually does represent but a small fraction of the total savings made possible by mechanical [materials-handling] equipment."[13] Capitalists discovered that such equipment also yielded savings by reducing inventories, accidents, breakage of parts, and floor area requirements, as well as simplifying records. Once known, of course, all of these advantages became capitalist reasons for extending the use of these devices.

These nonrepressive advantages were, however, generally secondary in motivating the rush to install conveyors, work slides, and rollways throughout the U.S. automobile industry. There was a repressive advantage that, once discovered, became the primary capitalist motivation for making this change in the labor process—the control that mechanized materials handling gave capital over the pace of labor. Prior to the installation of these devices, the pace at which materials had been carried from one work station to the next had depended largely on the workers themselves. It was they who pushed the trucks and handed the parts along. By thus controlling the speed at which work progressed on the line, workers were able to resist capitalist pressure for intensified labor. As we have seen, the progressive layout of work had increased, to a certain extent, the intensity of work, by reducing the distances parts travelled between work stations and by creating a certain pressure in the flow of work. But as long as workers were personally handling the work, there was always the possibility that they could use this weapon to slow down work intensity. As one engineering journalist wrote of the rotating-gang assembly method at Ford: "Motor cars were assembled by gangs of men who ran around the plant with trucks, leaving the necessary parts near every car in process of assembly. . . . The assembly cars moved from car to car and *one slow or lazy unit could hold up the whole line.*"[14] Mechanized materials handling solved this capitalist problem by progressively removing control of the speed of work transport from the workers and centralizing it into the hands of capital. With this control, capital then was able to increase the intensity of work, despite worker resistance. The unit labor time was thus reduced, but solely by repressing the antagonistic relations of production characteristic of capitalism. Once auto capitalists became aware of this repressive-control advantage, it became the main motivation for the extension of these devices.

Even the more primitive, nonmotorized work slides and rollways gave capital greater control over work intensity, which was the main factor behind the large savings of labor time achieved by their use. Of course, there were other factors associated with the installation of such devices that also contributed to labor savings. For example, the increased division of labor that often accompanied the introduction of work slides and rollways undoubtedly increased labor productivity. And the elimination of transportation labor also contributed to labor-time savings. But the central importance of capitalist control over work intensity in achieving labor savings on such devices can be demonstrated by the installation of a gravity rollway on the Ford flywheel-machining line. In this case, the labor time required to machine the flywheel was reduced by over one third, without increasing the division of labor or taking into account the labor saved by eliminating the truckers. That this reduction was due to the intensification of labor allowed by the rollway is revealed by engineering journalists, Arnold and Faurote, who conducted an extensive study of the Ford shops.

> Before the roll-ways were installed the straw boss could never nail, with certainty, the man who was shirking, because of the many work-piles and general confusion due to the shop floor transportation. As

soon as the roll-ways were placed the truckers were called off, the floor was cleared, and all the straw boss had to do to locate the shirk or operation tools in fault, was to glance along the line and see where the roll-way was filled up. As more than once before said in these chapters, mechanical transit of work in progress evens up the job, and forces everybody to adopt the pace of the fastest worker in the gang, and the roll-way had the expected effect of reducing the labor-costs by better than 33–1/3 per cent. . . . Placing work in progress on a slide-way and moving components along by hand as they are placed on the slide-way after an operation completion has the same effect on pace as that obtained by the moving assembly and the gravity roll-way. All the boss has to do to spot the slow man infallibly is to seek the forward end of the congestion of units in transit. This invariably results in increased labor-hour-productivity, besides cleaning up the shop floor and dispensing with the trucking labor.[15]

Auto capitalists and managers realized that by eliminating the discretionary time during which workers handled parts, even the nonmotorized work slides and rollways gave them greater control over the intensity of labor. Workers were forced to maintain a rapid pace or risk attracting the attention of the boss with a pile-up of parts. These devices resulted in a furious, capitalist-controlled pace on progressive lines. One visitor to Ford's Highland Park plant in 1914 wrote of the work on the rollways: "It's push and hustle and go. The man behind may shove his work along to you at any moment—you must not hold him back; at any moment the man in front may be ready for another piece to work on—he must not be kept waiting." The workers' reactions to these speed-up devices were predictable. The foreman of Ford's motor-assembly department, which had been put on a rollway in 1913, recalled: "The men didn't like it because they had to work harder. The pieces were there and they didn't have time to walk back and take a rest in between."[16]

The power-driven conveyors introduced shortly after these first mechanized materials-handling devices gave capitalists and their managers even greater control over work intensity. The work was never removed from the moving conveyor, so workers had no opportunity to slow down the flow of production. They had to perform their work rapidly, before the part was carried beyond their work station. Here was the ultimate pace-setting device.

It is necessary, however, to distinguish between two basically different types of power-driven conveyors. First, there were those that transported materials past workers in production departments— workers performed their operations on the materials as they moved.

Second, there were those moving conveyors that transported materials between production departments in the factory. For example, overhead monorail conveyors carried completed engines from the motor-assembly department to the final assembly line. In the process of this transit, no work was performed, the purpose being solely to get the materials from one place to another. This second type of conveyor was mainly a neutral technological instrument and must be considered primarily a nonrepressive-control device. Its main purpose was transportation. And with reference to it, there was much truth to the capitalist claim that such mechanical transportation relieved workers of back-breaking labor. This type of conveyor, however, did have a repressive-control element, which played a part in removing the control of work intensity from workers. Work could not proceed until materials had arrived in the production areas, and the quick and continuous delivery of materials ensured that work progressed without delays. However, this effect was largely secondary to the sheer transportation capacity that they provided. In the case of the first type of conveyor, the importance of these two labor-saving elements was reversed. Conveyors that carried materials past workers as they labored also helped to save them the often hard work of moving parts about. But the primary purpose of this moving line was to take control of work intensity out of workers' hands and allow capital to increase it by repressing the resistance of a recalcitrant, exploited work force. It was thus primarily an instrument of repressive control.

Automobile capitalists and managers often denied publicly that the moving line was used as a speed-up device. They stated that the increased worker-hour output associated with the moving conveyors had resulted from the increased division of labor, the decrease in labor time expended in carrying work, and the decrease in worker fatigue. It is true that these factors were responsible for part of the increased worker output associated with moving conveyors. But they certainly were not the only factors at work, as is clearly demonstrable from the data available in several instances. Take, for example, the introduction of the very first moving final assembly line at Ford. On this line, worker-hours per car were reduced from 12.5 to 5.8, a 53 percent reduction. It is impossible that any part of this reduction was due to an increased division of labor. There was little division of labor on this first line. The same six assemblers travelled the entire length of the line with the same car. In fact, this was a marked decrease in the division of labor, as compared to the rotating-gang system that had preceded it at Ford. Neither can this reduction in worker-hours be completely attributed to the elimination of transportation labor. In the rotating-gang system of assembly, only one hundred of the six hundred workers (about 17 percent) were employed exclusively as component carriers. Even if this transport labor had been eliminated completely, which it was not, we would expect only a 17 percent reduction in worker-hours. But the reduction was 53 percent. That leaves a large part unaccounted for. Most of this is explainable by the increased intensity at which Ford workers were forced to labor. It was no longer the workers, but the Ford managers, who determined the speed at which cars had to be assembled by turning the windlass or setting the speed of the motor driving the chain.[17]

Auto capitalists and managers were not, however, so deceptive in their talk about the assembly line among themselves. They and the industry's trade journalists, who had the interests of auto capital in mind, were anxious to inform other capitalists in and out of the industry of their great achievement in wresting the control of work intensity from the workers. To do so, they were quite candid about their motives and intentions. Not long after the introduction of Ford's moving final assembly line, *The Automobile* informed its readers bluntly: "It is a pace-setting scheme, the workman must do his job in so many seconds or loses out. The moving chain will not wait for him for other workmen have their work to do." The industry's major trade paper went on to state that many other auto manufacturers were increasing their production by "instituting various forms of pace-setting methods whereby production is quickened."[18] Upon visiting Ford's River Rouge plant in 1921, an industrial-management journalist wrote the following of the extensive system of moving conveyors that filled the plant: "Still another economy may be attributed to these systems and that is the elimination of any possibility of loafing or soldiering on the job when each operator is faced with the necessity of keeping up with the procession or else seeing his stock pile up to a point where it becomes distinctly noticeable by the immediate management." Henry Ford himself admitted in an uncharacteristically candid moment that "we regulated the speed of men by the speed of the conveyor. . . . "[19]

The labor-intensifying advantage that the moving conveyor gave to capital was also recognized by scholars studying the industry. One economist wrote in a classic study of the automobile industry published in 1928:

> Progressive assembly systems of this kind, which now prevail to a greater or lesser extent in all the largest factories, *represent the extreme limit to which the extension of the management's control over productive oper-*

ations can be carried. Not only are the design, shape, size and quality of the work predetermined, but the rate at which each operation must be performed by the workers is rigidly controlled by a power machine, which even may be driven from another building.[20]

Similarly, an MIT engineering professor wrote:

As a pacing device, the conveyor is unique, though uniform rates of production can be obtained without it. A powered conveyor paces each operation to assure a steady optimum output. . . . It holds the workers at their jobs and requires them to perform their work in the time allowed. It enables them to build up a rhythm and enables the management to discern quickly any bottleneck operations. To some manufacturers, pacing is the chief advantage of line production, and it is their aim wherever practical to get the job on paced production.[21]

Auto capitalists consciously used the moving line to eliminate any discretion or control that workers exercised over work intensity. By doing so, they were able to step up production to a pace that workers would never have imposed on themselves. This intentional process can be well demonstrated by the installation of the final section of the moving final assembly line at Ford. Before this installation, a number of assembly jobs were performed outside the factory, after the cars had come off the end of the moving line. Motor and rear-axle inspection, the assembly of the body to the chassis, and other minor assembly jobs were performed at stationary positions on the street. And test drivers drove the completed cars around at their own discretion. Ford managers complained that "this procedure afforded plenty of gaps and vacancies for discretionary proceedings on the part of all men working outside under the head assembler." Unlike the moving conveyor inside the shop, this work on the street did not push inexorably forward, controlling the intensity at which workers labored. To solve this problem of discretionary gaps and vacancies in the hands of workers, Ford managers installed another section of moving line. On the street they laid out an angle-iron track over which the cars slowly crept under their own power. As the cars moved along, the minor assembly and inspection jobs were performed. Testing was done at a stationary position, thus eliminating the disorderly and discretionary test drives. A marked speed-up of labor was the result of this elimination of worker discretion by the moving line. "A very considerable list of chassis-assembling operations, performed formerly between the shop door whence the cars came out and the body chute, are now performed on the John R street track, with that notable time-saving which always followed keeping work in progress in one well-defined line and thus leaving as little as possible to the whim or choice of the individual workman."[22]

Once auto capitalists had seized control of work intensity by means of the moving line, it was very easy for them to speed up work to an inhuman pace. This was done in several ways. First, they simply increased the speed of the chain-driving motor, without altering the operations or number of workers on the line. Parts thus came at a faster rate, and workers had to work harder and faster to keep up. For example, when Hudson first installed its moving assembly lines around 1916, a line speed of three feet per minute was considered the maximum at which workers could work efficiently. This was gradually increased until in 1924 a speed of twenty feet per minute had been attained! One business journalist concluded that "a glance at early factory practice as regards chain speeds shows that even the present 'slow' lines are like express trains in comparison."[23]

Second, auto capitalists and managers speeded up work on the moving lines by assigning more operations to workers. The speed of the line was left the same, but several workers were removed, their operations being divided among those remaining. Therefore, workers had to work much harder and faster in order to complete the increased number of operations in the same amount of time.

However, speeding line work by either driving the line faster or giving more operations to each worker soon ran up against the obstacle of human fatigue. The human body could only lift, place, and secure so many parts in a given time, without becoming so fatigued that careful work was impossible. Thus, the upper limit to which work on the moving lines could be speeded up was determined by the physiology of the commodity of labor power. In order to raise this physiological limit on work intensity, capitalists began to look for mechanical assistance. Assembly work was very difficult to mechanize completely because of the complex movements involved. But auto manufacturers could and did speed up the handwork of assembly through the introduction of hand-held power tools. In the early 1920s, pneumatic and electric tools for driving screws, nuts, and bolts came into use in the auto industry, replacing screwdrivers and wrenches. These tools allowed workers to do their jobs much faster. For example, with pneumatic boltdrivers, assembly-line workers at one company were able to tighten all the body bolts on twelve hundred cars a day, whereas previously the same number of workers with wrenches had tightened bolts on only three hundred cars daily. With the speed of individual work operations thus increased, the line could be further speeded up. To a certain extent, these tools made labor more productive—that is, they allowed workers to do more work in the same time with the same effort. But there was a certain amount of lifting and positioning of parts involved in assembly, the effort for which was not reduced by power tools. Hence, by allowing a quicker line speed, these tools actually forced workers to work more intensively, that is, with greater effort.[24]

Another repressive-control advantage that the moving line brought capital, apart from greater control of work intensity, was easier supervision of workers. The conveyors that moved materials past work stations eased the job of immediate supervision by mechanically guaranteeing work intensity. Before their introduction, the speed of production had been guaranteed mainly by the close supervision of the foreman. Even though work slides and rollways made the "shirk" easier to spot, getting him or her back in pace with the line depended on the strength of the foreman's lungs and language, that is, on verbal threats and abuse. Not infrequently, the foreman's fists were also called into service to persuade a worker to speed up. For this reason, foremen were generally known as "pushers" throughout the industry. However, the introduction of the moving line considerably eased the foreman's job of maintaining the speed of production and reduced the personal confrontation and conflict between him and his workers. The mechanical line, not the foreman, set and maintained the pace of labor. Auto industry foremen themselves were quick to cite this as an advantage of the line. One thus stated: "The line does a lot of your work for you. The men have to keep up with it. If I stand down at the end of my section, I can see if anything has been done wrong by one of my men, and I can find out why."[25] One auto-worker-turned-sociologist similarly stated:

> The line provides a superb form of technical and impersonal control for management. One of the latent functions of the line is that it makes it unnecessary for the foreman to act primarily as a "pusher." As one auto worker says: "The average guy fighting the line has two foremen. One is the regular foreman, the other is the damn line itself. They both keep pushing you." It creates an additional role for the foreman in which, to some extent, he acts as a trouble-shooter or a problem-solver engaging less in giving orders. Consequently, conditions emerge that permit the foreman to maintain a more friendly relationship between himself and the worker.[26]

The moving line thus allowed capital to minimize the number of supervisors. In 1914, Ford employed only one foreman for each fifty-eight workers in his plant. The moving line also reduced the level of conflict on the shop floor. Workers realized that it was no longer the foreman who determined work intensity, but those higher managers who set the line speed. The personal antipathy of the workers was thus shifted upward in the industrial hierarchy. Being no longer immediately confronted with the representative of capital's inexorable push for greater exploitation, workers found it more difficult to focus their resistance and were thus more acquiescent to increased work intensity.[27]

Another repressive-control advantage that may have entered into the introduction of the moving line, as well as the introduction of other materials-handling equipment, was enlarging the potential labor market from which auto manufacturers could draw workers. As long as auto work involved pushing and hauling heavy loads around the shop, it could be done only by relatively large, strong men. However, the installation of materials-handling equipment, which removed much of the burdensome work of transportation from the backs of workers, allowed auto manufacturers to draw on a much broader supply of labor. Smaller men and even women could be employed. This meant that labor surpluses could be more easily generated, surpluses that "put fear in the hearts of workers" and forced them to submit to intensified labor. In addition to creating more labor market pressure on men, the employment of women, made possible in part by this equipment, also lowered capital's wage bill, because of the lower wages consistently paid women in the auto industry. In James Bright's study of mechanization, he noted that several managers stated specifically that they introduced materials-handling equipment so that "anyone, not just a muscle man" could handle the job. Also, the employment of women was often mentioned by managers as a specific goal of these changes in the labor process. For example, one auto parts manufacturer stated that the installation of an overhead conveyor system in the enameling of windshield frames "made possible the employment of women for handling most of the work, whereas men were needed previously for a great many of the operations."[28]

The main result of the introduction and extension of the moving line in the automobile industry was the annihilation of worker control over the intensity of their own labor. Auto work ceased to be humanly paced, with respect to the needs and desires of the human worker, and began to be paced inhumanly, by a machine in the control of a class of humans that could not afford to be human in its drive for greater production and profits. The natural rhythms of the human body and mind—work and rest, alimentation and elimination—were subordinated to the mechanical rhythms of the line controlled by capital. Rest was niggardly rationed out in portions carefully calculated to restore the physiological ability to work, and no more. The biological need for food was only grudgingly recognized by capital, which provided minute allotments of time—usually ten to fifteen minutes—sufficient only for the quick refueling of the human machine. Ford line workers were strictly forbidden to speak to one another. Every human function was carefully regimented and controlled so as not to impede the inexorable forward progress of the line.[29]

The largely unpredictable function of elimination often proved to be a matter of grave concern to an industrial mechanism that knew only the even, predictable rhythms of the stopwatch. Ford workers on the line had to obtain permission to go to the toilet. If it were granted, relief workers took their jobs, and they were allowed exactly three minutes away from their work! "In the eyes of Henry Ford the human alimentary canal is a 'disassembly line' which in every man should perform a given operation in a standard length of time." One auto worker who complained because he could not get away from the line to go to the toilet was told by his foreman: "We don't regulate the line by your bowels; you regulate your bowels by the line." Ford workers were often followed to the toilet by a "serviceman" (a member of the company security force), who checked to make sure workers were actually there "on business." Once a serviceman caught an unwitting worker sitting on the toilet simply resting, with his pants up. He was summarily fired. Only in the bizarre, topsy-turvy world of the capitalist auto factory, where humans served machines and a small minority ruled the vast majority through these inhuman means, did a person have to carefully avoid being caught with his or her pants up![30]

Not all aspects of mechanized materials handling contributed to the dehumanization of work. As we have seen, there were aspects of nonrepressive control that both motivated and resulted from the installation of this technology. Some of these nonrepressive aspects actually made work more human by improving safety and eliminating much of the hard, physical labor of transporting materials. Others simply made work more efficient by decreasing overhead costs. But the antagonistic relations of production of capitalism ensured that the moving line was developed primarily as a repressive weapon in auto capital's battle to seize complete control of the labor process from an exploited working class.

Variation in Application of the Moving Line

The degree of capital's success in using moving conveyors to seize control of work was determined, however, by its relative strength vis-à-vis labor. Auto manufacturers were generally successful in installing moving lines and hence controlling work intensity in areas of the labor process where the power of workers had already been reduced by standardization, the division of labor, and mechanization. However, in those areas in which the variation and uncertainty of work continued to demand discretion, workers remained powerful and were able to resist capitalist attempts to control work intensity through conveyorization.

Before work tasks could be put on a moving line, they had to be carefully standardized. All variation had to be removed from each job, so that the time and movements required could be exactly specified and coordinated. Variant and uncertain work could not be so standardized. Neither could it be minutely divided, for it required workers to exercise discretion about what to do and how. And this discretion gave workers the power to control their own labor, which they used to prevent capitalist managers from seizing control of labor intensity through conveyorization.[31]

Motor assembly, for example, continued on simple rollways as late as 1919, long after moving conveyors had been installed in final assembly. This was because the assembly of an internal combustion engine continued to require relatively skilled handwork to ensure the accuracy of close tolerances. These skilled, uncertain tasks left much discretion in the hands of workers, and their consequent power prevented this work from being as minutely divided as other work and from being paced by a moving conveyor. Manufacturers' attempts to put this work on moving lines at this stage were frustrated by frequent delays caused by workers removing engines from the line in order to make individual adjustments.[32]

The power of skilled workers also delayed the application of moving conveyors to the production of trucks. Unlike passenger cars, trucks were not standardized in design and manufacture until much later in the century. They were produced in a great variety of models, and many were custom-made to customer specifications. Such varied and uncertain work demanded skilled workers, whose jobs could not be standardized and minutely divided. And the power of these workers prevented capital from mechanically seizing control of labor intensity. Moving conveyors were unknown in truck factories through most of the 1920s. Simple roller conveyors were used until the late 1920s, at which time the production of the larger manufacturers reached a volume sufficient to allow separate production lines for each model. Such specialization eliminated much of the variety and uncertainty of truck production, thus allowing for a minute division of labor. These changes in work eroded workers' power and laid the basis for the introduction of moving lines in truck production to control work intensity.[33]

Finally, moving conveyors were not used in the production lines of machine shops until the late 1930s, because of the discretion required of workers. Machine operators had to remove the part from the line, clamp and load it into the machine, feed it to the cutters, unload and replace it on the line. Even on specialized machine tools, these tasks of loading, clamping, and feeding parts were at the discretion of workers, who consequently had some control over work intensity. And they used this discretion and control to block conveyorization. As a result, machine shops used roller conveyors to connect machines in progressive lines until the late 1930s.[34]

Extended application of the moving conveyor and the concomitant capitalist control over work intensity depended upon eliminating the surviving pockets of worker discretion. Capital was able to achieve this elimination through higher levels of mechanization.

CHAPTER 6
Machines Come of Age: Toward Automatic Manufacturing

With the invention of the moving conveyor line, capital won a decisive battle in its war with labor over control of the labor process. But victories won in the assembly processes had yet to be extended to the machining lines. The nature of early machine-tool operation made the use of moving lines impossible, for it left numerous gaps through which that irrepressible enemy of capital—"the human element" —could assert itself. The subsequent mechanization of auto work was aimed at closing up these gaps in machine-tool operation. It was a gradual maturation of a labor process whose principles had been marked out by previous struggles. Slowly, bit by bit, capital cleaned up the remaining pockets of worker discretion, until the manufacture of automobiles took place with very little direct worker intervention. The machines became more and more self-activating, automatic. The shops were transformed from centers crowded with human workers to sparsely populated expanses of self-moving machines.

POWER FEED AND SEMIAUTOMATIC
MACHINE TOOLS

We have already followed the mechanization of work to a point at which specialized, multiple-operation machines had removed much

of the human skill and know-how from work. Tool movement was
so limited by the mechanism itself that little was required of the operator save to clamp the part in the fixture and to pull the lever or
turn the wheel to bring the cutting tool in contact with the part, or
vice versa. At the same time that machine tools were being specialized and given multiple tools, another qualitative change was being
made—the replacement of hand feed with power feed. Instead of
the operator turning a capstan wheel or pulling a lever to control the
contact of the tool with the part, he or she simply activated a power
mechanism that automatically fed the part or tool. Thus, another aspect of the control of work was taken from workers and incorporated into the machine controlled by capital.

The power-fed machine tool was not an invention of the early
twentieth-century American auto industry. The principle of power
feed was quite old, having appeared as early as 1795. But, it had
been used largely on specialized machine tools. Universal machines
commonly employed hand feed, which allowed skilled operators to
finely adjust operations to a wide variety of work and materials.
Thus, power-fed machine tools came into use in the auto industry
only when machines specialized for the production of one part began to replace universal machine tools.

When the early auto shops achieved sufficient volume to make
specialization feasible, they began adapting previously existing
power-fed machine tools to their uses. For example, as early as 1903,
the innovative Olds shops were using automatic turret lathes, or
screw machines, to machine pistons. Such machines had been in
use since 1871, but their adaptation to piston machining was new.
Once the pistons were loaded in the lathe and the switch thrown,
the machine automatically and successively took a rough cut on the
outside diameter, cut the piston ring grooves, took a facing cut off
the inside end, and cut the piston free from its supporting boss. All
this proceeded without the least intervention of the operator, who
simply loaded and unloaded the pistons. Similarly automatic lathes
were adapted early on to the production of many of the round parts
of the automobile: flywheels, gear shafts, valves, screws, nuts,
and bolts. Automatic gear-cutting machines, which had appeared
around 1860, were adapted to auto work around 1910. These machines automatically fed the cutter into the gear blank, stopped at
the proper depth, reversed the feed, turned the blank into position
for the next cut, and once again fed the tool to the blank. They continued until all the teeth of the gear had been cut.[1]

As production volumes grew and allowed greater and greater
machine-tool specialization, auto manufacturers began to add auto-

matic feed to machines constructed exclusively for auto work, such as specialized millers and grinders. Millers became increasingly automatic during the early 1910s. By 1916, these machines had advanced to the point where the worker simply clamped the work on a platen or table and threw a switch. From there on, the process was automatic—the table was rapidly traversed (moved to working position), changed to a slower speed and fed past the cutters, rapidly reversed, and stopped. With the ganging of work, the table was provided with numerous work-holding fixtures. The operator loaded all the fixtures and threw the feed switch. The table moved forward, feeding all the parts past the millers, and then rapidly reversed to the starting position. Often, detachable fixtures were provided, so that while one set of parts was being milled, the operator could set up another. Multiple-operation milling machines also incorporated automatic features. A machine with a revolving fixture that milled and bored cylinders incorporated a power feed, with the result that "after the job is set up it only requires the active attention of the operator when it becomes necessary to swing the set of cylinders from the boring to the milling side and to set up the new job, an operation requiring 4 minutes."[2] The all-important grinding machine also became increasingly automatic over the first fifteen years of the twentieth century. The feed and reverse on the specialized crankshaft and camshaft grinders were made automatic. As early as 1905, automatic sizing of grinding work had appeared. Instead of requiring the operator to reverse the feed, remove the part, and measure it, a device was invented that automatically reversed the feed once the desired diameter was reached. Further, a grinding machine was constructed that automatically brought several grinding wheels to work in succession on a part, applying the principle of a turret lathe.[3]

Most of the above machines may be classified as "semiautomatic," a term I shall use to refer to a machine that performed one or more operations on a part without human intervention, once it had been started (see table 4.1). The prefix "semi" denotes the fact that the operations did not proceed continuously without human intervention—the operator had to start and stop the machine. During the time between the end of one cycle and the beginning of the next, he or she had to unload the finished work and load the unfinished part. Thus, the operator still retained some control over the mechanism; it was not completely self-activating.

AUTOMATIC MACHINE TOOLS

The next step up the scale of mechanization was the introduction of fully automatic machines, which required no human intervention in order to complete a work cycle (see table 4.1). These machines were not started and stopped by workers. They either started and stopped themselves, or they ran continuously. On the semiautomatic machine, the worker loaded the work when the machine was idle; on the fully automatic machine, he or she loaded the parts while the machine was working. This required the machine to have more than one fixture, so that the worker could load and unload one, while work proceeded on the others.

The miller with a multiple-fixture table was one of the first machines to be made completely automatic. In 1915 Dodge reported the use of a miller that held nine cylinder blocks and nine cylinder heads. The operator loaded the first fixture on the table and started the machine. As the first set of parts fed through the millers, he or she continued to load the other fixtures. When all the fixtures were loaded, the worker proceeded to the other side of the machine, where the finished parts emerged, and began to unload these and put rough castings in their place. By the time this unloading and reloading was completed, the table had reversed itself and run back through the millers. In this way the machine ran continuously and was not started and stopped by the operator. Ford reported a similar reciprocating-table miller in use in 1915.[4]

Another way that capital rendered machines fully automatic was by making the fixtures rotate instead of reciprocate. Earlier machines fitted with revolving fixtures and automatic feed had allowed workers to load and unload one fixture while the other was automatically machined. However, these machines were not completely automatic, for they required the operator to turn the fixtures by hand. A giant step was made on the scale of mechanization when the rotation of the fixtures was taken out of the worker's hands and incorporated into the machine. The resulting automatic indexing machine not only automatically fed the tools into the part and returned them to starting position once the cut was completed. It also indexed the turntable, moving the finished part into loading position and the rough part into machining position. The operator did not start or stop the machine, nor did he or she control the speed at which the table turned. All this was done automatically by the machine itself, once it had been properly set up by the tool setter.[5]

Soon the principle of multiplying the operations on a single machine was incorporated into this automatic indexing machine. The result was a highly sophisticated machine tool—the multi-station automatic indexing machine. Instead of one work station, the machine had several, plus an idle or loading station at the front. The turntable held enough parts for all these stations. The operator simply unloaded the finished part from the fixture at the loading station and replaced it with a rough part. This part was then automatically indexed through the successive work stations, located around the perimeter of the turntable. As soon as the tools at one station had automatically fed to the work and reversed, the turntable indexed, bringing the part to the next station, where another cut was automatically taken. All stations worked simultaneously on a different part. By the time each part reached the loading station again, it was complete. This machine thus proceeded through a number of different work tasks continuously, without the slightest intervention of the worker. He or she merely stood at the front, removing finished work and replacing it with rough parts as the turntable rotated into the loading station.

Multi-station automatic indexing machines appeared in American auto shops around 1912, and their use quickly spread to a variety of operations: drilling, turning, milling, boring. A typical example of the labor savings that these automatic machines could achieve is provided by the use of an automatic indexing miller to replace a semiautomatic reciprocating miller at Hudson. The latter machine was "idle during both loading and unloading operations and the operator was idle while the machine was working." The automatic miller eliminated the idle time of both operator and machine.

> It has capacity for ten pieces. While the operator is loading one "station," the machine is working on the other nine pieces. By using a special jig, all the operator has to do is load and unload the idle station. The old plain type miller cost $2,900, the new $15,500; but one man now operates two of the new machines and produces as much as five men could produce on the old machines. The savings ratio is thus 10 to 1 and figures $4 per hundred blocks. On last year's output the total savings was $72,800 and of course justified the purchase of the new machine.[6]

Although some grinding was done on multi-station indexing machines, it was generally the new method of centerless grinding that rendered this machine process automatic. This method ground parts by rotating them between abrasive wheels instead of between centers. The part was simply dropped between the rotating wheels, and their motion moved it through the machine as it was ground. The machine thus ran continuously and did not have to be stopped for loading and unloading. The operator was merely required to drop new pieces of work in as the others automatically fed out. Centerless grinding machines were in use in auto factories in the early 1920s, grinding valve stems, piston pins, bolts, and other cylindrical parts.[7]

AUTOMATIC CLAMPING AND LOADING DEVICES

Throughout the 1920s, the machinery of the auto shops continued to grow more and more automatic. However, auto manufacturers again ran up against the human obstacle in their attempt to speed up production. The automatic machine tools had eliminated the need for the worker to set up, regulate, feed, and even start and stop them. But they still required a human to supply their voracious appetites with unfinished parts and to remove finished ones. This loading and unloading soon proved to be an obstacle to increased production. The problem was that the machines could complete parts faster than the operators could or would load and unload them. New tool steels and other machine improvements reduced actual machining time further and further. But the human operator could not keep pace with the high production rate. So machines had to run below their maximum speed. As one commentator stated of automatic machines, "under present conditions the limiting factor in their use will be in many cases the ability of the machine operator to load and unload the work."[8]

As always when capitalist production ran up against the barrier of worker inability or unwillingness, the solution was to take control of this part of the labor process from workers' hands and transfer it to the machine. Thus, auto capitalists set their engineering staffs to work inventing automatic clamping and loading devices. The simpler and the first of the two problems to be solved was that of automatic clamping. Clamping, or chucking as it is called in certain cases, is that process whereby the part is secured for work in a fixture or other holding device. In the early days, this usually involved turning a capstan wheel, pulling a lever, or tightening bolts or screws. Some of this work required considerable strength and effort. When it became clear that the workers' ability to clamp or chuck work was falling behind the machines' ability to cut the metal, automatic devices that cut down on clamping time were devised.

One of the first automatic clamping devises was the magnetic chuck. The fixture that held the part was simply magnetized, so all the operator had to do was drop the part in. Magnetic force held it in place during machining. This was suitable only for relatively small parts, which could easily be held by magnetism. For larger parts, other solutions were found, such as the quick-acting mechanical chuck. This device was powered from the machine's motor. On activation by a lever or button, the jaws of the clamp were quickly driven together until they contacted the part and stopped. On fully automatic machine tools, the power chuck was tied in with the cycle of the machine, so that it closed and opened automatically without operator activation. All that was required of the operator was to drop the part in the fixture at the proper time in the machine cycle. Pneumatic clamping devices worked similarly.[9]

The next step in the process of taking control of machining out of the hands of workers was to make automatic not only the clamping, but also the initial loading of the parts into the fixtures. This was first accomplished with small parts by the use of hopper or magazine feed. The parts were placed into a hopper or magazine, which had an opening at the bottom to allow one part to pass out. The hopper or magazine was automatically opened at the proper time to let the part drop into an automatic chucking or clamping device. This type of loading device was especially adaptable to centerless grinders, which required only that the part be dropped between the wheels. It was also used on automatic indexing machines. The hopper was placed over the loading station and dropped a part in the empty fixture as it was indexed by. Upon completion, a devise automatically ejected the parts from the turret. Screw machines were rendered even more automatic by being equipped with automatic magazine feed, which fed a new rod into position as the preceding one was used up.

The larger parts like the engine block were not so readily adaptable to automatic loading. But an advance that similarly cut down on the unproductive time of loading and unloading was the fully integrated machine line. Instead of placing machine tools alongside a roller conveyor and requiring workers to lift parts on and off of it for machining, the machines were built right into the line itself. The work tables of the machines were raised to the same height as the roller conveyor. Short stretches of conveyor connected the tables of adjacent machines, so the workers could simply roll the parts from the conveyor right into the machine and out again. This principle was used early (circa 1914) to connect a few machines, and it spread until the whole line was integrated into one system in the late 1920s. To make loading as quick as possible, the machine tools were built so they straddled or formed part of the conveyor itself. Later developments included the activation of the machines by contact with the parts as they were rolled forward. Clamping, machining, and unclamping proceeded automatically.[10]

AUTOMATION

By the early 1930s, automotive manufacturers had wrested from workers control of nearly every aspect of machine-tool operation: loading, clamping, feeding, sizing, reversing, unclamping, unloading. The machines were amazingly automatic, governed no longer by workers but by themselves. However, there remained one gap in the machining process, one segment that required intervention by workers—the transfer of parts from one machine to another. Workers on the machine lines had to push the parts along the conveyor, or load the hoppers or magazines from the finished-work receptacles of the preceding machines. This gap was soon closed, however, by a revolutionary innovation in the labor process—automation. Since it was first coined by auto manufacturers and engineers, this term has expanded greatly in meaning. But "automation" was originally used in the auto industry to refer specifically to the automatic transfer of parts from one machine to another in a production line.

The story of automation in the automobile industry—and, indeed, in industry as a whole—finds its origins in the early 1920s in the amazing frame factory of the A. O. Smith Corporation of Milwaukee. Until 1920, the Smith Corporation had manufactured automobile frames by stamping out parts on worker-operated presses and hand-assembling them in a stationary position. However, spurred by the increasing demand for frames brought about by the mass production of autos, President L. R. Smith asked himself around 1916: "Can automobile frames be built without men?" After five years of intensive research and engineering, Smith managers and engineers had constructed a factory that answered this question with a qualified yes. This amazingly automatic factory was fully integrated, synchronized, and correlated from start to finish, performing the five hundred and fifty-two operations on the average frame in one hour and fifty minutes, with virtually no worker intervention. The production line began at the automatic inspection machine, which measured and stacked steel according to size and curvature. After passing through an automatic pickling department, the treated steel progressed through the press department. There, parts were carried through a series of automatic presses, whose mechanical fingers lifted them off the conveyor, placed them in the die, and returned them to the conveyor after the press had stamped them. The frame parts then progressed through the automatic assembly lines, where they were riveted into completed frames. The conveyors intermittently halted at assembly stations, where the jaws of automatic riveting machines advanced, clamped shut to rivet parts together, and then retreated to allow the conveyor to move the frame forward to the next station. Finally, the assembled frames were conveyed through automatic washing and painting processes.

The A. O. Smith frame factory did not completely fulfill the capitalist dream of production without human workers. It was still necessary for workers to position parts for some machines and transfer parts from one line to another. But only two hundred were required to produce the same daily output of seven thousand frames that had required twenty-five hundred workers by the old methods. This remarkable labor saving is attributable mainly to the revolutionary innovation of automatic transfer of parts in machine and assembly lines.[11]

The details of the Smith Corporation's revolutionary technology were not made public until 1928, and not long after this, the principle of automatic transfer of work between machines began to spread in auto shops. In 1931, Seneca Falls Machine Company introduced a lathe with an automatic device that transferred work from one machine to the next. Sets of metal fingers on the lathe could take a part—a piston, for example—from a moving conveyor, load and unload it, and then transfer it to the next machine in the line. The technical editor of *Automotive Industries* enthusiastically described this lathe as "human in operation." "Robotlike, it loaded and unloaded by means of metal hands. A new era in piston making was ushered in thereby."[12]

The next step forward in the process of automation was the introduction of the transfer machine, a completely integrated and synchronized line of machine tools that functioned as a single machine. A transfer machine was made up of a number of work stations laid out linearly and connected by automatic transfer devices. Each work station was composed of a number of tool heads mounted around a metal arch or tunnel. The transfer devices connecting the stations were moving conveyors, hydraulically driven with an intermittent motion. Parts were loaded in the front of the machine and from there carried automatically through the series of stations. The conveyor moved the part forward to the first station, where it stopped and was automatically clamped into machining position. Then the tool heads automatically fed in and out of the work, which was subsequently unclamped and transferred to the next work station, as the next part on the line moved into the first station behind it. All the various stations and conveyors were controlled and coordinated by an intricate system of electric interlocks and limit switches. The transfer machine was also equipped with a system of telltale lights to pinpoint sources of trouble. Between the various machining stations and tied into the entire system were devices that automatically washed the parts and rotated them into position for the next machining operation. The entire transfer machine was generally operated by only a few workers, whose jobs consisted of loading and unloading the parts and observing the work to make sure it proceeded properly.

The first transfer machines were introduced around 1938. In that year Natco, a machine tool company, brought out an eight-station machine that automatically performed ninety-four drilling, core drilling, chamfering, counterboring, and reaming operations on ninety cylinder blocks an hour. It was attended by a single operator. Greenlee, another machine tool company, also began to produce transfer machines tailored to the needs of the auto manufacturers. The use of these machines spread in the industry in the early 1940s. Encouraged by their initial successes with this technology, auto manufacturers worked with machine tool producers to place more and more operations on transfer machines. By 1943, a fully integrated transfer machine of over one hundred seventy-five feet in length was in use at Studebaker and Wright Aeronautical on the production of aircraft engines. The machine, which cost eight hundred thousand dollars to build, contained fifty separate stations for machining cylinder heads. Fully loaded it held two hundred and three heads and was controlled by one operator seated before an instrument panel.[13]

The number of such transfer machines in engine-machining lines increased throughout the 1940s. In 1947, Buick introduced the first line to be made up entirely of transfer machines. It was one thousand feet long and performed nearly every machining operation on the engine block without human intervention. Workers were required only to inspect the blocks and push them from one transfer line to the next over stretches of roller conveyor. However, even this small amount of worker intervention was eliminated with the construction of Ford's Cleveland Engine Plant in 1948. Unlike the Buick plant, the Ford lines incorporated automatic transfer devices between the separate transfer machines. Another novel feature of the Cleveland plant was automatic selection on the lines. At points where the line divided for special operations on different engines, automatic equipment selected the proper route for each engine. The entire Ford engine line was one automatic, integrated machine, which required virtually no direct human intervention.[14]

From these first automated engine lines, the principle of automatic transfer spread to different production processes within the auto shops. In 1946 Ford began to introduce automatic transfer between the machine tools in lines machining smaller parts. For example, seven centerless grinders for pistons were linked together in a line by a moving conveyor belt. Each machine was equipped for automatic magazine loading and automatic ejection. Pistons were merely placed on the belt, on which they travelled to the first grinder and were deflected by a bar into its magazine loader. They were fed into the grinder, automatically ejected, guided by a chute back onto the conveyor, and proceeded to the next machine. The work continued in this way until all seven machining jobs were completed. The entire line was attended by one operator. Similar techniques were extended to the production of manifolds, valves, and oilpans. In 1948 Ford also introduced automatic transfer in its pressed metal shop. Presses were connected by moving conveyors or transfer units. Each machine was equipped with an "iron hand" that lifted the stamping from the conveyor, placed it in the die, lifted it out after stamping, and returned it to the conveyor to be carried to the next press. A part could thus traverse an entire series of presses without human handling. Automatic spot welders were similarly equipped and linked together to render welding an automatic process. Crankshaft lathes were also fitted with mechanical arms that picked up the crankshafts from troughs, loaded them into the machine, and unloaded them onto transfer devices after machining.[15]

OTHER AUTOMATIC MACHINES

Although most of the innovations in automatic machinery took place in the machine shop, similar steps toward self-activating machines were evident in most parts of the automotive manufacturing process. In the pressed metal shops, presses were given automatic cycles so that they ran continuously. Workers merely loaded and unloaded the stampings in the intervals between the fall of the ram. Eventually, human loading and transfer of work on presses were replaced by automatic roll feed, which supplied the stamping blanks, and mechanical transfer arms, which loaded and transferred parts between presses. The welding of these pressed parts was also made increasingly automatic. Specialized, semiautomatic welding machines were constructed to replace the more universal, worker-controlled ones. All the variables of the work—timing, pressure, power, amount of wire, melting rate—were built into the machines. All the operators were required to do was place the parts in the machine and pull a lever or press a button. The welding cycle then proceeded automatically. Some machines for welding small parts utilized the automatic indexing principle. The machines ran constantly and the operators merely loaded and unloaded the revolving fixtures as they whirled past.[16]

The paint and trim shops also underwent increasing mechanization. Body painting operations were increasingly placed upon one continuous line, which carried bodies through automatic cleaning, sandblasting, painting, and drying stations with few, if any, attendants at the machinery. Automatic buffing and polishing machines also replaced workers with hand tools in the finishing of many accessories. Assembly processes were generally resistant to high-level mechanization, although manufacturers made some inroads. Automatic screwdrivers and arbor presses were introduced into some subassembly lines. And in 1947, Chevrolet introduced a semiautomatic station on the final assembly line for welding and riveting frames.[17]

Even the heretofore refuges of skilled workers were not safe from invasion by increasing mechanization. Toolroom operations, such as tool grinding and die sinking, began to be done by automatic machines. The intricate process of cutting or sinking dies for presses and forges had previously been done by highly skilled workers, using only hand tools and gages. But in the mid-1920s, the Keller profiling machine was introduced, which could automatically reproduce a hand-sunk die. By 1935, a machine was in operation in the auto shops that could automatically take a three-dimensional die cut, guided only by a blueprint. The once-skilled process of sharpening cutting tools for machine tools was also done increasingly by semiautomatic machines.[18]

Inspection, once a skilled process performed by workers with great knowledge of intricate gages, was also turned into an automatic machine process. Special inspection machines fitted with electric and air gaging devices gradually replaced manual inspection. When the operator placed the part in one of these, it indicated whether the part was acceptable or not. Inspection work was reduced to mere sorting. One trade journalist wrote that these machines "speed productivity greatly and assure conformity to established standards since the machine coldly accepts or rejects without exercising judgment."[19]

REPRESSIVE AND NONREPRESSIVE CONTROL IN AUTOMATIC MACHINES

As with the steps in the mechanization of auto manufacture, this trend toward automatic machines was motivated by a complex combination of repressive and nonrepressive control. Auto capitalists and managers again cited increased precision and decreased unit labor costs as the major advantages fueling their drive toward machines free of worker intervention. But a close examination of this mechanization process reveals that both advantages were at least partially accomplished through the increased repressive control over workers that these machines brought to capital.

Increased Precision

Auto manufacturers often claimed that making machines more automatic increased the precision of the parts produced. As Henry Ford stated, "accurate, large-scale production must have automatic or nearly automatic machines in order to reduce the cost and the errors of human labour."[20] They admitted that accurate work was technically possible on less automatic, worker-operated machines. But capitalists and managers argued that automatic machines made accuracy necessary by eliminating the possibility of "human error" inherent in worker-controlled machines. As one trade journalist wrote of an automatic furnace, "human skill and judgment with their chance of error has [sic] been practically done away with, and the experience of the workman has little or nothing to do with the tempering of steel in this plant."[21]

It was technically possible for workers exercising skill and judgment to produce precise, accurate work under the best of circumstances—if they were willing, alert, rested, and careful. However, the social relations of production of capitalism ensured that these optimal circumstances were difficult to achieve. The antagonisms between capital and labor generated by this system generally made auto workers recalcitrant and unwilling to put in their best efforts in order to benefit their employers. Further, the constant, unrelenting drive for more and more surplus value guaranteed that workers would not be rested, alert, or attentive. The intensification of labor and the long hours that resulted from this drive inevitably rendered workers physically fatigued not long after the working day had begun. And the minute division of labor resulting from this same pursuit of profit made work a monotonous, boring repetition of the same few tasks; inattention and negligence were its natural by-products. Therefore, in order to guarantee that work was precise and accurate under these social conditions of production, it was necessary for capital to further remove control of work from workers by making machines increasingly automatic.

The statements of automotive capitalists and those who spoke for them reveal that automatic machines increased the precision of work mainly by removing its control from fatigued, bored, recalcitrant workers. Capitalists thought that automatic feed of machine tools, for example, constituted a definite advantage over hand feed for this reason. Henry Krueger, a leading machine tool engineer, stated: "Mechanical feed must be better than hand feed, for gears and cams are not affected by morning-after hangovers and afternoon weariness." Automatic clamping was also said to increase accuracy by eliminating the possibility of errors due to varying worker effort. As an ad for a broaching machine with such a device stated: "The operation of manual clamping and unclamping fixtures requires considerable effort—usually much more than the mere handling of the work. At a high rate of production, operators become arm-weary, slow down, spoil work. All this is eliminated with automatic clamping and releasing. . . . " Similarly, one of the benefits of automatic transfer machines was said to be the infallible and untiring performance of routine tasks. "Machines, like this one, work as if they had minds of their own. And minds of metal never tire, never change, never make mistakes . . . *and thrive on routine.*"[22]

Capital's attempt to increase precision by transferring the last remnants of control from tired, bored, exploited workers to automatic machines is well illustrated by the following statement by an executive of an auto parts manufacturing firm, justifying the introduction of an automatic assembly machine. He stated that the assembly of the voltage regulator is too delicate to expect a human to keep it up to a precise accuracy all day. Yes, they can do it one time and they can do it ten times, but can they keep it up a hundred times? We've noticed that this kind of thing would happen: One of the girls will be chatting with her neighbor or she'll take an extra long break. That puts her behind a little bit, so what does she do? She speeds up. As a result her adjustments go off. This means lack of uniformity. On the automatic machine . . . we are going to do this assembly operation mechanically, under a controlled atmosphere and at a controlled temperature. There just isn't a comparison in the uniformity and quality of the job we're going to get out of this automatic machine as compared to having people do the job.[23]

This executive admitted that the "girls" could do the work perfectly well for a while. But they simply could not keep up this accuracy under the conditions imposed by capitalist production—that is, long hours, intense work, confinement to a single, monotonous job. Under these social conditions, the automatic machine better guaranteed the necessary precision.

The increase in precision yielded by more automatic machines was thus achieved mainly through repressive control. Unlike some of the first steps of mechanization, these steps toward automatic technology did not improve the technical capabilities of human labor. They increased precision by shifting control of work to machines and thus insulating its accuracy from the social conditions of capitalist labor: recalcitrance, fatigue, boredom, negligence.

Decreased Unit Labor Costs

The main goal capitalists sought, however, with the introduction of automatic machinery was not increased precision, but decreased unit labor costs. As in the early period of mechanization, a relatively tight labor market prevailed throughout much of this later period, and auto worker struggles based on these favorable market conditions kept wages generally high. Industry capitalists could not, therefore, reduce unit labor costs by driving down wage rates. High wages stimulated them to achieve this goal through higher levels of mechanization, which reduced the labor time expended on a unit of production.

Although the general trend throughout this period was toward greater mechanization, stimulated by high wages, this trend was not without fluctuation. The development of automatic technology was uneven, fluctuating with wage rates, which in turn varied with the business cycle. In recessionary and depressionary periods, when labor surpluses swelled and weakened labor's market power, capitalists' efforts at mechanization waned, for they were able to reduce labor costs by driving down wages. This was especially true of the depression of the 1930s. One industry analyst noted that machine development during the depression "has lagged and in many cases almost halted." Noting that "cost-reducing methods of a high order have always been a concomitant of high wages," he attributed this lag to the decrease in auto workers' wages.[24] In boom periods, however, when labor shortages strengthened workers' struggle for higher wages, auto capitalists increased mechanization efforts in order to reduce unit labor costs. Thus, there was a spurt of mechanization beginning with the First World War and continuing unabated through the 1920s. Another spurt occurred during and immediately after the Second World War, when defense production and postwar prosperity dried up labor surpluses and pushed wages up. Thus, one industry commentator wrote in 1947: "Since increases in individual productivity have not kept pace with increases in wages, the only recourse to industry, therefore, is greater mechanization. If output is to be raised, the application of more automatic machines and power-driven tools is imperative."[25]

Like the early machines, capitalist use of automatic machines reduced the labor time expended on a unit and, consequently, unit labor costs, in two ways—by increasing the intensity and the productivity of labor. It is beyond doubt that in many instances, taking the knowledge and skill out of workers' hands and transferring them to automatic machines simply increased the productivity of labor, that is, the amount of work that could be turned out by a worker in a given time with the same expenditure of effort. Consider, for example, the automatic buffing machine. The process of buffing a chrome auto bumper by hand was very laborious, even when workers were assisted by hand-held power tools. The heavy tools still had to be held to the bumper and moved around to cover the entire area, which took considerable time and effort. However, on the automatic buffing machine, the bumper was simply fed by the operator onto a moving conveyor that took it past a series of spinning buffing wheels. This machine increased worker-hour output nearly 400 percent over the hand method, without requiring a greater effort of the operator. On the contrary, the operator's job was considerably eased. Or take the automatic transfer machine in the engine-machining line. Instead of hoisting a block or head from the conveyor, placing it in the machine tool, clamping it, throwing the feed lever, unclamping it, then hoisting it back to the line, the operator simply had to push the part into the front of the machine. The machine automatically took care of every aspect of a series of machining operations. Nash Motors reported that the installation of a Greenlee transfer machine reduced the machining time per one hundred cylinder heads from 42.92 to 7.58 worker-hours.[26]

The increased labor productivity achieved by rendering machines more automatic was obviously a neutral, nonrepressive-control measure, despite the fact that its benefits were appropriated mainly by capital. The self-activating machines increased workers' output per hour without affecting the social relations of production by making more efficient use of human labor. However, it is equally clear that auto manufacturers' transfer of skill and discretion from workers to automatic machines also cut unit labor costs by giving them greater repressive control over the intensity of labor. Capitalists consciously developed and used automatic machines to take the control of the pace of work out of the hands of labor and transfer it to the machine, which they controlled. They could then intensify work virtually at will, with little effective resistance from workers. Auto manufacturers utilized automatic machinery to intensify labor in three ways: (1) by speeding up work, (2) by stretching out workers, and (3) by expanding the supply of labor.

Speed-up. Intensification of labor was often achieved by increasing the speed at which the machine processes worked, thus forcing the workers attending the machines to work faster in order to keep up. Automatic machines allowed managers, not workers, to set the pace of work. As one commentator stated: "In all of these [automatic] machines a similar theory has dictated the design. The operator is relieved of practically all responsibility for the rate of feed. Tool life is prolonged and the production rate is increased. Instead of the man setting the pace for the machine, the opposite is the case. . . . "[27]

Each step toward the goal of completely automatic machinery was guided by a capitalist desire to speed up the pace of work by taking its control away from workers. A manufacturer of a drilling machine with an automatic feed appealed to this desire, advertising "an automatic feed mechanism that paces the operator, requiring him to maintain the pace set by the production department." With the automatic feed in control of production pace, workers lost much of their power to resist exploitation by slowdowns. During the post-World-War-II period, which was marked by heightened labor-capital conflict, a typical ad for a semiautomatic machine proclaimed: "You can't always control production slow-downs—but anytime you can eliminate six or seven manual operations, and replace them all with a single push-button control, your production line is going to move faster, your costs are coming down."[28]

The automatic indexing machine was also introduced to help capital further speed up work. On this fully automatic machine, workers no longer had even the freedom of starting and stopping the mechanism. It ran constantly at a speed set by capital and forced workers to work at its pace, loading and unloading parts. The innovative Bullard Machine Tool Company advertised that its automatic indexing machines controlled production costs. "The Mult-Au-Matic is not subject to the fluctuating temperaments of different operators. The machine sets the pace for the operator."[29] A milling machine with the automatic indexing feature was described as follows in one trade paper:

> The table has a fixed feed, so that there is no possibility of the operator increasing or decreasing the production of the machine, as any holding device passing the loading station will immediately attract the attention of the man in charge of the section and, in addition to this, as the functions of the machine require so many stations per hour to pass the loading station, that number of pieces must be loaded and unloaded. There is, however, *a provision in the feed mechanism by which the rate of feed can be increased or decreased by those in authority.*[30]

The inhuman pace at which "those in authority" could set the machine and consequently drive the workers is well illustrated by the following account by a worker who operated a multi-station automatic indexing machine that welded brake shoes.

> You pushed the starting button and the table began to revolve. With your right hand you picked up a reinforcement and put it in a depression in the die coming at you from the right, which it fitted very snugly. By then your left hand was supposed to have grabbed a brake shoe from the truck to your left to be placed in the fixture on top of the reinforcement. Then your right hand picked up the finished shoe out of the next fixture coming from the right; you tossed this welded shoe down the chute at your right. This completed one cycle of the operation, and you started all over again. . . .
>
> This gadget was timed to turn out eight hundred welded shoes per hour [!]. To make his production, a skillful operator had to keep it going almost constantly. This required a degree of dexterity which a beginner believed it impossible to attain—except for the cold fact that the old operator could do it. To master it, you had, in effect, to perform that old stunt of rubbing your belly and patting your head at the same time; that is, you had to learn to do one thing with one hand

while doing something else with the other. The way the machine was timed, you just could not keep one hand idle while the other worked.[31]

Automatic loading and transfer devices allowed manufacturers to speed up labor even further. As long as the control of loading and transferring parts rested in the hands of fatigued and recalcitrant workers, it raised an obstacle to increased production speed. This obstacle was overcome by pneumatic and mechanical clamps, magazine and hopper feeds, and ultimately, automatic transfer machines. The capitalist motive toward work intensification that lay behind these technological devices was revealed in interviews given to James Bright by the managers of Ford and another large auto company. Bright concluded from the interviews that one of the main managerial objectives in introducing automation was "reduction of variation in worker performance." Managers complained that when machine operation depended upon human action, the "energy, skills, attention, and attitude of the worker at the moment limit the speed of a machine." Machinery in engine plants, for example, commonly operated at only 60 percent of capacity.

> It was believed and intended by Ford engineers that use of automatic machine tool loading and parts handling would raise productivity by eliminating some of the variation associated with human effort. Sickness, Monday morning hangover, the after-lunch loginess, the Friday night rush, the end-of-the-day fatigue—the impact of these human weaknesses so common to all of us could be avoided, Ford manufacturing people held, if machines did the heavy work and controlled the delivery and movement of materials. Furthermore, the opportunities for human error, mistakes, and accidents would be reduced.[32]

The "human element" was an ideological expression by means of which capitalists tried to justify automation by making the traits of their workers seem natural and universal. In reality, however, the resistance, inattention, negligence, and fatigue of auto workers were in large part the peculiar results of this particular social system of production. Beneath this ideological distortion, the real capitalist motive for automation is clear—to strip workers of the power to control work pace by taking even the routine handling of parts between machines out of their hands.

Stretch-out. Automatic machines were also used by auto manufacturers to intensify labor by facilitating stretch-out, the practice of forcing workers to attend more than one machine. As long as workers actually operated machinery—that is, set up, loaded, fed it, etc.—they were physically tied to one machine, for they were continuously occupied with the direct regulation of work. However, when machines operated themselves, through the installation of automatic features, the continuous presence of workers was no longer required. While the machine automatically performed the work, they could either stand idle or be forced to attend to other machines. The antagonistic relations of production in auto shops dictated that this stretch-out potential inherent in automatic machines would be used to intensify labor.

In some cases, stretch-out seems to have been the primary motive for the introduction of automatic machines. For example, *Automotive Industries* concluded about a grinder with power feed that the "automatic features of the machine are incorporated with the idea of reducing the number of motions required of the operator to a minimum so that two machines can be operated simultaneously by one man."[33] Similarly, automatic sizing devices, which stopped work as soon as the desired dimensions were attained, seem to have been motivated in large part by attempts to stretch out workers. "To make it possible for one man to operate three or four machines, it was necessary to develop some method of automatically controlling the size of work. Accordingly, sizing devices were developed which automatically keep the work to a given size as it passes through the grinder."[34] Being forced to attend more than one machine meant, of course, that operators had to work harder, more intensively. Instead of being able to relax a bit as they fed and adjusted the work in progress, they had to hurry off to load and unload another machine. As many as eight machines were often assigned to one worker. In one carburetor manufacturing plant, workers were so stretched out that they had to have rolling chairs on tracks to cover the distance between machines.[35]

Expanding the labor supply. Finally, automatic machines, like the division of labor and earlier steps in mechanization, were used to intensify labor by expanding the supply of labor power available to the industry. As noted above, automotive manufacturers were faced throughout much of the period up to 1950 with shortages of workers with sufficient training to fill their rapidly growing shops. These labor shortages gave workers greater market power, which furthered their struggles for higher wages. However, this market power also had a profound impact on the workers' struggle for control on the shop floor. During periods of severe labor shortages, the main sanction by means of which capital exerted control over workers—the threat of firing—was weakened. Consequently, workers were strengthened in their resistance to increased exploitation. This was especially true during both world wars, when auto worker resistance of various sorts—soldiering and sabotage, strikes, absenteeism and turnover—reached epidemic proportions.[36]

One method used by auto capitalists to combat this resistance based on labor shortages was the progressive deskilling of auto work, which made possible the employment of relatively unskilled workers who were in greater supply. By allowing manufacturers to draw on the large reserve army of unskilled workers, deskilled work processes "put the fear of unemployment" back into workers and hence strengthened the power of capital on the shop floor. And this power was used to enforce demands for intensified labor upon workers. The division of labor and early mechanization had greatly furthered this process of deskilling. But it was only completed with the introduction of fully automatic machines, which so eliminated the necessity for the slightest worker skill that on many jobs "one hour's instruction will make the 'greenest' operator equal to the most expert 'old-fashioned' operator."[37]

Expanding the labor supply and thus increasing capitalist control over work intensity became a particularly important motive behind the automatization of machines during World War II, when manufacturers faced severe labor shortages. Thus, one ad for an automatic transfer machine in 1941 stated: "When you can't hire skill, have the brains built into your machines. Machines, like this one, work as if they had minds of their own. . . . In times of shortage of skilled labor you can use this type of design service to advantage."[38] One of the sources of unskilled labor that auto capitalists drew upon to fill labor shortages during both world wars was the largely untapped industrial reserve army of women. Most manufacturers agreed that the way to get women quickly into the labor-starved auto plants was to make work as simple and automatic as possible. Appealing to this motive, one ad in *Automotive Industries* for an automatic lathe pictured two women in work clothes and read:

> "Mine's the softest job in the shop! I admit it! I know less about machining than anyone in the shop. But I get more of it done and that's the truth."
>
> That's right! And it's happening in hundreds of busy plants today where the Gisholt Hydraulic Automatic Lathes have taken over—each doing the work of several manually operated machines—releasing skilled machinists for other work where their skill is needed.

Anyone can learn, in a very short time, to operate the Gisholt Hydraulic Automatic Lathe. What's more, one operator can usually tend two, or even three, machines. For it requires but little more than loading the machine and removing the work.

It's another wartime lesson that will stand many users in good stead long after the war is over.[39]

As was noted in the discussion of the division of labor in chapter 3, deskilling work in order to expand the labor supply was not an inherently repressive measure. There was a nonrepressive aspect to this use of mechanization—meeting the labor requirements of the industry so it could continue to expand production. However, the antagonistic relations between labor and capital ensured that this expanded labor supply made possible by automatic machines would also be used repressively to intensify work.

In these three ways, auto manufacturers developed and used automatic machines repressively to seize control of labor intensity from workers. As a result, auto labor was intensified and unit labor costs decreased. But unlike the nonrepressive aspects of automatic machinery, which increased the productivity of labor, these repressive aspects lowered labor costs solely by repressing the resistance of workers to increased capitalist exploitation.

As with other mechanical devices, these automatic machines employed some features that simultaneously furthered both repressive and nonrepressive control. For example, the same automatic transfer machine that increased productivity by relieving workers of transportation labor also allowed capital to increase labor intensity by totally controlling the speed of machinery. And the same automatic clamping devices that increased productivity by relieving workers of the arduous task of securing work in machines also allowed capital to increase the intensity of machine-operating labor by eliminating workers' control over the timing of machine cycles. However, some aspects of automatic technology seem to have furthered mainly the repressive control of capital. Automatic feed and multi-station automatic indexing features were mainly devices whereby capital wrested control of the work pace out of the hands of workers. Automatic feed did not make machines more productive or precise than hand feed controlled by willing, alert, and rested workers. It merely allowed capital to speed up work beyond the point at which recalcitrant, bored, and fatigued workers would or could work. The same holds true for the multi-station automatic indexing machines. Their only advantage was that they allowed capital, rather than workers, to set the pace of production, forcing workers to keep up with the speed of the whirling fixture.

THE INFLUENCE OF MARKET DEMAND
ON DESIGN AND TECHNOLOGY

Before concluding this discussion, it is necessary to briefly examine another imperative besides lower production costs that shaped the development of automotive production technology. This imperative was market demand. As long as the market for automobiles in the United States was large and growing, the major problem of manufacturers was to produce as many cars as rapidly and cheaply as possible. Both the design of the product and the technology of its manufacture were tailored to this goal of high-volume, low-cost production. However, as market demand began to decline, stimulating sales became a major concern, and design and technology had to be altered to accommodate this goal as well.

Mass production of a product requires a large market, for only high volume makes the installation of expensive work and technological processes economically feasible. The techniques of mass production also require a simplified and standardized product design. Only an invariant and unchanging design can be produced with highly specialized machines, work processes, and workers. The large and growing market in the early years of the industry allowed manufacturers to mass-produce automobiles. And mass-production techniques dictated very simple and standardized automobile designs. Thus, when market demand was unproblematic and production was the major problem, production technology generally determined the design of the product.

From the beginnings of the industry until the mid-1920s, auto manufacturers made major design changes in the automobile in order to adapt it to low-cost, mass-production techniques. Under capitalist relations of production, production costs were lowered by techniques that gave capital the greatest control over the labor process. Design and production engineers thus set to work to design a car whose production eliminated the necessity for worker skill and discretion. The general nature of this influence of production technology on design was explained by a trade journalist.

> Today a design is not good unless it has, outside of its performance, the qualifications which make it possible to produce the product at a

low cost. It is customary and proper, therefore, that in these days [1922] before an automobile is put into production, after the engineering department has fully gone through its tests and becomes satisfied with the performance standpoint, the design should be turned over to the manufacturing expert to see that it is adaptable to high speed production methods and tools.[40]

Specific examples of the manner in which deskilling technology shaped automobile design abound. Automobile bodies, for example, were redesigned to eliminate the large amounts of skilled labor that they had originally required. Wooden body panels, whose production required skilled woodworkers, were replaced by sheet-metal panels, which could be stamped out quickly on presses operated by unskilled operators. However, curved metal panels were not easily formed on presses; they required extensive hand-hammering by skilled workers. So in order to eliminate the necessity for these skilled sheet-metal workers, designers simply eliminated the curves in the body design. The boxlike appearance of the early, low-priced automobiles was the result, not of a lack of aesthetic sense by designers, but of the imperative of deskilling labor.[41]

The same imperative was behind Henry Ford's infamous statement: "Any customer can have a car painted any color he wants so long as it is black." In the days before fast-drying lacquer paints, painting an auto body was a very time-consuming and skilled process, requiring numerous hand-applied coats and long drying periods between them. There was one alternative method of finishing a body that eliminated much of the time and skilled labor involved—enameling. Entire body sections could be dipped in tanks of enamel and quickly dried in ovens. However, enamel could be applied successfully to auto bodies in only one color—black. So Ford's dictum that all Motel T's be painted black was the result not of a dislike of color, but of an attempt to reduce the skill and time requirements of production.[42]

By the mid-1920s, however, the rosy market conditions that allowed auto manufacturers to subordinate design to the imperative of deskilling work had begun to fade. Sales to first-time buyers, on which the early industry had depended for its phenomenal growth, began to decline. While in 1910 about two-tenths of one percent of all American families owned an automobile, by 1923, 74 percent were car owners. The main problem of the industry shifted from the production of enough low-priced autos to meet market demand to the sale of the cars it produced. Increased sales depended largely upon selling new cars to people who already owned one. But to do this, the manufacturers had somehow to convince existing owners that their cars were "old," although they retained years of functional use.[43]

The solution to this sales problem was a set of marketing techniques pioneered in the mid-1920s by General Motors president, Alfred Sloan. These marketing innovations consisted of annual model changes, consumer upgrading, and model diversification. Automobile models were changed every year, usually by superficial alterations in body design. And each year the models became more expensive, largely due to the addition of nonessential accessories. Finally, to spread a company's sales over the entire range of the market, a model was offered in every price category, from the cheapest to the most expensive.[44]

All of these new marketing policies required a change in the relationship between design and technology. Design could no longer be unilaterally molded to the requirements of cost-cutting production techniques. It now had to be manipulated to stimulate consumer demand. And the diverse and regularly changing designs that were adopted to do so placed certain limits on production technology. Highly specialized machines, rigidly constructed to perform one task on one specific part, proved impractical for automobiles whose design changed at least partially every year. They had to be scrapped or completely rebuilt quite frequently, which was very expensive. The problem faced by auto manufacturers was that of devising a technology that was flexible enough to allow frequent and rapid production changes, but that did not relinquish control of the labor process back to skilled machinists.

This challenge was met in two ways. First, beginning in the mid-1920s, manufacturers began to replace highly specialized machine tools with universal tools adaptable to specific tasks with special fixtures and tool arrangements. The special fixtures and toolings ensured that the skill continued to be built into the machine, rather than reverting to the workers. But because only the fixtures and toolings were specialized, the machines could be easily and rapidly adapted to changing designs. The second solution was unit-type machinery. A specialized machine was constructed from a number of standardized machine units: tool heads, motors, transmissions, feed mechanisms. When design changes dictated changes in tooling, the machine could be quickly dismantled and a new one constructed from the basic units to meet the new requirements. The rebuilding job was performed by the skilled workers and technicians of the tool department. The production workers remained unskilled, for they continued to labor at machines that centralized all skill.

Even the elaborate transfer machines could be constructed from units in this manner, so that changeover to a new model was relatively simple and rapid.[45]

Therefore, even though a change in the market for automobiles forced changes in production technology, capitalists managed to fulfill the crucial imperative of maintaining control over the labor process under these changed conditions. To have surrendered control to a resurrected force of skilled workers would have undermined the specifically capitalist labor process that capitalists had struggled to create, and the high profits that were its consequence.

CHAPTER 7
Human Consequences of the New Technology

Between the industry's beginnings and 1950, automotive capitalists completely transformed the work and technology of manufacturing automobiles. Meeting the imperative to maximize surplus value under the social condition of class antagonism, they shifted control of the labor process from labor to capital by removing much of the skill and discretion from work. This transformation yielded the results intended by capitalists. Skilled craft workers were replaced by unskilled specialists. Manufacturers were thereby able to draw on the greater supply of unqualified workers from Europe, rural America, and American households. And the final payoff came in increased worker-hour output and decreased unit labor costs.

CHANGING SKILL REQUIREMENTS AND OCCUPATIONAL DISTRIBUTION

Data from various sources clearly reveal that the capitalist goal of deskilling work was largely achieved by the transformation of work and technology. Measuring the changing skill requirements of automotive manufacturing occupations is not without methodological problems. Available data vary widely in definition, measurement, scope, validity, and reliability. Although these problems make it impossible to obtain precise measurements, data are sufficient to provide a rough estimate of the nature and pace of the decline of skill in the auto labor process.

For present purposes, skill will be defined as a set of mental and manual abilities, acquired through training and/or experience, that in some manner facilitate the performance of a task. There are many levels of skill, but here a skilled worker will be defined as one who possesses mental and manual abilities that require on the average at least one year of training and/or experience to acquire. Using this definition in conjunction with the available data reveals a rapid and early decline in the proportion of skilled workers in the auto labor force.[1]

In the very early days of the industry, the machining and assembly of auto parts were carried out by a force comprised largely of skilled machinists and mechanics. These were versatile, all-around, skilled workers, who generally learned their skills while serving an apprenticeship of up to seven years. Although no good data on the composition of the earliest auto shops are available, it is safe to state that the majority of workers fell into the skilled category. As late as 1910, when work rationalization had already begun in many factories, a report by the Michigan Department of Labor classified nearly three-fourths of those employed in the state's automobile industry as skilled. A similar picture of the proportion of skilled workers in these early shops is given by the 1910 census. Using the occupational statistics for the automobile industry and a knowledge of the early labor process, I have calculated that a little over 60 percent of the wage earners were skilled. Similarly, Stephen Meyer has calculated from a 1910 Ford Motor Company list of workers that approximately 60 percent were in skilled occupations (if foremen are included).[2]

This large complement of skilled workers in the auto shops was rapidly devastated, however, by the deskilling measures of the first half of the second decade of the century. Data from the innovative Ford Motor Company reveal, for example, that when it reclassified its entire work force by skill in 1913, only 28 percent of all workers were considered skilled. Approximately 50 percent of Ford wage earners were classified as mere "operators," while the remainder was divided between laborers and helpers. Ford was not alone in instituting early deskilling changes in the labor process, as is revealed by a 1915 survey of the metal trades in Cleveland. The study concluded of the city's automobile shops that, as a result of scientific management methods, "the skilled craftsman forms an insignificant part of the working force, which is made up chiefly of the sort of labor that can be taught to run a single machine or perform a

TABLE 7.1.   Estimated Time to Learn Automobile Manufacturing
Occupations, 1915

Learning time	Percentage of work force
1 month or less	44
2 months	15
3 months	12
4 months	2
6 months	14
6 months to 1 year	2
1 year	4
2 to 3 years	4
3 to 4 years	2
4 years	1

SOURCE: R. R. Lutz, *The Metal Trades* (Cleveland: Survey Committee of the Cleveland Foundation, 1916), p. 97.

single assembly process within a few days, weeks, or at the most, months."[3] Based on data furnished by several auto factory superintendents, the Cleveland study calculated the approximate time required to learn the various occupations of the industry. Table 7.1 summarizes these findings. By our definition, at most only 13 percent of the automobile work force in the Cleveland factories in 1915 was skilled. These skilled workers consisted mainly of skilled trade workers (electricians, carpenters, millwrights, blacksmiths), tool makers, and painters of various types.

In a very short time, then, auto manufacturers achieved a precipitous decline in the proportion of skilled workers in their factories—from perhaps two-thirds to one-eighth. This debacle of deskilling was the result of monumental changes in the labor process that they introduced during this period. Interchangeability and standardization, the division of labor, progressive layout, specialization of machines, the moving conveyor line—all of these innovations emerged during this period to greatly reduce the necessity for skill and discretion on the part of workers in most automobile manufacturing occupations. However, after this initial debacle, the proportion of skilled workers in the shops leveled off and remained fairly constant, as revealed by data collected by the Bureau of Labor Statis-

TABLE 7.2. Percentage of Skilled Workers in the Wage-Earning Automotive Factory Work Force, 1922–1950

Year	Percentage skilled
1922	11.0
1925	9.4
1928	9.5
1930	10.6
1940	12.4
1950	11.6

SOURCE: U.S., Bureau of Labor Statistics, Bulletin nos. 348 (1923), 438 (1927), 502 (1930), 706 (1942), 1015 (1951) (Washington, D.C.: Government Printing Office).

tics presented in Table 7.2. The main bulk of skilled workers had been eliminated by the time of the first survey in 1922. And despite yearly fluctuations, the percentage of skilled workers in the industry's work force remained (and continues to remain) around 12 percent.

These data conform well to the general curve of skill that James Bright noted in his important study of mechanization and automation. His findings indicated that as the mechanization of work developed from hand tools on through machines to automation, the level of skill required of workers quickly rose to a peak or hump and then slowly declined. The metalworkers, for example, required considerable dexterity when working with hand tools. When power was added to these tools, but their guidance was left to the operator, the worker had to have increased levels of dexterity, attention, and discretion to control tool action. When the tool was incorporated into a physical framework limiting its movement (that is, a universal machine), the knowledge required of the operator increased still further. The worker, now known as a machinist, had to know how to adjust and direct the more complex machine. This level of mechanization marked the peak or hump of skill, which occurred very early in the American auto industry. From this point on, increasing levels of mechanization directly entailed lower levels of worker skill. As machinery became specialized and automatic, the discretion, control, and knowledge of the operator were increasingly reduced. Machinists were replaced by semiskilled machine operators, whose jobs consisted simply of loading, machine actuation, workfeeding, patrolling, and inspecting. At the highest levels of mechanization, the worker became totally unskilled. Machines automatically started, fed, released, and transferred work, so that the operator became a monitor who merely observed the machine in action and ensured that it functioned smoothly.[4]

This does not mean, however, that the increasingly automatic labor process did not place certain demands on the worker. It did. But these demands were not the sort that could be called "skill," by practically any definition of the term. Unlike the less developed machines, which required attention to and concentration on the details of work itself, the increasingly automatic machines demanded above all a worker who was alert and attentive solely to the rapid pace of mechanical motions dictated by the machine. As Henry Ford stated, "the requirement is not for skill but for a higher alertness than is necessary in, say, a ditch digger or a crossing tender."[5] The worker had to be able to maintain a consistently high level of attention to rapid and mechanical movements that did not seriously engage his or her interests or demand concentrated mental effort. The worker at the automatic machine also had to have a level of manual dexterity and coordination sufficient to keep pace with the speeding machine.

Apart from alertness to mechanical pace and manual dexterity, the automatic machinery of automotive production further required absolute subordination of workers to the commands of capitalists and their managers. One academic investigator of the industry concluded that a requirement of the successful machine tender was "to follow without wavering printed instruction emanating from an unseen source lodged in some far off planning department. . . ."[6] Engineering journalists Arnold and Faurote, who made an extensive study of the Ford shops, stated this requirement a bit more forcefully: "But willful insubordination is, of course, absolutely intolerable, and Ford workers must be, first of all, docile."[7] The increasingly automatic technology rendered the various parts of the manufacturing process so interdependent that the failure of a single worker to do exactly as instructed could bring the whole mechanism to a grinding halt. As Henry Ford stated: "We expect the men to do what they are told. The organization is so highly specialized and one part is so dependent upon another that we could not for a moment consider allowing men to have their own way."[8]

Finally, workers at the advanced technology of the industry were required to be stable and reliable. "It is of vital importance to successful factory management that workmen should be steady in their habits and dependable in the point of continuous service," stated

Arnold and Faurote of the Ford shops.[9] The large investments in fixed capital entailed by the increasingly sophisticated technology demanded a rapid and predictable depreciation through continuous operation of facilities at full capacity. This could be achieved only if workers were stable and predictable in their efforts. Not extraordinary effort, but stable and calculable work performances were required of workers. Coming in every day, being on time, working from bell-time to bell-time at the standard rate, staying with the same firm year after year—these were the traits required of workers on the advanced technology of the automobile industry.

There were those who disputed the above contention that the skill levels of the work force declined with advancing mechanization. Proponents of the so-called "upgrading thesis" contended that, on the contrary, the skill level of the working class as a whole was raised by mechanization. As James Bright pointed out, this thesis seemed to be a mixture of two related but distinct contentions about the effects of mechanization: (1) that the skills within many job categories (especially operators) increased, and (2) that there was a relative shift between job categories toward the more skilled. Both contentions would seem to be refuted by the data we have cited, which demonstrate that, regardless of how jobs are categorized, the proportion of skilled workers in the auto labor force declined drastically. Nevertheless, an examination of these separate theses will serve to clarify the nature of the deskilling process.

The thesis that operators of increasingly sophisticated technology required greater skill is refuted by the statements of independent researchers and automotive capitalists alike. The manufacturers of automobiles and machine tools quoted in chapters 4 and 6 revealed that not only was the deskilling of operators the result of the increasingly automatic machines, but it was the intended result. Even workers on the most sophisticated automated transfer lines, to which upgrading proponents generally pointed to confirm their thesis, required no special training or unusual education. This was the finding of Bright in his investigations of two automated engine plants and three automated auto parts plants. He quoted Ford's top management as stating that, in the plant as a whole, automation had reduced training requirements, because less skill, less dexterity, and less knowledge and care were required of the workers. The findings of William Faunce's study of the changeover to automated lines in an engine plant were similar. The management informed him that no new or greater skill was required of machine operators as a result of the changeover. Workers generally shared this view, reporting no significant differences in the amount of training or time

required for a new operator to learn the job. They contended that
their new jobs on the automated lines required more "skill," but
usually meant by this more alertness and attention, not more mental
or manual ability. Faunce concluded that there was little reason to
suppose that automated jobs required greater skill. In fact, he stated
that because the manual skills required with conventional machining techniques were no longer needed, the converse may well have
been true.[10]

However, many advocates of the upgrading thesis contended that
what was required of workers was a new type of skill, unrelated to
the old conception of mental and manual abilities. Alain Touraine
was probably the first proponent of this thesis. In his study of the
evolution of work in France's Renault automobile factories, he concluded that workers in the automated labor process no longer possessed the technical skills and knowledge for executing work. But
they required a new "social skill." Workers were given responsibility
for a certain amount of automatic equipment, whose operation they
merely monitored. Their skill, Touraine argued, consisted of a certain amount of good will toward the entire organization, which facilitated rapid communication to higher-ups (technicians, specialists,
foremen) about problems on the line. This and other social skills allowed the operators to effectively work with the entire, interdependent social organization that was responsible for production. What
Touraine actually seemed to be saying was that the "newly skilled
worker" had to be a sort of back-slapping, hail-fellow-well-met, who
got along with everyone, (especially his or her superiors,) and did
not rock the organizational boat. Touraine is free to call this a "skill"
if he wants, but it seems to amount to little more than a willingness
to totally submit to the control and discipline of the capitalist organization of work. It bears little resemblance to the earlier mental and
manual abilities possessed by workers, which allowed them a certain amount of independence in the workplace.[11]

Many upgrading advocates contended, however, that mechanization increased skills not within, but between job categories, by
increasing the relative number of workers in qualified occupations.
Undoubtedly, advanced technology resulted in a relative shift from
blue-collar factory occupations to white-collar occupations in the
economy as a whole.[12] But we are concerned here mainly with the
wage-earning factory labor force. Did mechanization of auto work
shift workers into the more skilled occupations within the factory labor force?

Data on the occupational distribution of the wage earners in automotive factories summarized in table 7.3 reveal some distinct

TABLE 7.3. Percentage of the Wage-Earning Automotive Factory Work Force in Key Occupational Groups, 1910–1950

	1910	1922	1925	1928	1930	1940	1950
Laborers	17.8	10.7	11.6	10.2	8.4	—	—
Assemblers	4.1	14.0	15.0	16.0	14.4	16.9	13.0
Machine-tool operators	3.8	25.7	23.8	21.1	21.7	11.8	10.6
Inspectors	1.4	5.3	5.6	5.3	5.4	5.0	3.6
Tool and die makers	1.8	2.0	2.6	2.3	3.8	4.6	2.3
Maintenance and repair workers	5.1	—	—	—	—	8.9	10.1
Machinists and mechanics	34.4	2.3	2.5	2.3	2.5	—	—
Press operators	.3	2.0	3.1	2.8	3.4	5.3	6.2

SOURCE: Data for 1910 from U.S., Bureau of the Census, *Thirteenth Census of the United States: 1910*, vol. 4, "Population, Occupational Statistics" (Washington, D.C.: Government Printing Office, 1914): 336–39; data for all other years from U.S., Bureau of Labor Statistics, Bulletin nos. 348 (1923), 438 (1927), 502 (1930), 706 (1942), 1015 (1951) (Washington, D.C.: Government Printing Office).

changes, but none constituting an upgrading of the work force. One major occupational change was the decline of the proportion of laborers from nearly 18 percent in 1910 to about 8 percent in 1930. Although no good data are available after this date, due to a reclassification of this occupation, indications are that this trend continued. The proportion of auto workers engaged in common physical labor, such as carrying, handling, and cleaning up greatly decreased from the beginning of the industry to 1950, due to the mechanization of most of the physical labor required in production, especially materials handling.

A second notable change was the sudden jump in assemblers in the early years and the subsequent leveling off in that occupation. This great increase was due in large part to the fact that most workers in early shops engaged in assembly were classified not separately, but as part of the large group of skilled machinists and mechanics. Only after assembly became an unskilled job, divided between numerous detail workers, was a separate occupational category used to refer to such work. The persistence of assemblers as a relatively large part of the work force resulted from the difficulty of mechanizing assembly work, human labor being largely indispensable for such tasks.

The table further reveals an enormous growth in the occupation of machine-tool operators in the early years, and a slow decline thereafter. The leap in this occupational category was partly due to the fact that in the early industry skilled workers on machine tools were classified as machinists. As with the job of assembler, the category of machine-tool operator emerged as a result of the deskilling and specialization of formerly skilled workers. However, the proportion of the automotive work force actually working on machine tools, skilled or unskilled, seems to have grown in the early years, due to the mechanization of various tasks and the shift away from manual labor. The gradual decline of this occupation after its peak in 1922 can be attributed to increasingly higher levels of mechanization, which reduced the proportion of machine operators through increased productivity, speed-up, and stretch-out.

The proportion of the factory labor force composed of inspectors also increased substantially in the early years of the industry and declined in the later years. This growth is explained by the fact that in the early days, insection was not a separate occupation. Skilled machinists inspected their own parts as they produced them. Only later, under the sweeping division of labor, did inspection become a separate task. The decline of this category in the later years was due to the increasing mechanization of inspection labor.

One occupation that evidenced a constant growth throughout this period of the auto industry was press operator. This growth resulted from the gradual transfer of auto parts formerly produced by forging, casting, and handworking of metal to the cheaper, unskilled pressing or stamping process.

Finally, the table reveals notable changes in skilled occupations. First, the category of machinists and mechanics underwent a cataclysmic decline between 1910 and 1922, and remained fairly constant thereafter. This decline was the converse of the sudden jump in semiskilled and unskilled machine-tool operators. The specialization and automatization of machines reduced and finally eliminated the necessity of skills in operators and turned them into mere attendants. Second, tool and die makers evidenced a steady increase up to 1940, then declined steeply. This gradual increase is also explained by the direction of the evolution of auto work and technology. As capital transferred the skills of workers to increasingly specialized and automatic machines, the elite force of workers who produced and outfitted these machines increased. Thus, the skills formerly distributed widely in the production shops were concentrated into a small force in the tool shops, which grew as this transfer of skill intensified. Eventually, however, the tool shops also underwent the deskilling process. Under the pressure of wartime skilled labor shortages, auto manufacturers discovered that tool and die work could also be divided, specialized, and mechanized. Hence, the proportion of skilled tool and die makers declined and the number of mere machine opertors in the tool shop rose.[13]

The other skilled occupational category to undergo a notable change was maintenance and repair workers. The increasingly sophisticated machinery of auto production seemed to demand more skilled maintenance and repair. This occupation also grew because of the separation of machine maintenance and repair from the operators of machines. As a result of both factors, the proportion of the factory labor force engaged in maintenance and repair grew proportionally. Although table 7.3 has a large gap, data from this and other sources confirm that the percentage of these workers grew, especially with the introduction of automation.[14]

Taken as a whole, these data on occupational shifts within the wage-earning factory labor force of the auto industry do not support the thesis that mechanization increased the proportion of workers in skilled occupations. On the contrary, the major trend revealed by these data is an increase in the proportion of workers in semiskilled and unskilled occupations. The proportion of common laborers diminished, probably to the benefit of the occupations of machine-tool operator and press operator. But this shift did not really signal an increase in skilled occupations, because the operation of a machine or press required simply unloading parts or, increasingly, merely watching the automatic process. The growth in the proportion of both assemblers and machine-tool operators does not indicate a growth of skilled occupations, but rather an increase in specialized occupations at the expense of skilled machinists and mechanics. Unskilled press operators grew proportionally at the expense of skilled molders, forgers, and sheet-metal workers. The growth of the category of inspectors indicated a mere transfer of the relatively skilled task of inspection from machinists to a specialized occupation. The proportion of skilled tool and die makers grew, but it did so as the result of a massive deskilling of the vast majority of production workers. And while automated technology slightly increased the proportion of skilled maintenance and repair workers, it resulted in a much greater replacement of skilled machine operators with unskilled ones.

The upgrading thesis would thus seem erroneous in both of its variants for this period of the American auto industry. Neither skills within operator occupations increased, nor was there a relative shift toward more skilled occupations. On the contrary, the evolution of work and technology in the American auto industry resulted in a catastrophic decline in the overall skill of the factory labor force.

CHANGING DEMOGRAPHIC COMPOSITION
OF THE WORK FORCE

The capitalist transformation of auto work and technology resulted in changes not only in the skill requirements and occupational distribution, but also in the demographic composition of the labor force. The earliest auto shops were generally filled with skilled male workers, descended from early English colonists, or with northern European immigrants. And they were drawn mainly from the industrial centers of New England and the Midwest. However, as auto manufacturers transformed the work and technology of the industry, they were able to draw on the larger supply of workers of more diverse ethnic, regional, racial, and sexual characteristics to fill the newly deskilled jobs.

One of the first groups of unskilled workers to enter the mass-production auto shops was the "farm boys" or "buckwheats," migrants from the rural hinterlands of the United States. From the farms and villages of Michigan, Indiana, Illinois, Minnesota, Wisconsin, North and South Dakota, and all of the northwestern states came these workers. They were drawn to the industrial centers by the pull of high wages and the push of economic conditions on the farm. Many of these workers formed part of the transient "suitcase brigade," a contingent of young, unmarried men who flowed into the city during the industry's busy seasons and migrated back to the farm when business went slack.[15]

But the main group of workers that filled the newly created unskilled jobs in the industry was the immigrants from southern and eastern Europe. In the decade or so before the First World War, these immigrants flooded the industrial centers of the Midwest, where the auto industry was concentrated. Detroit was a major center for immigrant workers, due largely to the active recruitment practiced by the Employers' Association of Detroit. The great majority of the new arrivals were displaced peasants from Poland, Austria, Hungary, the Balkans, and Italy. The census of 1910 revealed that of all employees in U.S. auto factories, over 27 percent were foreign-born, and another 29 percent were of foreign or mixed parentage. These immigrant workers were concentrated in the low-liest, most unskilled jobs of the industry. In 1920, 47 percent of the laborers in American auto factories were foreign-born and another 15 percent were of foreign or mixed parentage. Foreign-born workers composed 28 percent of the industry's operatives (unskilled workers at machines), with another 27 percent in this occupational category of foreign or mixed parentage. A 1915 industrial survey in Cleveland, a center of auto production in the early days, estimated that from 50 percent to 75 percent of the unskilled auto workers were immigrants. The biggest factories generally employed the greatest number of immigrant workers. Ford's Detroit factories, for example, were manned by an overwhelming majority of foreign-born workers. A 1914 survey of Ford workers' national origins revealed that nearly three-quarters were foreign-born and more than half came from southern and eastern Europe.[16]

The First World War stopped the flow of immigrants to the rapidly expanding auto shops, forcing capitalists to turn to alternative sources of labor supply. These were found in rural workers, blacks, and women. To further attract workers from the rural hinterlands of northern industrial centers, auto manufacturers offered various incentives, such as special deals on the tractors they manufactured. Special efforts were also made to recruit southern blacks into the auto shops. Until the First World War, blacks had constituted only a tiny fraction of auto workers. The census of 1910 showed that blacks made up about one-half of one percent of all employees in the industry. But during and after the First World War, auto manufacturers increasingly looked to southern blacks as a solution to their labor shortages. Some sent agents to the South to enlist blacks, hiring trains to bring them back *en masse*. Promises of high wages, as well as the abysmal economic and political conditions in the South, caused many blacks to respond to the appeal. Detroit was a principal point of destination for black migrants, with the black population of the city increasing an estimated 400 percent between 1913 and 1918. And many found their way into the auto shops. By 1920, census data showed that nearly 8 percent of the laborers and over one percent of the operatives in American auto factories were black (composing 4 percent of the two categories combined). Like immigrants, blacks were confined to the lowliest of jobs in the factories. Postwar labor shortages and restrictions on immigration caused auto manufacturers to continue to draw upon black labor. By 1930, blacks made up 6.9 percent of the combined categories of laborers and operatives, and 4 percent of all auto industry employees. The proportion of black workers stabilized during the next decade, until war-induced labor shortages once again increased the black workers in the industry. According to the War Manpower Commission, black workers in large Detroit factories increased from 5.9 percent in May 1942 to 8.4 percent in March 1943. By 1950, black auto workers comprised about 9 percent of all employees of the industry.[17]

About the same time that blacks were beginning to be drawn into the auto labor force, southern whites were also being recruited to fill the labor shortages. The greatest influx of these workers seems to have been in the years between 1924 and 1929. From Tennessee, Kentucky, Arkansas, Alabama, and Missouri came the "hillbillies," as they were called. Auto manufacturers were particularly fond of these workers, for they were initially less class-conscious and more docile than indigenous northern workers. These characteristics were due largely to their total unfamiliarity with industrial work and their low standard of living, which made them very appreciative of their relatively high wages. Although the recruitment of these southern whites was halted by the depression of 1929, it resumed once again as the industry began to recover in 1935. Capitalists actually hired southern migrants in preference to veteran workers laid off during the depression, because of the growing militancy and resistance of the latter. It was estimated that by 1935, these workers numbered from fifteen to thirty thousand in Detroit. Like the other rural migrants, southern workers were generally young, single men, who initially sank no deep roots in the northern industrial centers. Many formed part of the transient work force and returned to their parents' farms when business was slack.[18]

Like blacks, women were drawn into the automobile industry mainly by wartime labor shortages. Before the First World War, women made up about one percent of the factory workers of the industry. They were generally confined to the assembly of small parts and various upholstering and trimming jobs, work considered appropriate for women. However, the labor shortages of the First World War brought greatly increased numbers of women into the industry. Auto manufacturers advocated the employment of this largely untapped industrial reserve army as a major solution to their problems. Women were put to work in all jobs, except those requiring the most strenuous physical labor. And to the surprise of the manufacturers, they proved themselves capable of every task they were assigned. By 1919, census data revealed that the proportion of women in the wage-earning factory labor force of the industry had risen to 4.4 percent. However, this figure undoubtedly underestimates the number of women in factories during the war, because after the hostilities ended, many were pushed out of their jobs by returning soldiers. Statistical reports from individual auto factories showed that during the war a labor force composed of as much as 12 percent women was not unusual. Women were thus viewed by auto manufacturers as an industrial reserve army, to be drawn on when male labor was in short supply, but turned out as soon as this problem was solved.

The relative number of women in auto factories slowly increased in the 1920s and 1930s, until the labor shortages of the Second World War once again caused capital to draw on women to "man" the machines of the industry. The percentage of women among production workers in the auto industry jumped from 6 percent in 1940 to 24 percent in 1944. But once again, women were later displaced by homecoming men. By 1950 they accounted for about 9.5 percent of all factory workers. Most women workers were in the parts factories, where they were employed mainly as assemblers of small parts.[19]

The labor force of the American automobile industry thus changed from one composed almost solely of white males of American and northern European descent to one in which southern and eastern European immigrants and their offspring predominated, and in which there existed growing minorities of American blacks and women. The transformation of work and technology allowed manufacturers to draw upon these sources of unskilled labor in order to alleviate their chronic labor shortages. Work was rendered so devoid of skill that a worker totally unfamiliar with industrial work of any type could be taught to do the vast majority of auto manufacturing jobs in a few days. This meant not only that the growth of the industry was facilitated, but also that an important aspect of workers' power was eliminated. With the potential supply of labor greatly expanded, the power of workers with scarce skills to exert an influence on auto production was dealt a death blow.

Increasing Worker-Hour Output

The ultimate aim of the transformation of work and technology in the automobile industry, of course, was to increase the production of surplus value or profits. By changing the labor of producing automobiles in a way that transferred control from workers to themselves, auto capitalists sought to lower the labor time expended on a unit, thereby decreasing unit labor costs and increasing the rate of surplus value. Evidence indicates that they were phenomenally successful in this aim.

The incredible increases in worker-hour output (the obverse of lower unit labor time) achieved through the transformation of the labor process are revealed in table 7.4. Here are reproduced three separate worker-hour output series for the automobile industry.[20] Because of their different data sources and methods of computation, these indices could not be consolidated into one series. But taken together, they cover much of the period under examination here. Each series employs an index that indicates the change in the output of the industry with labor expenditures (in worker-hours) of the base year and the labor efficiency of each year. For example, in series A, the index value of 112.5 for 1954 means that, because of increases in labor efficiency, 12.5 percent more output would have been produced in this year with the same number of worker-hours employed in 1929, the base year.

These output indices should be used with more than an ounce of caution. They are based mainly on survey data collected by the Bureau of Census and the Bureau of Labor Statistics, and they are subject to all the pitfalls of such official survey data. Furthermore, these measures contain a problem specific to the auto industry—the unstandardizable and changing nature of the unit of production. Over the years, the average automobile changed drastically in construction and complexity, so that the worker-hours required per unit

TABLE 7.4. Worker-Hour Output Indices for the U.S. Automobile Industry

SERIES A
1929 = 100

Year	Worker-hour output
1899	7.8
1909	8.3
1919	33.0
1929	100.0
1937	98.9
1947	94.6
1954	112.5

SOURCE: John W. Kendrick, *Productivity Trends in the United States* (Princeton, N.J.: Princeton University Press, 1961), 482, based on data from U.S., Census of Manufactures.

SERIES B

1914 = 100

Year	Worker-hour output	Year	Worker-hour output
1904	40	1923	265
1909	35	1924	258
1914	100	1925	280
1919	141	1926	302
1921	190	1927	278

SOURCE: "Productivity of Labor in 11 Manufacturing Industries," *Monthly Labor Review* 30 (March 1930): 14, based on data from U.S., Census of Manufactures and Bureau of Labor Statistics.

SERIES C

1929 = 100

Year	Worker-hour output	Year	Worker-hour output
1919	42.7	1928	83.9
1920	46.4	1929	100.0
1921	56.8	1930	105.9
1922	61.2	1931	94.6
1923	69.8	1932	82.4
1924	70.8	1933	100.0
1925	74.2	1934	99.8
1926	78.5	1935	112.4
1927	79.4	1936	115.7

SOURCE: U.S., Works Progress Administration, National Research Project, *Production, Employment, and Productivity in 59 Manufacturing Industries* (Philadelphia: Works Progress Administration, 1939), pt. 2: 144, based on data from U.S., Census of Manufactures and Bureau of Labor Statistics.

varied from one year to the next independent of labor efficiency. The indices we are considering have been adjusted for the different proportions of open cars, closed cars (which required much more work), and trucks in the total product for each year. But they have not been adjusted for the increasing complexity within each product category, which resulted in more worker-hours per unit at a given efficiency level. Therefore, these figures generally underestimate the worker-hour output increases in the industry. However, despite these problems, these statistics may serve our purpose of obtaining a general idea of the increases in production per unit of labor time.[21]

Series A indicates that worker-hour output changed very little in the first decade of the automobile industry, during which automobiles were mainly handcrafted by skilled workers. Although some innovators were beginning to divide labor, adopt progressive layout, and use specialized machine tools during this period, on the whole the labor process of the industry was not drastically changed. However, the decade from 1909 to 1919 saw a phenomenal growth of nearly 300 percent in worker-hour output, as evidenced by both series A and series B. This was the decade of the great changes in the labor process. The minute division of labor, the specialization and increasing automation of machines, the standardization and interchangeability of parts, the progressive layout of work, and various forms of mechanized materials handling—all these combined to produce the phenomenal increase in output per unit of labor input during this period. In the next decade, from 1919 to 1929, worker-hour output continued to leap forward, although at a slower rate than the preceding decade. The major innovations that totally transformed the labor process had already occurred. The 1920s were characterized mainly by their extension and intensification. Worker-hour output increased by about 200 percent, according to series A, and by 134 percent according to the more carefully adjusted index of series C.

The next ten years were disastrous ones for the automobile industry, as for the American economy as a whole. During the depression, worker-hour output dropped for several reasons: (1) the decline in volume of production, (2) the larger number of refinements on cars, (3) the reduction in the length of the average work week, and (4) the increase in part-time workers resulting from the government-induced "share-the-work" program. By the mid-1930s, worker-hour output had reached the 1929 level, but it increased very slowly thereafter. No good data are available for the 1940s, but there seems to have been another decline in output per unit labor input during the war and for several years afterwards. Ford Motor Company reported an overall decline of 34 percent in output per worker during the war years. General Motors reported a similar decline of 37 percent in worker-hour output between 1941 and 1945. Although GM recognized that less-experienced workers, poor organization and tooling, and interruptions in materials supply were contributing factors, it attributed 21 percent of the 37 percent loss to reduced productive worker effort. By the 1950s, labor output in the auto industry was back on the upward track, although increasing at a much slower rate.[22]

Some of the difficulties of these official statistics for the industry as a whole are overcome by examining series data on unit labor time within individual automobile firms. These data confirm the great advances shown by the survey statistics we have cited. For example, one firm expended 4,664 worker-hours in the production of a car in 1912. Worker-hours per car slowly decreased to 4,199 by 1914, but a leap in efficiency reduced the figure to 3,241 in 1915, a reduction of 23 percent in one year. This was undoubtedly due to the introduction of conveyor systems in this period. In 1916 another leap reduced unit labor time to 2,375 worker-hours, a 27 percent decrease. Thereafter, worker-hours steadily declined, until in 1923 it took only 813 worker-hours to build the automobile that had required 4,664 worker-hours in 1912, a decrease of nearly 83 percent in unit labor time in only eleven years![23]

These data prove beyond doubt that auto manufacturers were overwhelmingly successful in their aim of increasing worker-hour output in their shops. But what were the causes of these increases? A large part was surely due to increases in the productivity of labor in the strict sense of the term—that is, the quantity of products yielded by the same quantity of labor in a given time. Without working any harder, workers were simply able to turn out more products per hour because of the factors we have discussed: improved machines, materials handling equipment, progressive layout, greater division of labor, etc. However, a substantial proportion of these increases in output must be attributed to increases in the intensity of labor that the changes in the labor process allowed capital to enforce upon workers.

Many analysts of the American automobile industry recognized that increased labor intensity was an important factor in raising labor output. In his widely cited study of automation, Harvard Business School researcher James Bright implicitly recognized the distinction between the productivity and intensity of labor in accounting for the increased worker-hour output of automated production in the automobile industry. He distinguished between "increased productivity" and "higher and more uniform performance" as causes of increased output.[24] While the former corresponds to our strict definition of productivity, the latter implies an increased intensity of labor. By taking control of the pace of work away from the variable "human element," automated production allowed capital to enforce a uniformly higher level of worker effort and thereby increase worker-hour output.

William Chalmers similarly concluded in his 1932 dissertation on the employment policies of the auto industry that "working pace had increased along with improved techniques and was partly responsible for the increased man-hour productivity."[25] He cited as evidence not only his conversations with automobile workers, who uniformly felt that their work pace was constantly increasing, but also the statement of an employment manager, who explained that the high wages of the industry were necessary to attract and hold workers under the "more difficult conditions of production," that is, speed-up. Sometimes auto manufacturers candidly admitted that increased labor intensity was partly responsible for increased worker-hour output. Reporting a conversation with an executive of a major auto firm (probably GM) that had recorded an output increase of 250 percent over ten years, one researcher wrote: "This executive recognizes, of course, that management, machinery, methods, and material have all contributed to this increase, but he holds that increased man-hour effort [that is, work intensity] has also played an important part."[26]

These phenomenal decreases in unit labor times furthered the capitalist goal of lower unit labor costs. Even though wages remained high and generally increased throughout this period, unit labor times fell more rapidly, resulting in steadily declining unit labor costs. In the years between 1919 and 1940, unit labor costs in the industry were cut by nearly 60 percent. The benefits of increased worker-hour output accrued mainly to capital in higher profits, rather than to workers in higher wages. One study of the distribution of these benefits in the industry between 1923 and 1937 concluded that while consequent gains in wages were negligible, the rate of return on capital "increased substantially."[27]

CHAPTER 8
Worker Resistance to the New Technology

By revolutionizing the work and technology of production, automotive manufacturers wrested much of the control of the labor process out of the hands of workers. And by doing so, they suppressed the ability of workers to resist these increased levels of exploitation. However, the new technology did not spell the end of auto worker resistance. All the expensive, sophisticated technical instruments could not overcome the basic social contradiction of capitalism. Auto capitalists built a gigantic, imposing edifice, a mechanism for producing automobiles faster and cheaper than many themselves had ever imagined. But they built upon a foundation cracked by the antagonistic relations of production. The entire structure of technology and work organization was founded upon a class of workers who had no direct interest in their own production, whose work, tools, and products were alien things, forced on them against their will. All the technical instruments of production could not overcome this contradiction between labor and capital, but only suppress it, only render workers powerless to act upon it.

In fact, some of the instruments of the new technology actually exacerbated the contradiction between capital and labor and increased the power of workers to act upon it. By revolutionizing the labor process, auto manufacturers in some ways inadvertently strengthened the hand of their class opponent in the shops. These contradictions in the new technology led capitalists and managers to institute further changes in the labor process, meant to repress workers' resistance by transforming not the technical relations of production, but the social relations within and between labor and capital.[1]

WORKER RESISTANCE TO THE NEW TECHNOLOGY

It was evident from the beginning to all involved that workers were dissatisfied with the transformation of the technical process of producing automobiles. Skilled American workers were obviously reluctant to witness the destruction of the old craft process of production, over which they had experienced considerable control. And even the unskilled migrant and immigrant workers who had no experience in industrial production of any sort were not content to become unthinking automatons in the new labor process controlled by capital. Some labor historians like David Brody and Stanley Aronowitz have argued that immigrants from rural Europe readily adapted to newly degraded work, because of their conservative cultural traditions and a utilitarian orientation to industrial work as a temporary means of amassing enough wealth for a prosperous homecoming. However, others refute this contention. David Montgomery argues that immigrant workers did not passively conform to the demands of the capitalist labor process, but rather they resisted them in a variety of ways, many of which they learned from American-born workers with longstanding traditions of struggle. The evidence from the automobile industry seems to support Montgomery's side of this debate. There seems to have been little difference in either the extent or types of resistance mounted by American-born and immigrant workers. Although immigrants from rural Europe had no industrial craft traditions with which to evaluate the new technology, like the craft workers, they were accustomed to more independent, self-paced, and varied work. Therefore, like their seasoned coworkers, they reacted quickly and forcefully to the monotonous, machine-paced enslavement of the new auto labor process.[2]

Auto manufacturers sought to cover up the mounting discontent in their shops and to convince the public that auto workers liked their repetitive, monotonous, fragmented, machine-paced jobs. Henry Ford, for example, asserted in his widely read series of autobiographical books that "terror of the machine" was confined to intellectuals; the generally dull workers actually liked their mindless work.

> The average worker, I am sorry to say, wants a job in which he does not have to put forth much physical exertion—above all, he wants a

job in which he does not have to think. Those who have what might be called the creative type of mind and who thoroughly abhor monotony are apt to imagine that all other minds are similarly restless and therefore to extend quite unwanted sympathy to the labouring man who day in and day out performs almost exactly the same operation.[3]

But Ford and the other manufacturers knew better. Their public smokescreen about auto workers' attitudes toward the newly degraded work proved very thin. In other places and times, auto capitalists and managers acknowledged the negative reactions of their workers to the changes they made in the labor process. For example, commenting on time study, which was an integral part of the new technology, Ford stated: "When a study was made of shop methods, so that the workmen might be taught to produce with less useless motion and fatigue, it was most opposed by the workmen themselves. Though they suspected that it was simply a game to get more out of them, what most irked them was that it interfered with the well-worn grooves in which they had become accustomed to move."[4]

Similarly stressing the refusal of workers to surrender shop traditions, Ford noted elsewhere:

When, a few years ago we made sweeping changes in our methods of manufacturing and greatly raised the standards of accuracy, one of the largest obstacles that we met was the refusal of men to adjust themselves to the new standards. We had to change a very considerable portion of our personnel simply because so many of the older men stubbornly refused to believe that the new standard of accuracy could be attained.[5]

Ford's remarks here, however, obscure the real basis of workers' opposition to new capital-imposed "standards" of work. It was not certain outmoded "standards of accuracy" that workers defended tenaciously against capitalist attack. It was the old self-determined standard of work intensity that they defended against the speed-up enforced by time study. *Engineering Magazine* journalists Arnold and Faurote were closer to the mark in their statement on Ford workers' opposition to labor-cost reductions: "the workmen, always suspicious, never aware that the highest labor-hour production is the highest human good, object to being 'speeded up,' even though the speeding up may actually mean an easier day's work for themselves. . . . "[6]

Similar worker objections to the increased pace enforced by the new technology were recorded in surviving statements from some of the front-line supervisors charged with implementing it. Of the new system of roller conveyors that sped up work in Ford's motor assembly department, the foreman, William Klann, recalled: "It was a terrible shock . . . some of the boys did not want to work on this kind of conveyor. . . . The men didn't like it," Klann continued, "because they had to work harder. The pieces were there and they didn't have time to walk back and take a rest in between." The workers so hated Ford production methods, which were seen as an attack on their freedom within the labor process, that they likened the plant to a prison. "Because we had a long stone wall around the foundry," recalled Ford factory manager P. E. Martin, "they used to call the Ford plant the 'House of Correction.'"[7]

It was not solely the loss of control over work intensity that made auto workers dissatisfied with their newly degraded jobs. It was also the boredom and monotony associated with the repetition of one minutely divided task day in and day out. Ford was aware of this worker complaint and, in contradiction to many other statements, went so far as to recognize its legitimacy. "We carried that principle [the division of labor] farther than ever it had been carried. . . . Workmen have very generally suspected or resisted scientific management and in this they have been more instinctively right than most managers are willing to acknowledge. It is right for a man to resist being made into a machine."[8] Harry Tipper, an early labor editor for *Automotive Industries*, drove home this same point in his first article for the trade paper. On the basis of several years experience in auto factory work and numerous conversations with workers, he wrote in 1918: "Very few of the operations which he [the worker] had to undertake provided any incentive in themselves, once they were mastered. In fact, they became so irksome from their cramped requirement of mental and physical concentration that the one outstanding thought of importance was—how to get away from the monotony." Tipper noted that the worker wanted merely "to escape from the monotony of his work and secure as much money as possible for the little work he is obligated to do."[9] Another industrial journalist similarly noted the reactions of auto workers to being turned into "machine-men" by monotonous, mindless, mechanical work. "Labor turnover, discontent, industrial unrest and kindred problems confront industry as a result—partially at least—of the intensive development of the machine-man."[10]

FORMS OF WORKER RESISTANCE

This worker discontent with newly degraded work was translated into action. Auto workers refused to sit by passively as their bosses wrested control of work out of their hands. They resisted the new capitalist-dominated work in a variety of ways—direct and indirect, individual and collective. Automotive capitalists recognized in all of these actions a basic threat to the new labor process that they were attempting to build. In order to realize the potential for greater exploitation inherent in the new technology, workers had docilely to accept it and its built-in control. Their refusal to do so placed the entire project in jeopardy.

Turnover and Absenteeism

Indirect and individualistic forms of worker resistance were most important in the early auto shops that were undergoing the rudimentary transformations of the labor process. Instead of directly and collectively confronting their bosses over the changes in work that stripped them of control, auto workers indirectly registered their discontent by individually quitting or by being absent from their newly degraded jobs. Workers voted against the new technology with their feet—they walked out and stayed away from the auto shops in droves.

High labor turnover was not confined to the rapidly changing shops of the automobile industry. It plagued many of America's industries during this period, but especially those in Detroit. The city's tremendous industrial growth in the years between 1908 and 1914 created severe labor shortages. And competitive bidding by employers for scarce labor power caused workers to change jobs frequently in search of higher wages. As one observer of the city's industrial scene noted: "Demand for labor in Detroit in 1912 and 1913 was so keen that a man who quit a job in the morning might have employment in another factory at noon. There were many men, generally unmarried and of unsettled abode, taking jobs and abandoning them abruptly without explanation, or notice."[11] Data gathered from fifty-seven Detroit plants by a member of Detroit's Executives' Club in 1916 revealed an average annual turnover rate of 252 percent.[12]

The labor turnover in the changing auto shops, however, was significantly higher than either the Detroit or the national average. Detailed statistics for the Ford Motor Company, for example, reveal that in 1913, 50,448 workers left the employ of the company. The average number of employees in this year was 13,623, making the annual labor turnover rate 370 percent. Over three-quarters of this turnover was voluntary—that is, the workers quit, as opposed to being discharged or laid off. John Lee, who headed Ford's Sociological Department, reported that monthly turnover rates as high as 69 percent were common during this period. These Ford labor turnover rates were probably a bit high in comparison with the rest of the industry. Statistics gathered by the U.S. Bureau of Labor Statistics reveal that in 1913 and 1914, labor turnover in fifteen automobile manufacturing firms and automotive parts firms averaged 156 percent. But this rate was substantially higher than the turnover rate in the other eighty-four industries surveyed, which averaged 93 percent. Labor turnover in the auto industry exceeded all industrial groups, except slaughtering and meat-packing.[13]

The high rates of labor turnover in the automobile industry cannot, therefore, be explained solely by the general instability of the labor market in Detroit or the United States as a whole. As most associated with the industry realized, the new technology and work organization being introduced into the shops in this period were in large part responsible for auto workers quitting their jobs in unprecedented numbers. Workers were resisting the degradation of their labor simply by refusing to work under the new conditions. As one commentator stated concerning Ford's turnover problem:

> Now excessive labor turnover is a symptom of the worker's state of mind. In this case the discontent was a tribute to the inherent independence and personal dignity of the high class mechanic. In his previous jobs he had been able to feel that he was still a human being. He could arrange his work to some extent to suit his personal tastes—sufficiently so to leave him some shred of self-respect. There were precious moments of joking with the man at the next machine. He could make a few unhurried trips to the toilet or the water-cooler. The foreman was apt to be a friend—at least when all went well. But in the Ford factory the worker found things very different indeed. The pacemaker was a machine, usually a belt or an overhead conveyor. The unfinished parts—brake-bands, pistons, or gear—arrived from an unknown spot in the distance. The worker performed some simple operation, perhaps put two of them together, and placed them back on the belt. As soon as he had finished this, another part had arrived. He had just time to grab it. There was no leeway, no variation. The belt was tireless.[14]

It was not skilled mechanics alone, however, who quit the newly degraded jobs in droves. Skilled craft workers probably resented the new technology the most, for it undermined their traditional skills and power within the shop. But in 1913, when turnover at Ford peaked, they made up only 28 percent of the work force. Obviously the unskilled workers, most of whom had no industrial experience, viewed the new labor process with similar disdain and reacted similarly. The inherently monotonous, mindless nature of the degraded work caused even workers with no shop traditions to flee in search of relief. A Detroit Juvenile Court judge was merely stating what members of the Employers' Association already knew when he addressed them in 1912 as follows:

> It is not at all surprising to me with our modern conditions that it is difficult to find the boy who wants to continue in one employment. Our modern shops are built on such an economical plan that we get one individual doing one thing until he becomes most efficient at that one thing. It is impossible to take a child and set him at one task and not have him chafe at that task. . . . Among the thousand or more boys who come to me in a year I find few that hold their positions more than three months. Generally they say they get tired of that one thing. They want to go into a shop where they get some other kind of a job, one perhaps as tiresome in the end, but it represents a change temporarily.[15]

This relation between the transformation of the labor process and labor turnover was clearest at Ford, which was at the forefront of technological innovation. In the years around 1910, workers began to desert the Ford shops in large numbers. This was precisely the period of intensified division of labor and the use of specialized machinery. Previously skilled work was being minutely divided and its discretionary aspects built into the machines. And Ford managers were beginning to use the power they gained from these changes to drive workers to their limits. However, turnover did not reach epidemic proportions until Ford introduced the moving line. Shortly after its introduction in 1913, annual turnover rates peaked at nearly 400 percent. The reason for the mass exodus was no mystery to Ford managers. James O'Connor, foreman on one of the first Ford chassis assembly lines, recalled the widespread rejection of the new technology. "We all would get new men every day. They kept coming and going. . . . There were a lot of people who wouldn't even try. They thought they couldn't do it." Workers had no incentive whatsoever to submit to the increased exploitation enforced by Ford's new technology. As one Ford historian wrote: "They could afford to pick and choose. Other jobs were plentiful in the community; they were easier to get to [Ford's plant was several miles away from central Detroit]; they paid as well; and they were less mechanized and more to labor's liking."[16]

Auto workers also registered their dissatisfaction with the new technology by "going on a bat," that is, taking unauthorized absences from work. Unable to bear the daily grind of their monotonous and intensified labor, workers simply took a few days off. Of course, some absences were involuntary, due to sickness, accidents, and alcoholism. But these were also forms of resistance—the unconscious, physiological revolt of the human body against the inhuman demands of the transformed labor process. During the pivotal year of 1913, daily absenteeism at Ford reached the unprecedented rate of 10.5 percent of the labor force, which meant that over 1,400 workers were absent from the speeding lines each day.[17]

Auto capitalists and managers rightly perceived this indirect revolt of workers as threatening the very basis of the new labor process that was just taking shape. They were investing millions of dollars in new technology that had the potential to greatly increase the output of labor and the profitability of production. But the realization of this productive potential was thwarted by the "human factor," which refused to submit passively to its new mechanical master.

High turnover rates meant that thousands of new workers had to be fitted into their jobs by degrees. Even though these jobs were basically unskilled and easy to learn, a break-in period was still required, during which workers became familiarized with their jobs, surroundings, and general company policy. This break-in time was costly to capital, for new workers generally required greater supervision and instruction, increased the wear and damage to equipment, wasted and spoiled more parts, and decreased the rate of production. The head of the standards department at the Packard Motor Car Company estimated that labor turnover caused his factory's equipment to operate on the average 25 percent below expected capacity, costing the company between $1-1/2 and $2-1/2 million a year in labor costs and another $2 million in extra equipment. The head of Ford's employment office during this period stated that it cost the company about thirty-eight dollars to break in each raw recruit. At this rate, turnover cost Ford about 2 million dollars in 1913 alone, a full one-third of the original investment in plant and machinery at the Highland Park factory. Other estimates of the per capita cost of labor turnover revealed that Ford's was probably one of the lowest in the industry.[18]

Absenteeism was also seen as a threat to the potential labor savings of the new technology. For example, Ford's high daily absentee rate meant that managers had to have on hand 1,400 more workers than were actually required by the plant's equipment. This entailed an additional annual labor cost of around $1 million. Further, the constant shifting of workers to cover absences created crucial delays and inefficiencies in the highly interdependent labor process. Henry Ford thus wrote sternly that his company was "most insistent in the matter of absences. A man may not come or go as he pleases. . . . The organization is so highly specialized and one part is so dependent upon another," he explained, "that we could not for a moment consider allowing men to have their own way. Without the most rigid discipline we would have the utmost confusion."[19]

Restriction of Output

The unorganized and indirect revolt of absenteeism and labor turnover was supplemented by more collective and direct forms of resistance as the industry emerged from its childhood. For reasons we will detail shortly, auto workers began to fight their bosses instead of fleeing from the industrial battlefield. And they soon learned that their chances of winning were better when they joined with other workers to fight collectively. Workers were not ready yet for a full-scale industrial war, in which they would confront their employers directly with an organized army. But they did engage in a subterranean guerilla war in order to reassert some control over production.

Most of this subterranean resistance involved the restriction of output—that is, working below the rate prescribed by capital. As auto manufacturers transformed the labor process in order to seize control of the pace of work and intensify it, workers struggled to retain some control over work pace and resisted capitalist speed-up. Soldiering, goldbricking, ca'canny—whatever it is called, the practice of restricting output is as old as capitalism itself. Auto workers merely followed a tradition of working-class behavior in this respect. The motives and feelings of workers underlying such restriction were captured by the following poem, composed by a machine-shop worker and discovered on the shop bulletin board.

Harmony?

I am working with the feeling
That the company is stealing
Fifty pennies from my pocket every day;
But for every single pennie
They will lose ten times as many
By the speed that I'm producing, I dare say.

155

For it makes me so disgusted
That my speed shall be adjusted
So that nevermore my brow will drip with sweat;
When they're in an awful hurry
Someone else can rush and worry
Till an increase in my wages do I get.

No malicious thoughts I harbor
For the butcher or the barber
Who get eighty cents an hour from the start.
Nearly three years I've been working
Like a fool, but now I'm shirking—
When I get what's fair, I'll always do my part.
Someone else can run their races
Till I'm on an equal basis
With the ones who learned the trade by mining coal.
Though I can do the work, it's funny
New Men can get the money
And I cannot get the same to save my soul.[20]

Restriction of output in the auto shops undergoing a transformation of the labor process had two meanings, both to workers and their managers. Superficially, it was a conflict over how much work would be done for how much pay. As the poem reveals, workers had an intuitive sense of the rate of exploitation, and they were constantly measuring their output against the wages they received. If they felt the production required of them was too much for their wages, they held output down to a more "reasonable" level. But more profoundly, output restriction was a struggle over who was to control production on the shop floor. Workers were seeking to reassert their traditional power over the labor process in the face of the powerful forays into this territory by capital and its new technology. Both meanings were intertwined and imbricated in the complex struggle over production in the auto shops.

This struggle was particularly acute in incentive-wage shops, where wages were tied directly to output through piecework, bonus, and premium systems. Under such compensation schemes, which predominated in early mass-production auto shops, workers restricted output in order to protect their wage rates against cuts and thus to keep them from having to work harder for the same pay. But the struggle to protect rates was simultaneously a struggle for more worker control over the intensity of labor, for favorable rates allowed workers some discretion in their work pace and relieved them from working at a breakneck speed just to earn a living wage.

Output struggles in incentive-wage shops took two basic forms: time-study manipulation and quota restriction. Workers attempted to manipulate time-study experiments to get high piece or bonus rates. It was the job of time-study engineers to set the rates so low that workers had to work very intensively just to earn a living wage. However, when being studied for the purpose of setting rates, workers deliberately slowed down and made the job look difficult so that a high rate would be set. In this way, they were able to earn a decent overall wage without working too hard. Describing his experience with this form of resistance, one auto worker wrote:

> The time-study man was the agent of the company. And the stopwatch was the instrument by which the company got as much as it could out of my hide. So I knew I had to fight the stopwatch. One day the time-study man came to time me while I was filing lock nuts. The lock nut was about four inches in diameter and my job was to file off the sharp burrs on the edges. When the time-study man stood over me, stopwatch and clipboard in hand, I slowed down every motion I made without seeming to do so deliberately. I reached in the pan with my left hand, picked out a nut, held it in my left hand, and filed with the right. It was the simplest kind of operation and on the basis of my movements the time-study man set a price on the job. Once the price was set I had no difficulty "making out," as the workers used to say. Instead of holding the nut in my hand when filing, I made a "die" by cutting out a form on a board. With the nut held securely in the form I could file with both hands and turn out five nuts in the time it took to turn out one before. It was similar with other jobs: Those of us who worked on the bench could find all kinds of shortcuts—ways we never revealed to the time-study man. Although my day rate was only fifteen cents an hour, thanks to piecework I used to bring home from twenty to twenty-five dollars a week, a fantastic pay for a kid in those days [circa 1914].[21]

It can be inferred from the frequent mention of such practices in a wide variety of other sources that this form of resistance became widespread in the auto industry once time study came into use. Often, time-study manipulation required collective organization, both to spread the word when the time-study man was coming and to slow down the work of a team of cooperating workers convincingly.

But in order to protect their rates and prevent speed-up under these systems, workers also had to restrict production below certain quotas. Auto managers established upper limits beyond which they would not let workers' piece or bonus earnings rise. If earnings rose above the limit, they cut the rates, requiring workers to work harder and produce more in order to earn the same overall wage. To prevent piece or bonus rates from being cut, workers established and enforced their own production quotas. This effort at restriction often involved a high degree of collective organization and discipline, for one overzealous "rate-buster" could ruin the job for all workers. One auto worker described the group restriction in his gang and the motives behind it.

> I was framing boxes with a buddy, and they kept cutting the rate until we had to frame one every 15 minutes and go after our own stock. If we stopped for a drink of water, we got behind. Some fresh guys came in and killed the job. Believe me, nothing like that happens in the bunch where I'm working now. If anybody, new or old, starts to "put out," the whole bunch bumps him. We are turning out four cars a day and earning 90 cents an hour. We could earn $2.50 an hour if we "put out," but, as it is, our job's one of the best in this town, and we made it so by holding it down.[22]

As this account reveals, maintaining control over work pace, as well as protecting wage rates, was an important motive behind quota restriction.

Workers frequently received information from sympathetic foremen or time-study personnel about the upper limit on earnings, and they organized themselves to keep within the limit. Many workers kept their own precise records of production and disciplined themselves to avoid exceeding limits and provoking rate cuts. When they did surpass the limit, they often protected their rates by "banking"—hiding finished work and not turning it in. Not only did banking protect piece and bonus rates, but it also ensured pieceworkers a certain constancy in earnings. On good days, when production went smoothly, auto workers built up a bank. Then on days when production was hampered by machine breakdowns, delays in stock delivery, or bad stock, they drew on the bank to supplement the work turned in and stabilize their earnings.[23]

When other methods failed to protect piece rates and to control the work pace, workers sometimes resorted to work stoppages. Prior to the 1930s, these sitdowns and walkouts were generally brief, unorganized, and defensive in nature. Most were only department-wide and were caused by managerial attempts to cut piece rates. There was generally no collective bargaining, with workers either finding employment elsewhere or straggling back to their old jobs on management's terms. Typical of this sort of resistance was the reaction of door hangers in the Seaman Body Company to a cut in piece rates announced in 1926. As one participant recalled:

> When the men were notified of this most of them refused to work. They didn't walk out but just sat around talking about what ought to be done. There was no union or talk of a union. There was some hostility toward those men who turned in too many pieces and thus brought about the cut in piece rates. Some of us got tired of standing around. We went home at noon and returned the next morning. Most of the men had returned to work at the reduced piecework rate.[24]

Unorganized, fragmented, and undisciplined, these spontaneous work stoppages generally had little impact either on the immediate precipitating issue or on the more fundamental struggle over control of the labor process.

The use of incentive wages in the auto industry was largely eliminated by 1935. These systems assumed that workers retained some control of work pace and sought to stimulate their efforts by tying pay to output. However, once capital introduced technology that took the control of pace out of workers' hands, incentive wages became obsolete and were replaced by straight-time wages. But workers continued to restrict output nonetheless. Though wage rates were generally safe from cuts, they continued to struggle against managerial pressures to increase the amount of work required to earn the hourly or daily rate. The issues remained the same—how much work for how much pay and, more profoundly, who controlled production. Workers fought to keep the rate of production down, so they would not have to "work their asses off," so capital would not push them faster and faster. As one old-timer put it: "You just work so fast and you do just so much work. Because the more you do, the more they'll want you to do. If you start running, they'd expect you do a little bit more."[25]

Although capital increasingly built the pace of production into the machinery itself, workers were not completely powerless to struggle against it. Auto workers devised numerous methods to restrict production by slowing down the inhuman pace of the machinery. One was simply to refuse to work as fast as the machine dictated. On the moving conveyors, this was known as "taking the job into the hole." Each worker on the line had a specific work area within which he or she was supposed to finish the assigned operation, before the conveyor moved the part or car beyond it. If workers did not labor at the dictated speed, they had to move down the line out of their work areas to finish. Consequently, workers crowded into each others' work areas, stumbled over one another, and generally disrupted the operation. "Going into the hole" was a conscious, planned method that workers often used to protest the speed of the line and to force a slowdown.[26]

Auto workers also disrupted moving lines and forced slowdowns by skipping operations on cars. Sometimes skipping was an individual act of frustration. Often, however, it was an organized, collective action—"the skippie." One Hudson worker recalled: "One day, by placing the hoods closer together on the line, the management increased production from 140 to 160 an hour. The men figured that the increase of twenty was one-seventh of normal production and, amid laughter, skipped every seventh hood, which immediately messed up production ahead of them. The hood-line superintendent raged at first, then helpless, went back to 140."[27]

Sometimes the passive action of skipping operations was combined with outright sabotage of production. One participant-observer in an engine plant reported plant-wide organization to systematically sabotage production. Motors were defectively assembled or damaged in route—gaskets were left out, wrong-sized spark plugs put in, bolts left loose, plug wires assembled in the wrong firing order. Inspectors rejected three out of every four or five motors, and they did their own share of sabotage. The result was a huge accumulation of rejected motors needing repairs. Auto workers aimed their efforts not only at slowing down production, but at stopping it altogether for brief periods. One summer, workers in this engine plant organized a plant-wide rotating sabotage program to periodically stop production. They alternately took responsibility for shutting down the entire line in order to get relief from work in the unbearable heat (up to 115 degrees at times).[28]

Although not all attempts by auto workers to control their own work were as dramatic and well-organized as these, soldiering and slowdown in general seem to have been widespread. In William Kornhauser's 1954 survey of Detroit auto workers, 55 percent said that the workers in their shops could turn out more or better work if they wanted to.[29]

What emerges from these patterns of output restriction is an image, not of irrational resistance to authority, but of a rational, collective effort by workers to retain some control over their own production. Automobile capitalists and managers perceived workers' restriction of output as a fundamental challenge to their centralized control of the new labor process. Despite their attempts to seize control of the pace of work through new forms of work organization and technology, workers resisted this control and refused to labor at the dictated speed.

Industrial Unionism

As the industry matured, this guerrilla war of output restriction threatened to turn into a full-scale, direct industrial confrontation between organized armies. Industrial unionism loomed on the horizon as a challenge to the new industrial regime. Auto capitalists had successfully crushed most of the craft unions that had existed in the early shops through a combination of direct assault by the Employers' Association and indirect undermining of the position of skilled workers in the labor process. But just when they were beginning to enjoy their freedom from craft unionism, the new creed of industrial unionism arose to threaten their unilateral power in the shops.

An early attempt to organize the industry's workers on an industrial basis was made by the AFL-affiliated Carriage, Wagon, and Automobile Workers' Union (CWAWU). In the years after its founding in 1910, the union made some headway in the smaller shops, conducting a few strikes and winning some minor benefits. Its fortunes grew during 1912 because of its successful strikes in auto body shops. But as it prospered, the CWAWU became involved in jurisdictional disputes with AFL craft unions and was suspended from the Federation in 1918.[30]

A much greater threat to the new regime of automobile production came from the radical syndicalism of the Industrial Workers of the World (IWW). Its leadership of some of the largest and most publicized labor struggles of the early twentieth century sent fear into the hearts of employers of unskilled workers in all industries. Auto manufacturers were not exempt. The news columns of their trade papers closely reported the IWW's strike activities, while editorials and other articles attacked the organization in a way that revealed a real fear of its potential.[31]

These fears were justified by Wobbly activity in the auto shops. Early IWW organizing drives in Detroit in 1909 and 1910 left little permanent organization or activity. In 1911, a Wobbly organizer invited to Detroit by a group of auto workers did establish a small local. But it was not until March 1913, when the IWW sent in some of its top organizers to help the local, that the labor situation heated up. The organizers, including Matilda Rabinowitz and Jack Walsh, decided to focus their campaign on Ford. They carried their message of industrial unionism to the gates of the Highland Park plant, denouncing Ford to workers on their lunch breaks as the "Speed-up King" and calling for an eight-hour day. The Wobblies attracted a crowd of three thousand Ford workers and a contingent of Detroit police, who immediately arrested them on charges of obstructing traffic. But the stalwart group was back at the Ford gates the next day at noon, only to find that their listeners had been greatly depleted by a Ford order suspending the outdoor lunch privileges of workers.

Diverted but undaunted, the IWW organizers turned their attention to the second largest auto maker in the city and organized the first important strike in the history of the Detroit auto industry. At Studebaker, workers had general grievances about speed-up and long hours, and a particular complaint about a change in the pay period. But the conflict came to a head over the firing of one of their informal representatives. In protest of this firing, most of the thirty-five hundred workers on the day shift of Studebaker's No. 3 plant walked out on June 17, 1913. A militant core of Wobblies at Studebaker had helped to fan the flames of discontent, and in mass meetings the striking workers voted to conduct their struggle under IWW auspices. Mass pickets and marches succeeded in bringing another three thousand or so workers out of the other Studebaker plants. But the spread of the strike was halted by the police, who broke up mass pickets and marches by clubbing and jailing workers. At the end of a week, the striking workers voted to go back to work without winning their demands, realizing the futility of launching a strike in the middle of the summer slack season, when jobs were few and unemployment high. However, the spectacle of thousands of workers marching in the streets and shutting down plants was to haunt auto capitalists for years to come. It was partly responsible for the introduction of new methods for overcoming the incipient revolt.[32]

A serious union threat did not reemerge in the industry until the years immediately following the First World War. By this time, the CWAWU had reformed itself into an independent union, the United Automobile, Aircraft, and Vehicle Workers' Union (UAAVW). Its militant brand of industrial unionism found fertile ground in postwar auto shops. Intensified war production had substantially deteriorated working conditions, and war-induced inflation had eroded real wages. Around these grievances, the UAAVW organized a series of strikes and walkouts confined mainly to the body factories and parts plants. Among the companies struck were Liberty Starter, Wadsworth Body, Electric Auto-Lite, Fisher Body, Ford Plate Glass,

Wilson Body, Timken-Detroit Axle, Willys-Overland, Packard, and Studebaker. Most of the major automobile manufacturing firms were exempt from direct labor action, although many, including Ford, were seriously damaged by their inability to obtain parts from struck companies. As a result of its efforts, the UAAVW claimed in 1920 a membership of about forty-five thousand (out of a total auto work force of approximately three hundred and forty thousand). Membership was concentrated among the painters, trimmers, and woodworkers in the small custom body plants in the East and in the body factories of Detroit.[33]

In his 1932 dissertation on labor in the auto industry, William Chalmers investigated eleven of the strikes of this period and found the major ostensible issue to be wages. However, as he dug deeper into the causes of the strikes through interviews with leaders, Chalmers found that the demand for higher wages actually condensed a more basic struggle within the labor process, at least for the body workers involved. These painters, trimmers, and woodworkers generally retained some skill at this time. Due to the difficulties of standardizing and mechanizing the jobs of the body and trim shops, especially those building custom bodies, the workers there held onto their skills longer than the average auto worker. However, by the late 1910s, the division and mechanization of labor had begun to erode these workers' skills and control. During this deskilling process, manufacturers began to cut the high piece rates that had been characteristic on such jobs. Workers were forced to labor more intensively in order to maintain their wages at traditional levels. Thus, Chalmers found that when the workers demanded higher wage rates, they were actually protesting the speed-up and seeking to retain some of the control over the pace of production that they were losing to capital. Like the other forms of worker resistance, this wave of strikes and stoppages was a struggle by auto workers to retain some degree of control over their own work. And I will argue later that the labor strife of the late 1930s and early 1940s, which led to the unionization of the automobile industry, was similarly motivated.[34]

Automotive capitalists and managers were well aware of the basic challenge to their control over the new labor process constituted by the struggle for industrial unionism. What they feared from the organization of workers was not higher wages and benefits, but worker interference with their absolute control over the labor process of the industry. Henry Ford thus stated that he was not opposed to labor unions as such. "It is organizing to limit production—whether by employers or by workers—that matters."[35]

Charles Sorensen, one of Ford's top production executives, went on to elaborate upon the motives behind the company's anti-union policy. "He [Ford] wanted to make sure that the [union] mob that had moved into Detroit would not find in the plant anyone receptive to their bargaining. Everything Henry Ford and I had done to build up that plant and its organization would be jeopardized if we allowed the unions to have a voice in management."[36]

Ford and other auto manufacturers had gone farther than any other American industry in shaping a labor process that removed control of work from workers' hands. They feared that unions might interfere with the forward thrust of this continuing process by demanding a voice for workers in management. As William Chalmers concluded from his study of managerial policies of the industry in the late 1920s:

> the greatest fear the owners and managers of the industry have had from unionization is the restrictive measures which they believe to come from labor organization. This they have felt would so handicap an industry which is trying to put its greatest emphasis on speed of operation and rapid change in technique, that it was worth while spending a great deal in wages and in conditions to make sure it did not occur.[37]

POWER BASES OF AUTO WORKER RESISTANCE

Despite the best efforts of automotive capitalists and managers to construct a labor process that would overcome the resistance of the recalcitrant "human element," auto workers continued to struggle against their subordination and exploitation in many ways. The new technology proved incapable of completely crushing the power of workers. It left intact or strengthened certain bases of working-class power rooted in the general laws of motion of the capitalist mode of production. And, ironically, the highly divided and mechanized process of producing automobiles created new bases of working-class power, while simultaneously destroying others. The combination of the contradictions of the general laws of motion of capitalism with the contradictions of the specific process of auto production provided the power bases for continued worker resistance in the automobile industry. These shifting and changing contradictions also accounted for the changing forms and intensity of worker resistance.

Contradictions of the General Laws of Motion of Capitalism

The power of auto workers to continue to resist exploitation in the shops was partially based upon certain laws of motion inherent in the capitalist mode of production. But far from being autonomous developments imposed on humans from the outside, these laws of motion were the unintentional results of intentional human action in the form of capitalist competition and class conflict. In their conscious attempts to overcome the struggle of their workers in order to beat out their competitors, capitalists introduced measures that unintentionally set into motion economic laws that strengthened that struggle. Three such laws, which provided important sources of workers' power, are those of uneven development, the concentration and centralization of capital, and business cycles.

The law of uneven development determines that capitalists introduce labor-saving methods faster in some branches of industry, and faster in some firms within each branch, than in others. This unevenness is due in part to the different forms and intensities of worker resistance that capitalists encounter in their drive to produce greater profits. The American economy in general and the American automobile industry in particular were characterized by such uneven development. In the general economy, many American industries lagged considerably behind the innovative methods of the auto industry. And in the auto industry itself, there remained throughout the early period a large number of small firms that lagged behind the leading firms in labor-saving technology and organization. As late as 1923, there were still one hundred and eight companies manufacturing automobiles. Due to the small volume of production of most of these companies, introduction of the new technology was unfeasible. Most continued to operate with a high proportion of skilled workers and a labor process at least partially controlled by them. Similarly lagging behind the productive innovations of the leading auto firms were the companies manufacturing custom-made trucks and luxury cars.[38]

This uneven technological development of the branches of American industry and of the firms within the automobile industry created the conditions for the initial indirect and individualistic forms of worker resistance. Workers were able to escape the developing despotism of the advanced auto firms through turnover and absenteeism, because the underdeveloped firms and industries provided

165

them with alternative employment opportunities. Due to generally tight labor market conditions, workers found it easy to get jobs in other auto companies or in industries that paid just as well and were less intense, rationalized, and monotonous. In Detroit alone, less degraded and exploitative work was available in stove manufacturing, railroad car and locomotive shops, machine shops, and wagon and carriage factories, as well as in less advanced automobile firms. Under these conditions, auto workers found that the quickest and easiest solutions to the new repression on the shop floor were to quit work or take a few days off, for they knew that they would not be fired for want of replacements. Uneven economic development thus made the indirect methods of turnover and absenteeism the most popular forms of revolt for early workers.[39]

Although uneven development continued to characterize the auto industry and the American economy as a whole, its effect upon auto worker resistance was considerably diminished by a second law of motion of capitalism—the concentration and centralization of capital. This law of political economy determines that competition between the firms of an industry inevitably leads to the growth of large firms (concentration) and the takeover of smaller firms by larger ones (centralization). The firms with the more advanced and productive labor processes, introduced largely in an attempt to repress worker resistance, have a competitive edge over the underdeveloped firms, which are consequently forced out of business or taken over. The result is the domination of an industry by a few giant firms.[40]

The American automobile industry is a prime example of this law of capital accumulation. The industry began as a multitude of very small producers, each with a very minimal capital investment. As late as 1909, some two hundred and fifty firms were engaged in the manufacture of automobiles, and entry remained easy, with four hundred and ninety-nine firms entering the industry between 1900 and 1908. But a pattern of concentration and centralization emerged between 1908 and 1912, when the revolution in production techniques began. The new technology had the effect of concentrating and centralizing capital into a small group of large firms, because it demanded huge capital investments and large outputs to operate profitably. The share of the market controlled by the four largest firms increased from 43 percent in 1908 to 60.6 percent in 1913. The smaller firms were increasingly forced out of business by the lower costs and prices brought about by the new labor process.

The recession of the early 1920s and the boom of the later years of the decade saw the crystallization of the pattern of bigness. While one hundred and eight automobile manufacturing companies were in operation in 1923, only twenty-three existed in 1928. When the stock market crash hit in 1929, the Big Three auto makers produced about 72 percent of the total output of the year. The depression delivered the *coup de grace* to the small producers. When demand for autos started to rise in the 1930s, production was almost entirely in the hands of the Big Three. In 1939, they controlled over 90 percent of the market. A similar but less rapid concentration-and-centralization process characterized the auto parts division of the industry.[41]

The effect that this process of concentration and centralization of capital had upon the resistance of auto workers was twofold. On the one hand, it largely eliminated the small, technologically underdeveloped firms, which had provided the basis for the indirect, individualistic resistance of labor turnover and absenteeism. But on the other hand, this process created the basis for more direct and collective forms of worker resistance. The concentration and centralization of capital concentrated larger and larger numbers of workers into a few huge factories, bringing them into close communication with one another and stimulating the growth of class consciousness and collective action.[42]

The new labor process required large investments in fixed capital (plant and equipment), which had to be rapidly depreciated, before being outmoded by constant innovation. Rapid depreciation of fixed capital was especially important after the adoption of annual models, which dictated changing a substantial amount of machinery on a regular basis. It demanded the highest possible volume of production, which manufacturers achieved by increasingly concentrating all production at a few sprawling industrial sites. Industrial concentration not only created the requisite high volumes, but it also cut down on the time and money required to transport parts between different factories. The zenith of this development was Ford's River Rouge plant outside Detroit. Completed in 1920, this plant covered some six hundred and sixty-six acres and was the site of the manufacture of the vast majority of parts for the Model T. At its peak in 1929, the Rouge employed nearly one hundred thousand workers, and the problems of merely getting this huge work force in and out of the plant became so great that Ford had to start a new shift every fifteen minutes. Not all automobile factories attained such a scale, but table 8.1 reveals well the steady trend toward larger and larger factories in the industry.

The effects of this concentration of workers may be traced in the perceptions of automotive managers and capitalists, who were quick to realize the labor dangers inherent in the huge factories. In his first

TABLE 8.1.   Percentage of Automotive Factory Work Force in Large Factories, 1909–1950

Year	Percentage of all auto factory workers in establishments employing:	
	Over 1000	*2500 and over*
1909	32.6	—
1914	47.7	—
1919	64.1	—
1940	89.0[a]	72.6[a]
1947	84.0[b]	64.4[b]
1950	84.2	62.7

SOURCE: U.S., Bureau of the Census, *Census of Manufactures, 1914*, vol. 2, "Reports for Selected Industries and Detail Statistics for Industries" (Washington, D.C.: Government Printing Office, 1919): 737; idem, *Fourteenth Census of the United States: 1920*, vol. 10, "Manufactures, 1919" (1923): 870; idem, *Census of Manufactures: 1947*, vol. 2, "Statistics by Industry" (1949): 754; U.S., Bureau of Labor Statistics, Bulletin no. 706 (1942), 22; Bulletin no. 1138 (1953), 3.
[a]Automobile manufacturing division only.
[b]Includes all employees, not merely factory workers.

autobiographical book, the man in the vanguard of this industrial concentration, Henry Ford, stated the problem vaguely. The concentration of industry into huge urban centers led to certain "social ailments." These cities were "untamed and threatening," and prone to "violent plagues of upheave and unrest."[43] However, in the private pages of their trade publications, other auto capitalists specifically identified the major danger of industrial concentration as labor unrest. They saw labor trouble as a contagious disease that needed a natural growth medium to flourish. "In the case of industrial disputes, the natural medium seems to be the crowded industrial city." This was particularly so during recessionary periods, wrote one trade journalist, when the concentrated mass of unemployed, discontented workers was a powder keg awaiting a spark. "Concentration of production in large units in large cities does have the effect of drawing men in huge numbers to these centers for employment. And even in good times there is always a spread between total employment and total 'employable' population. In bad times, that spread is larger." The journalist advised capitalists not to draw excessive numbers of workers to the centers in boom periods, with the goal of "promoting social stability all along the line."[44]

Another danger of concentrated and centralized production beyond general labor unrest was its susceptibility to disruption. With the production of the whole vehicle, or just one vital part, concentrated in a single factory, a strike or slowdown could bring the production of the entire firm to a grinding halt. A trade journalist for *Automotive Industries* noted:

> Every time labor problems come to the foreground, conversation gets around to the disadvantage of too much centralization of industry and the possible advantages of decentralization. . . . Concentration of manufacturing in a few large plants, as is common in many automotive enterprises, undoubtedly increases the dangers of interruption of the whole production program through labor troubles. Shutdown in manufacture of a single part, under these circumstances, means a block in the entire manufacturing scheme.[45]

This danger became apparent in the wave of strikes in the years between 1918 and 1920, when the shutdown of key body and parts plants drove major producers to the wall. The lesson was further driven home during the sitdown strikes of 1936 and 1937, when the union consciously focused its efforts on plants that concentrated the production of key parts.

To combat these dangers of concentrated and centralized automobile production, capitalists launched programs of decentralization. Ford was in the forefront of this drive. In the early 1920s, he set up a string of small, rural, water-powered parts factories in Michigan. Other manufacturers lacked Ford's nostalgia for rural American and the "simple life," but they also began to realize the advantage of decentralized production during the Great Depression, when labor troubles increased. Many large auto firms began to decentralize the production of key parts into several widely separated factories. Of course, there were other advantages of decentralizing production to smaller plants and towns, namely, lower wages, taxes, and realty values. But these advantages had existed all along. Judging from the rush toward decentralization in the 1930s, labor unrest was the major cause. Decentralization was always basically limited, however, by the economies of large-scale production, so that it never seriously threatened to reverse the trend toward large production units.[46]

The third general law of motion of the capitalist mode of production that provided a power base for workers' resistance was that of business cycles. Capitalism has been plagued by the cyclical fluctuation of production ever since its beginnings. And these cycles exercise an effect on workers' power through the medium of the industrial reserve army, the body of unemployed workers. When industry is in the downswing phase of the cycle, capital cuts back production and lays off workers, thus increasing the size of the industrial reserve army. Because of the glut of labor power on the market, workers compete with one another for the few jobs available. This competition weakens the power of labor in its struggle with capital, and capitalists are able to impose lower wages and more intense labor upon workers. In the upswing of the cycle, capital expands and employs more workers, thus absorbing much of the industrial reserve army. Labor power becomes a scarce commodity, and the power of workers is enhanced. In order to hold onto and attract workers in a highly competitive labor market, each capitalist is forced to make concessions to worker demands for higher wages, better working conditions, and less intense exploitation. Workers intensify their struggle for these demands because they know that their employers are reluctant to fire them for want of replacements. Thus, the contradictory, cyclical nature of capitalist industrial development ensures that periodically workers will be empowered in their struggle by the shrinking of the industrial reserve army.

The early automobile industry was generally characterized by a shortage of labor power, which accounted in large part for the power of workers to resist exploitation through turnover and absenteeism. However, the early industry's chronic labor shortage was exacerbated by the cyclical swings of the American economy as a whole. The first such swing to deeply affect the auto industry was the industrial boom during the First World War. War production pulled the economy out of its stagnation and generated unprecedented levels of production and employment. These conditions exacerbated the labor-supply problems of Detroit's big auto producers, who were already hard-pressed to secure an adequate work force for the new labor process. Government analysts estimated that in the spring of 1918 there was a shortage of about twenty thousand workers in Detroit's industries; one year later, the estimated shortage had jumped to fifty thousand. Auto manufacturers were desperate for labor power—they competed for workers in the ad columns of the daily press, pirated workers away from each other with promises of high wages, sent labor agents to the South to recruit rural black labor power, and even breeched their own sexist employment policies in order to put women to work in many parts of their factories.[47]

The clear-headed editor of *Automotive Industries* retrospectively captured the essence of these times. "For many years labor was underneath in the industrial struggle and some employers felt themselves secure in their power. The war brought to labor its first real opportunity to exercise power and the natural reaction from these previous years was for it to exercise that power to its fullest extent. . . . "[48] Labor turnover and absenteeism increased to epidemic proportions in the industry. "Workers are finding it so easy to secure jobs," another trade journalist wrote, "and a competition between the employers has forced wages to so high a standard that the average employee changes his position once every six weeks—that is, labor turnover is now averaging 60 percent per month in some factories, while absentees are in some instances averaging 400 percent per month."[49]

During this upsurge in their power, however, auto workers did not confine their resistance to the individualistic, indirect methods of turnover and absenteeism. More direct and collective forms of struggle also were increasingly used. There were reports from automobile factories of increased industrial "accidents," defective products, and reduced production. The Lincoln Motor Company reported that:

> Mishaps—whether caused by sabotage or carelessness—occurred constantly. Machines would be thrown out of adjustment overnight so that the operation next morning might go on for hours turning out scrap before inspection could catch it. Screws were loosened, bolts were removed which would allow parts to fall and be damaged. Loose nuts were found in the crankcases of engines, feed pipes were plugged. On one occasion, cans full of powder were found in the coal supply, and fire extinguishers were plugged with cotton. Emery dust was found in the machines.[50]

This period was also marked by an increase in the number of strikes and work stoppages. Made bold by the wartime and postwar labor shortages, workers showed themselves increasingly willing to strike or stop work in order to press their demands for higher wages and slower production pace. U.S. Bureau of Labor Statistics data revealed that the number of strikes in the industry increased from three in 1917 to thirteen in 1918 and thirty-one in 1919, falling back to nineteen in 1920.[51]

A similar upsurge in auto worker's resistance based on the power afforded them by labor shortages occurred during the industrial boom of the Second World War. Once again, turnover and absenteeism soared in the auto plants, which were mainly engaged in war production. In the automobile and body manufacturing plants, the monthly quit rate rose from 1.4 percent in October 1940 to 5.5 percent in October 1946; the corresponding figures in the auto parts plants were 1.8 percent and 4.3 percent, respectively. Absenteeism was also rampant. In General Motors plants, short-term absenteeism doubled in the fifteen months prior to December 1942; and the company estimated that absenteeism accounted for losses of from 2 to 7 percent of the total production time. There was also an increase in soldiering, slowdowns, and restriction of output in the auto shops. Workers used the power afforded them by the tight labor market to struggle against capital's control of the pace of work. Ford Motor Company reported an overall decline of 34 percent in output per worker during the war period. General Motors similarly reported a decline of 37 percent in worker-hour output between 1941 and 1945. And although GM management recognized other problems as partially responsible for this decline, it saw "reduced productive worker effort" as the main cause. Managers and capitalists commonly recognized that production standards were generally loosened during the war as a result of worker resistance.[52]

When capital proved adamant against worker demands for decreased pace during the Second World War, auto workers resorted to strikes and walkouts. Bureau of Labor Statistics data showed that the number of work stoppages in the automobile industry leaped from twenty-nine in 1940 to two hundred twenty-eight in 1944, while worker-days lost due to stoppages increased from 104,000 to 1,360,000 in the same period. The vast majority of these stoppages were wildcat strikes, unauthorized by the union, which had signed a no-strike pledge in 1942. Data further revealed that in at least 34 percent of the stoppages, the main issue was either worker discipline or productivity.[53]

I have focused upon the two periods of wartime boom because the effect of the shrinking industrial reserve army upon auto workers' struggle was most pronounced then. However, this relationship holds generally for all periods of rapid growth and expansion of the industry.

Contradictions of the Auto Labor Process

The general capitalist laws of motion of business cycles, uneven development, and the concentration and centralization of capital generated contradictions, which strengthened and unified worker resistance to managerial power on the shop floor. However, the nature and strength of auto workers' resistance can be explained fully only by the combination of these contradictions with those specific to the labor process of the automobile industry. In their construction of a labor process intended to weaken the opposition of workers, auto manufacturers inadvertently created a new base for working-class power through the leveling or homogenization of the work force. As was detailed in chapter 7, the progressive rationalization and mechanization of labor largely reduced the hierarchy of craft groups and skill levels to the homogeneous labor of minding machinery. Both the proud craft workers and the lowly laborers lost ground to the ever-growing groups of assemblers, machine-tool and press operators. Beneath the statistics on occupational shifts lies a story of a growing objective community of auto workers. No longer were they separated by widely varying degrees of control over their own work. Most were subjected to the indiscriminate despotism of the pace-setting machine. The yoke of crowded, dangerous shop conditions came to unite workers in a common bondage to capital. Differences in knowledge and training were replaced by a common superfluity of training and an increasing interchangeability of workers. The craft pride and prejudice that once had flourished found little fertile ground in the new labor process, with its minutely divided, monotonous, machine-minding uniformity.[54]

In a capitalist society, in which the measure of all things is money, perhaps the best indicator of the increasing homogeneity of auto workers is the distribution of their wages. Few data are available on the wage distribution of workers under the old craft process of production. However, it can be inferred from what is known generally about industries encompassing many varied crafts that wages were widely dispersed. The wage differences between the crafts reflected their differing market conditions and training requirements. The variance in auto workers' wages was further increased by the wide differences between the wages of craft workers and those of unskilled helpers and manual laborers.[55]

As the development of the new technology eliminated both skilled craft workers and unskilled helpers and laborers and replaced them with relatively unskilled machine tenders, the variance in wages was rapidly and substantially reduced. By the time of the Cleveland survey of metal trades in 1915, the use of the assembly line and specialized machinery had already reduced the percentage of skilled workers to about 13 percent of the factory labor force. The wage structure reflected the leveling effect of this technology. Of all auto workers included in the sample, the hourly wages of 59 percent were encompassed in a five-cent range, between twenty-five and thirty cents. The rest of the distribution was as fol-

TABLE 8.2.   Absolute and Relative Dispersion of Hourly Wages of Automotive Factory Occupations, 1919–1950

	Combined divisions	
	Interquartile range (cents)	Relative dispersion index (percentages)
1919	5.3	9.7
1922	6.2	9.1
1925	8.4	11.5
1928	7.9	10.4

	Automobile mfg. division		Automotive parts division	
	Interquartile range	Relative dispersion index	Interquartile range	Relative dispersion index
1934	9.9[a]	13.7[a]	8.1[a]	13.3[a]
1940	9.0	9.4	17.0	20.0
1950	14.0	8.8	35.0	22.3

SOURCE: U.S., Bureau of Labor Statistics, Bulletin nos. 348 (1923), 438 (1927), 502 (1930), 706 (1942), 1015 (1951) (Washington, D.C.: Government Printing Office); "Wages and Hours in Automobile, Car, Electrical Apparatus, Foundry, Machinery, Machine Tool and Typewriter Industries," *Monthly Labor Review* 10 (June 1920): 82–94; N. A. Tolles and M. W. La Fever, "Wages, Hours, Employment, and Annual Earnings in the Motor Vehicle Industry, 1934," *Monthly Labor Review* 42 (March 1936): 521–553.

NOTES: The relative dispersion index is a standardized measure calculated by dividing the interquartile range by the median of the distribution and multiplying the quotient by 100.

BLS data before 1928 combined the automobile manufacturing and auto parts divisions of the industry. After that date data for the two divisions were reported separately.

[a]Male workers only, data on female workers unavailable.

lows: under twenty-five cents, 23 percent of the work force; from thirty to thirty-five cents, 10 percent; and thirty-five cents and over, 8 percent.[56]

The general trend of the distribution of auto workers' wages from this early point was toward further compression. Table 8.2 shows the movement of the absolute dispersion (measured by the inter-quartile range) and relative dispersion of the hourly wages of auto-motive factory occupations. It should be noted that these data reveal only the variation between the average wages of different occupa-tions. They do not measure the personal variation between workers in the same occupation. This deletion of personal differentials may tend to exaggerate slightly the compression of the wage structure of the industry. This is especially true of the years before 1934, when piece and bonus wage systems were common in the industry and created greater variation within occupations than straight-time wages. However, despite this problem, the data clearly show that the wage structure of the automobile industry had become very compressed by 1919 and remained so throughout the period under examination here. This general fact is also confirmed by reports on the wage structures of individual plants in which no occupational averaging was done.[57]

This leveling of auto workers' wages did not, however, corre-spond to any absolute impoverishment. Auto workers made fairly consistent absolute wage gains over the years, but these gains were collective, affecting all workers more or less equally. The wages of all auto workers increased proportionally, without changing their relative distribution. Because of this compressed wage structure, marked by collective as opposed to individual gains, Ely Chinoy found that auto workers saw their ability to improve their liveli-hoods as a collective affair, to be accomplished through collective effort rather than through individual attempts to rise in the corpo-rate hierarchy. The objective leveling of wage differentials, which in-dexed homogenization of working conditions, skill, status, and con-trol, gave rise to a tendency for auto workers to subjectively define themselves as a community with shared interests.[58]

Automotive capitalists and managers themselves realized that their efforts to transform the labor process in order to better control workers had had the contradictory effect of strengthening workers by creating a community of interests among them. Harry Tipper, the early labor editor of *Automotive Industries*, warned his fellow capital-ists of the grave implications of their attempts to standardize and mechanize the process of building automobiles. "We have already standardized to such a degree in our attempt to use human beings easily in industry, that standardization has in many cases developed into a dangerous suggestion of uniformity . . . [and] has been one of the chief elements in the growth of trade unionism and the develop-ment of socialism." The standardization of labor, Tipper argued, cre-ated unionism and socialism by leveling pay to a uniform basis and causing workers to view their compensation as the result of their collective power rather than their individual value.

> When the conditions of the work are sufficiently uniform and the basis of reward sufficiently standard, the sense of individual value becomes so small a part of the total value of the operation that the sense of personal responsibility is almost destroyed. . . . The present valuation for any group of workers is based almost entirely upon the so-called law of supply and demand, modified by the power and strength of labor organizations in the group. . . . [Thus, this system] puts a premium upon strikes, labor organization and warfare.[59]

A second contradiction in the new technology that provided workers with a source of power was its increased interdependence and consequent vulnerability to disruption. The method of line production made each work station absolutely dependent upon the preceding station to deliver work to it and upon the succeeding station to take its work away. No stock was stored between stations or departments, and the continuity of the entire elaborate process was dependent upon the carefully timed flow of work. If just one station broke down, the whole mechanism ground to a halt. As one production engineer wrote: "To set up equipment in a progressive sequence is courting trouble; if any one of the machines within the line breaks down, the flow is interrupted and all subsequent operations must stop. Also parts coming down the line quickly create congestion before the disabled machine. If the line conveyor itself gives way, work will be held up in every station."[60]

This total interdependence of the labor process meant that a small number of rebellious workers could disrupt production. If they merely quit working, or sabotaged the moving lines so as to stop them, they could tie up production immediately in their particular department and progressively disrupt the entire interdependent factory. This contradiction of interdependence lay behind many of the incidents of sabotage examined above. Workers used this power to create periodic stoppages in order to gain some free time, force capital to slow down the pace of production, and protest other working conditions. But the purpose for which this source of power proved most useful was for shutting down production completely in strikes. This was a key tactic used by auto workers in the wave of sitdown strikes of 1936 and 1937 that won the unionization of most of the industry.

The third and final contradiction of the new technology in the automobile industry that empowered workers in their struggle with capital was the cyclical reemergence of uncertainty. Auto capitalists sought to eliminate from the production process all variation and uncertainty, for these elements allowed workers some control over their own labor. But, they were not completely successful in this aim. The introduction of annual model changes in the mid-1920s to stimulate lagging sales created a cycle of uncertainty that provided a basis for worker resistance.

Every year a portion of the production process had to be restructured in order to accommodate the new model. Machine tools had to be rebuilt and rearranged to produce the new parts. Presses had to be fitted with new dies and their operations and sequences adjusted accordingly. Particularly affected were the final assembly lines, where model changes forced a complete overhaul of this highly coordinated, minutely timed department every year. The number of workers and operations, the division of labor, the nature of operations and tools, the timing of each operation, the overall balance, the speed of the line—all these aspects of the moving assembly line had to be restructured to produce a smooth-flowing, unproblematic production unit under the changed circumstances. Despite the best capitalist efforts to plan every detail of the production of the new model, many aspects remained uncertain and dependent upon the experience of trial and error for their final determination. The reemergence of these uncertainties during model changeovers gave workers a brief resurgence of production power, which they used to struggle for decreased line speeds and greater autonomy. Initially, managers did not have exact knowledge about how much could be produced how fast. They often sought to impose the production rates for the old model on the new process. Taking advantage of the uncertainty of managerial knowledge, workers contended that because of the changed nature of work, the old rates could not apply. Thus, at every model changeover, workers used this resurgence of uncertainty as a weapon to struggle with capital over the pace of production. As two students of the industry—one a seasoned auto worker himself—wrote: "The speedup becomes a particularly acute issue when new models are introduced. Since the new models always require at least a few changes in the productive process, it is often extremely difficult to use the work rate of the previous model as a basis for comparison. On such occasions, a struggle over work rates, with the union claiming speedup and the company slowdown, bursts into the open."[61]

This cyclical reemergence of uncertainty, as well as the homogenization of the work force and the interdependence of production, constituted contradictions in the new technology that ironically increased the power of auto workers. The combination of these contraditions, which were specific to automobile production, with the general contradictions of the capitalist economy gave workers the power to struggle in the shops and caused the forms of that struggle to become more direct and collective. In chapter 12, I will examine how the historical juncture of these contradictions during the late 1930s resulted in a monumental revolt of auto workers—the mass sitdown strikes that led to the unionization of the industry.

The capitalist transformation of the technology of auto production was thus not sufficient to break the back of labor's resistance. Auto workers continued to struggle against capitalist control of work, and the new technology ironically provided them with new weapons. Automotive capitalists and managers realized even as they revolutionized the technical relations of production that complete control of work required additional control measures that transformed another part of the labor process—the social relations within and between labor and capital.

CHAPTER 9
Bureaucratization of the Authority Structure

One of the first aspects of the social relations of the labor process that auto manufacturers transformed in order to control the resistance of workers was the authority structure. In the early process of changing auto technology, capitalists and managers largely ignored the exercise of authority over it. They retained the structure of authority from the early shops, which proved wholly incapable of meeting the requirements of the new technology and quelling the revolt against it.

The new technology of the automobile labor process increasingly centralized the direction and evaluation of work into the hands of managers and other specialized workers loyal to capital. But the methods for disciplining workers remained largely unchanged through the mid-1910s. The administration of sanctions remained decentralized, controlled by foremen who ruled their workers with arbitrary and harsh authority. Such a structure of authority proved woefully unsuited to the requirements of the new technology, as the rising tide of worker resistance made clear. In the face of sky-rocketing turnover and absenteeism, capitalists realized that they had to make concessions to workers in order to hold them to their newly degraded jobs. But these concessions could not be made uniformly as long as foremen exercised arbitrary authority over discipline and sanctions. Capitalists needed a new centralized, rule-governed structure of authority—in short, a bureaucracy—in order to create the stable and predictable relations demanded by the new technology.[1]

The Early Authority Structure

In the earliest, small shops of the industry, authority was generally wielded directly and personally by the entrepreneur himself. The small scale of production and the small size of the work force enabled the auto capitalist personally to direct and oversee the entire manufacturing operation. Thus, one commentator wrote of one of the earliest auto firms in the U.S., the Winton Motor Carriage Company: "Encouraging the whole corps of engineers, designers and artisans by his personal supervision is Mr. Winton, whose interest in the success of his product is so largely a part of himself that he devotes himself constantly and enthusiastically to its manufacture."[2]

Usually aided by a handful of supervisors or foremen, the entrepreneur personally planned and directed production, evaluated work and workers, and administered sanctions: hiring, firing, pay rates and bonuses, fines, and suspensions. All of this was done on a very arbitrary, informal basis. Authority was personalistic, not systematic. Compliance with orders was obtained through a combination of harsh coercion and personal loyalty. For example, in the early days of his small shop, Henry Ford was known to be a "manhandler" at times, but he generally relied on personal intimacy and association to control his workers.

> All accounts agree that Ford himself was in these years [circa 1904] still the life of the force. Though busy chiefly in the experimental room, he frequently moved about the factory, jesting, telling stories in off moments, and playing practical pranks on the hands, but scrutinizing every operation. "Everybody used to call him Hank or Henry," writes one early employee, "and he used to know everybody by name." . . . His eye caught every hitch in operations, and he was quick to devise new expedients. In certain moods he was harshly arbitrary, and this "mean streak" was to grow. In general during this period, however, he seems to have been considerate of the workers. He seldom gave a direct command. Instead, he would say, "I wonder if we could get this done right away," or, "It would be fine if you could do so-and-so." These hints were effective. "The men would just break their necks to see if they could do it. They knew what he wanted. They figured it was a coming thing, and they'd do their best."[3]

Such a personalistic structure of authority—Max Weber called it patriarchalism, or in some cases, patrimonialism—was not unique to Henry Ford or his firm. In the early Olds machine shop, the use of this personalistic method of control by the elder Olds often annoyed the young son, R. E., who already had his eye on a more standardized, impersonal method of production. "Pliny [Olds], a sociable old fellow by nature, loved to stop his workmen to recount an interesting story. Frequently R. E. found himself chafing as a handful of men in the shop would pause for half an hour to listen to Pliny's account of some local happening."[4] In this early period, the positive sanctions of personal friendships and loyalties usually overshadowed harsh coercion as a way of exerting control over workers.

The emphasis upon the positive sanction of loyalty in this patrimonial system was a consequence of the early labor process and its concomitant balance of power on the shop floor. This early craft method of production was largely controlled by the skilled workers themselves, because of the unstandardized and variable nature of the work. Because the balance of power on the shop floor was favorable to workers, it was impossible for the entrepreneur to control them wholly or mainly through physical coercion and brutal discipline. Such negative sanctions cause the alienation of workers from authority, which could be disastrous so long as their scarce skills were largely responsible for the quantity and quality of production. They could retaliate by restricting production, lowering its quality, or simply quitting. A control strategy that would not alienate these powerful workers was devised that relied on the normative sanctions of personal ties and loyalties. Workers were not motivated by external force, but by the internalization of the norms and goals of their employer. Through personal interactions on the shop floor, the early capitalist created in workers a sense of identification with himself and the firm. In this way, they were persuaded that they were actually working for themselves or their kind instead of an alien capitalist, for "us," instead of "them."

This normative, patrimonial control system was all the more possible in the early shops because the class distance between capitalists and workers was small. Early auto entrepreneurs were themselves mainly skilled mechanics and engineers, who had only recently crossed the class line from worker to capitalist. They shared with their employees a common shop culture, which facilitated the establishment of personal ties. The balance of power in the early labor process made this type of normative, patrimonial control a necessity. And the small size of these firms, as well as the small social distance between employer and employees, facilitated its use.[5]

The burgeoning automobile firms soon outgrew the conditions of this patrimonial control by entrepreneurs, growing too large for one individual to supervise personally all operations and maintain friendly relations with all workers. Control had to be delegated to supervisory personnel in more direct contact with the work and workers, usually superintendents and foremen. As Ford historians Allan Nevins and Frank Hill wrote of the company circa 1906:

> As the size of the labor force increased, however, control of the men had to be more largely deputed. Once the worker was put on the payroll, equipped with a badge, and sent to his department, he was under the all but absolute authority of his immediate foreman. The size of his wage-check, the severity of the production standard assigned to him, the time given him to learn his job, his chances of promotion or transfer, his tenure—all this lay within the range of the foreman's discretion. Above all, the foreman's right of arbitrary and unchallengeable discharge was accepted as the cornerstone of efficient labor practice. This was true of most large American factories at the time; it was true of practically all big motor works.[6]

The foreman came to replace the entrepreneur as the administrator of discipline in the auto shops. The direction and evaluation of work still remained largely in the hands of the skilled workers themselves. The foreman participated in both functions as the "first among equals." He was the most skilled and knowledgeable of the workers in his crew, and he played the role of consultant rather than commander with respect to the actual execution of work. But as a discipliner of workers, the foreman wielded unchallenged power.[7]

Although the administrator of discipline in the auto shops changed from entrepreneur to foreman or superintendent, the system of control remained largely the same—normative, patrimonial control. In these years in the middle of the first decade of the twentieth century, the work forces of the auto companies grew, but the labor process remained largely skilled and controlled by the workers themselves. Because skilled workers continued to exercise considerable control in the labor process, authority over them had to be decentralized into the hands of foremen as the force grew. The balance of power on the shop floor still required normative sanctions, based on personal ties and loyalties. But due to the size of the work force, such ties could be maintained only by supervisors in close, direct contact with the workers. Foremen had to be given control over all sanctions, because only they had the personal relations with workers upon which to base their administration.

Foremen not only determined wages, promotions, work assignments, and training. They also administered the crucial sanctions of hiring and firing, since this power was an indispensable tool in creating the personal loyalties required in the normative, patrimonial system. The easiest method of establishing such loyalties was to draw on the bonds of communities outside the factory—communities of race, religion, nationality, neighborhood, and family. Hence, it was common for auto shop foremen, and all industrial foremen of this period, to practice nepotism and favoritism in hiring and firing. One investigator of early industrial employment practices found that

> hiring by foremen in some cases builds up cliques based upon nationality, religion, fraternal organization, etc., within the department, either because the foreman gives preference to men of a certain nationality or religion or to members of a certain organization, or because he hires such men unintentionally by asking men already employed to bring in friends.[8]

This favoritism was probably not a consciously calculated control strategy but was adopted simply because foremen and workers got along better with their own kind. And it was precisely this amiable cooperation between kindred personnel that was demanded by the control system of this period.

At first, foremen, like the entrepreneurs before them, relied upon a lax and personal style of supervision, based upon personal friendships rather than upon close, coercive control of workers.[9] But the benevolence of the foreman's reign began to decline rapidly in the years around 1910 in the larger shops, and a harsh system of petty despotism arose to take its place. The chief motivating sanctions ceased to be normative ties and loyalties and increasingly became brutal coercion and the cold cash nexus. The nature of this transition was most evident at Ford, where the early, lax system of supervision came to an end with the rise of a succession of brutal and coercive factory superintendents. Allan Nevins and Frank Hill wrote:

> Inasmuch as the number of employees ran up toward 3000 in 1910, the proportion of unskilled and foreign-born constantly rose, and the turnover was heavy . . . , discipline was essential; the force had to be treated much like a little army. Couzens and Ford by 1908 seemed remote figures to the man at the multiple drill. It was P.E. Martin and Charles Sorensen to whom the men looked, and these superintendents tried to combine strictness with rough—sometimes very rough—justice.[10]

The philosophy behind the new regime of industrial despots at Ford was aptly summarized by Samuel Marquis, a former Ford executive. To the new Ford factory superintendents, wrote Marquis, "the morale of the organization meant nothing. They flouted loyalty on the part of the employees as being of no value. They stoutly held that men worked for two reasons—their wage, and the fear of losing their jobs." Any humane treatment of workers was thought to weaken the authority of the boss and the discipline of the shop. For the new supervisors, Marquis concluded, "the sole end of industry was production and profits, and the one sure way of getting these things out of labor was to curse it, threaten it, drive it, insult it, humiliate it, and discharge it on the slightest provocation; in short—to use a phrase much on the lips of such men—'put the fear of God into labor.' And they were always thinking of themselves as the little gods who were to be feared."[11]

In the Ford shops, Charles Sorensen gained a particularly odious reputation as a brutal, quick-tempered driver of workers. He was known to show his scorn for some performance in the factory by tipping over a worker's bench, or crashing a stool over it. One day, strutting through the huge Rouge complex like a feudal lord surveying his domain, Sorensen spied a worker sitting on a nail keg splicing some wires. This was a violation of the strict company rule prohibiting workers from sitting down at any time. Without warning, Sorensen angrily kicked the keg out from under the worker, who fell to the floor. The worker bounced to his feet and threw a punch that floored Sorensen. "You're fired," the latter roared as he scrambled upright. "The hell I am," the worker responded. "I work for the telephone company."[12]

Such coercive control over workers was exercised by foremen as well as superintendents during this period. "Many foremen were arbitrary, prejudiced, and brutal," reported Nevins and Hill of the Ford shops of the day. Nor was this sort of behavior confined to Ford. One worker reported that most of the foremen at Packard "as well as at other auto plants I would come in contact with, had this thing about being kind of cold, as a demonstration of how tough they were. They would love to lay you out in public for any chicken-shit reason." At Keim Mills, William Knudsen (who eventually became a top Ford executive) used similar methods to turn out pressed-steel auto parts. Differences between Knudsen and the workers he supervised were often settled with their fists, reported his biographer.[13]

This change from a normative to a coercive system of patrimonial authority in the auto shops was the result of a radical shift in the balance of power on the shop floor. It is no coincidence that the change came precisely at the time when auto work was beginning to be deskilled and degraded on a large scale. In the years between

1908 and 1910, the rationalization and mechanization of work undermined the control over the labor process exercised by skilled workers. Because workers were no longer as powerful as before, foremen and superintendents could resort to more coercive tactics, for they did not have to fear alienating them.

It was still necessary, however, at this stage, that power be decentralized and personal (patrimonial) as opposed to centralized and impersonal, for vital areas of uncertainty in the production process continued to exist. Now, more than ever before, foremen played a crucial role in the direction and evaluation of work. The skills of workers had been undermined by rationalization and mechanization, but production had not yet become so standardized that it could be controlled by centrally established rules. The labor process still required at least one technically skilled and knowledgeable worker in each crew to perform as yet unrationalized tasks: machine setting, maintenance and repair, tool changing and sharpening, work inspection. These tasks generally fell to the foremen. Because they controlled these vital areas of work direction and evaluation, foremen had to be given the control over discipline and sanctions to motivate workers' compliance with their directions. Unchecked by the power of workers below and of top managers above, foremen and production superintendents were the rulers of their small domains, wielding absolute and arbitrary authority.[14]

BUREAUCRATIZATION OF WORK DIRECTION AND EVALUATION

This decentralized, patrimonial system of authority, with foremen acting as petty despots, was increasingly undermined by the changing labor process. The areas of uncertainty in production that required the dispersion of authority in the hands of skilled and knowledgeable foremen were progressively eliminated, allowing the direction and evaluation of work to be centralized into specialized staff departments removed from the shop floor. Better raw materials, more accurate and specialized machine tools, interchangeable and standardized parts—these and other factors guaranteed the invariability of production necessary for the establishment of central authority.

Ultimate authority over production became increasingly invested in one individual—the chief engineer, general manager, or superintendent. But in the larger plants, this man was assisted in his duties by a series of staff departments that emerged in the later years of the first decade of the twentieth century. No longer did foremen direct the workers under them in the exact way to do the work. This kind of direction came from a central department, variously called the engineering, planning, or production department. Whatever the name, the function of this department was to determine the best and most efficient methods of production. Thus, of the direction of work at Ford circa 1910, one executive wrote:

> When we change an old operation or put into effect a new system or plan of manufacture, our engineering department draws up the work on a theoretical basis, provides the machines and submits them to the manufacturing or factory department with full data as to the operation of the machines and what the output should be from a theoretical standpoint, making due allowance for mechanical defects and human indifference, as established by experience.[15]

One sure indicator of the growing centralization and bureaucratization of the direction of work in the large auto firms was the increasing use of written instructions. The issuance of written rules and orders by staff departments far removed from the shop floor allowed the growing organizations to be controlled centrally by a very few people. Foremen generally received from the production department daily schedules of the work to be turned out in their departments. They were also given detailed written instructions on machine set-up, methods and sequence of operations, time of performance, and number of workers required. Often these instructions were broken down into individual instruction cards given to workers.

Just as important as the bureaucratization of the direction of work was the bureaucratization of its evaluation. It was one thing to issue central commands on how work was to be done; but to make the emerging bureaucratic system work, it was necessary to evaluate the quality and quantity of work actually produced against the commands issued. In order to do this, the large auto companies began to establish in this period separate inspection and accounting departments. The inspection department evaluated the quality of work produced and guaranteed that it was within the limits set by the production department. Once the task of individual foremen, inspection began to be centralized into autonomous departments, beginning in the later years of the first decade of this century. Sometimes inspection was spatially segregated from the production floor, as at Pierce-Arrow and Willys-Overland. But often the inspection force was dispersed throughout the various production departments, as at Ford. In 1914 a force of some six hundred Ford inspectors blanketed the process of production from start to finish.[16]

Bureaucratic accounting systems were also established by auto manufacturers to ensure that work was done in the specified quantities and within the time standards dictated by the production department. In the Maxwell-Briscoe factory in 1912, one hundred clerks were employed full-time, collecting and analyzing such data for a production force of two thousand workers. These factory clerks closely observed the operations of production workers, recording their exact times on the job order issued by the production department, and comparing them with established standards. In 1917, seventeen hundred of Ford's approximately forty-one thousand factory workers were clerks of various types. In production departments, workers kept individual records of their daily output, which were collected by subforemen and transferred to a standard form. These forms were then delivered to factory clerks working in each department, who compiled from them long-term production records for each worker. These records were sent to the cost department, where labor-cost and time-of-production totals were computed and compared to standards.[17]

The new bureaucratic system for the direction and evaluation of work not only centralized authority, but it also legitimated the new authority it established. The authority of capitalists and managers at the top was now shrouded by the seemingly neutral form of quantitative commands and calculations through which it was exercised. It was easy for workers to resist the personal commands of a brutal, driving foreman, but it was more difficult for them to fight the impersonal, quantitative directions and evaluations issued by the various staff departments. Social relations of authority were increasingly mystified by the language of science. Thus, when auto manufacturers introduced "quality control programs," which statistically plotted each worker's output against established tolerances on a chart beside his or her station, one trade journalist wrote:

> Quality control . . . removes the necessity of high-pressure supervision or appeals to idealistic and economic strategems. Through its use some of the problems of production are reduced to a statistical procedure. The quality control chart circumvents the individual and exerts no personal pressure, therefore it cannot elicit any counter-attitude. . . . There is no argument with the facts because the production story is on record.[18]

BUREAUCRATIZATION OF WORKER DISCIPLINE

For a time, the larger auto factories were faced with an incongruent authority structure. Power over the direction and evaluation of work was becoming increasingly centralized and bureaucratized by staff departments removed from the shop floor, while power over the discipline of workers remained patrimonial and decentralized in the hands of individual foremen, who wielded it arbitrarily and brutally. This unstable situation created pressure to centralize and bureaucratize discipline in the shops, for several reasons. First, the system of decentralized, patrimonial discipline by foremen was no longer necessary. This system was based upon the foremen's control of work direction and evaluation, which had been dictated in turn by the uncertain nature of the labor process. When this uncertainty was eliminated and the direction and evaluation of work centralized, it was no longer necessary for foremen to discipline workers to motivate their compliance with directions that they had not issued. Second, this patrimonial system of discipline was no longer possible in the rapidly growing auto factories. Just as the burgeoning labor force grew out of the personal control of the entrepreneur, so too did the number of workers under each foreman grow too large to control by means of personal supervision and contact. Third, and decisively, the system of decentralized, patrimonial administration of discipline was no longer desirable in the changed labor process. The new technology required a work force that was above all stable and predictable. As engineering journalists Arnold and Faurote wrote in reference to the Ford shops: "It is of vital importance to successful factory management that workmen should be steady in their habits, and dependable in the point of continuous service."[19] Such stability was necessary to plan the profitable investment and depreciation of the huge amounts of fixed capital in the new labor process. Furthermore, because the process was interdependent and susceptible to disruption, absolute stability of the work force was necessary to ensure continuous and uninterrupted production. A shortage of labor at any one point, or a strike or slowdown motivated by grievances, could tie up the entire factory. The system of discipline that had left to scores of individual foremen the administration of sanctions based on their personal whims and prejudices was egregiously ill-fitted to meet these new requirements.

Auto capitalists were made suddenly aware of these shortcomings of the old system of discipline beginning around 1914, when the worker revolt against the new technology reached epidemic proportions. Auto firms in the vanguard of technological innovation were hit hard by high worker turnover and absenteeism. As the decade progressed, these problems were compounded by war-induced labor shortages. From the auto shops went up the cry of capitalists for labor stability. "The one *greatest* problem in American industry at the present time [1917] is how to get, and how to keep, a labor supply which will do the work at hand in the best and most profitable way."[20] Auto manufacturers found that the absolute power of discipline in the hands of foremen hindered this stabilization. They complained that foremen discharged men arbitrarily and without warrant due to petty spite, ignorance, jealousy, and prejudice. The coercive methods utilized by foremen to discipline workers were said to drive many to quit. As one commentator put it, the industry could no longer afford to use the old "hammer-and-tongs labor policy. . . . Bismarck is dead; so is Machiavelli; neither blood-and-iron nor an opportunist policy of using any means, good or bad, to attain a desired end can gain success in the conduct of industry's human relationships."[21] The foremen's control over wages was also found to hinder stability in the labor force. Wages set arbitrarily, often on the basis of favoritism and personal deals, caused resentment among workers and resulted in turnover.

Capitalists and managers discovered that they could not repress the new revolt and stabilize the work force with the old decentralized, patrimonial system. So under the pressure of worker resistance, they began to construct a bureaucratic structure of discipline. The control over worker discipline was stripped from foremen and centralized into a staff department that administered sanctions on the basis of written rules, not personal ties. This central employment department could quickly adjust the company's labor policy to changing labor market conditions in order to maintain a stable and predictable force of workers. Through control of hiring, it could be more or less demanding of applicants, depending on the availability of labor. By controlling the crucial sanction of firing, the employment department could "maintain a check on the way in which discipline is being maintained in the plant . . . ," varying strictness so as to maintain a stable force under the shifting balance of power on the shop floor. This department could raise or lower wages as required to hold an adequate work force under varying labor market conditions. As one academic commentator on labor relations stated: "Because the employment department is best informed concerning wage rates in the market and because it is first to feel the effects of a scale too low to attract and hold labor, the supervisor of labor who manages the employment department is likely to take the initiative in making recommendations for wage advances necessary to keep pace with the market."[22] Wage rates could also be standardized so that all workers doing the same job received the same wage, thus removing a source of worker grievance.

Ford was one of the first auto firms to seek a solution to the problems of turnover and absenteeism by setting up a centralized employment department. In October 1913, the Ford Employment Department was established under the direction of George Bundy and given power over hiring, firing, absenteeism, and wages. No longer were Ford foremen allowed to go to the plant gates and hire workers for their crews. The Employment Department took written applications from all job-seekers and kept them on file. When a foreman was in need of additional hands, he filled out a requisition and sent it to his superintendent for approval, who in turn sent it to the Employment Department. There, written applications were screened, and the applicant selected was interviewed by the superintendent, who could either accept or reject the applicant for employment in his department. Absolute power over firing was similarly taken away from Ford foremen. Under the new system, a foreman had the power only to terminate a worker's employment in his crew. To do so, he filled out a form, giving his complete reasons, and sent it with the worker to the Employment Department. There the case of the worker was reviewed and, if at all possible, he or she was given a job in another part of the factory. Complete termination from Ford employment could be authorized only by a committee consisting of Henry Ford, the vice-president of the company, the employment manager, and the factory superintendent. This centralization of the power to fire resulted in an immediate reduction in discharges.

Having thus reduced the labor turnover due to arbitrary firing, Ford next moved to reduce voluntary turnover by centralizing control over wages. The power to determine wage rates was taken from foremen and given over to the Employment Department. A six-grade wage classification system, based ostensibly on skill, was instituted to standardize pay and thus eliminate the wage inequities that had often resulted from foremen setting wages. Foremen were allowed to recommend workers for raises to the Employment Department, but the latter held final authority over wages, basing its decisions in part on the records of individual worker efficiency. Also, the department could initiate general wage increases in factory departments experiencing high turnover in order to hold workers to their jobs.

This new, centralized department was also given control over absenteeism in the Ford shops. Each morning it received a list of absent workers from the factory departments. A doctor, nurse, or investigator was sent to the homes of these workers to investigate the causes of their absences. If they were sick, medical attention was given. If they were not, they were required to report to the Employment Department and answer for their absences. Ford managers reported a substantial reduction in absenteeism as a result of this program.[23]

Other automobile firms were not far behind Ford in centralizing control over discipline to meet the challenge of worker resistance. The Paige-Detroit Motor Car Company created its employment department in 1919 and gave it control over hiring, firing, and wages. It also served as a court of appeals for worker grievances. The department's work was facilitated by the maintenance of detailed employee records. The company enthusiastically reported that the employment department was responsible for a reduction of twelve percentage points in the monthly turnover rate. At the Packard Motor Car Company, an employment department was placed in charge of hiring, wages, "keeping men contented," and adjusting grievances. Wages of individual workers were determined in large part by the written records kept by the department on worker efficiency, absences, and tardiness. The Saxon Motor Car Company established an employment department in 1916 and reported a reduction of 140 percentage points in annual labor turnover in its first year of operation. The Haynes Manufacturing Company reported that the establishment of its employment department in 1915 cut its turnover to one quarter of its original magnitude in one-and-a-half years.[24]

The numer of automobile companies with central employment departments grew throughout the war years and on into the 1920s. When the Bureau of Labor Statistics took a survey of hiring and separation methods in two hundred and twenty-four establishments in 1932, all eleven of the auto firms included had central employment departments, as compared to only 63 percent of the total sample. In most of the auto firms, the employment manager or personnel director had full power to hire employees. Ten of the eleven firms reported that they recorded reasons for employees leaving and attempted to adjust difficulties. But there was greater variation in the power to discharge. Two of the auto firms still vested this authority in foremen, while six gave it to employment managers and two to higher officials.[25]

The establishment of employment departments in auto firms resulted not only in the centralization of worker discipline, but also in its depersonalization. The administration of sanctions became based upon written rules and records, as opposed to the personal judgment of this or that manager. Wages generally ceased to be determined by favoritism and arbitrary imposition and became based upon rule-governed classification schemes, which ensured that workers doing similar jobs received comparable pay. Wage increases and promotions were increasingly governed by rules that took into consideration length of employment, individual efficiency, standardized performance tests, and employee conduct. Hiring also became more standardized and rule-governed. Standard interviews and written tests were often used to evaluate job applicants along such dimensions as their trade knowledge, psychological profiles, and work histories. Layoffs were increasingly determined by systems of rules based on such criteria as length of employment, number of dependents, and individual efficiency. And firing and other disciplinary measures also became governed by codes that standardized punishments for specific numbers and types of infractions.[26]

This bureaucratization of authority did not, however, proceed evenly throughout the auto factories. Bureaucratic structures developed unevenly, varying largely according to the nature of the labor process. In the labor processes that were deskilled and over which workers wielded little control, authority was rapidly depersonalized and centralized. However, those parts of the shops in which workers retained significant skills and hence control over work—tool shops, maintenance and repair work, some jobs off the production lines—authority remained more patrimonial, with supervisors relying on personal ties and loyalties. Because workers in these processes controlled areas of discretion and uncertainty, they could not be supervised by centralized rules. Authority remained more decentralized in the hands of immediate supervisors, who wielded normative sanctions so as not to alienate these more powerful workers.[27]

Centralized, depersonalized bureaucratic authority could, however, be used to repress the resistance of deskilled workers to the new technology. By placing the direction, evaluation, and discipline of workers on a centralized, rule-governed basis, auto manufacturers were able to adjust authority to the balance of power on the shop floor and thus ensure the stability of the labor force demanded by the new technology. As a result of the bureaucratization of authority, capitalists better realized the productive potential of the new technology. But these consequent increases in output were not due to more efficient use of resources, for the most part, but to greater repression of worker resistance. Thus, like the mechanical instruments of production examined earlier, this organizational instrument embodied a large element of repressive control.

This is not to say, however, that the emerging industrial bureaucracies were exclusively repressive instruments and increased productive output solely by overcoming social antagonisms. Max Weber was correct to argue that technical superiority—sheer efficiency—was a major factor in the growth of bureaucratic organization. In all large-scale enterprises, control by standardized, written rules and instructions increased the speed, unity, and continuity of production by large numbers of cooperating workers. Further, the administration of sanctions like hiring, firing, and setting wages on the basis of impartial rules would seem to be not only more efficient, but also more just than the personalistic system, which bred favoritism and nepotism. In many instances, auto workers seemed to prefer the centralized control by the employment department to the arbitrary rule of foremen. The impartial administration by rules would seem to be a nonrepressive aspect of industrial bureaucracies, increasing the efficiency of production without affecting the antagonistic relations of production. But Weber also recognized that bureaucracy grew in capitalist society because it is "a power instrument of the first order . . . a system of domination [that] is practically indestructible."[28] Rigidly centralized authority provides its masters with a superior method of dominating their opponents, thus realizing their particular interests. Therefore, the advantages yielded by the bureaucratization of authority in the auto industry were the result of a complex combination of repressive and nonrepressive controls.

VARIATION OF AUTHORITY WITH THE BUSINESS CYCLE

The way in which auto capitalists and managers used the new bureaucratic structure to repress worker resistance is revealed by the fluctuation in the severity of authority with the business cycle. The bureaucracy allowed a controlled adjustment of authority to the vicissitudes of worker resistance. And, as we have seen, one of the major factors affecting the strength of that resistance was the business cycle.

When a boom period created a tight labor market and thus strengthened worker resistance, the top executive in charge of labor policy could loosen the reins of authority by liberally interpreting the rules. Such relaxed authority was characteristic of the industry during the two world wars. In order to hold a sufficient work force, auto managers relaxed the administration of sanctions, and workers were able to break disciplinary rules flagrantly with impunity.

Conversely, when recession and depression swelled the ranks of the industrial reserve army and weakened labor's resistance, auto capitalists found it easy to tighten discipline by interpreting the rules strictly. In hiring, the employment department became more choosy, requiring more experience, higher levels of demonstrated skill, and spotless employment records from applicants. Wage policies were circumvented or blatantly abrogated in order to cut wages. And because they no longer needed to restrain firings to hold an adequate labor force, manufacturers reverted to a more arbitrary, decentralized control over firing. Labor policies centralizing control over firing remained ostensibly in effect—officially foremen had only the power to recommend dismissal. But these recommendations were rarely challenged or reviewed by the central employment department. In effect, foremen once again came to wield largely arbitrary power over workers through the use of this sanction.

The manipulation of auto workers' fear of firing during depressionary periods resulted in some of the harshest discipline known in industrial America. During the depression of 1920 and 1921, for example, the atmosphere of the Ford shops turned decidedly more repressive. When a full working force was rehired after the shutdown caused by the depression, Ford workers found the pace of production accelerated, the enforcement of rules tightened, and the entire atmosphere harsher. Rough treatment of labor was encouraged. And supervision became much closer, with the number of workers under each subforeman cut from an average of thirty to fifteen. Petty rules against talking, singing, whistling, and sitting were ruthlessly enforced by "spotters," hired specifically to report on rule violations. Constant speed-up and stretch-out were forced on workers by threats of discharge or layoff. The Ford shops operated at 80 percent of their predepression capacity with 60 percent of the previous work force. Conditions at Ford do not seem to have been atypical of the auto industry in this period. An informal survey conducted by *Automotive Industries* revealed a general trend toward greater output per worker-day. "The spectre of possible unemployment has had a wholesome effect upon the attitude of workers and they are more concerned than they had been for years over the possibility of losing their jobs."[29]

After a period of more lax discipline during the middle and late 1920s, dictated by renewed labor shortages, the discipline of auto workers once again became ruthless and arbitrary during the depression of the 1930s. Foremen regained control over firing and layoffs and used it to drive workers mercilessly under the fear of losing their jobs. One auto worker reported: "There was no rhyme or reason in the selection of the fortunate ones chosen to continue working. The foreman had the say. If he happened to like you, or if you sucked around him and did him favors—or if you were one of the bastards who worked like hell and turned out more than production—you might be picked to work a few weeks longer than the next guy."[30] The direct connection between consciously cultivated fear of unemployment and the intensification of labor in the auto shops during the Great Depression was revealed by the extensive investigation of the industry conducted by a committee of the National Recovery Administration.

> One of the psychological problems faced by the automobile worker today is the gamble that he knows he is facing as he goes to work each day. He sees the men waiting at the gate for an interview for employment. If he is feeling badly on a particular day and slows down his gait, his straw-boss or foreman tells him, "Step on it. If you don't want the job, there are thousands outside who do," or "Look out the window and see the men waiting in line for your job." Whether or not it be true, large numbers of individual workers are convinced that it is the plan of various plants to maintain lines outside of the employment gates whether or not men are being hired, so as to make the "step on it" a little harder.[31]

Auto manufacturers exercised ruthless, arbitrary, coercive discipline over workers throughout the industry. Production was speeded up to unprecedented levels. Strict rules against talking and sitting were closely enforced. Fear of the growing union movement led capitalists to create dense networks of labor espionage that repressed freedom within and outside of the factories. Plant security forces were transformed into gestapo squads, which employed physical coercion and intimidation to repress dissent and enforce speed-up. Nowhere was this depressionary authority more brutal than at Ford, where Harry Bennett and his gang of toughs in the Service Department unleashed a reign of terror unparalleled in American industrial history.[32]

This reversion to largely arbitrary and decentralized power in auto firms during depressionary periods did not mean that bureaucratic systems of authority were dismantled. Formally, power over hiring, firing, and wages remained centralized and under the control of the employment departments. However, during the depression, top officials in the bureaucracy seem to have allowed the *de facto* decentralization of power into the hands of foremen, because the centralized, rule-governed structure was no longer necessary to ensure a stable and compliant labor force. The pressure of the labor market proved more than sufficient to hold workers to their jobs, no matter how coercive and arbitrary authority became. The bureaucratic authority structure remained formally in existence, however, so when the labor market tightened and labor's resistance strengthened, top officials could rein in foremen and reassert central authority over sanctions to accommodate the restricted labor market.

THE CHANGING ROLE OF THE FOREMAN

Although the exercise of authority in the automobile industry varied with the business cycle, the overall trend was a decline of the decentralized, patrimonial authority of the early shops and the rise of centralized, bureaucratic authority. As a result, the role of the foreman, who was the immediate manifestation of capitalist authority on the shop floor, underwent a profound change, altering the interaction and conflict of labor and capital.

The foremen of the early auto shops were very powerful. Because of the varied and uncertain nature of the craft labor process, they participated with skilled workers in controlling the process of production. Their power was increased by the early changes in auto production that rendered workers less skilled, for they were the only personnel left on the shop floor with sufficient technical knowledge and skill to direct and evaluate work. Continuing mechanization and division of labor, however, eliminated the areas of uncertainty controlled by foremen and allowed the centralization of the direction and evaluation of work. Technical expertise was thus no longer required of foremen. As early as 1916, the Cleveland survey of metal trades revealed that in the more rationalized factories, "foremanship itself has been specialized. In the larger plants foremen are chosen more for their ability to handle men than for their technical and trade knowledge." The survey report went on to state that the foreman's "principal duty is to keep the machine-like shop organization going with as little friction as possible. . . . He is an adjuster, teacher, and referee, rather than a boss. He must be courteous, just and fair. He has little to do with standards of output, which are fixed by statistical and time-study methods, or standards of quality, which are fixed by the engineering department."[33]

Soon, however, even the foreman's function of disciplining workers was eroded by the increasing bureaucratization of authority in the auto shops. As we have seen, the revolt of auto workers against the new technology revealed the weaknesses of the decentralized system of discipline and caused managers to seek a more stable and centralized control over sanctions through bureaucratization. In matters of discipline, the foreman was no longer judge, jury, and executioner, but merely the bureaucratic administrator of disciplinary rules formulated by the employment department.

The unionization of the industry added a new layer of bureaucratic authority, which limited the foreman's power even to interpret the rules of discipline. The grievance procedure established in most union contracts allowed the union to challenge any disciplinary decision made by a foreman before higher company authority. As the National Labor Relations Board wrote in one decision:

> With respect to the discipline and grievances of the rank and file workers under his supervision, the scope of the foreman's authority at Packard is established and circumscribed both by written rules and regulations laid down by the Company and by the contract between the Company and the Union of the rank and file, in negotiation of which the foremen, of course, play no part.[34]

For a given infraction, the foreman merely assessed the standard penalty provided in company rules. If the union steward did not agree with the foreman's action, he or she immediately appealed it to higher management. This bureaucratic grievance procedure led foremen to complain that their power was being by-passed or short-circuited, with higher management taking original jurisdiction over grievances. This erosion of power by both the company and the union bureaucracy led the National Labor Relations Board to the following conclusion about the position of foreman in auto shops of the mid-1940s: "Whereas he was formerly an executive with considerable freedom of action, he is now an executory carrying out orders, plans, and policies determined above; he is more managed than managing, more and more an executor of other men's decisions and less and less a maker of decisions himself."[35]

This change in the foremen's position in the automotive factories had two important effects on the balance of power between labor and capital on the shop floor—one favoring capital, the other favoring labor. First, managers benefited from the reduction of the conflict between foremen and workers and the maintenance of a more amiable atmosphere in the shop. The close, personal supervision of workers by foremen in the early shops had been a constant reminder of class antagonisms. The shop floor was often the scene of violent and bitter conflicts between workers and their foremen. However, with the progressive bureaucratization of the foreman's power over workers, this conflictual atmosphere waned.

Workers realized that foremen were no longer responsible for the orders they gave, but that they merely relayed and enforced policies established higher up. Chalmers found in his study of labor in the auto industry of the late 1920s that there was usually no personal antipathy between the workers and their immediate foremen— "they recognized that many of the conditions under which they worked were general company decisions."[36] The target of worker resentment and conflict was generally shifted up in the bureaucratic hierarchy, leaving a more amiable and conflict-free atmosphere on the shop floor. In their study of auto assembly-line workers, Charles Walker and Robert Guest reported that almost three-quarters stated that their foreman got along very well or fairly well with his workers. And many who commented unfavorably on their foreman ascribed the offensive behavior not to the foreman himself, but to his superiors. Walker and Guest concluded that even "when a foreman appeared to be reinforcing disliked characteristics of the line—its pace, repetitiveness, or fatigue, for example—the worker tended to exonerate him by implying that such factors were beyond his personal control."[37]

This removal of personal antipathy between foremen and workers created a shop atmosphere more conducive to production. Furthermore, without this immediate personal confrontation with capitalist authority, workers found it more difficult to focus and concentrate their discontent. It is much easier to get angry with a living, breathing human being than with a distant and vague company policy or system.

The second effect of this changing position of the foreman was not so much to the liking of auto capitalists. For as foremen found themselves increasingly on the receiving rather than the giving end of orders, the distinction between them and their workers began to blur. Already quite close to their workers in class background and culture, the foremen's decline in organizational position created a tendency for them to identify with workers rather than managers. Capital's front-line troops in its battle against labor began defecting to the enemy.

Signs of trouble appeared on the horizon as early as 1938, when foremen at the Kelsey-Hayes Wheel Company organized and were granted a charter by the CIO. By the summer of 1939, the CIO foremen's union had nine hundred dues-paying members and was well-established in eleven Detroit plants. However, the real push to organize auto industry foremen came with the formation of an independent union, the Foreman's Association of America (FAA). Beginning in the Ford war production plants in 1941, the FAA grew and spread to most of the major auto plants in Detroit. During 1943 and 1944, the union conducted strikes at Ford, Chrysler, Briggs, and other smaller Detroit plants. During these struggles, ominous signs of solidarity emerged between auto workers and foremen. Many workers honored the FAA's picket lines and refused to cooperate with foremen not striking. And the Michigan CIO Council passed a resolution expressing moral support for the foremen's organizing drive. In March of 1945, the National Labor Relations Board ruled that foremen could collectively bargain under the provisions of the Wagner Act, and the FAA quickly won the right to represent foremen at Ford and Packard. The union demanded of management the standard rights that the UAW had won for its members in the late 1930s.[38]

An investigation of the disputes between foremen and management by a special panel of the National War Labor Board in 1944 found that the conflict had been precipitated by the immediate conditions of wartime production. Workers' wages higher than foremen's pay, managerial by-passing of foreman authority, the fear of demotion or layoff after the war—these were some of the immediate conditions that had pushed foremen to the breaking point. But the underlying cause of their discontent was, as the National Labor Relations Board noted in 1945, the declining authority of foremen. In real power, foremen differed little from the average wage laborer. They constantly had to take the heat from above, with little or no say in their own conditions of work or pay. It is little wonder, then, that foremen began to view themselves as having more in common with labor than management and resorted to labor's traditional means of dealing with the boss—organization and striking.[39]

With its front-line troops increasingly defecting to the enemy, auto capitalists had to take quick action to attract them back to their camp. A united front of foremen and workers would have put capital in a dangerously weak position on the industrial battlefield. One capitalist solution to this problem was the introduction of largely symbolic distinctions between foremen and workers. Ford, master of the symbolic, led the way with a series of gestures. Time clocks and time cards for foremen were abolished. They were given special parking spaces, individual desks and lockers, special eating facilities, and distinctive overalls. Foremen carried cards instead of wearing the usual worker identification badges. And new vacation plans were also made for them.

Auto capitalists also used monetary compensation in a largely symbolic way to reinforce the distinction between workers and foremen. Ford gave all lower-level salaried employees a 10 percent raise to reestablish the monetary distinction between foremen and work-ers. General Motors placed all foremen on a salary and established a pay formula to ensure that they earned considerably more than their workers. These and similar measures by top managers seemed to succeed in winning foremen back to the management camp. In the years after the Second World War, the membership and power of the foreman's union declined.[40]

CHAPTER 10
Wages and Welfare

Automotive manufacturers used their new bureaucratic authority to institute changes in the social relations between labor and capital in order to combat worker resistance. The centerpieces of the new social policies were wage reforms and welfare programs. Auto capitalists and managers hoped that higher wages and improved working conditions and benefits would provide the incentives for auto workers to submit to the mechanized despotism.

Although auto manufacturers often sought to place a veneer of humanitarianism and philanthropy on these policies, their real purposes were never far from the surface. First, higher wages and greater benefits were bribes to buy off the resistance of workers to the new technology. Capital reasoned that if workers no longer reaped the intrinsic satisfactions of work controlled and conceptualized by themselves, they could be made to tolerate the new process of production by substituting for the old rewards the extrinsic reward of money. Second, in a more subtle vein, employers sought through wage and welfare policies to reconstruct the normative ties between labor and capital that had been attenuated by the growth of the shops. Perhaps the feeling of community between employees and employers, which had been seriously weakened by increased personal, social, and cultural distance, could be reinvigorated by paternalistic measures demonstrating that employers had the best interests of their workers at heart. Finally, and most profoundly, the new wage and welfare policies of the automotive firms sought to mold a new type of worker, whose character and culture would be adapted to the new technology and bureaucracy. These programs provided the pretext and incentives for altering workers' habits of work and leisure in order to create the stable and predictable work force required by the new labor process.

WAGES

Marxist political economy conceptualizes labor power in capitalism as a commodity, which, like all commodities, has a value that forms the basis of its exchange in the market. The value of labor power is the amount of socially necessary labor time required to produce the package of subsistence goods that sustain the laborer and his or her family. There are two determinants of the size and makeup of this package of commodities. First, an absolute lower limit on the level of consumption is set by the physiological needs of the worker. In order to have the physical capacity to work, the laborer must have minimal material needs met. Second, the subsistence goods necessary to reproduce labor power are also determined by the social-historical needs of the worker. The size and makeup of the subsistence package depend upon the traditional standard of living, which varies from country to country according to the level of social and historical development. While a certain minimum level of subsistence may provide the physical capacity to work, the willingness to work at a given intensity under given conditions depends upon a level of consumption considered by the worker to be commensurate with the traditional standard of living. This traditional standard is determined in large part by class struggle, with workers constantly seeking to add new needs to what has customarily been considered an adequate level of consumption, and capitalists just as persistently seeking to force the value of labor power down to the physiological minimum.

The value of labor power provides the basis around which the market price of labor power—wages—fluctuates. The fluctuations in wages above and below the value of labor power are determined, like the price movements of all commodities, by supply and demand in the market. But the effect of these market forces on wage movements is not direct; rather it is mediated by class struggle. Only through struggle with capitalists are workers able to force wages above the value of their labor power during times of labor shortages, and only against worker resistance are capitalists able to force wages below the value of labor power when there is a glut on the labor market.

Wages thus hinge vitally upon class struggle. In the short run, wages fluctuate around the value of labor power according to class struggle based on market forces. In the long run, wages change with the value of labor power, which (disregarding fluctuations in the value of commodities) is determined by class struggle based on broader political and social forces.[1]

The new wage policies adopted by auto manufacturers were clearly a response to the struggle of their workers. It became clear to them that the wages they were accustomed to paying were not sufficient to motivate workers with a willingness to work under the new conditions of production. Auto capitalists were demanding a new quality of labor power from workers—one that was stable, dependable, absolutely subservient to capitalist commands, and able to bear up under intensified, repetitious, monotonous, unceasing production. And workers revolted against these demands. Part of their power to do so was based upon the economic conditions of the labor market, as we have seen. But workers' power was also based on general social and political conditions. The leveling of the work force, the interdependence of the new production process, and the concentration and centralization of capital all helped to strengthen auto workers, not only in their particular economic struggles with their bosses, but also in the general political struggle with the bourgeois class. Due to this balance of power favorable to labor, auto workers were able through their struggle to force an increase in the value of their labor power, that is, to exact from capital an increased standard of living as the price of their willingness to labor in the transformed factories.[2]

Ford's Five Dollar Day

The first concession to struggling workers in relation to this increased standard of living came in a dramatic step by the leader in the transformation of auto work, the Ford Motor Company. Ford was in the forefront of technological change in the auto industry and thus experienced the greatest jolt of worker resistance to the new technology. The company was therefore forced to pioneer new social relations to motivate worker compliance with the new process of production. This balance of social forces combined with Henry

Ford's personal impulsiveness and flair for the dramatic to shake the industrial world on January 5, 1914 with the announcement of the Five Dollar Day.

Ford's monumental innovation of paying workers five dollars a day for their labor power was not, however, this company's first attempt to quell the revolt of workers by increasing their wages. As early as 1908, when the process of rationalization and mechanization was just getting under way, Ford began to increase the wages of factory workers through annual bonuses based on seniority. By paying workers a percentage of their annual earnings that increased with their years of employment, Ford attempted to encourage stability in its restless work force. In 1911, the basis of the bonus was changed from seniority to output, with payment going only to carefully selected employees who had shown themselves willing to bear the increased demands of Ford's production methods. In October of 1913, the first act of the new Employment Department was to reorganize completely the wage structure and give all workers an average wage increase of 13 percent. Although these piecemeal wage measures had some positive effects, they did not quell the rising tide of worker resistance expressed in high turnover and absenteeism. Something much more drastic and innovative was required.[3]

Although the exact details of the initial decision to pay Ford workers five dollars a day are unclear and disputed, the most reliable and carefully researched accounts agree on the basic facts. On January 4, 1914, Henry Ford presided at a meeting of a handful of top Ford executives called for the purpose of discussing wages for the new year. Ford had Charles Sorensen, his production superintendent, place on a blackboard projected cost figures, which showed that as production volume increased, costs fell, and profits rose. Thinking current wages too low in comparison with this steeply rising level of profits, Ford ordered Sorensen to transfer anticipated profits to the labor-cost column, raising daily wage rates progressively from the current average of $2.34 to a minimum of $3, $3.50, $4, then $4.50. James Couzens, a top Ford executive who was obviously hostile to these wage increases, challenged Ford to make the daily minimum wage $5. He immediately did so, and the next day the company shocked the industrial world with its public announcement of the fantastic wage.[4]

There is some uncertainty about Henry Ford's motives in instituting the wage plan. In order to sway public opinion, he often portrayed the Five Dollar Day as a humanitarian act or "a voluntary act of social justice." But most data clearly reveal that it was increased production and not justice that Ford was seeking with the new wage. In statements to news media made after the announcement, Ford contended that the plan "is efficiency engineering, too. We expect to get better work more efficient work as a result." A pamphlet explaining the Five Dollar Day to Ford workers stated: "The Ford Motor Company does not believe in giving without a fair return. So to acquire the right to participate in the profits [new wage] a man must be willing to pay in increased efficiency." And in answer to a question about the plan's motives, Henry Ford told the editor of the *Dearborn Independent* that he had "concluded that machinery was playing such an important part in production that if men could be induced to speed up machinery, there would be more profit at the high wage than at the low wage."[5]

Clearly then, what Ford managers were seeking with the Five Dollar Day was increased worker effort. And how they thought the plan would achieve this is revealed in subsequent statements by Henry Ford. When asked about the motives for the plan by the Congressional Commission on Industrial Relations in 1916, Ford answered:

> The knowledge that market rates of wages were not sufficient for men to properly care for self and dependents and that the environment in which its employees were thus made to live, gave rise to mental anxiety and a physical condition that made it utterly impossible for the human agency to deliver all of the effort that it was capable of in fulfilling the best and larger functions for which it was designed at work, at home, and in the community.[6]

Similarly, Ford told Samuel Marquis, who had once headed the department administering the plan, that five dollars a day

> is about the least a man with a family can live on these days . . . [and] maintain himself and his family under proper physical and moral conditions. . . . . By underpaying men we are bringing on a generation of children undernourished and underdeveloped morally as well as physically; we are breeding a generation of working men weak in body and in mind, and for that reason bound to prove inefficient when they come to take their places in the industry.[7]

Ford thus recognized that the standard of living of his workers was not sufficient to reproduce their labor power—not just physically, but also morally. Ford's old wages could not support a standard of living sufficient to induce workers to willingly meet the demands of the new technology, as the revolt of Ford workers revealed. Ford was forced to raise wages in order to motivate labor effort up to the potential of the new technology.

This motivation toward increasing worker effort by decreasing worker resistance can also be detected in the details and administration of the Five Dollar Day. Ford did not simply raise the daily minimum wage of all workers to five dollars when the plan went into effect on January 12, 1914. Workers had to meet certain strict requirements in order to be eligible for the "profit-sharing plan," as the new wage was called. Only the following groups were even considered for participation in the plan: married men who lived with and took good care of their families, single men over twenty-two of proven "thrifty habits," and men under twenty-two and women who were the sole supporters of dependents. These requirements were based ostensibly upon "need"; only those workers who needed the wage to support themselves and/or dependents were eligible for their "share of the profits." But their effect was also to restrict the higher wage to workers dependent upon it for their livelihood. This provided a check against turnover, since those dependent upon the higher wage would be much less likely to leave Ford than those for whom it merely constituted additional income above and beyond their basic livelihood. Another requirement for participation in the plan aimed at reducing problematic turnover and stabilizing the work force was a minimum six months' residence in Detroit. Clearly this selected and rewarded stable workers.[8]

But even if workers were, by these requirements, eligible for the plan, they were not paid the new wage until they were investigated by the Sociological Department and certified as "coming up to certain standards of cleanliness and citizenship." Ford stated that the five dollar wage served as "an incentive to better living. . . . a man who is living aright will do his work aright."[9] By thus making the new wage conditional upon a certain character and cultural style, both within and outside of the shop, the company sought to mold its workers to the requirements of the new production methods. This intention was brilliantly grasped by Italian communist Antonio Gramsci, who wrote of such programs of Ford and others:

> The new methods of work are inseparable from a specific mode of living and of thinking and feeling of life. One cannot have success in one field without tangible results in the other. In America rationalisation of work and prohibition are undoubtedly connected. The enquiries conducted by the industrialists into the workers' private lives and the inspection services created by some firms to control the "morality" of

their workers are necessities of the new methods of work. . . . The
American phenomenon . . . is *also* the biggest collective effort to date
to create, with unprecedented speed, and with a consciousness of
purpose unmatched in history, a new type of worker and of man.[10]

For Gramsci, Ford's high wage was "the instrument used to select
and maintain in stability a skilled labour force suited to the system
of production and work."[11]

The new rationalized and predictable technology required workers whose characters and culture were similarly rationalized and
predictable, in the style of the Anglo-Protestant middle and upper
classes of the United States. The nonworking lives of workers had to
be standardized to form a basis for their hours inside the factory. As
Ford stated, "a man who knows how to employ his free hours well
will know how to employ his working hours to best advantage."[12]
The new forces of production demanded, for example, a stable rationalization of sexual desires within the bounds of the monogamous family. As Gramsci noted, if a worker was happily married,
he would not "squander his nervous energies in the disorderly and
stimulating pursuit of occasional sexual satisfaction. . . . The exalta-
tion of passion cannot be reconciled with the timed movements of
productive motions connected with the most perfected automa-
tism."[13] Consumption in general also had to be disciplined and controlled so as not to lead to indulgences that would interfere with
work. Ford's five-dollar wage was the inducement for workers to
bring their characters and culture into line with the requirements of
the new technology.

In order to enforce this connection between culture and character
and the new wage, Ford formed the Sociological Department and
charged it with investigating workers' qualifications for the program. Under the initial direction of John R. Lee, the department began with thirty investigators, but it grew quickly to a peak of one
hundred and sixty employees around 1920. These investigators
made extensive, in-depth, and detailed reports of every aspect of a
worker's home life. In general, they looked for and sought to encourage the cultural traits of the Anglo-Protestant upper and middle
classes dominant in the U.S.: a stable nuclear family, a Ben Franklin
type of thrift, "American" standards and customs of consumption, industriousness, dependability, stability, and disciplined self-
denial. As indices of this desired cultural style, investigators gathered detailed information on a worker's marital status, dependents,
nationality, religion, citizenship, housing, savings, indebtedness,
life insurance policies, health, recreation, drinking and smoking

habits, home conditions, and neighborhood. On the basis of these investigations, workers were classified into three groups: those qualifying unconditionally, those qualifying conditionally, and those not qualifying. The conditional qualifiers were regularly investigated to ensure that they maintained their "Ford morality." Those originally disqualified were also subject to repeated probes, and if at the end of six months they had not attained the cultural standards, they were fired.[14]

The Five Dollar Day was thus used as a battering ram to break down the working-class and immigrant cultures of Ford workers and to inculcate them with the culture of the Anglo-Protestant upper and middle classes. The preindustrial culture of immigrant workers and the working-class culture of American craft workers were threats to industrial capitalism in America at a number of levels. At the level of production, both cultures imbued members with erratic work rhythms—they were used to bursts of frantic activity, punctuated by long lulls of inactivity. Such work habits were unacceptable in the new process of production, which demanded a steady, invariant level of effort. At the level of consumption, these cultures were characterized by communal and social styles, which were at odds with the private and individual fulfillment of needs through the market required by capitalism. At the level of politics, the immigrant and working-class cultures threatened to form the basis of a strong working-class political movement, challenging the political dominance of big capital and its allies. Ford's wage-induced cultural offensive aimed to break down resistance at these three interrelated levels, to make Ford employees not only good workers, but also good consumers and good citizens.[15]

Another way in which Ford managers intended the Five Dollar Day to quell worker resistance was by reestablishing normative ties between capital and labor within the shops. The growth of the auto factories had broken down the ties of intimacy based on face-to-face interactions between employer and employees. Patrimonial, normative control had of necessity begun to be replaced with the cold and rational control of bureaucratic rules. But if such normative ties could not be reestablished in the realm of work, Ford managers reasoned, perhaps they could be reconstructed by a paternalistic concern of management for the leisure and home life of workers. As one trade journalist wrote in reference to Ford's Sociological Department:

> Years ago, when industries were small, there was a close contact between the employer and employee. The employer knew nearly every

one of his men more or less intimately and knew of his requirements. There was more of a personal element in the connection than now, when industries have grown to large proportions and it is impossible, perhaps futile, for an employer to come in personal contact with such great numbers—30,000 to 50,000 individuals. For this reason it was advisable to organize at the Ford plant a special department whose function it is to keep in personal relations with the employees.[16]

If paternalistic policies could create an image of the company as a benevolent father, who personally looked after the individual needs of all in the Ford family, perhaps the real lines of class division could be blurred and workers would cease their revolt.

Whatever the original motives behind Ford's Five Dollar Day, the results of the plan accounted for its survival and general dissemination in the American auto industry. And these results were beyond the expectations of the Ford managers themselves. First, the plan drastically reduced both turnover and absenteeism. In 1914, the profit-sharing plan's first year of operation, the annual rate of labor turnover was cut from 370 to 54 percent. In 1915, the rate dropped to 16 percent. Thus, in two years of operation, the plan reduced turnover more than 90 percent, and the vast majority of this reduction came in the form of reduced quits. A similar reduction was achieved in absenteeism. Daily absentee rates were reduced from 10.5 to 0.4 percent in the first year. Ford managers attributed these reductions in turnover and absenteeism directly to the Five Dollar Day, which obviously had worked to halt the "revolt of the feet" and stabilize the Ford work force.[17]

The second great effect of the Five Dollar Day was increased worker morale, resulting from renewed normative ties between labor and capital. Their increased standard of living produced in workers an identification with the company and consequently a greater willingness to work, even under conditions of increased labor intensity and capitalist domination. Ford historians Allan Nevins and Frank Hill wrote that the plan created a cooperative attitude among workers. "For the first time since the early days of Model T, Ford workers felt a sense of personal identification with a great hopeful enterprise, managed in their interest as well as that of the owners. A spirit of comradeship spread throughout the factory."[18] Not all Ford workers were pleased with the plan. There is evidence that many resented the investigations of their personal lives as violations of their personal liberties. But the majority seemed willing to put up with this nuisance in order to earn the high wage. On balance, the general effect of the plan on workers' attitudes was strongly positive.

Third, Ford's "incentive to better living" did indeed seem to have an effect upon the character and culture of workers, both within and outside of the shops. Under the mildly coercive hand of the Sociological Department, Ford workers were cajoled into a thrifty, frugal, and stable style of life. As indicators of this change, Ford compiled statistics showing that during the first year of the plan's operation, home ownership increased 85 percent; life insurance policy holders, 124 percent; workers with bank accounts, 49 percent; and married employees, 30 percent. In the same period, the total savings of Ford workers increased over 200 percent. The keepers of Detroit's moral order praised the positive effects of the Five Dollar Day on workers' standards of conduct. Judges, police officers, and clergymen all hailed the decline of intoxication, gambling, and crime among Ford workers.[19] Within the shops, the high wage was found to reduce the natural resistance of workers to labor-cost reduction measures. Engineering journalists Arnold and Faurote noted:

> These pay conditions make the workmen absolutely docile. New regulations, important or trivial, are made almost daily; workmen are studied individually and changed from place to place with no cause assigned, as the bosses see fit, and not one word of protest is ever spoken, because every man knows the door to the street stands open for any man who objects in any way, shape or manner to instant and unquestioning obedience to any directions whatever.[20]

This docility of Ford workers was not, however, due solely to the internal character constraints that Ford selected and cultivated in workers. It was also the result of the external constraint of the huge industrial reserve army that the Five Dollar Day brought literally stampeding to the Ford factory from all over the United States. The morning of January 6, the day after the announcement of the plan, ten thousand job-seekers crowded around the gates of Ford's Highland Park plant in hopes of being hired at the incredible wage. Despite signs declaring "No Hiring," crowds continued to form, until on January 12 a riot broke out among frustrated workers.[21] Such disorderliness outside the factory served as a powerful incentive for orderliness within. The new wage created a great surplus of labor power in Detroit, and Ford workers knew that if they hesitated to obey their boses' commands or submit to their mechanical masters, they could quickly be replaced by one of the thousands of unemployed workers clamoring at the gates. The Five Dollar Day generated a massive industrial reserve army, which was used to enforce absolute obedience within the shops.[22]

All of these effects of Ford's wage plan—reduced turnover and absenteeism, improved morale and normative bonds, changes in character and culture, increased industrial reserve army—combined to produce the result most gratifying to Ford management, a tremendous increase in worker output. With Ford workers laboring more willingly and stably, with resistance to the capitalist domination of the labor process greatly reduced in both its direct and indirect forms, the great productive potential of the new technology was unleashed. John R. Lee, first head of the Sociological Department, estimated that after only seven weeks of operation the plan had increased production 25 percent. Ford himself estimated that the plan alone was responsible for a 15 to 20 percent increase in production, despite a cutback in working hours. The company released detailed statistics purporting to show the effects of the Five Dollar Day on worker effort in its first year of operation. These revealed that worker-hour output in the motor department had increased 32 percent; in cylinder timing, 67 percent; radiator core assembly, 107 percent; fender, 48 percent; paint shop, 77 percent; gasoline tanks, 87 percent. As a Bureau of Labor Statistics investigator reported, "foremen and heads of departments . . . insist on the correctness of the claim that the large increases in production . . . while made possible by constant improvement in methods and machinery, were due very largely to the increases in wages. . . ."[23]

These increases in worker output do not seem to have immediately compensated for the cost of Ford's wage increase, for unit labor costs rose 35 percent during 1914. But the wage plan purchased an asset whose value would be fully realized only over a longer period of time—the submission of workers to capitalist control over the production process. Once secured, this submission allowed Ford to increase the intensity and productivity of labor without encountering resistance. Perhaps it was this fact that led Ford to conclude some years later that "the payment of five dollars a day for an eight-hour day was one of the finest cost-cutting moves we ever made. . . ."[24]

Dissemination of Fordist Wage Measures

Ford's Five Dollar Day blazed a path that many other auto manufacturers followed with varying degrees of closeness. As they adopted the new technology and encountered worker resistance, they followed Ford's lead in adopting new wage measures to quell the class revolt. The industry was quick to assimilate the lessons of Ford's innovative wage plan. Numerous articles on it appeared in the trade journals and business press, in which journalists laid bare the logic behind the plan. Wages had to be calculated, the argument went, to pay workers "as little as is consistent with the obtaining of maximum service."[25] Raising wages above the average level raised worker effort by increasing morale, loyalty, and docility, and decreasing turnover and absenteeism. Thus, in the long run, high wages might be the cheapest, actually lowering unit labor costs.

Because of the lag in adopting Fordist production methods, most of the other large auto firms did not feel compelled to adopt new wage plans until around 1918. By this time, their advancing production methods had combined with war and postwar labor shortages to greatly increase the resistance of their workers. General Motors moved in 1918 to deal with this problem, taking Ford as its conscious model. As Alfred Sloan, who would later become GM's president, recalled: "Ford's announcement of a minimum wage of five dollars a day in 1914 had attracted men from all parts of the continent. Turnover in the Ford plant was cut down almost to the vanishing point. But at Flint, too, there was every desire to keep men, to stabilize the industry, to capitalize the boom."[26] This desire led to the introduction of GM's Bonus Plan, which provided annual awards of company stock to employees who "contributed to the success and prosperity of the Corporation in some special degree by their ability, industry, and loyalty." To further quiet labor unrest and create normative bonds between labor and capital, in 1919 GM established its Employees' Savings and Investment Plan, which gave "employees an opportunity of sharing in the development of the business." Workers with at least three months' employment with GM were allowed to make deposits in an interest-bearing savings account. The company matched their savings with investments in GM stock held in the employees' names. The plan not only created worker identification with the firm through partial "ownership." It also established incentives for worker stability—only those with sufficient seniority could participate, and the amount of a worker's investment fund that could be withdrawn upon quitting increased proportionally with seniority. Thus, in assessing these GM compensation plans, historian Sidney Fine wrote that GM was "undoubtedly motivated by an understandable desire to link its employees more closely with their employer and thus, hopefully, to lessen the possible appeal of outside unionism to its workers at a time when labor organizing was on the upswing and to reduce labor turnover in its burgeoning work force and in such boom towns as Flint."[27]

Not far behind General Motors in instituting a new compensation plan was Willys-Overland, another of the top auto producers in this period. In January 1919, the company introduced a profit-sharing plan whose aim it was "to create among the men the feeling that they are working with the company instead of for it." As one trade journalist wrote in explanation of the plan, the rise of large factories had undermined personal contact as a basis for an identification between employee and employer. So John Willys sought to recreate this ideological identification through a monetary "community of interest." "He is making it as much of interest to the laborer in his plant to have the Willys-Overland Company show a large profit as it is to the capital element in the concern."[28] In addition, the profit-sharing plan also sought to decrease labor turnover, for participation was permitted only after six months' continuous employment, and a worker's share in the "profits" increased with each month's employment in excess of one year.

Studebaker Corporation was facing problems similar to those of all the large automobile producers in the period, and it moved to deal with them in similar ways. As early as March 1917, the corporation established an annual wage dividend for workers based upon years of continuous employment. And in January 1919, because of increasing labor problems, Studebaker increased the wage-dividend rates and added a stock-purchase plan to increase employee compensation. Clearly stating the conditions and purposes of these plans, the president of Studebaker wrote:

> Continuous service is necessary to entitle employees to payments under the plans. . . . Obviously, therefore, only steady, true, and capable employees receive payments under the plans, which indeed are the reward of merit rightly earned. Experienced, loyal employees do more and better work and are worth more than the prevailing wage rate which floaters also receive. Lower labor turnover, lower costs, and better products for the corporation and its customers result from the co-operative plans and the management naturally strives continually to minimize the turnover. . . .[29]

These wage and compensation policies seem to have been fairly widespread in the automobile industry during this period. William Chalmers concluded from numerous interviews with Detroit auto executives during the late 1920s that there existed a general and conscious policy throughout the industry of paying high wages in order to win the cooperation and acquiescence of workers and thereby lower labor costs. The result of this policy was an industry wage structure that compared quite favorably with other American industries. In 1914, the year Ford introduced the Five Dollar Day, the auto industry ranked seventh in average yearly wages paid to employees. By 1919, it had moved to fifth, and in 1925 it ranked first. Automotive manufacturing remained one of the best paying industries even during the Great Depression, ranking second in 1931, and first again in 1935. A study by a Bureau of Labor Statistics researcher confirmed that the capitalist motives behind this high-wage policy were not even remotely philanthropic. From interviews with managers of firms instituting profit-sharing plans, Boris Emmet concluded that their principal motives were:

(1) to stimulate the elimination of waste and to foster economy,
(2) to increase efficiency,
(3) to stabilize the working force, and
(4) to improve relations between management and its employees.[30]

The actual effectiveness of these wage and compensation plans in realizing these goals is difficult to assess with any certainty because of the lack of reliable before-and-after data. But auto manufacturers generally believed that the plans were effective in reducing turnover and absenteeism and improving labor output. And one participant-observer in the auto shops of this period concluded that the wage and compensation policies did have the intended effects of developing in auto workers feelings of gratitude and appreciation toward their employers and consequently stimulating greater effort on their part. At any rate, it is undoubtedly true that these wage policies in no way hurt industry profitability. The intensity and productivity of labor rose much faster than wages, so unit labor costs declined and profits rose. In all probability, wage plans helped to achieve these results by winning the compliance of workers to the intensified and degraded labor of the new technology.[31]

Changing Forms of Wage Payment

The form as well as the general level of wages in the industry was determined by class struggle and by capitalist efforts to overcome it. In the early auto shops with craft production, the straight-time rate was practically the only form of wage. Workers were paid a set rate for each day or hour worked, regardless of their output during that period. This wage form was the result of a labor process that gave workers considerable power. Due to the variable and uncertain nature of work in these craft shops, it was impossible for capitalists to set exact output standards and tie wages to them. They were forced to pay wages on a time basis.[32]

The increasing rationalization and mechanization of auto work undermined the technical and social basis of the straight-time wage. Uniform time wages hindered the efforts of auto manufacturers to raise worker effort to the potential of the new technology, for they provided no incentives for increased worker output. Thus, the labor editor of *Automotive Industries* noted the tendency for the "uniformity of wages to lead into a uniformity of output below the possible average of a proportion of the men, in other words, the tendency for a uniform wage to bring about a minimum output suited to the average of the less efficient."[33] Straight-time wages also united all workers in a collective resistance to capitalist speed-up and in a collective push for higher wages, because the only way workers could raise their wages was to unite to increase the time rate of their group. As industrial efficiency expert Henry L. Gantt wrote: "The horizontal wage system, under which men on certain work get a certain wage and under which it is practically impossible for any individual to get much more than the average wage of the group, has its effect in causing the workmen to combine to get the average wage increased."[34]

In order to break the united resistance of workers and to realize the productive potential of the new technology, auto capitalists needed a new wage form based on the output of the individual worker. And fortunately for them, the same technology that created this problem gave capitalists the power to solve it. The rationalization and mechanization of work eliminated its uncertainty and allowed capitalists to calculate precisely the minimum time necessary to accomplish the standardized tasks. They could then force workers to adhere to these standards by directly linking their wages to output. Auto capitalists began to replace straight-time wages with these incentive wages in the mid-1910s, as the new technology began to break the control of skilled workers over the work pace. And incentive wages became increasingly popular with manufacturers throughout the 1920s.

The most widely used form of incentive wage in the early period was individual piecework. Under this simple system, individual workers were paid a standard price for each piece of work they produced. Piece prices or rates were set by the time-study department at a level that forced workers to labor at what it determined to be maximum intensity in order to earn a normal wage. Individual piecework forced workers to speed up by breaking their united front of resistance. As a former Packard worker noted, "piecework tends to encourage going it alone in a sort of individual entrepreneurship. . . . the result was little or no sense of mutual interest or support."[35]

Piecework systems, however, had the disadvantage to capital of having a constant labor cost per piece, as long as piece rates remained the same. In order to secure lower unit labor costs as output increased, auto capitalists had to resort to rate cutting. They allowed the piecework earnings of workers to rise only to a certain limit, beyond which they cut back the rates, thus forcing workers to labor harder to earn the same overall wages. But as we saw in chapter 8, rate cutting often motivated collective efforts by workers to restrict output and thus maintain their piece rates at a level at which they could earn a decent wage without working too intensively. Ironically, then, the piecework systems introduced to overcome collective restriction of output often ended up increasing it.[36]

In order to overcome these problems, auto manufacturers increasingly replaced individual piecework with individual bonus systems during the 1920s. For each job in the shop, the time-study department set a production quota and an hourly base-pay rate. For each percentage point of output above the quota, workers received a varying percentage of their base-pay as a bonus. The advantages for employers of such individual bonuses over individual piecework were twofold. First, the methods of determining bonuses were often so complicated that workers were unable to calculate exactly what their wages should be. As a result, wage cutting could be carried out without arousing the united opposition of workers. As one critic of the industry noted, "it is always safer for an employer to dip a little off a complicated bonus than to reduce straight time or piece rates."[37] Second, some bonus systems reduced the labor cost per unit as output increased. Under these differential premium systems, as they were known, a worker's overall earnings increased as his or her output rose, but the pay rate per unit of output decreased. These systems thus allowed employers to cut unit labor costs without resorting to rate cutting, which often aroused the united resistance of workers.

These individual piecework and bonus plans seem to have been initially successful in overcoming worker resistance and raising worker output to the potential of the new technology. In 1926, *Automotive Industries* reported that worker-hour output in the industry had increased over 200 percent in the last ten years and concluded that "the readiness of automotive manufacturers to investigate and adopt incentive methods of wage payment has been one of the major factors in bringing about this increase in efficiency."[38] But as the automobile industry grew and changed throughout the 1920s, incentive wages pegged to individual output became outmoded. The new technology made output dependent on the efforts of a group of interdependent workers laboring cooperatively under the compulsion of pace-setting machines. Thus, it made little sense to pay workers incentive wages designed to stimulate individual efforts. Incentive wages were increasingly put on a group rather than individual basis.

Group incentive wages were introduced in the auto industry in 1918, but they did not become widespread until 1922 or 1923. The first plans were simple group piecework. A group of cooperating workers was paid a set price for each piece they produced, and the sum was differentially divided among them. However, group bonus systems became increasingly popular with manufacturers throughout the 1920s. Each worker was paid his or her base rate plus a share of the group's bonus earnings proportional to the rate. By 1928, a Bureau of Labor Statistics survey of ninety-four auto establishments found that of the forty-two with bonus systems, twenty were on a group basis.[39]

Apart from being better adapted to the increasingly socialized process of production, these group incentive wage plans had two additional advantages over individual incentive systems that accounted for their popularity among auto manufacturers. First, they greatly reduced the costs of administration, for records had to be kept only for large groups of workers instead of for each individual. Second, and perhaps decisively, group incentive wages shattered the solidarity of workers and caused them to speed up each other. Because the wage of each individual worker depended upon the output of the group, slower workers were resented, for they lowered the wages of all workers in their group. In order to speed up slower producers, group members cursed, cajoled, and intimidated them. Auto capitalists were well aware of and took great delight in the worker dissension created by group incentives. A manager at Packard wrote that under the new group bonus system "where there were shirkers in a department the men themselves have either compelled them to work or get out."[40] Reporting on the results of a group bonus system at Hudson, a journalist wrote in the *Wall Street Journal* that

> when the individuals in a group fall behind in their work, all of the others begin to 'holler,' for they know their pay is affected. The erring member of a group gets the 'spotlight' in this case, and if he does not correct his ways quickly he is soon forced out by the 'public opin-

ion' of his fellows . . . or if it is found that fewer men can produce
the objective the gang quickly insists that the surplus manpower be
laid off.[41]

Despite their popularity among auto capitalists, incentive wages
began to be replaced by straight-time rates in the early 1930s in an
attempt to quiet the incipient worker revolt. Auto workers disliked
incentive wages because of the pressure for production they exerted
and their mystifying complexity. They especially hated group incentives because of the dissension they caused. During the early 1930s,
unions were making strong inroads into the auto industry on the basis of these and many other grievances. Thus, for the purpose of
"avoiding all such friction and argument with its workers" and
eliminating "potential nuclei of major troubles," auto manufacturers
switched to straight-time wages. Oldsmobile was the first company
to switch, apart from Ford, which had maintained time rates from
the beginning. The rest of the automobile manufacturers generally
followed in quick succession in 1934. The parts producers, however,
lagged behind, maintaining their usual payment by piecework much
longer. As late at 1950, about half of the workers in the parts and
truck divisions of the industry were still on incentive wages.[42]

Like the level of wages, then, their form was determined by class
struggle in the shops and capitalist attempts to overcome it. The de-
bilitation of skilled workers by the new technology allowed manufacturers to introduce incentive wages, which broke the united front
of worker resistance by stimulating individual efforts. Group incentives were particularly effective in pitting workers against each other
and raising the intensity of labor. However, when auto workers
began to organize to oppose such repressive wage systems and
other aspects of auto work, the goal of overcoming worker resistance dictated a shift back to time wages in order to deflate discontent and the organizing drive that it fed.

WELFARE WORK

Wages were not the only incentive that auto capitalists manipulated
with their new bureaucratic power to overcome the rising tide of
worker resistance. They also devised programs of nonwage incentives called welfare work. Industrial welfare work first emerged in
the late nineteenth century in America's rapidly growing industries,

in which labor unrest forced owners to grant new benefits in order to regain control over workers. As the auto industry expanded and mechanized, it faced the same problem and adopted similar welfare programs as a solution.

The general aim of all such welfare schemes was to overcome labor's resistance to capital by creating a sense of loyalty and identification between the two classes. To accomplish this, capital instituted various programs to improve the "welfare" of workers. But like the wage carrot, these welfare incentives had a mass of strings attached that bound workers to the needs of capital. Most welfare benefits were conditional upon workers' adaptation to the demands of the new technology, both within and outside of the factory.

Welfare programs had been present in the American automobile industry almost from the beginning. But their purpose shifted in conjunction with the social relations within the labor process. In the early craft shops, welfare work was meant to stimulate the individual effort and initiative of skilled workers in order to improve the quality and quantity of production. As the tiny auto firms expanded in the early 1910s, capitalists found their normative, patrimonial control over workers slipping, but the power of skilled workers prevented them from exerting greater central authority. Auto manufacturers responded to this crisis in authority by introducing welfare programs, which sought to renew the normative identification of labor and capital.

In the years around the First World War, however, welfare work underwent a qualitative change. These programs were invested with a greater sense of urgency, because the new technology of production combined with labor shortages to arouse the resistance of workers in the shops. If welfare work had once been a nice way to bring labor back a little closer to capital, now it began to be viewed as a way to curb the mounting resistance of workers. Furthermore, the type of worker behavior these industrial betterment policies sought to cultivate changed. They no longer aimed to stimulate the individual worker to increase the quality and quantity of production, for both were increasingly guaranteed by the technology itself. Rather, welfare work sought to cultivate worker acquiescence to the demands of the new labor process. Using a varying mix of incentives and coercion, these programs induced and cajoled workers to alter both their work and their leisure lives to conform to the stable, dependable, submissive model required by the new production methods.

Welfare Work to Influence Work Habits

Many industrial betterment programs cultivated specific work habits desired by capital through direct rewards. Because labor turnover was a major form of early worker struggle and a threat to the new technology, auto capitalists sought through welfare programs to encourage employee stability by making benefits conditional upon it. Life insurance, for example, was introduced by auto capitalists with "the idea that it would contribute to the stability of the working force," as a Bureau of Labor Statistics study concluded.[43] Most group insurance plans had a minimum service requirement for eligibility and policy benefits that increased with years of service. For example, Packard insured its workers at the date of employment for $1,250; after six months' employment, for $1,500; after one year, for $1,600; and increasing $100 each year, until after twenty years' service, the maximum of $3,500 was reached. Packard managers considered their insurance plan an important factor in stabilizing the work force, as did most auto managers with similar plans.

The pension and vacation plans introduced as part of the welfare package of many auto firms were similarly pegged to service and attendance requirements in order to stabilize the work force. As Boyd Fisher of Fisher Body Works explicitly stated, "it is advisable to tie the vacation plan up with the measures to reduce absenteeism by making the length of the vacation with pay vary with the number of weeks of satisfactory attendance." Most auto firms also required a minimum employment period before vacations were awarded, and increased their length with years of employment. Pension plans for workers were also introduced with the aim of reducing turnover. Although pensions did not become widespread in the industry until after unionization, several auto firms introduced them early on as "encouragement for remaining in the service of the company for a long period of years. . . ."[44]

As part of their welfare work to stabilize the work force, many automotive firms established programs to encourage workers to buy houses, under the assumption that home ownership entailed obligations that discouraged turnover. One trade journalist thus wrote that "from the standpoint of stability, ownership of homes and other community obligations of a definite stabilized character are of more importance than the ownership of stock in a concern."[45] A few of the larger auto firms—Ford, GM, Studebaker—experimented briefly with company-constructed housing. But most firms merely encouraged and assisted home ownership. Ford, for example, assisted its workers with legal aid and financing. The Reo Motor Company encouraged home ownership by establishing a real estate exchange department, providing free legal services, and offering loans to finance purchases. These company-assisted finance plans obligated workers to remain with the company in order to keep their homes. Evidence that such housing schemes were actually effective is offered by Chalmers, who found that GM's program created among workers not only good will and cooperativeness, but also a reluctance to leave the company because "the workers dislike to leave an established home and equity."[46]

Financial aid and services of a general sort were also part of the welfare packages designed specifically to reward stable and dependable work habits in auto workers. A Ford plan of making loans to workers on the basis of future wages was thought to bind workers to the company. Managers stated that those borrowing under this plan were from the "shifting class of labor. . . . It is, therefore, reasonable to expect that this plan in operation will exercise some hold upon them. . . . if it results in creating a habit of steady employment and continuous service, it may also develop other traits that naturally associate with steadiness in any direction."[47] Auto capitalists also intended financial aid to increase labor output by relieving workers of financial worry. Editorializing about a loan plan in operation at Cadillac, *The Automobile* stated: "Financial worries in the mind of the worker are much like a wrench in the gears of a machine. Destruction of a productive ability, discord, costly mischief are the results. . . . The plan . . . develops a loyalty toward the company, frees the workers from hounding creditors and leaves them at liberty to think about their work."[48]

While some welfare programs directly rewarded work habits like stability, high output, and cooperativeness, others sought to encourage such habits indirectly in workers by creating an identification between labor and capital. The structures of work and authority in the transformed factories had eroded the paternalistic ties between workers and employers characteristic of small shops, replacing them with the calculated connections of cash and command. In order to overcome the resulting hostility between the increasingly estranged classes, auto capitalists sought to reestablish this loyalty on a larger scale, to create "a patriotism for the industrial establishment akin to the patriotism for home town or for country," as *Automotive Industries* put it.[49] Welfare work was the vehicle for the new paternalism for, as one trade journalist observed, it was "based on the principle that men who receive benefits are certain to feel gratitude.

. . ."[50] Capitalists hoped that even though many of the worker benefits they introduced were not specifically conditional upon new habits, they would create worker loyalty and gratitude that would ultimately result in more stability, better production, and less worker resistance.

This rationale seems to have motivated programs to improve working conditions, which were considered part of welfare work. Capitalists viewed improvements in the immediate working environment as a way to alleviate aggravating conditions and cultivate employee gratitude. Thus, beginning around 1915, auto manufacturers began to make their factories more pleasant places to work. Improvements were made in ventilation, light, the cleanliness of general surroundings, and temperature control. Safety work was launched on a large scale. Machines were equipped with safety stops and belt and chain guards; aisles were widened to avoid worker contact with machines; safety glasses and other apparel were required; warning signs were placed in dangerous areas; classes were formed to instruct workers in safe working methods. Medical facilities—generally emergency rooms staffed by nurses or doctors—were also added to automotive factories. And many manufacturers sought to improve general factory facilities for workers by providing them with washrooms, showers, lockers, drinking fountains, and lunchrooms. These improvements were thought to make workers more content, allow more efficient work, and induce them to stay put.[51]

The attempt to create an ideological identification between labor and capital also led to company sponsorship of recreational and social activities. Bringing together workers under company auspices to participate in common activities provided "the means of welding together more closely employee and employer," reported an *Automotive Industries* study of welfare work at Reo. Competitive athletics were particularly useful in creating this company *esprit de corps*. As a trade journalist reported of one company's program, "these athletic games, where the Fisk teams meet other aggregations and carry out big athletic events at Fisk Park, create a spirit of enthusiasm such as is felt by a member of the New York A.C. or a college man for the success of the enterprise with which he is connected. Enthusiasm means better results for the worker and for the organization."[52] After interviewing a number of General Motors workers about such activities, sponsored by GM's Industrial Mutual Association, Chalmers similarly concluded that they "were showing an attitude of acceptance to their jobs as a result of these I.M.A. activities through a response of preferring that to other jobs." For these reasons, such recreational and social activities were sponsored by most of the larger auto firms. As early as 1917, a Bureau of Labor Statistics study of welfare work reported that five of the nine auto firms surveyed had social gatherings, recreational facilities, or outings for workers. A similar survey in 1926 found that thirteen of the fourteen auto firms included had social gatherings of some sort, and nearly all had recreational activities also.[53]

Employee magazines and papers similarly sought "to bind workers close to the corporation, to make it the center of their interest and devotion."[54] Managers sometimes used this forum to "sell" the company and preach to workers about the necessity of hard work and self-denial. But the main purpose of these publications was to persuade workers to identify themselves as employees of the firm, on and off the job. They mainly contained trivialities about employees and their families, reports of employee group activities, company news, gossip, and humor. Discussion of issues divisive of labor and capital—wages, working conditions, politics, and economics—seldom found its way into employee magazines and papers. As one critic aptly concluded, their

> aim is to divert rather than to misrepresent. The cheapness of the magazines' literary aims and achievements, the cult of slang, the driveling sentimentality of the "human interest stories," the volume of utterly trivial anecdotes and practical jokes, are all meant to stabilize the working force, because they tend to choke off whatever critical and rebellious faculties are faintly stirring in the American worker.[55]

Employee representation plans, or company unions, were a part of welfare work also aimed at blurring class lines ideologically by creating worker identification with the company. Management sought to make workers feel that they participated in managing the firm by allowing them representation on a works council, which met at regular intervals with management to discuss the general conditions of employment and specific grievances of workers. Capitalists hoped that by allowing workers to participate in decisions affecting their conditions of employment, these works councils would provide for large-scale industry "a substitution for immediate personal contact between worker and employer which existed in the days of small establishments."[56] As with other aspects of welfare work, the great impetus for the establishment of works councils was the general labor unrest during the First World War. As Harry Tipper wrote in *Automotive Industries*: "In all cases these organizations had for their object the reduction of 'turnover,' the settlement of individual grievances, the increased co-operation between employees and employer, and the elimination or reduction of strikes." Works councils sought to accomplish these results by undermining the growing class solidarity of workers, replacing it with a solidarity between labor and capital on a company basis. Auto capitalists realized that, as a result of changes in the labor process, the worker's "interests have been separated from his industrial unit and absorbed by his occupational organization. His class consciousness had been aroused. . . ."[57] Faced with the threat of class-conscious unionism, employers sought to tie workers back to the company with works councils. As Tipper wrote:

> The manufacturer must decide whether he will bargain collectively, inside his own organization with his own workers, or whether he will bargain collectively with the outside organized labor body. He must decide whether he will fight for control against the constantly increasing political power of organized labor and the constant tendency toward more radical demands, or whether he will gather together with his own workers in a group unified in purpose so that it can fight for its own place in the industrial world.[58]

Many auto manufacturers found these works councils successful in creating a better spirit and greater confidence between workers and employers.

Welfare Work to Mold Leisure and Consumption

The efforts of automotive managers and capitalists to mold a new loyal, compliant, and dependable worker with welfare work did not end, however, at the factory gates. Manufacturers sought not only to influence the work habits of their employees, but also to mold their habits of leisure and consumption. The ultimate aim was the same—overcoming worker resistance and raising the output of labor to the potential of the new technology. But auto capitalists realized that their workers' leisure and consumption habits had an important influence upon their work performance.

> A man who works 10 hours a day for 10 years spends 4 years working, 3 years sleeping and 3 years eating and in recreation. The 4 years of work and the 3 years of recreation and eating are equally important to the company that employs this man. The remainder of his life is spent in sleep which automatically takes care of many of his bodily ills, but to make the 4 years of work as productive and effective as

possible, the 3 years of recreation and eating should receive the attention of the employer and it is around this idea that the industrial betterment movement of recent years is centered.[59]

Employers used welfare work as a tool to mold their workers' leisure life to make it support an efficient and stable working life.

The most extensive program of leisure-molding welfare work in the automobile industry was established by the Ford Motor Company. Much of Ford's prying into workers' home lives was directly tied to the Five Dollar Day wage program, as we have examined. The higher wage served as a pretext for Ford's cultural offensive against immigrant and working-class cultures, which contradicted the productive, political, and consumption requirements of industrial capitalism. But other aspects of this welfare work were independent of the new wage. The most important of these was the Ford English School or, as it was also known, the Melting Pot School. When Ford launched this program in May 1914, its ostensible purpose was to teach Ford's large number of immigrant workers English. And given the difficulties on the shop floor that could and did result from the great diversity of languages spoken by Ford workers, this concern was probably genuine. All non-English-speaking workers were required to attend the thirty-six-week course of morning and afternoon classes, which employed the Berlitz method of language instruction. However, from the beginning, language instruction was intertwined with attempts to "Americanize" immigrant workers—that is, to destroy threatening immigrant cultures and assert the cultural hegemony of the dominant Anglo-Protestant middle and upper classes. The language lessons were divided into three series, teaching different aspects of "American ways and customs." The industrial series taught specific work habits. The domestic series inculcated workers with norms of middle-class family life and leisure. And the commercial series sought to wean immigrants from ethnic merchants and standards and make them consumers of American goods from American merchants. So in the process of teaching English, Ford managers forced upon immigrant workers a culture that not only met the needs of employers for stable workers and consumers, but also smothered tendencies toward class conflict under a blanket of national or cultural chauvinism.[60]

Ford was not alone among auto manufacturers, however, in including a cultural offensive in his welfare programs. Many others similarly sought to shape the leisure and consumption of their workers. Indeed, Boyd Fisher, himself an auto capitalist and vice-president of the Detroit Executives' Club, reported in 1917 that with respect to Ford's "extension of factory influence into the whole life of the worker":

> All Detroit plants are beginning to follow him in this, and I honestly believe that they are profiting by his experience. . . . They recognize that turnover of labor is a special phase of the problem of inefficient labor and that the reduction of turnover is only the first step in a process of education and of economic pressure to elevate the standards of workmen. They aim not only to keep workmen, but to develop them. And they are prepared to go as far, even, as the workmen's home-life to solve their problem.[61]

After Ford, the Reo Motor Car Company had one of the most extensive and direct programs of Americanization. Before being put on the payroll, an alien had to "assure the management that he wants to become an American citizen, adopt American habits of living, and obey the laws of the land." If there were indications that an employee had breached this promise, the Reo Welfare Department sent an investigator to check upon his home life and, if necessary, instruct his family in American ways. Other automobile companies incorporated efforts to influence workers' leisure life into welfare programs that also molded work habits. They sought to cultivate wholesome social and recreational activities, not only to create ties of loyalty to the company, but also to bring workers back to the factory the next morning on time and refreshed for another day's monotonous grind. Savings and investment plans were intended not only to provide economic incentives for long service and stability, but also to "inculcate in their employees habits of economy and thrift."[62] The encouragement of home ownership was intended to cultivate in workers individualistic and privatistic habits of consumption, as well as to stabilize them geographically.

The connection between welfare work to mold workers' lives outside the factory and their productive efforts within the factory is illustrated by manufacturers' efforts to motivate immigrant workers with incentive wages. Many foreign-born workers were wholly unresponsive to economic incentives for greater production, "which seemingly should affect their selfish natures, but apparently do not, beyond a given point."[63] Many immigrants and natives alike were accustomed to a standard of living lower than their wages allowed. Thus, they felt no need to work harder to secure higher wages, when their base wages ensured a standard of living that was quite comfortable by their standards. To motivate workers to respond to the economic incentives offered for higher production, auto manufacturers had to cajole them into adopting a higher "American" standard of living. They could then be induced by incentive wages to work harder in order to earn sufficient wages to support this new standard.

That the capitalist motives behind Americanization programs were mainly economic and had little to do with philanthropy is revealed by an editorial in *Automotive Industries*.

> It is purely commercial, purely a production building undertaking. . . . Looking at Americanization in this coldly practical way, it can be said that it has been found to be a good, and in many cases a necessary, investment. Workers, to be good workers, to be the kind of workers that make for maximum production, must have the American point of view. They must have American ideals and ambitions. They must first of all speak and read our language. They must like our country well enough to become citizens of it. They must feel that their home is here and that this is the land in which they will experience the realization of their highest hopes.[64]

The overall effects of welfare work, whether aimed at cultivating work habits or inculcating modes of leisure and consumption, were somewhat ambiguous. On the one hand, these programs created more discontent than appreciation among some auto workers. The most common worker complaint was that, although formally voluntary, participation in welfare programs was in fact compulsory. Pressure by managers as well as the benefits tied to these programs forced workers into participating in them as a virtual condition of employment. Workers also objected to welfare work as an unnecessary outlay of money that would be better spent in the form of direct wage increases. Other common complaints focused upon the blatant paternalism of the programs and the exclusion of workers from participation in their administration.[65]

On balance, however, welfare plans seem to have been well-received by most workers, and they seem to have been somewhat successful in achieving their goals of increased cooperation and identification with the company, greater stability in the work force, and improved efficiency. At least auto capitalists and managers were pleased with the results of their efforts in this area. A typical assessment of welfare work was made by the president of Studebaker: "These expenses have decreased labor turnover, heightened loyalty and efficiency of labor, decreased men-hours per car produced and improved the quality of cars. These combined savings have undoubtedly offset the expense."[66] The Bureau of Labor Statistics summed up the opinions of the managers it interviewed by stating that welfare work generally reduced labor turnover, improved the stability of the work force, reduced time lost from work, lowered the accident rate, and was conducive to a better feeling on the part of the working force. These results were reportedly achieved with a relatively small overall expense in most firms.[67]

Both the wage plans and welfare work introduced by auto manufacturers were temporarily successful in repressing the resistance of workers and getting them to adjust to the requirements of the new technology. By cajoling workers into adopting more stable and predictable work habits, Americanizing and rationalizing their leisure lives, and identifying more closely with capital masquerading in paternal costume, these programs quieted the workers' revolt of the feet and more collective dissent. Workers complied more willingly with the demands of the intensified labor process, allowing capital to more fully realize its productive potential.

This is not to say, however, that wage and welfare policies were completely repressive, functioning solely to overcome antagonistic social relations. It is arguable that, in the process of achieving this main goal, these capitalist concessions to worker struggle raised the standard of living of auto workers and made their lives more livable, both within and outside the factories. The higher "family wage," which provided a morally acceptable standard of living for a worker and his or her dependents, probably spared many children the torturous deprivation of factory work. Small savings accounts, pensions, and financial aid may have eased slightly the anxiety of a hand-to-mouth existence in a highly seasonal industry. Doubtless many immigrants and migrants benefited from language instruction and assistance in adapting to urban living standards. The stable, monogamous household, with its increasing stock of consumer durables, probably provided temporary respite from factory despotism. Within the factory, safety work and improved facilities certainly made the hours of unrelenting, intensified monotony a bit more tolerable. But these nonrepressive benefits of wage and welfare programs must be weighed against the price capitalists demanded that workers pay in return: unquestioning submission to capitalist authority, an ever-increasing work pace, the destruction of life styles rooted in national traditions, loss of freedom in one's leisure time, paternalistic dependence, a repressive personality structure denying self-expression and enjoyment. Wage and welfare programs conceded to struggling workers an improved standard of material life, but at the exorbitant cost of lost group and individual freedoms. That the cost of a decent life came so high was solely the result of the antagonistic relations of capitalist production.

VARIATION IN WAGE AND WELFARE MEASURES
BY BUSINESS CYCLE

These wages and welfare programs were not permanent fixtures in the labor policies of automotive firms. They were basically temporary measures to combat the increased power of workers that resulted from the periodic shrinking of the industrial reserve army. When there was a shortage of labor power and workers were consequently strong, centralized authority allowed manufacturers quickly to replace the stick of coercion with the carrot of high wages and welfare. But when recession or depression swelled the ranks of the army of unemployed, capitalists placed this carrot in cold storage and put the stick of coercion back into service. Wage and welfare policies thus varied directly with the power of labor, which in turn fluctuated with the business cycle.

Most of the wage and welfare plans in the industry were introduced during and immediately following the First World War, when war-induced labor shortages combined with the incipient revolt of workers against the new technology to create labor havoc. Capitalists introduced higher wages and welfare work to quell the unrest. However, many of these policies met their demise in the depression of 1920. At Ford, the profit-sharing plan was abolished, along with the entire Sociological Department. A Bureau of Labor Statistics survey of the industry found that eight of the nine bonus plans in operation in 1919 had been discontinued in 1922. These programs were abolished, not because of the economic straits of individual firms, but because of the general shift in the balance of class power. As the labor editor of *Automotive Industries*, Harry Tipper, wrote in 1922:

> under the prevailing impression that labor is beaten, the desire for better relations and better understanding seems to have gone into the discard almost entirely. There is a widespread belief in manufacturing circles that labor is definitely beaten for a considerable time and that it is possible for the manufacturer to place himself in the position of virtual control again. This is the idea behind . . . the general abandonment of work in industrial relations within the plant, the advocacy of the open shop, and the bitterness expressed in many quarters toward the unions. . . . Control of labor through economic conditions only postpones the final settlement.[68]

When the boom of the late 1920s once again created labor shortages, wage and welfare plans were revived to combat labor's strengthened resistance to capital. But on the whole, the scope and intensity of industrial betterment never regained the peak it had reached just prior to the 1920 depression. Safety and general improvements in factory facilities and working conditions became part of the standard conditions of employment throughout the industry. But, as one industrial journalist concluded, "many of the innovations introduced during the war in the effort to stabilize a floating labor supply have been abandoned and . . . the disposition is to concentrate on the services and conveniences which have proved of real benefit to employers and management."[69]

Even these scaled-down programs were dealt a crushing blow by the Great Depression. The power of workers was so diminished by the huge army of the unemployed that such measures were no longer necessary to ensure their stability and acquiescence. After the depression, wage and welfare work in the auto industry was never again practiced on a scale commensurate with the predepression days. Some of the programs, especially company unions, were rehabilitated in the mid-1930s to try to head off the growing union movement. But this time the palliatives were not sufficient, and all the major firms were unionized by the early 1940s.

Unionization generally spelled the end of special wage and welfare programs in the auto industry. Capital lost the battle for the allegiance of workers to the union, an organization that defined itself in opposition to the company. This severed the ideological ties between labor and capital that the wage and welfare programs had tried to establish. Collective bargaining transformed wages and benefits from matters of paternalistic generosity into issues of struggle and negotiation between two opposing parties. Ironically enough, the triumph of unionism may have been furthered by the same wage and welfare plans with which capitalists hoped to defuse it.

CONTRADICTIONS OF WAGE AND WELFARE MEASURES

The compensation and welfare measures instituted by auto manufacturers seemed to help repress the resistance of workers to capitalist domination in the short term by creating a stable and compliant labor force. But these measures embodied contradictions that in the long term actually undermined capitalist control and strengthened workers' resistance. Many wage and welfare measures, for example, furthered the homogenization of workers by compressing the wage distribution. As one trade journalist wrote:

This is the fundamental difficulty with all general profit sharing, partnership and other systems for increasing the reward of active workers. These are not founded upon any greater analysis than the regular
wages. They bear no relation to the amount of time and effort which
must be given to acquiring proficiency in operation and education in
judgment. They do not take into account either the cost or the length
of time involved in acquiring the necessary background of experience
and, while they ameliorate conditions temporarily, they will not and
cannot provide a permanent remedy for the unrest which is constantly developing. Not only is this the case, but the whole wage system as it relates to operation, tends to remove the sense of individual
responsibility by placing all the workers within the same group upon
a uniform basis.[70]

This tendency toward homogenization was clearest in Ford's Five
Dollar Day plan. It was the intention of the plan to level wage differentials by giving the greatest benefits to workers earning the lowest wage, probably because they accounted for most of the turnover and absenteeism. Statistical reports on the plan revealed that it
reduced the gap between the highest and lowest factory wages
from 56 cents to 25 cents. Even though other plans probably did
not have similarly large effects on absolute wage differentials,
they undoubtedly narrowed these differentials relatively, for most
distributed equal benefits to workers at all wage levels. Some wage
and welfare plans established new personal differentials on the
basis of seniority, attendance, good behavior, etc. But their differ-
entiating effects were generally not large, because of the minimal nature of the requirements and the ability of most workers to easily
meet them.[71]

The second contradictory aspect of these programs was the social-
ization of workers' needs. Capitalism is based upon the provision
for human needs through individual purchases of commodities on
the market. While such consumption was encouraged by some welfare programs, others actually undermined individualized commodity purchases by establishing a social provision of needs. These programs distributed medical care, recreation, housing, food, and
financial services not individually, through the market, but socially,
through the firm. Workers often came together to share in common
such facilities as housing, lunchrooms, cooperative stores, recreational facilities, company hospitals and clinics. Despite the fact that
welfare programs socialized needs only within a small group—
the firm—they nevertheless tended to undermine the very basis
of capitalism—the commodity. Moreover, by bringing workers
together in the lunchroom, on the playing field, and in the club

house, albeit under the company's aegis, auto capitalists furthered worker interaction and solidarity. In both ways, then, welfare work originally intended to strengthen auto capitalists and capitalism in general also tended to undermine both.[72]

Finally, employee representation plans, or company unions, also contained contradictions. Although these plans were intended to create ideological ties of loyalty between labor and capital and to defuse attempts at legitimate labor organization, they were not without their unintended consequences. Despite the limited scope of issues they dealt with, works councils did give workers some rudimentary experience in bargaining with management. And they probably whetted the appetites of workers for genuine representation and bargaining. As one contemporary labor relations scholar has noted, a little industrial democracy never seems to be enough. Once workers get a taste for bargaining and representation, they want more. In the auto industry, the expectations for representation heightened by the works councils were probably partially responsible for the success of the union movement. Furthermore, company unions may have helped to ensure that the emerging legitimate labor organizations would be industrial rather than craft unions. By including all the workers in the factory in a single organization, the company union served to remind the different occupations and crafts of their common interests rather than their differences.[73]

In these ways, the wage and welfare programs introduced by automotive manufacturers united and strengthened workers' opposition. It became clear to capital that these measures alone would not ensure the stable, acquiescent labor force required by the new technology. So early on manufacturers began to devise a subtle strategy to divide and conquer workers—the bureaucratization of the job structure.

CHAPTER 11
Bureaucratization of the Job Structure

The authority structure of the auto firms had already been bureaucratized. In the place of a decentralized, patrimonial dispersion of power, capitalists erected a centralized, rule-governed, hierarchical structure, commanded at the top by owners and their managerial agents. However, this bureaucratization of authority did not reverse the increasing homogeneity of the mass of wage earners over which it exercised control; in fact, it furthered this process of homogenization. Workers previously differentiated by wages, working conditions, and severity of command were united in their subjection to the uniform and rule-governed authority of the bureaucracy. And as we saw in the preceding chapter, some bureaucratic policies introduced to quell worker resistance backfired and actually strengthened the workers in their fight.

In order to combat this continued resistance, auto manufacturers extended bureaucratization down into the ranks of the wage earners themselves by introducing a rule-governed job hierarchy. Although the new technology rendered auto production jobs more and more alike technically, capitalists undertook to arrange these basically similar jobs into a fragmented hierarchy of occupational categories, each with a different rule-defined wage rate. By thus widening and bureaucratizing wage differentials, they hoped to undermine the basis of common worker action. Combined with a system of promotion, such a job structure could be doubly divisive, for not only would workers have their common interests hidden by largely artificial wage differentials, but their efforts to obtain higher wages and greater control could be channeled away from collective struggle toward individual efforts to gain personal advantages through promotion.

Creation of the Bureaucratic Job Structure

The divide-and-conquer motivation behind the creation of the bureaucratic job structure was nothing new in the auto industry. Incentive wage systems also sought to divide the interests of workers, who were becoming technically more homogeneous. But, as we saw, such systems often backfired by uniting workers against arbitrary rate cutting. Harry Tipper, labor editor of *Automotive Industries*, recognized the dangerous homogenization of workers' wages caused by the new technology, but warned against incentive wages as a means of combating the problem.

> Standardization was introduced as the factory system produced machinery which would repeat the same operation with sufficient rapidity to permit a much larger production. This standardization in the operation led to a uniformity in the rate of pay and, as the rate of pay had always been based upon time, the uniformity in the time rate became more or less general. It is true that piece-work was employed all through the evolution of the factory system in a great many lines, but the evils which arose from the piece-work method of payment . . . induced the labor unions to fight it and eliminate it wherever possible. . . . The evils of the early piece-work system have been responsible for the development of opposition and a continuance of that opposition in trade union circles to any such methods of payment. They have also been one of the most important sources of the bitter suspicion and distrust which grew up between the worker and the employer.[1]

But, Tipper continued, without some way of splitting up the homogeneous pay structure, industrial conflict was inevitable, for wage differentials resulted solely from labor market forces and the struggle of occupational groups. "The payment of wages as a comparative matter between various occupations according to the demand for, and the organized strength of the group, emphasizes the injustice, increases the unbalance and puts a premium upon strikes, labor organization and warfare." What was needed, Tipper concluded, was some new, "logical" basis for establishing the comparative value of different jobs, with the unspoken but implied condition that this basis should sufficiently fractionalize the workers.[2]

One of the first auto firms to place job classification on such a "logical basis" was the Ford Motor Company, which introduced a bureaucratic job hierarchy as part of its reorganization plan in October 1913. Like the other aspects of the plan, the bureaucratic job structure was a response to the mounting worker resistance and the general administrative disorder of the expanding shops. Allowing individual foremen to determine wages had created chaos, producing sixty-five different wage rates in the factory work force. Petty discrimination and injustice were rampant; workers doing the same job were paid widely varying wages. To gain control over the situation, the power to set wages was removed from the foremen and centralized into the Employment Department, which promptly erected a bureaucratic job classification system to guide its decisions.

Ford's job hierarchy was based ostensibly on a combination of skill and efficiency. Six classes of work were established on the basis of skill, and each of these was further divided into three subclasses based on individual efficiency. Each subclass had a specific wage rate. Incoming workers were assigned a particular class of work on the basis of their skills, and placed in its lowest efficiency subclass. They were expected, however, to advance in the hierarchy from one subclass to the next and from one class to the next as they gained skills and efficiency. Foremen kept records on individual workers and recommended them to the Employment Department for promotion. Workers incapable of progress were transferred to other jobs and ultimately fired.[3]

Not long after this job classification system was put into operation, however, it ran into an obstacle—there were not enough positions in the skilled classes of work to accommodate all those entitled to promotion. Workers piled up in the top subclasses of the unskilled classes. Ford was compelled, therefore, to further differentiate the system by adding a fourth subclass to the unskilled classes known as the "service rate," which was reserved for workers who had attained a high grade of efficiency and had also been employed at Ford for at least two years.[4]

The capitalist motives behind Ford's new job classification system were twofold, but both were related to an underlying desire to overcome the resistance of workers. On the one hand, the bureaucratic system was intended to correct the blatant inequities and discrimination of having pay rates determined by foremen. By basing wages upon a centralized, rule-governed classification scheme that ensured comparable wages for similar work, managers hoped to eliminate the worker discontent caused by rate inequities. Such a reordering of the chaotic wage structure was clearly in the interests of workers as well as managers.

But the byzantine structure of Ford's job classification system cannot be accounted for entirely by attempts to ensure equity and order. The goal of paying similarly skilled work at a comparable rate could reasonably justify a division of the work force into three or four classes. But because of the continued leveling of skill requirements by mechanization and rationalization, the goal of equity cannot account for the eighteen separate subclasses and wage rates. Clearly, there was a second motive involved—an attempt to keep the interests of workers divided through wage differentials between basically similar jobs. Although allowing foremen to determine wages had established such differentials, their blatantly arbitrary nature aroused workers' discontent. Managers needed a system of differential wages that appeared to be rational. As two engineering journalists wrote:

> Rate inequalities cause much hard feeling. No man is happy when a fellow worker doing the same job gets a higher rate of pay. But if he can be shown that in addition to the work done, the other fellow has qualities that make him more valuable to the firm, he will not resent the difference nearly so much. He can be shown why these qualities make the other man worth more money and be assured that when he acquires them he will be put in the same class.[5]

Ford's classification scheme based on skill classes and efficiency subclasses provided the legitimation required of a system of wage differentials for similar jobs.

The policy of promotion within Ford's job hierarchy furthered its purpose of quelling the rising discontent of workers. First, promotion up the minutely graded steps of the ladder provided an illusion of upward mobility that could have a pacifying effect on workers, especially in a society with a strong meritocratic ideology. Second, even if workers did not personally experience promotions, their mere availability was a tool of control for managers and capitalists. Promotions were used as incentives to stimulate greater effort. As two engineering journalists wrote, "a job evaluation spurs the good employee to master his job in order to qualify for one calling for a higher wage rate, either as ingrade or labor-grade promotion."[6] Third, the entire system had the ideological function of legitimating positions in the industrial hierarchy on the basis of individual merit. If workers were in low-paying jobs, the bureaucratic ideology held that it was their fault alone, for if they were smarter or more industrious, they would be able to climb to higher rungs on the job ladder. Thus, commenting on Ford's new job ladder, one industrial journalist noted:

> Under this system the employee can be made to understand clearly
> that his own wages and those of every other man in the shop depend
> entirely upon the work he does, that an improvement in his work will
> be rewarded without fear or favor by a stipulated amount correspond-
> ing to the improvement shown and that increased production and a
> wider range of ability will bring about a definite advancement and a
> definite increase in earnings.[7]

Although Ford's new bureaucratic job structure seems to have
been moderately successful in quelling worker discontent, it was
completely overshadowed several months after its introduction by
the Five Dollar Day. For a period, then, the divide-and-conquer
strategy of the job ladder took a back seat to wage and welfare programs, which often had a leveling effect upon wages. However, as
Ford's wage policies lost their initial efficacy for containing labor unrest in the late 1910s, the company returned once again to a divisive
job structure. On May 24, 1919, a new classification scheme of nine
skill classes was established, and profit-sharing payments were
equalized for all classes. Ford thus abandoned its wage schemes
for a straight job hierarchy that maximized wage differentials between workers.[8]

The late 1910s and early 1920s brought an increased interest and
awareness in such hierarchical job structures in American industry
as a whole. Sumner Slichter, an academic labor relations specialist,
promoted job hierarchies as a solution to labor turnover and unionism during this period.

> This policy [of filling vacancies by promotion], should it become gen-
> eral, will greatly increase the seriousness to the worker of the loss of
> his job, for it will substantially enhance the difficulty to experienced
> workers of finding new work of the same grade as they previously
> performed and yielding corresponding wages. Employers so far have
> not fully appreciated as a means of combating unionism the tremen-
> dous possibilities of the plan of organizing the work in their plant into
> minutely subdivided jobs each of which can be easily learned, of
> organizing these jobs into systematic lines of promotion, of training
> each man for the job ahead of him in advance, and then filling va-
> cancies by the hiring of men for the lowest positions and moving
> others up.[9]

The auto industry also became increasingly conscious of the control advantages of job hierarchies. Numerous articles in *Automotive
Industries* detailed the structure and operation of such plans in related metal-fabrication industries and sang their praises. A bureaucratic job classification system at Bullard Machine Tool Company, a

major supplier of equipment to the auto industry, was praised as cultivating contentment and good will among workers. Six classes of work were established on the basis of skill, with each having an assigned range of wage rates. Within that range, the pay of an individual was based on an incentive wage system. A promotional policy provided for filling all vacancies with workers from the next lower class who demonstrated exceptional ability. This system thus legitimated a worker's position within the structure of differential wages by claiming to offer "full opportunity for advancement along definite lines to those showing ability" and to provide "a wage rate limited only by ability and occupation."[10]

The ideological or legitimation function of bureaucratic job ladders was further clarified in a description of a similar plan in operation at the Fellows Gear Shaper Company. Here work was divided into seven wage classes, "according to the difficulty and skill involved in the various operations." Newly hired employees entered the system at a level determined by previous experience and progressed up the job ladder through promotions, which were based on standardized technical tests and foreman recommendations. The company noted two marked benefits of the bureaucratic job ladder. First, its introduction reduced turnover considerably. Second, the plan "definitely affects the general contentedness among the employees. . . ."[11] To illustrate this second benefit, the plant superintendent related the story of a belligerant old drill-press operator who had been working on the same machine for twenty years. After he was heard complaining about his job and his lack of advancement, the superintendent offered him a chance to take a training course for promotion. The worker promptly refused it, stating that he preferred to stick to his old job. The superintendent replied to him:

> You have had your chance, but you didn't want to take it. You want success and advancement, but you are not willing to take the trouble and work that goes with it. Now, there isn't any use of you going around to these young fellows here, telling them that it is no use for them to work hard, produce more, or try to advance. When you say "Look at me, I'm right where I was twenty years ago," the young fellows in the plant can say, "Yes, we are looking at you. Why don't you come along and take this course with us; probably there is an opportunity for you if you want it."[12]

A trade journalist concluded from the story that "the influence of the discontented man is obviated by the mere facts of the case. It isn't that the management tells the men that hard work and ambition will mean advancement and opportunity; the big thing is that the opportunity really is there. Where the facts of the case are against the discontented man, his views have little chance of spreading."[13] The job ladder thus functioned ideologically to prevent the spread of discontent among workers. It was meant to convince workers that their positions were determined solely by their individual abilities and efforts rather than by class relations, and that the best way to better themselves was to forsake collective action with other workers and to strive for individual advancement through promotion.

As these and other advantages became evident, more and more auto manufacturers adopted bureaucratic job structures as solutions to their labor problems. In many firms, job ladders were short, distinguishing only broad skill and authority divisions. But even these simple ladders seem to have been fairly successful in quieting labor unrest and stimulating greater effort. A policy of promotion among a few simple categories at the Brown-Lipe-Chapin Company, an auto parts manufacturer, reportedly "removes the irritating lid which so often holds down a man's ambition, makes him discontented with his work, and restless in performing it." The Autocar Company reported that its policy of promoting foremen from within the firm created greater incentives as well as a more submissive spirit among workers. "The advantage of this policy is that it presents a definite promise to every workman that he will have an opportunity to rise through increased effort. . . . The policy of promoting from within is an excellent one, and will go far toward obtaining better spirit among the workmen."[14]

Other auto companies went to greater extremes to combat worker resistance, creating highly differentiated and complex job structures. In 1922 the Franklin Company instituted a complex job classification system based ostensibly on skill. Promotion between the numerous levels was based upon worker seniority as well as effort, thus providing an incentive for two worker traits desired by capital. The White Company also put an elaborate job structure into operation in the late 1920s. Instead of dividing jobs into skill classes, the White system classified individual workers into ten different wage categories "according to their recognized abilities." An individual was promoted from one wage category to the next "by demonstrating his capability to do the work of a superior category. . . ."[15] With this system, which paid workers on the same job different wages, managers abandoned the myth that classification was based on skill requirements of jobs. The White wage structure recognized that a worker's worth to the company was determined not by skill alone, but also by the personal traits demanded by the new technology:

stability, regularity of effort, submissiveness. The system cultivated such traits in workers by rewarding them with promotions to higher wage categories.

The impetus toward divisive job classification systems in the automobile industry continued up to and through the period of unionization. Efforts in this direction intensified, however, immediately following unionization, when manufacturers were struggling to break the infant organization, and during the Second World War, when labor unrest was again high. The Ford Motor Company, for example, continued to push bureaucratization of the job structure with the addition in 1946 of "scientific methods" of selection and promotion of personnel. Incoming employees as well as those applying for training programs leading to promotions were given a series of tests that enabled management

> to establish a high percentage of accuracy in appraising the man's qualities in such thing as mental alertness, aptitudes for specific kinds of work and learning, certain personality traits which will be helpful on specific kinds of jobs, inventories of the basic interests which the man has, and specific measurement of his knowledge, skill, and abilities in various subjects or kinds of work.[16]

It is clear from these tests that Ford managers were looking not so much for technical knowledge and ability, but for willingness to submit to managerial authority. Personality traits measured included "cooperative tendencies," "dependability," "emotional stability," "extroversion," "self-reliance," and "social adjustment." An official in Ford's Training Department further noted that these tests justified workers' positions in the job hierarchy and thus promoted contentment.

> In some cases a change of jobs is indicated [by testing]. In others it becomes evident that the man is in exactly the line of work for which he is best suited. In either case the man is happier and his morale is greatly increased. He is sure of his own judgment. He has a greater inclination to accept responsibilities. He has increased his industrial stature for he has the security of knowing that he can, through the aid of selective testing, plan his future more effectively. Obviously this is an increased asset to both the worker and the Ford Motor Company.[17]

Two other studies of the auto industry support the conclusion that managers and capitalists consciously maximized wage differentials. Robert MacDonald found in his study of collective bargaining in the auto industry that management consistently pressured for the maintenance and enhancement of wage differentials between workers doing the same or comparable work, as well as between workers with different job skills. William McPherson reached the same conclusion in his study of labor relations in the industry. "Management is more desirous than is the union of maintaining appreciable job differentials. Management believes that such differentials are essential to provide an adequate incentive for superior work."[18]

Therefore, like the division of labor between different jobs, the classification of these jobs into wage categories was determined primarily by the antagonistic relations of capitalist production, not by the technical requirements of work. The same capitalist imperative to repress the resistance of a recalcitrant working class that had dictated dividing crafts into a plethora of specialized jobs also dictated fractionalizing these basically similar jobs into a multitude of wage categories. Both measures were repressive attempts to break the basis of workers' power. In the craft system, such power lay in the control of individual skilled workers over production, which was destroyed by the division of labor. In mass production, workers' power lay in their unity within a highly socialized system, which was attacked with divisive job structures.

These bureaucratic job structures, just like the division of labor, did have their nonrepressive aspects. To the extent that they replaced arbitrary, personalistic wage determination with rule-governed systems treating all workers on the same job uniformly, they were in the interests of workers as well as capitalists. And to the extent that wage categories coincided with actual skill differences and thus rewarded knowledge and training, they were nonrepressive, serving to motivate productive effort. However, given the objective leveling of skill differentials in auto work, such nonrepressive job structures would have contained three, possibly four, categories. Indeed, before the bureaucratization of job structures in the late 1910s, capitalists themselves generally divided the factory force into three or four broad skill categories, like "mechanic," "operator," and "laborer." More elaborate divisions, based not merely upon job skill but on individual output, seniority, absenteeism, and submissiveness, were clearly repressive attempts to fractionalize the interests of workers and channel discontent away from collective struggle into individual job-ladder climbing.[19]

Educational Work

That more than mere technical skills and knowledge differentiated the levels of the bureaucratic job structure is demonstrated by the factory training courses that were often required for promotion. Most of these courses offered by auto firms did provide useful technical training, necessary to fill positions distinguished from normal production jobs by true skill differentials. However, in addition to technical skills and knowledge, trainees in these courses received a generous dose of "character-building." Manufacturers took the opportunity to inculcate in workers specific work and personal habits required by the new, specifically capitalist labor process. In order to pass the course and rise to the new position, workers had to demonstrate above all a willingness to submit to capitalist control over production. As David Noble has written, through corporate education, managers

> sought to habituate both the working population and potential workers to industrial discipline and to educate them to carry out the directives of management most efficiently. . . . They saw in education, properly guided according to corporate imperatives, the key to corporate prosperity and stability; by means of education they sought to eliminate the problems of "labor turnover," and "lack of training," to bring about greater productivity and industrial efficiency.[20]

Formal training of skilled workers emerged only with the mass production process. In the early craft shops, training had been accomplished through an apprenticeship system, in which young workers learned the trade by working with older, more experienced craft workers. Although there were often examinations and requirements administered by managers and capitalists, training was largely in the hands of the skilled workers themselves. The mechanization and rationalization of the labor process destroyed the apprenticeship system. Jobs became so deskilled and specialized that an apprentice could not obtain the knowledge and skill to become an all-around mechanic by merely working with other workers.[21]

The highly rationalized and mechanized production process still required skilled workers to cut the dies and build and set up the specialized machines operated by unskilled workers. In fact, the industry expanded so fast in the early days that despite the decline in the proportion of skilled workers in the shops, the absolute number of them required increased rapidly, and shortages of this precious commodity developed. Many auto manufacturers were content for a while to obtain skilled workers by external recruitment, rather than internal training. But some began to realize the value of training their own workers. The first educational programs in the industry were introduced as part of welfare work and viewed as ways to reduce turnover and increase worker contentment. But the training aspect of the programs soon overshadowed the welfare intent, and capitalists began to view them as a way to provide their shops with badly needed skilled labor power. By maintaining strict control over educational programs, capitalists and managers realized that they could produce workers who were not only technically competent, but also ones socially conditioned to the alienated labor that existed in the rapidly changing labor process.

Internal conditioning was particularly vital to the capitalist control over skilled workers. Unskilled workers could be controlled largely through the external constraints built into the technology. But because the jobs of skilled workers involved greater uncertainty and discretion, they could not be controlled by means of such standardized technology. Capitalists and managers had to rely on normative control for these workers—the internalization of ideas and attitudes that corresponded to capitalist interests. The only way to ensure that these workers who made their own decisions and controlled their own work would use their discretion to further the interests of manufacturers was to inculcate in them the values of Anglo-Protestant bourgeois culture, which corresponded to the requirements of the capitalist-controlled labor process. Auto manufacturers thus turned their training programs into schools of capitalist culture and social relations as well as technical schools of auto production.[22]

One of the first educational programs in the auto industry aimed seriously at training workers—technically, culturally, and socially—was launched by Henry Leland's Cadillac Automotive Company. In May 1907, Leland established the Cadillac School of Applied Mechanics in order to solve the company's skilled labor shortage. The school offered a two-year training course divided between classroom and shop instruction. In the classroom, students studied such subjects as mechanical drawing, blueprints, and general physics. In the shop, they gained practical experience in all facets of automotive production. However, it is evident from a close examination of the requirements, methods, and curriculum that more was being taught than technical skills. The school attempted to mold the workers' culture and character in order to habituate them to the alienated labor of the auto shops.

Admission requirements were strict. In addition to meeting certain age and education standards, applications had to be of "good moral character." Self-indulgence in the forms of smoking or chewing tobacco or "using intoxicating liquor" was prohibited. Among the subjects listed in the course catalogue were "character building" and "rules of success." "In his talks with young men, these rules were a common theme for Henry Leland. His theory was that one essential ingredient of success was mastery of one's self as well as one's job." Or better said, a primary purpose of the training was the internalization of the mastery of capital over labor. Students were also habituated to the capitalist organization of work. Their hours were the same as Cadillac factory workers—ten hours a day, five days a week, plus six hours on Saturday. The Cadillac School also taught students to respond properly to monetary incentives, the cornerstone of a system of alienated labor. They were paid an hourly rate and received wage increases and bonuses on the basis of their grades, which included evaluations not only of their mechanical ability and knowledge, but also of their "perseverance, tactfulness, and character." "As is evident from all these provisions, the Lelands wished to encourage the virtues of promptness and reliability as well as good clean habits."[23]

Nine years after the establishment of Leland's Cadillac School, Henry Ford entered educational work with the establishment of the Henry Ford Trade School. It was originally part of Ford's welfare work, established to give underprivileged boys a chance to learn a trade. But the humanitarian veneer was soon dropped, and the school became an undisguised effort to train skilled workers for the Ford shops, especially tool and die makers. Beginning with six boys in 1916, the school rapidly expanded, reaching an enrollment of four hundred by 1920. Combining classroom and shop instruction, the general course lasted two years, after which many boys continued in specialized training in one of several trades.

Like Leland's Cadillac School, the Henry Ford Trade School aimed not only at technical training, but also at the cultivation of a certain moral type of worker—the stable, dependable, subservient worker required by the system of alienated labor that capital had introduced into the shops. In order to ensure that the boys would stick with the program and not leave, Ford only accepted underprivileged boys— those whose families really needed the small pay that students brought home. Further, as at the Cadillac school, the boys were socialized into the world of alienated wage labor. They were paid on an hourly basis, and satisfactory marks at the end of each six-week period automatically entitled a boy to a raise. Students were graded not only on their class and shop work, but also on "industry," a catch-all term for conduct appropriate to the capitalist shop. "'Industry' is another and perhaps much better term than the 'deportment' mark so long used in many schools. In the Henry Ford Trade School it is extremely important. . . . It includes 'attitude,' and is defined as 'Industry—the effort put forth'; and 'attitude—effort and conduct combined.'"[24]

Bourgeois attitudes toward time and money were also inculcated in Ford's school. "From the beginning every boy is taught that time should at all periods of his life be a thing to be minutely considered. Time is a very positive and finely calculated element. It is an extremely valuable element. It should be used for all that it is worth."[25] Labor time was indeed a valuable commodity to Ford, who sought to ensure in his school that skilled workers internalized the discipline that made its use as profitable as possible. In the same cultural vein, the school encouraged that self-denying trait of thrift by distributing to students funds that they were required to deposit in savings accounts. In summary, the Henry Ford Trade School supplied the auto manufacturer with a steady supply of labor power that was not only technically skilled, but also imbued with the social and cultural values and traits required by the new process of alienated labor.

Other large automotive firms used similar educational programs to solve their problems of obtaining skilled workers adapted to capitalist relations of production for the upper ranks of their job hierarchies. In 1916 the Reo Motor Car Company established its Apprenticeship School for boys "16 or 17 years of age, of good character and possessing mechanical ability." Preference was given to sons of Reo employees. The three-year course consisted of the usual combination of classroom instruction and shop experience in all aspects of automotive production. The importance of the school in building normative ties of gratitude and loyalty between labor and capital was revealed by one graduate, who praised the Reo managers for giving workers a chance to improve themselves and creating a "spirit of harmony" in the shops. A similar training school was established at Studebaker in 1915, offering three-year courses to young workers of the corporation who demonstrated "good moral character." General Motors offered employees education courses through the Flint Institute of Technology, which later became the General Motors Institute of Technology. The institute provided promotional training for older workers, as well as apprentice training for young workers just beginning with the company.[26]

Through these training courses, auto capitalists not only provided themselves with qualified workers to fill the upper reaches of the job ladder, but they also guaranteed the reproduction of capitalist relations of production. By controlling the education required for passage between levels of the bureaucratic job hierarchy, they were able to ensure the advancement of only those who were acquiescent to managerial authority, responsive to monetary incentives, dependable, stable, and self-denying. By the time workers had traversed the obstacles of this formal training to rise in the hierarchy, they had thoroughly internalized the repression and discipline required in the capitalist labor process. Employers had no need to worry that the greater power associated with skilled jobs would be turned against them in struggle. Educational work even gave managers greater ideological control over workers who never entered the training courses. Employees' education was used as a symbol of the opportunity for advancement available to all who worked hard enough. If most workers never availed themselves of this opportunity, they could console themselves with the recognition that their failings were their own.

THE SUPERIMPOSITION OF STATUS DIVISIONS ON THE JOB HIERARCHY

The divisive effects of the bureaucratic job hierarchy were further exacerbated by the superimposition upon it of status groups, that is people sharing a similar lifestyle or culture. The largely arbitrary hierarchical distinctions were enough to create hostilities and resentments among a culturally homogeneous work force. But the coincidence of these divisions with existing racial, sexual, and ethnic divisions greatly enhanced their divisive effects. These status divisions evoked deeply rooted hatreds and hostilities, which, when compounded with the cleavages created by wage differentials, often prevented united worker action against employers. The discontent of the privileged group of native-born white males was somewhat assuaged by their exemption from the lowest-paying, hardest jobs in the shops. And the resentments of the immigrants, blacks, and women confined to the bottom rungs of the job ladder were deflected away from capital toward the privileged workers who monopolized the better jobs.[27]

It should not be thought, however, that auto manufacturers confined racial, ethnic, and sexual minorities to the bottom of the job hierarchy as an intentional policy aimed at further dividing the working class in their shops. There is little evidence to substantiate this. A more likely explanation of the maldistribution of jobs by status

246

groups is that the auto companies reflected the prejudices of the larger society. The ethnic, racial, and sexual stereotypes of American society were reflected in the employment practices of the auto firms, resulting in the discriminatory distribution of jobs. However, once this job structure, segmented by status groups, was in place, auto capitalists were not reluctant to use the hostilities and divisions it fostered to weaken the resistance of workers. They played off ethnic group against ethnic group, race against race, and sex against sex in efforts to speed up workers, cut wages, and break strikes. American automotive manufacturers cannot be accused of inventing racism and sexism. But they did turn these preexisting weapons against their workers in attempts to break a united class struggle.

Ethnic Discrimination

In the early days of the industry, immigrant workers from southern and eastern Europe were generally relegated to the lowest-paying, least desirable jobs in auto firms. The Russians, Poles, Croats, Hungarians, and Italians who flooded into Detroit in the early years of the twentieth century were usually employed as common laborers or as unskilled operators of the new specialized machinery of the industry. The 1916 Cleveland Survey estimated that from 50 to 75 percent of the unskilled workers in Cleveland's auto shops were recent immigrants. The 1920 Census of the United States revealed that about 72 percent of all common laborers and 55 percent of all operatives in the nation's auto factories were either foreign-born or of foreign or mixed parentage. The skilled jobs were filled by native-born American workers, or immigrants from northern and western European countries (Germans, Britons, Scots).[28]

This original ethnic division of the job structure was partially due to the different backgrounds that these groups brought with them to the auto factories. The peasant immigrants from southern and eastern Europe had no experience or skills in industrial production and thus were initially suited only for the unskilled jobs created by the rationalization and mechanization of auto work. The native-born Americans, Britons, Germans, and Scots brought to the auto factories experience and skills gained through employment in various industrial and craft occupations. However, this technical basis for the ethnic division of labor was eroded by the increasing industrial experience of the peasant immigrants. The perpetuation of ethnic stratification was due in large part to the general racism of American society, which led to discriminatory employment and promotion policies among automotive manufacturers. Another contributing factor was the transmission of advantages between generations in families of skilled workers: fatherly instruction in a craft, the inculcation of an occupational culture, higher educational levels supported by relatively higher family incomes, and family support during low-paying apprenticeship training.[29]

Once this ethnically stratified job structure was in existence, through whatever causes, auto capitalists realized that it could be helpful in preventing a united worker resistance. Thus, the labor editor of *Automotive Industries* wrote that "the number of races involved in the working population of this country and the difference in their traditional, political and social inheritance and their understanding, makes it difficult for them to come together in any well-ordered organization. . . ."[30] And during the sitdown strikes of 1937, the editor of this trade paper suggested to the industry's capitalists that "certain national groups among the workers, no matter how much apparent solidarity there might be on broad principles, would feel the urge of thrift and loyalty reassert itself, and might, unconsciously, begin to yearn for jobs and stability sooner than other groups."[31] He did not have to remind his readers that some ethnic groups would be more loyal precisely because they had been granted a privileged position in the bureaucratic job hierarchy.

This divisive effect of the superimposition of ethnic divisions on the job hierarchy is documented in Peter Friedlander's study of the unionization of an auto parts plant in Detroit's Polish enclave, Hamtramck. In the plant there existed a typical pattern of ethnic divisions coincidental with levels of the job hierarchy. The unskilled production jobs were filled by first- and second-generation Polish, Ukrainian, and Lithuanian immigrants, while the skilled occupations and crafts were dominated by workers of American and northern European heritage. The unionization drive emerged largely among the second-generation Poles in the production departments. Because the skilled workers were privileged in relation to the Polish workers, they demonstrated little sympathy with their grievances or their union efforts. But exacerbating this skill division was ethnic prejudice among the skilled, which was encouraged by the management. Even after the plant was organized and skilled workers joined the union, they remained reluctant members.[32]

The southern and eastern European immigrant workers possessed, however, two advantages that prevented their continued exclusion from the more privileged positions in the job hierarchy: their white skins and their masculine gender. These traits ensured that they would ultimately be accepted at all levels of the job hierarchy dominated by white males. Less fortunate were those whose black skins and feminine gender prevented them from shedding their distinct identities and consequently being assimilated into the job hierarchy. Reflecting the general racism and sexism of American society, auto capitalists discriminated against blacks and women in hiring. But even when members of these groups managed to gain employment in the automobile industry, they were almost always confined to the lowest ranks of the job ladder, with no opportunities for advancement.

Racial Discrimination

From the very beginning, the racism of auto manufacturers confined black workers to the bottom of the job hierarchy. Invariably they were given the dirtiest, hardest, hottest, most dangerous and disagreeable jobs: janitors, painters, sanders, foundry workers, manual laborers. The general attitude toward black employment in the auto plants was well reflected in a statement given by one white auto worker to an investigator. "I asked if Negroes were not employed anywhere in the plant. He said, 'Yes, some jobs white folks will not do; so they have to take niggers in, particularly in duco work, spraying paint on car bodies. This soon kills a white man.' I inquired if it never killed Negroes. 'Oh, yes,' he replied, 'It shortens their lives, it cuts them down but they're just niggers.'"[33]

The 1910 census of the United States showed that five hundred and sixty-nine blacks were employed in the auto industry (about 1/2 of 1 percent of the work force). Of these, about one-third were laborers and most of the rest were unskilled workers of various sorts. Although the 1920 census did not reveal the exact number of blacks in the industry (it was probably less than 3 percent), it did calculate that 7.7 percent of all laborers, but only 1.4 percent of all operatives employed, were black. The 1930 census revealed that black workers comprised about 4 percent of all auto workers and were overwhelmingly concentrated in the lowest jobs. Nearly three-fourths were in the lowest skill category, as compared to one-fourth of the white workers. And only one-eighth of the blacks were working at white-collar or skilled jobs, as compared to about one-half of white workers.[34]

This discrimination in the job ladder was reflected in wage differentials between white and black auto workers. Although no good data exist on the racial breakdown of hourly wages in the industry, in 1939, data on annual incomes revealed that white auto workers averaged $1,291, as compared to $1,092 for blacks. These figures probably understated the race differential in average hourly rates, because blacks were concentrated in occupations that were steadier and hence worked more hours per year. Although there were cases in which blacks were paid less than whites for the same work, the largest factor causing this wage differential was the maldistribution of blacks in the job hierarchy.[35]

The Ford Motor Company deviated somewhat from this general rule of racial discrimination in the auto industry. Ford employed more blacks than any other auto firm, accounting for nearly half of their numbers in the industry. And the company employed these black workers at nearly every level of the occupational hierarchy. They could be found working as machine-tool operators, press operators, assembly-line workers, tool and die makers, and construction trade workers, as well as janitors, laborers, and foundry workers. Blacks and whites commonly worked side by side at machines and on lines. And Ford managers brooked no worker interference or complaint about their more equitable racial employment policies. But despite their marked deviation from the industry pattern, Ford's policies toward blacks were not free of racism. The more equitable policies were put into effect only at the River Rouge plant, with outlying factories practicing the racist policies characteristic of the rest of the industry. And although blacks at the Rouge were offered greater opportunities, their occupational distribution was far from balanced. Black Ford workers were overrepresented in the same low-paying, rough, hot, dirty jobs in which they were found almost exclusively in other auto firms.[36]

There is little evidence to support allegations that automotive manufacturers discriminated against blacks in occupational placement in a deliberate attempt to exacerbate divisions within the working class. Capitalists merely reflected the general racism of American society, believing that blacks were incapable of performing any but menial labor. However, once race had been superimposed upon the job structure of the industry, auto capitalists and managers did not hesitate to use the resulting antagonisms to divide workers and weaken their common struggle. The discontent of white auto workers was somewhat cushioned by their privileged position in the job hierarchy. And there is some evidence to suggest that auto capitalists did not fail to remind white workers of their superior position vis-à-vis blacks, blurring class divisions by appealing to racial loyalties.[37]

This pattern of racial discrimination also made black workers resentful of the superior positions of whites, and these resentments were cleverly manipulated by capitalists to divide workers. These black attitudes and their manipulation became most evident during the sitdown strikes of the late 1930s. Most black auto workers took a somewhat neutral attitude toward these struggles for unionization, cooperating neither with management nor organized labor. They resented white monopolization of the better jobs in the shops and were skeptical of the willingness of white workers and their unions to give up their privileges. Black workers had no reason to believe that the United Automobile Workers would be different from other American unions, most of which had either excluded blacks altogether or confined them to segregated auxiliaries. And no union had done much to combat racist employment policies in its industry. In 1937, Roy Wilkins, then assistant secretary of the NAACP, expressed the skepticism of many blacks toward the auto unionization drive. "While some Negro workers in General Motors plants have joined the United Automobile Workers of America and some took part in the sit-down strikes in Flint, many more are hanging back, asking the usual question: 'Will the union give us a square deal and a chance at some of the good jobs?' "[38]

Black workers were also reluctant to join white workers in the unionization struggle out of fear of incurring management's displeasure and provoking a deterioration in their occupational status in the industry. Compared to the general societal pattern of racial discrimination barring blacks altogether from many industries, employment even in the undesirable jobs in the auto industry was an improvement. Blacks seemed to fear that any actions against auto manufacturers would provoke retaliation that would erode their relatively better employment chances in the industry. Further, a certain sense of gratitude and loyalty among black workers and the black community as a whole was created by these relatively favorable employment policies.

In two instances, auto capitalists blatantly manipulated these black fears, loyalties, and suspicions in attempts to break ongoing strikes. Shortly after the UAW struck Chrysler in 1939, company officials began to manipulate black alienation from the union and white workers in order to launch a back-to-work movement. Chrysler used its relatively favorable image among blacks in Detroit to persuade some community leaders to encourage blacks to return to work. Managers also recruited black strikebreakers by playing upon black frustrations and resentments of whites, promising them better jobs if they participated in the scheme. Since the small number of black strikebreakers they managed to recruit could not alone resume production, the apparent strategy of Chrysler managers was to break the strike by inciting interracial violence and then calling for intervention by the National Guard. The strikebreakers, one hundred eighty-seven in all, confronted six thousand UAW pickets at the Dodge Main plant, but racial violence was averted by close cooperation between UAW officials and some far-sighted leaders of Detroit's black community. Black strikebreakers entered the plant untouched, and Chrysler agreed to bargain with the union later the same day.[39]

These attempts by Chrysler managers to manipulate blacks' fears and resentments to defeat the union were paltry in comparison to Ford's complex plan to pit race against race to break the UAW strike of 1941. But the events of that year were merely the climax of a carefully constructed racial policy that was calculated to divide Ford workers. Henry Ford's less discriminatory racial employment policies were not based upon a belief in basic racial equality, for he was also infected with racism. Rather, a peculiar blend of paternalism and Machiavellianism lay behind his policies. Ford felt bound by philanthropic duty to support what he considered to be subordinate races. But he also expected these workers to show appreciation and loyalty in return for job opportunities that were generally denied them in the larger society. Ford sought to manipulate this paternalistic loyalty and dependency of his black workers in order to block the development of a united workers' movement. As two historians have concluded from a study of Ford's policies: "While no explicit connections have been uncovered between Henry Ford's concern about radicalism and industrial strife on the one hand and his philanthropy toward blacks on the other, he did see in black America an eager reservoir of workers committed to the American system. The auto magnate pictured blacks as a quiet, compliant people, loyal to employers and the nation."[40]

Ford sought to cultivate paternalistic loyalty and dependency, not only among his black workers, but in the entire black community of Detroit. He enlisted the support of black middle-class leaders—ministers, lawyers, doctors, shop owners—in keeping black Ford workers in line. Ford could count on their assistance, not only because these petty bourgeois men were dependent upon the wages of black Ford workers for their livelihood, but also because of a carefully constructed system of patronage. Several influential blacks were hired as personnel managers to recruit and manage "very high type" black workers. But these managers only hired blacks recommended by influential leaders in the black community. Through this patronage system, as well as by carefully distributed donations in the community, Ford managed to buy the loyalty of black leaders and accentuate their bourgeois hostility to trade unions.[41]

Although these carefully cultivated ties were undoubtedly beneficial in maintaining the day-to-day subservience of black workers on the shop floor, their greatest payoff came during the unionization struggle. As early as 1937, when the first wave of sitdowns struck the industry, Ford began girding his factories for battle. And his strategy included specific plans for utilizing loyal black workers. The Service Department began to hire blacks as armed factory guards for the first time. Ford also launched a propaganda war against UAW efforts to recruit blacks, playing on racial fears and loyalties. Handbills were passed out to black workers, proclaiming that "Henry Ford has done more for our Race than the Union," and asking "Have you stopped to think who is the Real Head of the Union, and does that race care anything about you?" A Loyal Workers' Club was formed among black Ford workers, and it held mass meetings in black churches. As union pressure mounted, Ford's race-splitting policies intensified. He hired some two thousand blacks to serve as strikebreakers. And at a banquet he gave for black leaders, Ford's black personnel manager "contrasted Henry Ford's benevolences with the animosities of 'foreign-born' workers who purportedly dominated the union and excluded blacks from skilled jobs, and he bluntly informed the ministers that their future depended on the company's victory."[42]

These policies produced in black Ford workers a combination of fear and loyalty that prevented them from joining the union movement. When the UAW struck Ford on April 1, 1941, all but a few blacks left the Rouge factory with the striking workers and assumed a neutral attitude toward the struggle. However, some black workers did remain in the plant and were joined by hundreds more the next morning at the company's urgings. Ford managers tried to turn these blacks inside the Rouge into a strikebreaking force with promises of high pay and tales of white reprisals. They were sent out twice to try to smash UAW picket lines. Ford officials also attempted to build a strikebreaking movement among blacks outside of the plant, whipping up racial antagonisms at mass meetings. However, both strikebreaking attempts were unsuccessful, due largely to the reluctant support of important black leaders won by the UAW. Upset by Ford's callous pitting of blacks against whites, fearful of a race riot, and convinced that the UAW would win anyway, these leaders joined the UAW in successfully defeating both attempts to break the strike.[43]

These cases of managerial manipulation of racial loyalties and resentments during the unionization struggle are only the most blatant examples of a general policy in the industry. In the more routine, day-to-day skirmishes on the shop floor, managers used the same resentments and loyalties created by the racially segmented job hierarchy to divide and weaken workers. Because of this discriminatory job structure, managers were often successful in supplanting class with race as the basis of workers' struggle.

Sexual Discrimination

The same managerial use was made of another status division within the auto factory job hierarchy—sex. As we saw in chapter 7, sexist employment policies in the industry began at the factory gates, with men almost invariably given preference in hiring over women. However, those women who did manage to circumvent hiring barriers and obtain factory jobs faced similar sexist barriers inside the shops. Women were confined to a narrow range of jobs related to the unpaid domestic labor they performed in the home. In the automobile manufacturing division of the industry, they were concentrated in body and trim departments, sewing and fitting fabric for the cars' interiors. Women also worked as small-parts assemblers and coremakers, jobs for which their "delicate touch" was thought to suit them. A 1940 Bureau of Labor Statistics survey of automobile manufacturing firms revealed that 72 percent of all women factory workers were concentrated in these jobs. In the automotive parts division, where a greater proportion of women was employed, their range of occupations was a bit wider. They were found in small percentages in many occupations, but remained concentrated in jobs considered "women's work," especially small-parts assembly. In both divisions, the jobs dominated by women were at or near the bottom of the wage hierarchy. As a result, the average hourly wage for women auto factory workers was about 65 percent of the male average throughout the 1920s.[44]

Sexist exclusion from the broad range of automotive occupations was not the only aspect of discrimination against women in the bureaucratic job structure. Even when they did manage to fight their way into the better jobs, in every case they were given a wage classification distinct from men and consequently paid lower wages for the same work. Bureau of Labor Statistics surveys chillingly revealed the broad differentials between the average hourly wages of men and women in the same occupations. For example, in 1922 male motor assemblers received an average hourly wage of sixty-six cents, female motor assemblers, forty-eight cents; male drill-press operators received sixty-four cents, female, forty-five cents; male screw-machine operators, sixty-nine cents, female, forty cents.[45]

It is evident from the justifications offered by auto capitalists that this discrimination against women was mainly the result of the general sexism of American society. Women were thought to be frail and weak of constitution and thus unable to withstand the physical demands of most automotive occupations. Furthermore, managers claimed women were unstable workers, having turnover rates greater than men because they quit to get married or worked only for extra money to pay unexpected family expenses. As a result of this instability, women workers would not return the investment that would have been required to train them for other occupations. Employers in the auto industry used similarly sexist justifications for paying women less than men for the same work. Women were said to need less money because they supported fewer dependents, to require male assistance in adjusting machines and lifting parts, to need more frequent rest breaks and shorter hours, and to require special safety and sanitation facilities. Most of these sexist justifications for discrimination against women in the job hierarchy were belied by the auto industry's experience with women workers during the First World War. In order to alleviate the severe wartime labor shortages, employers drew upon the reserve army of women and put them to work in the full range of automotive jobs. And managers enthusiastically observed that women were able to perform all but the most strenuous factory jobs under demanding production conditions, often with greater stability, willingness, and efficiency than men. However, this experience did not prevent auto managers and capitalists from quickly reinstating the sexual segmentation of the job structure as soon as the war was over.[46]

Although the discrimination against women in the job hierarchy seems to have originated in the general sexism of American society and not in a conscious capitalist strategy to divide workers, once in place these discriminatory policies were consciously manipulated by capital to weaken workers' struggle and resistance. For example, women were sometimes pitted against men in order to force speed-ups. During the First World War, when women were extensively used in traditionally male occupations, managers noted that they often produced more than men because they did not cooperate in the restriction of output. "The reported superiority of women in some of the instances cited was so great as to suggest that restriction of output by men may have played a part in raising the comparative efficiency record of women. . . . women are less inclined than men to practice arbitrary restriction."[47] The relative unfamiliarity of many women workers with the shop culture of the working class was probably partially responsible for their failure to restrict output. But the sexist barriers in the job hierarchy were also probably instrumental in motivating such "rate-busting." As *Automotive Industries* pointed out in an editorial, women were anxious to prove themselves capable of these new jobs in order to overcome sexist job barriers. "Women entering this line of work realize that they are opening up a new field for their sex and are on probation, as it were. They know their work is being watched and compared with that of male employees, and they are eager to show up well in the comparison."[48] Furthermore, women workers may have refused to cooperate with men in work restriction because of their resentment of the male monopoly on better jobs and male opposition to their advancement. But whatever the reasons for the reluctance of women to "soldier," auto managers used these divisions between the sexes created by the sexist job structure to speed up all workers. As one capitalist commentator wrote during the First World War: "Women are now an important factor even in the automobile shops and they have been responsible for a considerable amount of speeding-up. It is found an easy matter to train a women to get the maximum out of a machine, and this has had its influence on men who have systematically kept machines below their maximum output."[49]

In some instances, auto capitalists and managers sought to use the sexually segmented job classification system to cut wages by substituting women earning lower wages for men on certain jobs. For example, in the late 1920s, a Packard worker reported that women had been substituted for men on a number of operations and earned about half of the previous male rate. In one instance, women earning thirty-five to forty cents an hour operated milling machines, replacing men who had earned sixty to sixty-five cents. In 1927, men who trimmed doors at a Murray Body plant were discharged and replaced by women making scarcely half their wages. Similar reports of the replacement of men by women in order to cut wages came from A.C. Spark Plug, Briggs, and Buick factories in the late 1920s. Complaints by auto workers about the same managerial practice broke out again in the mid-1930s. Auto workers testifying before the National Recovery Administration's committee investigating the industry stated that wage cutting through sexual reclassification was rampant in the trim, upholstery, and machine shops. This was undoubtedly encouraged by the NRA's Automobile Code, which established a sexual differential in minimum wage rates. In April 1934, workers struck the Motor Products plant in Detroit over this managerial practice of replacing male with female workers in order to slash wage costs. A similar strike occurred at Ford's Canadian plant in Windsor on December 1, 1942. More than fourteen thousand workers stayed out for a week when Ford hired thirty-seven women earning fifty cents an hour to replace male stockroom workers earning seventy-five cents an hour.[50]

Auto capitalists and managers were able to use female workers to cut wages only because they systematically discriminated against them in the wage classification system. And women were probably more willing to be used in this way because of the normal policy excluding them from the broad range of occupations in the auto shops. They were anxious to gain access to jobs previously reserved for males, even at the cost of lowering wage rates. Because of the hostility often shown them by men in the factories, women could hardly have been expected to show great concern for the plight of displaced male workers. Thus, as with the status divisions of race and ethnicity, auto capitalists used the sexual divisions that had been superimposed on the hierarchical job structure to divide and conquer workers. The privilege and prejudice of the white, native-born males at the top of the job ladder, as well as the pent-up resentment and hostility of the ethnics, blacks, and women below, were manipulated to weaken the united opposition of workers against their bosses.

CHAPTER 12
The Impact of Unionization on the Labor Process

Despite all of the repressive-control measures taken by auto capitalists to overcome working-class resistance, auto workers managed to topple one of the key battlements in the fortress of capitalist domination of the industry—the open shop. Their victory in the battle for unionization marked the beginning of a new phase in the continuing war of labor and capital. Auto capitalists and managers no longer faced an unorganized force of scattered and divided workers fighting a defensive battle. Unionization marked the entrance onto the industrial battlefield of an organized army of workers, which was determined to go on the offensive to recapture lost territory. It is the impact of this more organized force of unionized workers upon the contested terrain of the labor process that forms the subject of this final chapter.

As we saw in our look at earlier attempts at labor organization in chapter 8, what the capitalists and managers of the American automobile industry feared from unions was not higher levels of wages and benefits. They were quite willing to pay for industrial peace with greater monetary compensation for workers. Their main fear was worker interference with their absolute control over the process of production. Auto capitalists and managers had spent millions to construct a labor process that centralized control in their hands, and to purchase the acquiescence of workers to it. They feared that all of their efforts and outlays would go for naught if a powerful body of organized workers demanded and won greater control over their own labor.

The Struggle for Unionization

Automotive manufacturers were justified in fearing union challenges to their dictatorial factory rule. The grievances behind the
union movement as well as the initial efforts of the young United
Auto Workers confirm that workers saw organization as a means to
greater worker control over production. Like the earlier push toward
organization following the First World War, the unionization efforts
of the 1930s were in large part attempts by workers to recapture part
of the control over the labor process that capitalists and managers
had wrested from them.

Undoubtedly the main worker grievance behind the unionization
struggle was speed-up. After taking testimony from auto workers
throughout the country on the labor conditions in the industry, the
Research and Planning Division of the National Recovery Administration concluded that:

> The grievance which was mentioned most frequently and which ap-
> peared uppermost in the minds of those who testified is the
> "speed-up." Everywhere workers indicated that they were being
> forced to work harder and harder to put out more and more products
> in the same amount of time with less workers doing the job. . . . If
> there is any one cause for a conflagration in the Automobile Industry,
> it is this one.[1]

The Great Depression brought labor market conditions that made
speed-up possible. With thousands of unemployed workers clamoring at the gates of auto factories for jobs, the workers inside could
do little to resist the relentless capitalist pressure for intensified labor. So when the leaders of the new United Auto Workers union
formulated a list of demands to serve as the basis for their organizing drive, the elimination of speed-up was at the top.

Speed-up was actually a complex grievance, encompassing many
of the fears and resentments of auto workers. But the common
theme in all speed-up complaints was the absolute and dictatorial
authority of capitalists and managers on the shop floor. As Sidney
Fine wrote in his scholarly history of the unionization struggle at
General Motors:

> The speed-up meant different things to different automobile workers.
> It was the inexorable speed and the "coerced rhythms" of the assem-
> bly line, an insufficient number of relief men on the line, the produc-

tion standards set for individual machines, the foreman holding a stop watch over the worker or urging more speed, the pace set by the "lead men" or straw boss on a non-line operation, and incentive pay systems that encouraged the employee to increase his output. However expressed, the complaints of the speed-up summed up the automobile worker's reaction to the fact that he was not free, as perhaps he had been on some previous job, to set the pace of his work and to determine the manner in which it was to be performed.[2]

The generic speed-up complaint also encompassed grievances about pay and job security. Workers judged the adequacy of their wages in relation to the work demanded of them, thus calculating a common-sense rate of exploitation. And most auto workers judged their pay to be inadequate for the intensity of work they were forced to maintain, especially during the Depression when wages were constantly cut and lines speeded up. The issue of job security was also bound up with speed-up complaints. During the Depression, layoffs and firings were generally determined by the ability and willingness of workers to intensify their labor. The slowest workers were laid off first. Older workers, many with years of seniority in a firm, were hit hard by this practice, because of their physical inability to keep pace with the intensified labor. Speed-up complaints thus encompassed worker grievances about job insecurity and the lack of a seniority system in auto factories. Most auto workers saw the union as a way of fighting these and the other implications of speed-up and regaining some control over their own work.[3]

The importance of workers' control as an issue in the unionization movement is also substantiated by the social locus of union support within the automotive labor force. There is evidence to suggest that those workers facing deskilling and speed-up were most active in the union movement. Workers in the body plants, for example, were in the vanguard of the sitdown movement, initiating many of the conflicts with manufacturers. And although their militancy can be partially explained by the hard and dirty labor required of body plant workers, at least of equal importance was the deskilling that their jobs were undergoing during this period. Previously skilled jobs like metal finishing were being mechanized and speeded-up, as well as undergoing wage cuts. In his study of the union movement in a parts plant, Friedlander found the greatest militancy among production welders, whose relatively skilled jobs were being progressively rationalized, mechanized, and speeded-up. In both cases, a surviving consciousness of skill and control propelled these workers into the vanguard of the union movement, which they hoped would protect them against further capitalist encroachments upon their power.[4]

Auto workers' grievances about their loss of control over work were not, of course, new to the 1930s. Deskilling, speed-up, incentive wages, arbitrary managerial authority—all of these conditions had existed in the industry since its phenomenal growth in the late 1910s. Why, then, did auto workers wait so long to mount a union movement to fight these conditions? The answer must be found in the unique context in which the Depression placed these sources of discontent. The phenomenal growth of the industry during its first three decades caused, as we have seen, a chronic labor shortage. These labor market conditions channeled discontent predominantly into an individual form of resistance, labor turnover. If a worker disliked the working conditions in one plant, instead of staying and fighting for their improvement, he or she simply quit and sought more favorable work elsewhere. However, the Great Depression, which was the first sustained period of economic downturn to hit the industry, changed all of this. Labor market conditions shifted from scarcity to surplus, and the lack of alternative employment opportunities cut off the traditional escape route from unfavorable shop conditions. For the first time, the threat of being fired, wielded arbitrarily by capital, became gravely serious. And the conditions that this threat enforced—speed-up, stretch-out, wage cuts, incentive wages—took on a new gravity. The Depression thus tightly shut the safety valve on the pressure cooker of the auto shops, causing the pressure slowly and ominously to mount. The force of discontent could no longer harmlessly escape through the factory gates in the form of turnover. It was redirected against the basic constraints of the capitalist labor process itself. The explosion came in 1936 and 1937, when auto workers shut down practically the entire industry with the sitdown strikes.[5]

This mounting discontent of auto workers was not, however, in itself sufficient to produce a successful struggle to unionize the industry. As we have seen in the preceding chapters, auto capitalists had shored up their defenses against worker resistance through the bureaucratization of authority and the job structure. And as the nascent union movement grew, they used these repressive tools to fight it. How, then, were auto workers able to win unionization against this powerful capitalist opposition? It was the contradictions of capitalism analyzed in chapter 8 that made a union victory possible.

First, despite managerial attempts to fragment working-class interests with divisive job ladders and wage differentials, continuing mechanization and rationalization of work inexorably increased the homogeneity of the work force. As table 8.2 reveals, the range of variation in auto workers' wages remained quite narrow. Thus, by continuing to introduce deskilling technology and work organization, auto capitalists and managers reproduced the objective conditions for worker unity at the same time that they struggled to overcome this unity.

Second, the general capitalist law of concentration and centralization of capital also strengthened union forces. The concentration of masses of workers into large automotive factories facilitated worker communication and organization. A few UAW speakers or leafleters strategically positioned outside the factory gates carried their message to thousands of auto workers in a few moments. So troublesome did the handful of union activists at the gates of Ford's River Rouge complex prove to be that the company resorted to legal restrictions and ultimately physical force against them. Within these huge factories, a few carefully placed union organizers carried the word to hundreds of workers. Furthermore, the concentration of corporate production in large factories greatly increased its susceptibility to interruption. When the entire car or even a few vital parts were produced in a single factory, as was often the case in the industry, closing that factory could bring the entire corporation's production to a halt. The UAW consciously manipulated this contradiction to its advantage in the struggle. As one participant in the unionization drive at General Motors subsequently wrote:

> The union's strategy held that the chief burden of the strike must be born by Flint's Fisher One and by Cleveland Fisher with the former taking the lead. . . . Possibly three-fourths or more of the corporation's production were consequently dependent on these two plants; an interlocking arrangement that was not unusual, moreover, in the highly specialized auto industry and especially among the leading corporations. . . . The entire blueprint of the union's organizing schedule depended upon this type of careful selection for its forces were terribly limited and the power it opposed so commanding.[6]

The sitdown strikes in these two plants late in December 1936, virtually paralyzed the entire General Motors Corporation. With the closing of a third strategic plant—Chevrolet No. 4, which was the sole production site for Chevrolet engines—a union victory was clinched.

A third contradiction making a union victory possible in the auto factories was the interdependence of the labor process and its consequent vulnerability to disruption. The method of line production relied so absolutely upon the carefully calculated continuity of work from one station to the next that if one of these stations broke down, the entire mechanism ground to a halt. Following the example of sitdown strikers in the rubber plants, a small group of dedicated unionists exploited this contradiction to shut down the highly interdependent labor process in auto plant after auto plant. A group of fifty workers sat down on the Fisher Body line and shut down the seven thousand-three hundred-worker plant. At Cadillac's Fleetwood body plant, ninety of the thirteen hundred workers sat down, forcing its closing in a few hours. And at the strategic Chevrolet No. 4 plant, two hundred UAW members concentrated at key points in the conveyorized engine plant shut down the facility, which employed about three thousand eight hundred workers. Describing the ease of the shutdown in one division, one participant wrote: "He [Gib Rose] reached up and pulled the switch and conveyor A-1 was dead. This was the signal for Dow Kehler who headed conveyor A-2. In five seconds she was down, too. When Kenny Malone saw that he pulled the switch on conveyor A-3 and the entire division was frozen."[7] Squads of unionists stationed at key conveyors secured the plant shutdown against worker and managerial opposition.

The unionization of the automobile industry was thus largely an attempt of auto workers to regain some control over their own labor. The labor market conditions of the Depression deflected the expression of these worker grievances away from indirect, individualistic channels into more direct and collective efforts. And the contradictions within the capitalist economy and auto labor process strengthened these efforts and made a union victory possible. Of course, there were other forces apart from these economic ones behind the union struggle and victory. Of particular importance was the balance of political forces. With the New Dealers at the helm, the state lent its weight to the construction of a partnership between government, capital, and labor, whose purpose it was to contain the upsurge of labor and popular movements and stabilize the fluctuations of American capitalism. As part of this policy, the federal government encouraged unionism as the organizational vehicle of the cooptation of labor into the lopsided partnership. However, my treatment of the union struggle here is not intended to be comprehensive and definitive, but merely to trace the impact of forces within the labor process, which is my focal concern.

EARLY UNION CHALLENGE TO CAPITALIST CONTROL

Having ridden to victory on a wave of discontent about the dictatorial control of capital over production, the young United Auto Workers union began immediately to challenge this control. In the shops and out, the UAW and its militants pushed hard to regain some power over production, thus calling into question the entire capitalist-controlled labor process that had taken some thirty years to build. The actions of workers on the shop floor confirmed that their intentions in joining the union struggle went far beyond collective bargaining for wages and benefits. They meant in large part to run the shops. As two close students of unionism in the industry observed of these first days: "In effect a rebellion occurred against managerial discipline in many of the shops. The newly elected union committeemen were 'biting at the heels of the foremen' with all sorts of beefs, complaints, grievances, and outright threats. Where this kind of direct action brought no results, sit-down strikes and 'quickies' were organized."[8] One story that came out of the newly unionized Ford shops well illustrates the radical intentions and expectations of auto workers following union victories. In one department, the workers chose as their committeeman a man who had done an outstanding job as a picket captain during the strike. Immediately upon his election, he walked over to the department foreman, pointed to his committeeman's button, and exclaimed: "Do you see this?" The foreman replied, "Ah yes, you are the new committeeman. Congratulations." The committeeman snapped: "Congratulations, hell. I'm running this department now—you scram the hell out of here."[9]

One area in which the union mounted a strong challenge to capitalist authority was that of work intensity. Because speed-up was the strongest complaint of auto workers during the union struggle, one of the first steps taken by organized workers was to try to regain some control over work pace. Rank-and-file militants used direct action on the shop floor to slow down the speeding lines and enforce their standard of a fair day's work. One Dodge worker stated that while, previously, foremen and superintendents had exercised autocratic authority: "Now they had to deal with our stewards, and this was hard for them to take, especially when we challenged them on production standards. We told them the contract called for a fair day's work for a fair day's pay, and by God a fair day's work was all they were going to get. . . . Sometimes foremen would jerk up the automatic conveyor a couple of notches and speed up the line. We cured them of that practice; we simply let jobs go by half-finished."[10] When such actions were not sufficient to force managers to slow down work intensity, workers and stewards resorted to sitdowns and stoppages, ignoring contract provisions prohibiting such interruptions of production. In the interval between the signing of the first major agreements in March 1937 and the beginning of May 1939, there were more than two thousand recorded sitdowns, slowdowns, or other production stoppages by unionized workers. And as the auto plants moved into war production in the 1940s, this struggle to control work pace intensified. During 1944 alone, there were one thousand forty-five recorded strikes and work stoppages in five hundred automotive plants. And the principal issue in most of these actions was production standards.

While rank-and-file union members struggled on the shop floor, UAW leaders fought at the bargaining table for a formal mechanism to ensure their participation in setting production standards. In practically every major contract negotiation between 1937 and 1950, UAW bargainers pushed for worker codetermination of standards. Strikes against Chrysler in 1939, GM in 1945–1946, and Ford in 1949 all involved as a major demand a union role in work-pace determination. The Big Three automobile manufacturers held firm against this demand. However, the UAW did win formal codetermination of standards in several of the smaller, independent automotive companies.[11]

The UAW never directly challenged the right of capital to determine the technology and organization of labor. But its attempts to exert control over work intensity indirectly challenged this unilateral right. One of the biggest advantages of the new technologies introduced by capital was their intensification of labor. The union's challenge of capital's right to determine dictatorially the intensity of labor threatened to limit severely the advantages to be reaped from the new technology and consequently capital's control over it.

The young union of auto workers also challenged unilateral capitalist control over worker discipline, through which intensified labor was enforced. The sanctions that loomed largest in the disciplinary arsenal of capital were firings and layoffs. The unilateral capitalist power to determine dismissals and layoffs during periods of slack business rendered workers virtually helpless to resist demands for more work. Because the resulting job insecurity was one of the major grievances behind the union movement, the young UAW moved quickly to curb this absolute authority of capital. The struggle over worker discipline, like that over work intensity, was waged simultaneously on the shop floor and at the bargaining table. In contract negotiations with automotive manufacturers, union officials fought for and won grievance procedures to curb arbitrary firing. The grievance structure provided a formal mechanism with several levels whereby workers could appeal the disciplinary actions of managers. In order to restrict the arbitrary managerial use of layoffs and rehirings, the UAW negotiated seniority systems. The details of these systems varied from company to company, but all basically determined the order of layoffs and rehirings by the length of employment within certain occupational and departmental groups.[12]

On the shop floor, rank-and-file workers did not wait for the negotiation of these formal mechanisms to launch an offensive to curb arbitrary managerial discipline. Even after these procedures were in place, they were often ignored in favor of more spontaneous and direct challenges to disciplinary actions. Alfred Reeves, vice-president of the Automobile Manufacturers Association, stated in 1937 that there existed a "dangerous attitude" among auto workers that managers did not have the right to fire.[13] This attitude grew during the Second World War, when strikes and stoppage protesting disciplinary actions skyrocketed.

During its infancy, the United Auto Workers union also challenged the bureaucratic job structure that capitalists and managers had established to motivate and control workers. The union struggled to make the job structure more egalitarian and to render movement within it dependent upon seniority. First, a struggle was launched to eliminate personal wage differentials. The union recognized that such differences in wages between workers on the same job were used by managers to create dissension and force speed-up. So it fought tenaciously to eliminate them, by replacing incentive wages with straight-time wages and by reducing merit and service differentials between workers. Second, the UAW fought to equalize the wage differentials between different job classifications, thus flattening the wage hierarchy that divided workers' interests. Against considerable capitalist opposition, the union generally pushed for across-the-board, flat-rate increases for all workers, which had the intended effect of favoring the lowest-paid workers and reducing the relative dispersion of wages. Furthermore, by filing a grievance contesting the reclassification of any job, the union forced management to adopt much broader and less differentiated classification systems.[14]

UAW pressure in negotiations relating to seniority systems also aimed to breakdown the bureaucratic job structure. One of the most important issues in this struggle was the size of the unit within which seniority applied. Managers sought to establish very narrow seniority units, which maintained a differentiated and closed job structure. The union, however, sought to define units as broad as possible, often plant-wide. This meant that when work in one department in a plant was cut back, workers not needed there could remain employed by replacing or "bumping" workers with less seniority in any other department or occupation in the plant. This tended to open up the job structure and make job security more dependent upon the equitable criterion of seniority than upon the invidious distinctions of the job structure. In an attempt to further restrict the capitalist use of the job hierarchy to control workers, the union also struggled to make seniority, rather than arbitrary managerial judgments, the basis for promotion.[15]

The United Auto Workers also generally fought to eliminate the racial and sexual inequalities in the job structure. The international union had unequivocal policies favoring racial equality in pay and opportunity. It pressed in contract negotiations for clauses barring racial discimination and made some efforts to combat racial bias in the shops. However, these policies were often pursued with less than maximum vigor, because of strong opposition on two fronts: rank-and-file union members and their local officials, and management. Both groups had vested interests in the system of racial discrimination, which they vigorously defended. The UAW similarly had definite policies barring sexual discrimination, but it was less enthusiastic in enforcing these against managerial and rank-and-file opposition than in enforcing anti-racist policies. The union fought to eliminate the blatantly discriminatory practice of sexual differentials on the same job. But the male-dominated union structure showed little interest in breaking down the sexist job structure that generally confined women to a narrow range of low-paying occupations.[16]

Most of these union challenges to capitalist relations were indirect, seeking mainly to modify the labor process. However, in several ways the early UAW directly challenged the property relations of capitalism, by putting forth social-democratic plans for worker participation in decisions on investments and the accumulation process, which are usually the sole prerogative of owners. The first such challenge came during the Second World War and was known as the Reuther plan. In 1940, the UAW endorsed Walter Reuther's scheme for using idle automotive-manufacturing resources for aircraft production. The challenge in the plan was an aviation production board, composed of equal numbers of presidential appointees from government, labor, and management and having full authority to manage aircraft production in auto plants. Despite the plan's defeat, the union came forward at the end of the war with another plan to get labor's foot in the managerial door. It proposed a sixteen-point program for converting industry from war to civilian production, which included provisions for a pool of labor and machinery cutting across corporate lines, a thirty-hour work week, government operation of monopolistic industries, fixing normal sales prices for some commodities, and priority production for urgent social needs. The entire conversion process was to be managed by a Peace Production Board, composed of representatives from labor, management, consumers, government, and agriculture. Once again, the plan went down to defeat in a barrage of capitalist protests. But undaunted in its attempts to win for labor a voice in management, the UAW fought for another plan threatening property relations in its confrontation with General Motors in 1945. In contract negotiations, the union demanded that a 30 percent wage increase be accompanied by a company promise not to increase automobile prices. By doing this, the UAW sought to mobilize broader consumer support for labor struggles, as well as to win participation in investment and pricing decisions. When GM rejected the proposal, the UAW struck, initiating one of the bitterest battles in the union's history.[17]

Although the international union organization played a role in all of these early struggles for greater worker control, in most, the initiative came from the rank and file. The early structure of the United Automobile Workers was relatively decentralized and democratic. The local unions were left largely unfettered by the international union organization to struggle for their own survival and bargain with local plant managements over a broad range of issues. The top of the UAW structure had its hands full with campaigns for recognition, bargaining over wages and hours, and factional disputes. Within this decentralized early structure, the key role was played by the shop stewards. They were the front-line troops in the union army, fighting toe-to-toe with foremen over workers' grievances and complaints. It was at this shop-floor level that the early battle over control of production largely took place. The grievance machinery was new and rickety, and centralized control had not yet been established in the union. As a result, stewards exercised much power and initiative, often calling local wildcat strikes over a grievance.[18]

Capitalist Counteroffensive to Retain Control of Production

The capitalists and managers of the American automobile industry made it clear from the beginning that they would not tolerate what they perceived as union challenges to their managerial prerogatives. Although they had lost the battle for unionization, they did not intend to lose the entire war for control of production. Automotive manufacturers retained a great deal of economic and political strength, and they were quite willing to use it to destroy the infant union organization, if it could not be tamed. They were determined to allow the union to survive only under the condition that it abandon its challenges to capitalist property rights and control over the labor process and accommodate itself to capitalist relations of production. As far as auto capitalists were concerned, the only role open for the union was that of copartner in maintaining the discipline and stability of the work force within a labor process dominated by themselves.

A capitalist ultimatum—accommodate to our rule or perish—was issued to the union in the first days after its early victories. It was well summarized by a statement authored by the editor of *Automotive Industries.*

> Can unionism be sold to us like improved machinery which is offered and gladly accepted as a means for providing increased production at reduced unit cost, better products at lower prices, and greater availability of useful goods to a larger portion of our population?
>
> Can unionism be sold to us as an agency for the promotion of industrial stability, as a maker of jobs and a creator of individual opportunity; as a stimulator of individual initiative; as a provider of more skillful and more reliable workers upon whom we can constantly depend for efficient and effective effort in the conduct of the nation's business?
>
> Can unionism be sold to us as an upholder and safe-guarder of fundamental Americanism, as a champion and protector of individual and minority rights, as an uncompromising advocate and supporter of the right of every worker to "that freedom of choice and action which is justly his?"
>
> If unionism had the material for a sales campaign build along those lines, it could be easily sold and would be readily accepted. But unionism as we see it today, surrounded by its atmosphere of industrial strife, its minority strikes, its slowdowns, picketting, internecine struggles, its restrictions, demands and threats, stands, unattractively to say the least, as something which finds for itself a most reluctant acceptance and that only on a take-it-or-else basis.[19]

Capitalist Pressure Toward Union Bureaucratization

Automotive manufacturers demanded from the union above all a stable, predictable, and compliant work force to work their machines and valorize their capital. In return, they were willing to ensure the organization's survival, as well as make concessions in the areas of wages, benefits, hours of work, seniority, and other employment conditions. But manufacturers were adamant that collective bargaining be confined to these issues alone. They would not tolerate union interference in the sacred managerial rights of setting production standards, discipline, methods of production, hiring, pricing, and product determination. One former labor negotiator for GM summarized the policy of the entire industry when he stated: "GM's position had always been, give the union the money, the least possible, but give them what it takes. But don't let them take the business away from us."[20]

The large auto corporations demanded this trade-off—survival and money for worker discipline and stability—from the outset. In a letter to the UAW president four months after signing the first union contract, GM president Knudsen threatened to cancel negotiations for a new contract if the union did not discipline workers engaged in unauthorized strikes. "For failure on the part of the Union to take such action, or to prevent strikes and stoppages to production, as herein provided for, the company shall have the right to terminate the agreement."[21] The weak and disorganized union, barely on its feet after a lengthy recognition battle, could little afford another struggle with one of the most powerful corporations in the United States. It had to yield to capitalist demands to discipline its workers. But this was difficult to do so long as the organization was so decentralized. Initially, full responsibility for controlling unauthorized strikes and disciplining participants was retained by the local unions, which were often the leaders in shop-floor militancy. So under heavy capitalist pressure, the union took its first step on the road to a centralized, bureaucratic structure. The International Executive Board signed a formal agreement with GM in September 1937, assuming responsibility for the control of wildcatters. When the conference of convention delegates, representing local unions, met and rejected this agreement, the board usurped its power and adopted resolutions in May 1938 reaffirming its full control over the discipline of wildcat strikers.[22]

Not only did the automotive manufacturers force the union to discipline wildcat strikers. They also forced it to recognize and endorse their own disciplinary actions against unauthorized strikes. In 1946 contract negotiations, both Ford and Chrylser demanded that in return for union security the UAW endorse a "company security agreement." Eventually included in both contracts, this clause gave the corporation the right to discipline and/or discharge any worker taking part in an unauthorized work stoppage and bound the union not to oppose such managerial actions. In 1947, General Motors similarly demanded and won union agreement to a provision giving management the unilateral right to discipline wildcat strikers without union challenge. With the political backing of the Taft-Hartley Act, even the small and less powerful independent manufacturers were able to win company security agreements. For example, in 1947 the UAW signed a contract with the Murray Body Corporation relieving the union of legal liability under Taft-Hartley for unauthorized breaches of contract (strikes) in exchange for guaranteeing the discipline and productivity of its members. The union agreed to authorize no strikes over production standards or "managerial rights," to exhaust the grievance procedure before authorizing any other strikes, to order workers to resume production in the case of a wildcat strike, and to allow the company to discipline wildcat strikers as it saw fit. A similar agreement was signed with Reo Motors in the same year.[23]

The automotive corporations also forced the union to centralize and bureaucratize the grievance procedure in order to ensure the discipline of workers. The decentralized system, leaving power in the hands of militant stewards on the shop floor, was unacceptable to capitalists and managers. By applying pressure, they forced the UAW to agree to a rule-governed structure that removed power over grievances from the shop floor and centralized it in the hands of top managers and union officials. The first step in this process of bureaucratization was the reduction of the number of shop stewards. While the UAW generally sought to create a vast network of stewards—about one for every twenty-five workers—managers sought from the outset to limit their numbers. By 1939, General Motors had won limitation of union representatives (committeemen) to one for every four hundred employees. The 1941 Ford-UAW contract provided for only one steward for every five hundred and fifty workers.[24]

The major step in bureaucratizing the grievance procedure, however, was the adoption of the impartial umpire system. First introduced into the 1940 GM-UAW contract at the suggestion of the union, this system resolved grievances over which top managers and union officials were unable to agree by referring them to an impartial umpire jointly chosen by union and company. It was incorporated into Ford and Chrysler contracts in 1943 by order of the War Labor Board. Dealing principally with disciplinary actions by managers, the umpire system had the effect of bureaucratizing the struggle over worker discipline. No longer did stewards on the shop floor directly challenge capitalist sanctions against workers; they merely referred grievances up the hierarchy. The decisions reached at the top of the structure became codified as precedents and rules governing the actions of lower officials in both union and corporate hierarchies.

Top union officials originally proposed and pushed the umpire system, probably as a way to curb the power of shop stewards and centralize union power. Managers accepted the system only reluctantly at first, but they eventually became its staunchest supporters, because it increased the predictability and stability of labor relations. As one industry analyst wrote: "The corporation has looked upon the grievance machinery as a great achievement in collective bargaining and as an effective stabilizing device in management-union relations." With grievances governed not by the unpredictable and often militant stewards, but by rules and precedents made at the top, union leaders were able to exercise greater control over the rank and file and thus ensure managers the stable and predictable work force they demanded as the price for union survival. Typical of rank-and-file reaction to the plan was a statement by a former UAW steward. "When the company and the union agreed to set up a so-called umpire system, we stewards became mere referral agents. The union contract got larger and more complicated, union procedure became more legal, grievances got channeled right up to the international union and finally to the umpire. It became more and more difficult to settle grievances on the job. . . ."[25]

Also enhancing the union's performance of its role as discipliner and stabilizer of the work force was the progressive centralization and bureaucratization of the system of collective bargaining. Of course, there existed a certain amount of centralization in bargaining from the very beginning. The UAW signed contracts covering all workers in a corporation. But in the early days, such corporate contracts covered only a few crucial issues: union recognition, wages, and benefits. A large number of issues dealing with workplace control—seniority, grievance procedures, production standards, job structure—were left in the hands of local unions to negotiate with their plant managements. But several years after the first contracts were signed, the decentralized structure in which the rank and file played a crucial role began to be centralized under the control of union officials. In 1939, the UAW created corporation departments to unify the demands of all locals in a corporation into a single package to be pressed on the employer. Each department was composed of a director, a staff of international representatives, an intracorporation council representing the locals within the corporation, and a national negotiating committee, elected by the council and responsible for bargaining with management for demands determined by the council. Agreements by locals supplementing the corporation-wide contract had to be approved by the council. By the early 1950s, further centralization of collective bargaining was accomplished through determining substantially the economic demands for all departments in the national convention or a special economic conference. The only real power within the bargaining process left to the rank and file was the ability to reject the contract negotiated by the department's negotiating committee.[26]

This trend of centralization and bureaucratization was evident not only in the union's dealings with capital but also in its internal structure. From a decentralized, democratic organization, the United Auto Workers gradually evolved toward a bureaucracy that concentrated power in the hands of top leaders. The national convention, composed of delegates from local unions, remained the sovereign body of the UAW, but it fell gradually under the control of top officials and became less representative of rank-and-file opinion. Much of union policy on important issues was formulated in committees appointed by the International Executive Board. The role of convention delegates was reduced mainly to accepting or rejecting these policies. The replacement of the annual convention with a biennial one in 1953 further removed the top union officials from responsibility to the rank and file.[27]

Automotive capitalists and managers actively encouraged and rewarded a bureaucratic union structure, for it facilitated the union's role as copartner in maintaining labor discipline and stability. Blunt statements made their position on union structure clear. Henry Ford II told a meeting of the Society for Automotive Engineers: "We do not want to destroy the unions. We want to strengthen their leadership by urging and helping them to assume the responsibility they must assume if the public interest is to be served. It is clear, then, that we must look to an improved and increasingly responsible union leadership for help in solving the human equation in mass production."[28] Upon the signing of the first Ford-UAW contract in 1941, *Business Week* was even more blunt in its call for the centralization of union power. Without a centralized structure, the magazine stated, the UAW would be unable to play the role of partner envisioned by the company.

Vast, sprawling, and now with the absorption of Ford employees probably the largest and potentially wealthiest union in the country, UAW has been discredited more than once by its policy of "home rule." Home rule worked to give each local enough autonomy so that it could defy the parent organization and embarrass it. . . . The only way Ford is going to get union protection in his plants, without which his union shop contract can mean complete chaos, is to have UAW transformed into a strongly centralized organization exerting iron discipline over its constituent locals and over its rank and file. For the Ford-UAW partnership to be profitable, UAW must first put its house in order.[29]

In order to encourage centralization and remove leaders from accountability to the rank and file, automotive capitalists and managers gave the union various "security measures." The more secure the UAW's existence in the industry, the less it had to generate continual rank-and-file support by pursuing popular demands and grievances, and the more it could afford to take the unpopular action of disciplining workers. In the forefront of provision for union security was the Ford Motor Company. Although it held out against unionization longer than the other automotive giants, when Ford finally accepted the inevitability of unions, it gave the UAW the best contract in the industry. The 1941 strike-settling agreement gave the UAW a union shop for all Ford workers in the U.S. and a dues check-off. Ford's union shop, *Business Week* observed, facilitated "union protection, a kind of plant policing by the union for the company."

> Where union membership is not a condition of employment, labor organization must ever be active if it is to anchor the loyalty of employees and keep them convinced that it is to their interest to pay their dues. To achieve this, it constantly seeks "grievances," and where they cannot be found it often manufactures them. . . . But once a union gets a union shop and check-off, the pressure for demonstrating its value to members and possible recruits is lifted.[30]

Top UAW officials held out the promise of such stable, centralized control of labor in pushing for similar security agreements in other companies. One student of the industry paraphrased union leaders' claims as follows:

> The union cannot assume full responsibility for observance of the agreement until it has the protection of the union shop. Any attempt of its officers to enforce production standards or to discipline members for a violation of agreement would, in the absence of this protection, result in withdrawals from the union and the weakening of the organization. With the granting of the union shop the union will be able to enforce compliance of its members with the agreement. Only then, union officers conclude, can their organization be thoroughly responsible.[31]

But an analysis of all UAW contracts for 1941 revealed that only 40 percent required union membership of all covered employees. It took an order by the National War Labor Board in June of 1942 to generalize these union security provisions throughout the industry.[32]

Some scholars critical of this bureaucratization of unions and labor relations have held union leaders mainly responsible. Following in the tradition of Robert Michels, they have depicted top labor officials as leading American workers down the road to bureaucratization and accommodation, either because of their accommodationist ideologies or their self-interested pursuit of power and privilege. For example, in recent works, both Martin Glaberman and Nelson Lichtenstein partially explain the bureaucratization of the UAW by the social-democratic ideology of leaders like Walter Reuther. Because they held a corporatist vision of top level union participation with management and government in the planning of the economy, they were eager to centralize power in their hands and were not reluctant to compromise shop-floor issues for this broader, social agenda. While it may be true that union leaders' ideology played a part in their actions, it was not the central factor. The process of bureaucratization and accommodation within the UAW began long before the advocates of "social unionism" gained control, when union leadership still contained an influential Communist faction. All union leaders, regardless of their ideologies, were forced to operate within the structural constraints of the extant American political economy. In order to ensure the survival of their organizations within a society so overwhelmingly dominated by corporate capital, they were forced to mold unions to play the only available role—that of partner to capital in disciplining and stabilizing the work force. The strength and demands of auto capital, not union leaders' ideology, were primarily responsible for the course taken by the UAW.[33]

This is not to say that capital was the only force behind the bureaucratization and stabilization of labor relations in the U.S. Lichtenstein convincingly demonstrates that the state played an independent role in this process. In order to ensure stable, high-level war production during the Second World War, he argues, the state enforced a labor policy that granted industrial unions security and benefits in return for centralized control of rank-and-file militancy. While it is true that the state's war policy was instrumental in the construction of a stable, centralized system of labor relations in the auto industry, it was not decisive. As I have demonstrated above, pressure toward a bureaucratic system of collective bargaining existed prior to the war and emanated not from the state, but directly from capital. The state's war labor policy hastened this trend, because during this period, its interest in peaceful, stable war production coincided with capital's interest in centralized, bureaucratic control over labor. Thus, National War Labor Board rulings extended the umpire system and union security provisions. But these measures had been in use before the war and continued after peace brought an end to direct state enforcement, mainly because industry capitalists and managers perceived them to be in their interests.[34]

The importance of capital's role in this process is substantiated by comparing the degree of bureaucratization of labor relations in auto companies of varying strengths. In the largest firms, which possessed top market positions and large economic reserves, labor relations were highly centralized and bureaucratized. Due to their overwhelming economic power, capitalists in these firms were able to withstand long strikes by the UAW over issues that challenged their power. The union was forced to play the role of discipliner and stabilizer that capital demanded of it, and to bureaucratize its structure in order to do so. However, in the smaller and competitively weaker automotive firms, labor relations were generally less centralized and bureaucratized. Because of their precarious financial and competitive positions, capitalists in these firms could not withstand a prolonged battle with labor. They were the first to recognize UAW locals and to give them contracts closer to union demands. These companies did not have the strength to force their locals to play the role of disciplinary agent, and consequently their labor relations were much less centralized and bureaucratized.

These generalities are substantiated by the comparative study of the labor relations of General Motors and Studebaker published in 1947 by Frederick Harbison and Robert Dubin. They found that union-management relations at GM were highly centralized and bureaucratized. The management pushed for formalistic and centralized relations, based upon written rules and procedures negotiated at the top levels of the union and management hierarchies. The corporation repeatedly demonstrated the will and power to endure long strikes to defeat union attempts to expand the scope of collective bargaining beyond these bureaucratic limits. On the other hand, labor relations at Studebaker were found to be much more informal and decentralized. Management based its dealings with the union, not on tenaciously defended principles, but on an informal, problem-oriented arrangement. Due to its precarious economic position, "the company could ill afford to have taken a do-or-die stand in an actual situation just as a matter of eternal principle."[35] When Studebaker managers did try to move the union toward more bureaucratic procedures, the local union successfully resisted. Because of its strength vis-à-vis capital, the Studebaker local maintained its autonomy from both union and management bureaucracies and remained responsive to the demands of the rank and file.

There exists the possibility, of course, that this suggested correlation between bureaucratization and capitalist strength is spurious—that it was not capitalist strength that determined bureaucratization, but rather firm size that determined both. It might be argued that the sheer size of firms like General Motors caused both management and union to centralize and bureaucratize their relations in order to render them efficient and coherent, while in small firms like Studebaker, more informal, decentralized dealings were possible. However, the effect of this size variable may be controlled by examining the extent of bureaucratization in large firms alone. And it seems that capitalist strength remains an important variable accounting for bureaucratization. For example, American Motors, a fairly large multiplant company, characterized by the same competitive weakness as many small firms, also possessed rather decentralized and nonformalistic labor relations. The five local unions of the corporation retained considerable autonomy, and they were not constrained by bureaucratic procedures negotiated by a centralized power structure. Even among the Big Three auto makers, the extent of bureaucratization of labor relations varied by the relative strength of management. In his study of collective bargaining in the auto industry, Robert Macdonald found that the international union exercised less firm control over local activities at Ford and Chrysler than at General Motors, with the result that labor relations in the former were less stable. Local insurgency and opposition to international leadership were more frequent and intense at Ford and Chrysler, even though all three firms had substantially similar formal structures of labor relations by 1950. Although Macdonald attributed this variation to the ability and foresight of individual company managers, the superior economic power of GM was surely a factor in its managers' ability to enforce a more centralized and bureaucratic structure of labor relations on the union.[36]

Reassertion of Capitalist Control Over Work Intensity

Under a strong capitalist counteroffensive, the UAW was forced not only to bureaucratize and discipline its members, but also to abandon its attempts to control the intensity of labor. Although it struggled year after year on the shop floor and at the bargaining table to win some voice in the determination of production standards, auto capitalists and managers were generally successful in retaining unilateral control over this vital factor. Worker participation in setting work intensity standards challenged indirectly the power that had been largely responsible for the industry's enormous gains in worker output—absolute capitalist control over technology and work organization. So not surprisingly, automotive manufacturers fought tenaciously to retain this control. In 1939 Chrysler defeated UAW demands for codetermination of production standards by withstanding a fifty-four-day strike. GM held firm in the 1945–1946 UAW strike against such demands, and Ford was similarly adamant during the 1949 strike. The most the union was able to win from the giants in this area was the right to be present at the retiming of a disputed standard or to appeal work-standard disputes through the grievance procedure.

The union's acquiescence in capitalist control of work intensity, as well as other managerial rights, became formally embodied in the contract through the sole prerogative clause. A typical example appeared in the 1945 GM-UAW contract.

> The right to hire, promote, discharge or discipline for cause, and
> to maintain discipline and efficiency of employees, is the sole re-
> sponsibility of the Corporation except that union members shall not
> be discriminated against as such. In addition, the products to be man-
> ufactured, the location of plants, the schedules of production, the
> methods, processes and means of manufacturing are solely and exclu-
> sively the responsibility of the Corporation.[37]

In agreeing to capital's sole right to determine "methods, processes and means of manufacturing" and to maintain the "efficiency of employees," the UAW formally renounced any claim to control technology or work intensity.

In return for acquiescence in this managerial prerogative, the union was given greater economic benefits. This trade-off was explicitly incorporated into the watershed GM-UAW contracts of 1948 and 1950. In 1948 GM managers proposed and the UAW agreed to two major innovations in collective bargaining as compensation for stable, cooperative union relations. The first was the cost-of-living "escalator clause," which provided wage increases pegged to changes in the Bureau of Labor Statistics cost-of-living index. The second innovation was the "annual improvement factor," which allowed workers to share in the benefits of increased industrial output. Each year auto workers were granted a flat cents-per-hour wage increase, calculated by multiplying the overall growth rate of the American economy in the previous year by the average wage in the auto industry. Although this did not tie wages directly to increases in GM output, the implication was clear—the union was willing to surrender to capital exclusive control over technology and work intensity in exchange for a cut of the resulting benefits. The 1950 contact, which incorporated and consolidated this provision, stated that "the annual improvement factor provided herein recognizes that a continuing improvement in the standard of living of employees depends upon technological progress, better tools, methods, processes, and equipment, and a cooperative attitude on the part of all parties in such progress."[38] GM chairman Alfred Sloan made the nature of the trade-off even more explicit, writing:

> I think the fact that our workers benefit on a definite and prescribed basis, resulting in an increase in their standard of living, gives us a more sympathetic cooperation in the introduction of labor-saving devices and other improvements that flow from technological progress, which on the whole have a healthy influence on the efficiency of the corporation's operations."[39]

These landmark contracts set the pattern of labor relations for the next thirty years in the industry. *Fortune* magazine hailed the 1950 GM-UAW agreement as the "Treaty of Detroit" and saw it as the beginning of a new era of cooperation between union and management in the industry.

However, as with the bureaucratization of labor relations, union acquiescence in capitalist control over work technology and intensity varied with the relative strength of capital. In the strongest firms, capital generally won formal contractual concessions from the union. However, even among the Big Three, which had similar contractual agreements, control over intensity and technology varied with informal struggle. GM's superior strength allowed it to maintain absolute control over production standards against union opposition, resulting in the fastest production pace in the industry. Because they were comparatively weaker, however, Ford and Chrysler were less successful in resisting informal union pressure and consequently had slower work paces. But the real differences in formal and informal capitalist control in this area existed between the big corporations and the smaller and weaker independents. Within the latter, the union was able to exert considerable influence on production standards. Workers in many of the smaller plants were successful in establishing informal controls over labor intensity, especially during the Second World War, when labor market conditions and a vital shop-floor organization strengthened workers. And formal mechanisms of union participation in setting work standards were won in several companies, such as Studebaker, Murray Body, and Briggs. However, the same weakness that forced these companies to negotiate with workers concerning work intensity also led to their bankruptcy or takeover by the strong corporations. So competitive pressures eventually made unilateral capitalist control over technology and intensity predominant in the industry.[40]

Union Successes in Altering the Bureaucratic Job Structure

One area of the labor process in which the union did not totally capitulate to the capitalist counteroffensive was the wage and job classification system. The UAW fought tenaciously to eliminate all the artificial wage differentials between workers that capitalists used to divide them and to stimulate individual efforts. And its efforts here were in large part successful. The union was able to eliminate almost completely personal wage differentials (between workers doing the same job). Thus, economist Robert Macdonald concluded:

> The reduction of personal differentials is largely an effect of unionism. While we can only guess at the way these rate differentials would have behaved over the last 25 years or so in the absence of bargaining, a careful weighing of union and management attitudes, as reflected in negotiations and in statements of wage policy, suggest that the union has been primarily responsible for the elimination of rate ranges on production jobs, the narrowing of the spread between starting rates and job rates, the shortening (and regularization) of qualifying periods, and the virtual abandonment of sex differentials, and has been partly responsible for the sharp decline in the use of incentive payments. It is likely that some reduction in personal differentials would have occurred in any case, but certainly not to the extent experienced under unionism.[41]

These union successes were won in the face of a managerial counteroffensive to maintain personal differentials. Automotive managers and capitalists claimed that service differentials (wage differences based upon length of employment) reflected real differences in output between new and experienced workers. Struggle over this issue during the Second World War resulted, however, in a War Labor Board decision favorable to the union. Service differentials on a given job could not exceed ten cents and could last no longer than sixty days. Capitalists also fought to maintain the right to pay differential wages based upon their judgments of workers' relative merits, claiming that this right was necessary to reward differences in effort and ability. However, the UAW claimed that these differentials led to divisiveness and favoritism, and with tenacious struggle was able to win their elimination in the large automobile manufacturing corporations by 1950. Although many companies had voluntarily replaced incentive wages with straight-time wages before unionization, auto capitalists and managaers nonetheless fought to maintain the right to use incentive systems. And during the Second World War, when worker output began to sag, Ford and GM began to push for the reinstitution of incentive wages. However, the vehement opposition from all levels of the UAW defeated these efforts and effectively eliminated such wage systems from the automobile manufacturing plants. However, companies in the automotive parts division were more adamant in their fight to retain incentive wages, because their production was less machine-paced and more competitive. As late as 1950, about half of the workers in the parts and truck divisions of the industry were still on incentive wages.[42]

Automotive capitalists and managers also resisted the union's efforts to reduce the differentials between different classifications in the job structure. As one student of the industry wrote: "Management is more desirous than is the union of maintaining appreciable job differentials. Management believes that such differentials are essential to provide an adequate incentive for superior work."[43] Without the carrot of promotion to better paying job categories, managers felt helpless to motivate more intensive labor. So they struggled to retain significant differences in the wage structure. They refused to allow the UAW a voice in the determination of the job structure, retaining the right to classify jobs as they saw fit and assign to them wages they considered appropriate. Most of the major agreements set only minimum wage rates for broad job categories, leaving it to capital to determine the spread of wages above the minimum. Auto managers also opposed the union's insistent demands for flat-rate rather than percentage increases in wages, for these had the tendency to flatten the wage hierarchy. GM chairman Alfred Sloan expressed particular displeasure with the "egalitarian effect" of such wage measures. In order to offset this effect, auto managers willingly granted the skilled elite of the wage hierarchy special adjustments to maintain their differentials over production workers. And in 1955, they were successful in changing the annual improvement factor from a flat-rate to a percentage basis, which served to maintain relative wage differentials between all workers.[44]

Automotive capitalists and managers also perceived the union's efforts in the realm of seniority as a challenge to the divisive job structure that they had managed to create. For the purposes of layoffs and rehirings, employers were generally successful in retaining very narrow seniority units that minimized movement between jobs ("bumping"), which they claimed disrupted production and reduced efficiency. Managers also vigorously fought the UAW's attempts to make promotion between levels in the job hierarchy dependent solely upon seniority. Seeing promotion as their chief means of rewarding workers for greater effort, employers generally were successful in retaining the contractual right to promote workers on the basis of "merit and ability," as determined by themselves. Only when these latter factors were judged to be equal were they bound to take seniority into account.[45]

However, despite this capitalist counteroffensive to retain wage differentials between jobs, the UAW achieved considerable success in compressing them. Of course, the technological changes in the labor process had already created a trend toward wage compression before unionization. But it is beyond doubt that automotive employers would have had greater success in arresting this trend and maintaining differentials had it not been for the tenacious efforts of the UAW. As Robert Macdonald concluded in his study of labor relations in the industry:

> The union's major impact has been to compress wage differentials within each of the two major work groups—production workers and skilled tradesmen. . . . in light of differences in union and management wage philosophies—revealed in management's criticism of the union's insistent demand for flat increases, its apprehensiveness about the effects of wage-leveling on incentives and morale, and its promotion of differential increases—it is reasonable to conclude that in the absence of collective bargaining (or of a union so steadfastly dedicated to cents-per-hour adjustments), wage compression would have been less acute, and absolute differentials would have undergone at least a moderate expansion.[46]

Macdonald's data, drawn from the files of the UAW Research Department, reveal that between the date of unionization (1937) and 1958, relative wage differentials within each of the two major occupational groups declined by about 60 percent. However, the wage differential between production workers and skilled trades workers substantially increased during this same period. This latter fact can be attributed to a number of forces: increasing pressure by skilled workers in the union to maintain their privileges, the disproportionate influence of the skilled trades within the UAW, and corresponding managerial pressure to maintain differentials between the two groups.

The United Auto Workers union was also successful generally in diluting the effectiveness of the incentive of promotion within the job bureaucracy. Although, formally, management retained the right to promote on the basis of "merit and ability," in practice the union won a promotion system based primarily on seniority. Attempts by managers to promote workers out of order of seniority inevitably resulted in the union filing grievances, which it vigorously pursued. And the umpires at the top of the grievance structure generally required management to show substantial evidence to prove the greater merit of workers it promoted out of order of seniority. As a result, employers relented to the union demand and generally followed seniority in promotions. However, the egalitarian effect of promotions based on seniority was limited by the narrow seniority units won by management. Workers could be promoted on a seniority basis only within their occupational groups and departments, which restricted vertical movement in the job hierarchy. Furthermore, barriers to movement between production jobs and the skilled trades were strictly guarded by mutual agreement of union and management. Formal apprentice training remained the sole route of mobility between the two occupational enclaves.[47]

Therefore, despite the continued existence of a broad differentiation between production and skilled workers, the union was able to eliminate many of the differentials in the job structure that capital preferred to maintain. This leveling impact of the UAW should not be dismissed by pointing to the continued privileges of the skilled trades, as some leftist labor scholars have done. The union successes in this area fundamentally changed the structure of domination on the shop floor, for they virtually eliminated the capitalist use of the job hierarchy as a device to divide and motivate workers to intensify their labor. With the wages among production workers substantially equalized and promotions between remaining wage grades based upon seniority, workers had little incentive to work hard to achieve a better paying job. As a result, auto workers generally abandoned hopes of bettering themselves through individual promotion. In their studies of auto workers' career aspirations, both Ely Chinoy and Robert Guest found that the large majority showed no active interest in promotions to different jobs. The compressed wage structure of the industry diverted workers' efforts for a better life from individual careerism to collective struggle. As Chinoy concluded:

> With such limited wage differentials, most workers can hope to earn more money primarily through general wage increases. For them, opportunity in the large plants in which they work has become to a great extent a collective affair in which the union plays a major role. Advancement is less and less an individual matter and more the collective gaining and holding of standardized agreements which provide for higher wages and for other benefits such as old-age pensions, hospitalization insurance, and life insurance.[48]

Guest's study substantiated the objective basis of auto workers' perceptions of advancement opportunities. He found that the wage increases experienced by auto workers with at least twelve years in the same plant were almost wholly the result of union-negotiated raises, rather than individual career advancement.[49]

All of the union's efforts to eliminate the divisive job structure robbed capital of its incentives for spurring workers to greater individual effort. As a result, speed-up induced by individual incentives was generally eliminated in the auto industry. As William McPherson concluded in his Brookings Institution study of the industry's labor relations:

> Managers maintain that the variations in the production of individual employees have been greatly reduced since the advent of the union. There is a tendency for the faster workers to hold their output down to standard. Because many employees are always below standard, management had depended on the extra output of others to keep average productivity up to normal. Since the advent of the union, managers have had more difficulty in inducing exceptional employees to produce a correspondingly exceptional quantity of product. It is probably the tacit, if not official, policy of many local union executives to discourage output above standard. Management objects strenuously to this tendency toward uniformity. Union restrictions upon dismissal and other penalties, insistence upon hourly wage rates, and enforcement of strict seniority appear to managers to have deprived them of a large measure of their control over productivity and to have removed the chief incentives for high efficiency.[50]

Capitalist Recalcitrance in Ending Racial and Sexual Discrimination

The union was less successful, however, in combating the capitalist counteroffensive to retain the traditional racial and sexual segmentation of the job structure. The international union's attempts to end the racist confinement of blacks to the least desirable jobs in the auto shops met opposition on two fronts. Many white auto workers were racially prejudiced and resisted the encroachment of blacks on their privileged job sanctuaries. But the main obstacle to greater black opportunities was the recalcitrance of employers. They were just as infected as their white workers with the pervasive racism of American society and had an even greater interest in maintaining racial discrimination in the job structure. Auto managers and capitalists had long used such discriminatory practices to keep workers divided against themselves and to drive down the wages of exclusively black occupations. Therefore, with a few exceptions, they resisted union demands to include in contracts clauses barring racial discrimination in seniority and promotion. The managerial right to promote on the basis of "merit and ability" was used in a discriminatory manner to exclude blacks from jobs traditionally reserved for whites. And local union officials, many of whom supported such racism, seldom filed grievances challenging this practice.[51]

That capitalist recalcitrance was the main force behind continued racial discrimination is confirmed by the events of the Second World War. Up to this time, the efforts of the international union to achieve black upgrading in the job hierarchy had met with little success. But during the war period, blacks made their greatest gains since the industry's beginning, breaking out of the foundries and paint shops into the production lines and machine shops. What accounted for these gains? The pressure of the international union was no greater during the war. Nor was the opposition of white workers any less adamant. The only major change in the balance of forces around racism was in the position of capital. The severe labor shortages of the war period created an economic interest among employers in upgrading blacks to fill the rapidly expanding positions of machine-tenders. Of course, the joint pressure of the federal government and top UAW officials was also required to speed along the process. But it was the desire of auto capitalists and managers to overcome labor shortages and thus capitalize on the opportunities of war production that made the decisive difference in black upgrading.

In 1941 the U.S. Office of Production Management negotiated with the UAW and automotive employers a Six-Point Transfer Program. The plan created advancement opportunities for blacks by basing transfers to war production in auto plants upon a worker's seniority in the entire industry, regardless of his or her former occupational position. Where auto employers were strongly committed to upgrading blacks under this program to fill labor shortages in their burgeoning shops, they let no amount of white worker resistance stand in their way. "Hate strikes" erupted among white auto workers protesting the upgrading of blacks into traditionally white jobs. But where managers were adamant in their support of the program, they cooperated with the international UAW and the federal government's Committee on Fair Employment Practices to bring the wildcat strikes quickly to an end. For example, when white workers walked out of the Dodge Truck plant on June 2, 1942, in protest of black transfers to war production, Chrysler managers stood resolutely behind their decision. International UAW representatives were called in and threatened the local with firings and expulsions from the union if it would not get its workers back to the shops. As a result, production was resumed in a matter of hours. Similarly cooperative efforts quickly ended hate strikes at Hudson and Timken Axle.[52]

However, in the few cases when automotive employers resolutely refused to abandon racist employment policies, the combined pressure of the federal government and the international union proved to no avail. At Ford, for example, managers successfully resisted pressure to abandon racist hiring policies. In a striking reversal of its previous employment policies, Ford virtually ceased hiring blacks after unionization and resisted government pressure to place blacks in war production. At Packard, managers reluctant to surrender the divisive benefits of the racially segmented job hierarchy adamantly opposed upgrading blacks into jobs traditionally monopolized by whites. As two historians of black Detroit have written: "Actions of Packard officials like Weiss's [Packard personnel director] made it quite evident that they were exploiting the racial prejudices of their workers in order to undermine the union. . . ." Under heavy government pressure, managers reluctantly upgraded blacks, but their encouragement of white resistance led to a massive hate strike of twenty-five thousand Packard workers in June 1943. White workers were forced back to the shops by strong intervention by the federal government and the UAW, but the intransigence of Packard managers blocked black opportunities for many years.[53]

Once the war ended, however, even those automotive employers previously receptive to black upgrading sought to return to a segmented job structure. No longer under the pressure of wartime labor shortages, managers ignored seniority provisions and sought to force blacks back down the occupational ladder. When UAW officials tried again to introduce or strengthen anti-discrimination contract clauses, they encountered managerial recalcitrance in all the major companies. However, vigorous union enforcement of contractual seniority rules on managers and workers helped blacks to maintain the footholds in the better jobs that capitalist self-interest had allowed them to gain during the war. By 1950, blacks were nearly fully integrated into automotive production jobs. However, they continued to be excluded from the elite of the work force, the skilled trades. The white workers who monopolized these jobs sought to exclude blacks entirely, and they found a powerful ally in employers. Although apprenticeship programs were formally opened to blacks after the war, barriers erected by managers and supported by white trades workers—entrance tests and educational requirements, for example—resulted in blacks' virtual exclusion from these upper reaches of the job structure. The UAW made efforts to expand black opportunities in this area, but it had to proceed gingerly in order to maintain the allegiance of the increasingly powerful and outspoken skilled trades workers.[54]

Automotive capitalists and managers also resisted union efforts to end sexual discrimination in the job structure. The major UAW goal in this area was to eliminate sex differentials between workers on the same jobs. Managers clung tenaciously to these artificial wage differences, claiming that they reflected legitimate differences in job performance between men and women. However, the union prevailed in this struggle. In a 1942 dispute over this issue between General Motors and the UAW, the War Labor Board ruled that women must receive wages equal to those of men performing the same job. The ruling not only resulted in back-pay awards for female auto workers but also set a precedent for future negotiations. However, little headway was made against the main type of sexual discrimination—the confinement of women to a narrow range of jobs within the auto shops. This was due not only to managerial recalcitrance, but also to the reluctance of the union to confront this issue. Male auto workers as well as managers had an interest in the sexually segmented job structure, and top union officials were much less willing to confront either group over this issue than they were over racism. However, when managers needed workers to alleviate shortages of male labor during the Second World War, they did not allow the sexist protests of their workers to prevent them from employing women in traditionally male jobs. But after the war, the upgraded women were generally forced back down into their occupational ghetto. As a result, the basic pattern of sexual segregation persisted and was not seriously challenged until the 1960s.[55]

Thus, in opposing changes in racial and sexual discrimination in the job structure, white male auto workers often teamed up with management. However, it is unrealistic to attribute the perpetuation of the racially and sexually segmented structure equally to both groups. Capitalist managers continued to hold decisive power in shaping the labor process in their factories, compared with whom workers were relatively powerless. It was managers who were the major causal force behind the perpetuation of the discriminatory structure. When managers perceived it to be in their interests to upgrade blacks and women to fill labor shortages, no amount of worker opposition could stop them. This is not, however, to absolve white male workers from moral responsibility for their racist and sexist attitudes and actions. What they thought and did certainly was morally abhorrent. But they generally did not have the power to implement their sexism and racism. Auto capitalists and managers did.

Adamant Capitalist Defense of Property Relations

On no front did automotive capitalists and managers put up a more tenacious struggle to repulse union challenges than on basic property relations. Employers perceived the UAW's social-democratic program to win worker participation in decisions on investments and the accumulation process as threats to their managerial freedoms and the free enterprise system as a whole. And they fought with all their resources to defend both. When the UAW announced its Reuther plan, which called for labor participation in managing war production, auto capitalists launched a broadside against it. William Knudsen, former GM president and head of the Office of Production Management, called the plan "socialistic." George Romney, managing director of the Automotive Council for War Production and general manager of the Automobile Manufacturing Association, stated that the plan constituted a "usurpation of at least part of the management function, authority and responsibility."[56] The UAW's plan for conversion to peacetime production, which gave labor a voice in a powerful Peace Production Board, went down to defeat in a similar barrage of capitalist acrimony.

The bitterest struggle over property rights, however, came with the UAW's 1945 demand that General Motors give workers a 30 percent wage increase without increasing the price of its products. When GM refused and the UAW struck, the battleground shifted from the bargaining table to the public media. The union sought to mobilize public support for its attempt to hold back the price increases of oligopolistic corporations and increase the purchasing power of American workers. It demanded that the company open its accounting books to public scrutiny to prove its contention that a wage increase was impossible without a price increase. GM launched a public relations counteroffensive, calling the union's attempt to interfere in pricing policy and tie wages to profits "socialistic." The corporation took out advertisements asking: "Is American business to be based on free competition or is it to become socialized, with all activities controlled and regimented?"[57] A commentator in *Automotive Industries* similarly construed the union's demands as challenging the property rights of capital.

> To most close observers the present struggle is much more fundamental and significant than the strikes over collective bargaining in 1937. If the union is successful in its contention that wages shall be directly proportionate to profits and that prices of the company's product shall be a factor in negotiations, the entire wage basing structure that has prevailed over the years will collapse. It will be replaced by a system giving labor a measure of control over wages, prices, and profits. This is the ultimate objective of the UAW-CIO—a voice in the affairs of management. That is what the fight is all about. And that also is why General Motors in a sense is fighting the battle for all American industry and the free enterprise system.[58]

Although these capitalist outcries about socialism and the demise of free enterprise were exaggerated, they did contain a kernel of truth. In demanding a union voice in pricing policy and calling a corporation's investment decisions to public account, the UAW was challenging rights generally reserved to property owners. And General Motors used all of its considerable power to fight off this challenge. The corporation endured a one-hundred-and-thirteen-day strike and lost millions of dollars in sales to defend its sole prerogative to determine the allocation of capital. This defense was simply too strong for the UAW, especially when other industrial unions were settling for simple wage increases. The defeat of the union on this issue in the 1945–1946 strike marked its last attempt to achieve broader power in the industry. Auto employers were successful in forcing the UAW into a narrow business unionism, which sought solely economic gains in exchange for accommodation to the basic structure of capitalist domination in the shops.[59]

RESULTS OF THE UNION CHALLENGE

Automotive capitalists managed to beat back the union challenge to their control of the labor process in almost every area. However, the

UAW was succesful in effecting one major change in the structure of class domination in the shops—the virtual elimination of the hierarchical job structure. Through tenacious pressure, the union managed to reduce substantially wage differentials both within the same job category and between different categories in the structure. And the union-instituted seniority system came increasingly to govern promotions between the few steps on the job ladder that remained. These changes virtually eliminated the positive incentives that capital had traditionally used to exact greater personal effort from workers. The use of the seniority system to govern the order of layoffs and rehirings also eliminated a major negative sanction that capital had traditionally used to drive workers. The major result of these union-induced changes was the inability of capitalists to motivate differential levels of effort among workers. The variation in the intensity at which workers labored declined.

Auto capitalists were probably more willing to give ground on union demands on the job structure than on any other aspect of the labor process, for several reasons. First, apart from union pressure, there were also real technological pressures working to flatten the job structure. The mechanization and rationalization of the work of manufacturing automobiles increasingly eliminated the control of workers over the output of machine processes. It made little sense, therefore, to pay wages to stimulate individual effort, when such effort made little difference in production output. Furthermore, the development of technology increasingly eliminated the real skill differences between workers, which formed the rational basis for wage differences. Second, the maintenance of an artificial wage hierarchy was more expensive than a flat structure, especially under the conditions of unionism. The payment of several strata of privileged workers at wage levels above the value of their labor power was an economic burden. And with the union concentrating its efforts on raising the wages of the lowest-paid workers, capitalists simply found it less expensive to allow the structure to flatten out by not increasing the wages of higher-paid workers to maintain constant ratios. Third and finally, capitalists were more yielding to union pressure to flatten the job structure and eliminate incentives to individual effort, because they retained the power to increase the collective intensity of labor with technological methods. From the beginning of the industry, automotive employers had relied upon technological innovations to speed up workers. And during the era of unionization, they retained an iron-fisted control over work intensity and technology. With a bureaucratized union structure, placated and strengthened with economic concessions, to assist them in enforcing collective submission to machine-paced labor, auto capitalists had no need for individual incentives to spur workers on. The union's major impact on the labor process was thus the reinforcement of the industry's traditional reliance upon technological control of workers. If it had cut off the ability of capital to motivate individual effort, the UAW surrendered to capitalist attempts to increase collective effort through unilateral control of technology and work organization.

The terms of the surrender, which provided the formula for the industry's success for the next twenty-five years, were set forth in the monumental GM-UAW contract of 1950—the "Treaty of Detroit." A centralized and bureaucratized union agreed to enforce on its troops a collective acquiescence in capitalist control of technology in return for a share of the economic benefits. In an industry that was the rising star of a booming postwar economy, this looked like a good deal for both labor and capital. The treaty did not free the auto slaves. Slavery continued in the American automobile industry. But it did manage to exact from the slaveowners a greater economic price for wage slavery, which made its bonds a little more bearable.

EPILOGUE
The Possibility of
Liberated Production

My historical study of automotive production has sought objectively to excavate and reveal the repressive social imperatives shaping the development of the labor process. But the unspoken foundation of this analysis has been the hope that a nonrepressive, liberated method of production is possible. Once the development of the technological hardware and organizational software of industrial production is revealed to be a process of social choice rather than a determined technical evolution, alternative industrial horizons based on alternative social structures are opened up. Choices among alternative forms of production depend upon the human values pursued by a society and ultimately upon the balance of social forces lined up behind different values.

This study has attempted to demonstrate that the development of the automotive labor process was determined in large part by the social structure of antagonistic class relations inherent in capitalist wage labor. Such a society, dominated by the owners and controllers of private property, invariably and inevitably values the enlargement of dead capital over the enrichment of living labor. Increasing surplus value—the alienated, inanimate storehouse of human abilities—becomes an end in and of itself, quite apart from and ultimately in opposition to the development of human abilities. But by distinguishing the repressive control necessary to overcome antagonistic class relations from the nonrepressive control necessary to produce efficiently, I have sought to uncover an alternative method of production lurking within the old as an unrealized potential. If we want it, a nonrepressive, liberated process of industrial production is possible, one that is at least as productive and efficient as the old process, but which enhances rather than suppresses human freedom and creativity.

The liberated process of production can and must be efficient and productive, for maximizing the material output per unit input of human and nonhuman resources must remain a goal of production in any society. Not because the expansion of material wealth should be an end in and of itself. It should not. The ultimate goal of a truly human society must be the development to the fullest extent of the inherent powers and abilities of human individuals. However, this development is to a large extent dependent on efficient material production. Humans are fundamentally physical creatures with material needs that must be minimally fulfilled in order for life to exist at all, and more generously fulfilled to make it enjoyable. Individuals cannot realize their human potentials as long as basic physical needs are unmet. So producing sufficient material goods rapidly and efficiently in order to fulfill the physical needs of all must be a goal of all societies for the foreseeable future.

Human beings are, however, physical creatures endowed with unique abilities and needs beyond mere physical existence. Humans possess the inherent capacity for consciousness and have the need to express and develop this capacity in free, self-determined activity. But human activity dominated by the sheer production of the material necessities of life is not free. Production of material goods demands the transformation of nature into a form compatible with human needs. And this transformation is to a large extent dictated by the natural laws of the material world, which are neither created nor controlled by humans. Therefore, producing material necessities inevitably involves the involuntary subordination of humans to natural laws, regardless of how much sophisticated technology mediates the relation of humans to nature. It is the realm of necessity, not freedom. In the production of steel, for example, humans must conform their activities to the natural properties of metals and to metallurgical processes or the end result is not steel. Thus, fulfilling the higher needs of individuals for free, conscious activity demands the reduction of the human time and energy expended in the realm of necessity—the production of physical necessities—in order to expand the time and energy available for the realm of freedom—conscious, free, unrestrained activity. To accomplish this, it is necessary to make industrial production as productive as possible in order to reduce to a minimum the human labor requirements of the production for material needs.

But expanding the realm of freedom does not mean reducing human productive activity of any sort in favor of idle leisure. What must be reduced to enhance human freedom is merely that part of productive activity constrained by natural laws. A society that takes as its highest goal the development of the abilities and capacities of the individual must develop productive forces that reduce the natural necessities of human labor and expand its free, conscious, discretionary side. Such a society would, for example, reduce the time spent building mere structures for physical shelter and expand the time spent designing and building creative architectural treasures; it would reduce the time spent cultivating plant and animal protein for human subsistence and expand the time spent cultivating the art of preparing and enjoying food.[1]

The development of productive forces under capitalism, however, has been the reverse of this human ideal, as this study of the auto industry has shown. Many technological and organizational "advances" have restricted rather than expanded the consciousness and freedom of individuals in the productive process, in order to repress the inherent class antagonisms. In a society in which these class antagonisms were eliminated or substantially reduced, these repressive-control measures could be eliminated, without adversely affecting productivity. These measures are technically unnecessary; they are above and beyond the controls necessitated merely by the efficient production of goods. They are necessary solely for production in an exploitative class society, in which the command and fruits of labor are unequally distributed. In a society without gaping inequalities of power and material rewards, repressive control would be superfluous, for all would voluntarily produce in a manner that maximized the public good from which all equally benefited.

This supposition about a nonrepressive, voluntary, liberated process of production remains, of course, largely speculative, for there are no classless industrial societies in which it could be validated. Most analysts of postcapitalist societies like the Soviet Union, Poland, and the German Democratic Republic agree that regardless of their rhetoric, they possess highly structured class inequalities, which place largely the same imperative of repressive control upon the labor process as ours do. However, within existing class societies—both capitalist and postcapitalist—there exist hints of the possibility of a liberated labor process. The heavy burdens placed upon organization and equipment by class antagonisms have led even some capitalist firms to seek ways to reduce hostilities and capture the voluntary compliance and cooperation of their workers.

And the evidence from these rudimentary experiments in workplace democracy largely supports the conclusion that if class antagonisms can be even moderately reduced, by giving workers an interest in their own production, industrial production can be made just as or more efficient by reducing the division of labor, mechanical control, and hierarchical command. At the Topeka dogfood plant of General Foods, for example, managers organized workers into teams and made them responsible for a wide range of decision making. The strict division of labor was replaced by a system of job rotation that rewarded workers for broad knowledge of production; bureaucratic hierarchy was replaced by democratic team decisions. The team system reportedly reduced unit costs, labor turnover, and accidents, saving the company $1 million a year. A similarly autonomous team was created to run a department of numerically controlled machine tools at a General Electric aircraft-engine plant. This pilot program was a last-ditch effort to control a technological innovation that had brought managers nothing but trouble, mainly because of conflict with workers. The program broke down old lines of industrial authority and classification and made workers almost completely responsible for every aspect of their own work. The results were reductions in scrap and labor turnover and increases in machine utilization, output, and worker morale.[2]

Despite the fact that they increased efficiency and productivity, these two experiments and a considerable number like them were gradually replaced by more repressive forms of workplace control. The barrier to the expansion of these more liberated production processes was and continues to be, not technical efficiency, but the social relations of property and their derivative prerogatives of control. At the Topeka General Foods plant, managerial pressure undermined democratic decision making and resulted in the division and bureaucratization of team responsibilities. It seems that the authority of both corporate executives and local managers was threatened by workers' control. "It became a power struggle," one former employee stated. "It was too threatening to too many people."[3] Similarly, at General Electric, managers unilaterally terminated the pilot program against strong union objections, replacing it with a traditional managerial hierarchy and division of labor. Again, the basic issue was not efficiency, but managerial control and ultimately private ownership. As David Noble has written: "To GE's top management, the union's desire to extend the program appeared as a step toward greater worker control over production and, as such, a threat to the traditional authority rooted in private ownership of the means of production."[4] The ultimate obstacle to a liberated labor process is not technical, but social—the social relations of private property in society's productive resources. If we truly want to construct a method of producing that both increases productivity and fulfills the human need for free, conscious activity, we must find ways to eliminate, lower, or circumvent this obstacle.

I will offer no pat prescriptions. They have a way of stifling rather than stimulating thoughtful discussion of alternatives. A plurality of new property forms are possible and necessary, each adapted to the particular political, economic, and cultural circumstances of production: worker cooperatives, community ownership, state ownership, private ownership with stringent social controls. But the intent of each must be the same—removing production decisions from private hands and placing them more under social control.

And when workers have greater control over the process of production in which they are engaged, what will the results be? Generally, it can be predicted that they will opt for forms of technology and organization that are nonrepressive and eliminate those repressive forms required solely by social antagonisms. But the distinction between repressive and nonrepressive control is not one that can be made resolutely once and for all. It is historically relative, dependent upon the specific level of development of the productive forces as well as productive relations. The distinctions I have made in the analysis of the auto industry have been approximations, based upon the particular period, not final determinations. A technique that presents itself as a nonrepressive-control measure in one period, ensuring productive and efficient use of society's productive resources, may become a measure of repressive control in a latter period in which forces and relations of production are more advanced. For example, divisions of labor that in an early period were necessary to increase the productivity of hand labor may become repressive in a society in which production is largely automated. The only way to ensure that the distinction between repressive and nonrepressive control is adequately readjusted for each historical period, and that outmoded nonrepressive controls do not turn into repressive controls, forming the basis for new inequalities, is to place the power to define and enforce this distinction in the hands of workers themselves.

But is all this speculation about liberated production merely a pipe dream? Even if it is possible, is it probable? Although in the short term there may be clear sailing for repressive forms of industrial production based on private property, in the long term there are storm clouds on the horizon. How long can an economy that demands increasingly varied products and flexible processes rely on rigidly automated factories with narrowly specialized workers? Can the necessary flexibility and discretion be built into automation, or will systems that attempt to replace human discretion be so complex as to be wholly unreliable and subject to failure? And in a substantially automated capitalist system, in which the demand for human labor is drastically reduced, how will the products of industry be distributed, if the reduced income of wage earners precludes market exchanges? Finally, is a social system that places economic decisions in the hands of private, individual owners or organizations suitable to a production process that depends increasingly upon the social coordination of interdependent resources on an international scale?

The very development of the capitalist labor process has placed the questions of workers' control and social ownership on the historical agenda. These questions can only be answered by the concerted, conscious efforts of humans struggling to make production meet their needs. This task will not be an easy one. But humankind always sets itself only such tasks as it can solve.

Notes

CHAPTER 1

1. For discussions of the technological determinism of orthodox Marxism, see Harry Braverman, *Labor and Monopoly Capital: The Degradation of Work in the Twentieth Century* (New York: Monthly Review Press, 1974), 14–25; Charles Bettleheim, *Class Struggles in the USSR, First Period: 1917–1923* (New York: Monthly Review Press, 1976), 19–45; Monika Reinfelder, "Introduction: Breaking the Spell of Technicism," in *Outlines of a Critique of Technology*, ed. Phil Slater (Atlantic Highlands, NJ: Humanities Press, 1980), 9–37. The quotation is from Karl Marx, *The Poverty of Philosophy* (Moscow: Progress Publishers, 1955), 95.

2. Braverman, *Labor and Monopoly Capital*, 45–58. For a similar account of the origins of conflict and control in work, see Richard Edwards, *Contested Terrain: The Transformation of the Workplace in the Twentieth Century* (New York: Basic Books, 1979), 11–16.

3. Braverman, *Labor and Monopoly Capital*, 59–69.

4. Ibid., 70–84.

5. Ibid., 85–138.

6. Ibid., 184–235.

7. Ibid., 228–229. For a critique of Braverman's position on technology, see Michael Burawoy, "Toward a Marxist Theory of the Labor Process: Braverman and Beyond," *Politics and Society* 8, nos. 3–4 (1978): 289–295.

8. David Gordon, "Capitalist Efficiency and Socialist Efficiency," *Monthly Review* 28 (July–August, 1976): 19–39. For another analysis that conceptualizes class domination as separate from and often opposed to profitable production, see David F. Noble, *Forces of Production: A Social History of Industrial Automation* (New York: Knopf, 1984), esp. 318–323.

9. Edwards, *Contested Terrain*, 12. For a similar critique of Gordon's for-

mulation, see Al Sysmanski, "Braverman As a Neo-Luddite?" *Insurgent Sociologist* 8 (Winter 1978): 45–50.

10. Karl Marx, *Capital*, 3 vols. (New York: Vintage Books, 1977–1981), 1:449–450. For an elaboration on this distinction in Marx's theory of the labor process, see David Gartman, "Marx and the Labor Process: An Interpretation," *Insurgent Sociologist* 8 (Fall 1978): 97–108.

11. Dan Clawson, *Bureaucracy and the Labor Process: The Transformation of U.S. Industry, 1860–1920* (New York: Monthly Review Press, 1980), 18–24; Edwards, *Contested Terrain*, 16–18; Andrew Friedman, *Industry and Labour: Class Struggle at Work and Monopoly Capitalism* (London: Macmillan, 1977), 77–78.

12. On the distinction between the intensity and the productivity of labor, see Marx, *Capital* 1:655–667.

13. Braverman, *Labor and Monopoly Capital*, 139–152.

14. For general criticisms of Braverman along these lines, see Richard Edwards, "The Social Relations of Production at the Point of Production," *Insurgent Sociologist* 8 (Fall): 109–110; Michael Burawoy, "Toward a Marxist Theory of the Labor Process," 266–276.

15. Edwards, *Contested Terrain*; David Gordon, Richard Edwards, and Michael Reich, *Segmented Work, Divided Workers: The Historical Transformation of Labor in the United States* (Cambridge: Cambridge University Press, 1982); Michael Burawoy, *Manufacturing Consent: Changes in the Labor Process under Monopoly Capitalism* (Chicago: University of Chicago Press, 1979).

16. Edwards, *Contested Terrain*, 136–147; Burawoy, *Manufacturing Consent*, 109–120.

17. Edwards, *Contested Terrain*, 132–147; Burawoy, *Manufacturing Consent*, 95–108; Katherine Stone, "The Origins of Job Structures in the Steel Industry," *Review of Radical Political Economics* 6 (Summer 1974): 73–75; Howard Wachtel, "Class Consciousness and Stratification in the Labor Process," in *Labor Market Segmentation*, ed. Richard Edwards, Michael Reich, and David Gordon (Lexington, Mass.: D.C. Heath, 1975), 95–122; Stanley Aronowitz, *False Promises: The Shaping of American Working Class Consciousness* (New York: McGraw-Hill, 1973), 162–183; David Gordon, *Theories of Poverty and Underemployment* (Lexington, Mass.: D.C. Heath, 1972), 72–77; Mario Barrera, "Colonial Labor and Theories of Inequality," *Review of Radical Political Economics* 8 (Summer 1976): 1–18.

18. Antonio Gramsci, *Selections from the Prison Notebooks* (New York: International Publishers, 1971), 286; Stone, "Origins of Job Structures," 75–76; Edwards, *Contested Terrain*, 91–97; Stuart D. Brandes, *American Welfare Capitalism, 1880–1940* (Chicago: University of Chicago Press, 1976).

19. Aronowitz, *False Promises*, 172–183, 214–263; Burawoy, *Manufacturing Consent*, 109–120; Michel Aglietta, *A Theory of Capitalist Regulation—The U.S. Experience* (London: New Left Books, 1979), 190–198; Stone, "Origins of Job Structures," 153–161; C. Wright Mills, *The New Men of Power* (New York: Harcourt, Brace & Co., 1948).

20. For a more extensive critique of these studies by Burawoy and Agli-

etta, see David Gartman, "Structuralist Marxism and the Labor Process," *Theory and Society* 12 (1983): 659–669.

21. Stanley Aronowitz, "Marx, Braverman, and the Logic of Capital," *Insurgent Sociologist* 8 (Fall 1978): 127–146; idem, "The End of Political Economy," *Social Text*, 1 (Summer 1979): 3–52.

22. Gordon, Edwards, and Reich, *Segmented Work*.

CHAPTER 2

1. On the history of mass production, see Roger Burlingame, *Backgrounds of Power: The Human Story of Mass Production* (New York: Scribner's Sons, 1949); Christy Borth, *Masters of Mass Production* (Indianapolis, Ind.: Bobbs-Merrill, 1945); Charles Kettering and Allen Orth, *American Battle for Abundance* (Detroit: General Motors, 1974); Siegfried Giedion, *Mechanization Takes Command* (New York: Norton, 1969).

2. I include in the term "automobile industry" all firms manufacturing and assembling motor vehicles, and all firms manufacturing component and repair parts and accessories for motor vehicles in which this is the primary line of business. The term "motor vehicles" includes passenger cars, trucks, truck tractors, buses, taxicabs, and other commercial vehicles for use on the highway.

3. On the origins of the American automobile industry, see John B. Rae, *The American Automobile* (Chicago: University of Chicago Press, 1965); idem, *American Automobile Manufacturers* (Philadelphia: Chilton, 1959); Ralph C. Epstein, *The Automobile Industry* (New York: Arno Press, 1972); E. D. Kennedy, *The Automobile Industry* (New York Reynal and Hitchcock, 1941); H. L. Barber, *Story of the Automobile* (Chicago: Munson, 1917); C. B. Glasscock, *The Gasoline Age* (Indianapolis, Ind.: Bobbs-Merrill, 1937); Robert P. Thomas, *An Analysis of the Pattern of Growth of the Automobile Industry, 1895–1929* (New York: Arno Press, 1977).

4. Allan Nevins and Frank E. Hill, *Ford: The Times, the Man, the Company* (New York: Scribner's Sons, 1954), 222–233.

5. Throughout the descriptions of the early labor process, I use masculine nouns and pronouns. This use does not reflect sexist bias, but is rather an accurate description of the gender of early auto workers, who were almost exclusively male.

6. Charles Kettering and Allen Orth, *The New Necessity: The Culmination of a Century of Progress in Transportation* (Baltimore: Williams and Wilkins, 1932), 39.

7. Harold W. Slauson, "Efficient System for the Rapid Assembly of Motor Cars," *Machinery* 16 (October 1909): 114.

8. Henry Ford, in collaboration with Samuel Crowther, *My Life and Work* (London: Heinemann, 1923), 79–80.

9. For descriptions of this early assembly process, see "The Winton Plant and its Product," *Cycle and Automotive Trade Journal* 8 (March 1904):

69–69; C. B. Owen, "Organization and Equipment of an Automobile Factory," *Machinery* 15 (March 1909): 497–498; "The Manufacture of Automobiles," *Scientific American* 90 (January 9, 1904): 29–30; William E. Chalmers, "Labor in the Automobile Industry" (Ph.D. diss., University of Wisconsin, 1932), 89; Nevins and Hill, *Ford*, 184–185.

10. Chalmers, "Labor in Autos," 89.

11. Mrs. Wilfred C. Leland, with Minnie D. Millbrook, *Master of Precision: Henry M. Leland* (Detroit: Wayne State University Press, 1966), 73–74; Robert Thomas, *Pattern of Growth*, 34–35, 67–68; Nevins and Hill, *Ford*, 222–223.

12. Overland advertising supplement to *The Automobile* 25 (August 1911), no page (following 288); Thomas J. Fay, "Special Machinery Used in Making Automobiles," *The Automobile* 21 (October 1909): 596; "Science in Spring Manufacture," *The Automobile* 32 (May 1915): 835–836, 839.

13. "Gasoline Engine Castings a Problem," *The Automobile* 20 (April 1909): 706.

14. Overland ad supp., no page; Alain Touraine, *L'Evolution du travail ouvrier aux usines Renault* (Paris: Centre National de la Recherche Scientifique, 1955), 61.

15. H. E. Blank, Jr., "40 Years of Machine Tool Progress," *Automotive Industries* 81 (October 1939): 345–352; Fred H. Colvin, in collaboration with D. J. Duffin, *60 Years with Men and Machines* (New York: McGraw-Hill, 1947), 120–124; Oberlin Smith, "Modern Machine Shop Economies," *Cassier's Magazine* 17 (February 1900): 295–299.

16. For a discussion of this level of mechanization, see James R. Bright, *Automation and Management* (Boston: Division of Research, Graduate School of Business Administration, Harvard University, 1958), 41, 46.

17. Touraine, *L'Evolution du travail*, 24–25, 57–66; Bright, *Automation and Management*, 188, 205.

18. On factory layout in general, see Richard Muther, *Production-Line Technique* (New York: McGraw-Hill, 1944), 7–9. On layout in early auto shops, see C. V. Avery, "How Mass Production Came Into Being," *Iron Age* 123 (June 1929): 1638; "A Comparison of Methods of Automobile Manufacture," *Industrial Engineering and the Engineering Digest* 7 (February 1910): 89; Owen, "Organization and Equipment," 496.

19. Horace L. Arnold and Fay L. Faurote, *Ford Methods and the Ford Shops* (New York: Arno Press, 1972), 101–112.

20. Overland ad supp., no page; Kettering and Orth, *New Necessity*, 86–92; "American Methods Count in Body Making," *The Automobile* 26 (February 1912): 560; J. Edward Schipper, "Quantity Production of Sheet Metal Bodies," *The Automobile* 38 (June 1918): 1188–1193; Norman G. Shidle, "How to Reduce Body Production Costs Topic of Body Session," *Automotive Industries* 48 (January 1923): 112–115; "The Winton Plant," 72–73; Mortier W. La Fever, "Workers, Machinery, and Production in the Automobile Industry," *Monthly Labor Review* 19 (October 1924): 15–16.

21. Marx calls this general control of early capitalists over work and work-

ers based upon the simple ownership of means of production the formal subsumption of labor under capital. This formal subsumption is transformed into the real subsumption of labor under capital only with the seizure by capital of control over the immediate labor process from workers. See *Capital*, 3 vols. (New York: Vintage Books, 1977–1981), 1:1019–1038. On the considerable power of early capital, despite workers' control over the labor process, see also Dan Clawson, *Bureaucracy and the Labor Process* (New York: Monthly Review Press, 1980), 160–166.

22. David Montgomery, *Workers' Control in America* (Cambridge: Cambridge University Press, 1979), 9–31. For an interpretation of this resistance as largely cultural, see Herbert Gutman, *Work, Culture, and Society in Industrializing America* (New York: Vintage Books, 1977), 3–78.

23. Nevins and Hill, *Ford*, 381–383.

24. The Ford maxims are quoted from Stephen Meyer III, *The Five Dollar Day: Labor Management and Social Control in the Ford Motor Company, 1908–1921* (Albany: State University of New York Press, 1981), 73–74.

25. Norman Beasley, *Knudsen: A Biography* (New York: Whittlesey House, 1947), 47; "Mills on All Three Sides," *The Automobile* 29 (August 1913): 279; Ford, *My Life*, 80.

26. Sheffield Corporation advertisement, *Automotive Industries* 88 (June 1943): 69.

27. George S. May, *A Most Unique Machine: The Michigan Origins of the American Automobile Industry* (n.p.: William B. Eerdman's, 1975), 33, 80–81, 342; Norman Beasley and George W. Stark, *Made in Detroit* (New York: Putnam's, 1957), 46–47; Nevins and Hill, *Ford*, 74–75, 270, 515.

28. Nevins and Hill, *Ford*, 220–251.

29. Jack Russell, "The Coming of the Line: The Ford Highland Park Plant, 1910–1914," *Radical America* 12 (May–June 1978): 30; Duane Yarnell, *Auto Pioneering: A Remarkable Story of Ransom E. Olds* (Lansing, Mich.: R. E. Olds, 1949), 65–68; Glen A. Niemeyer, *The Automobile Career of Ransom E. Olds* (East Lansing, Mich.: Michigan State University Business Studies, 1963), 21–22; Nevins and Hill, *Ford*, 376–377; Beasley and Stark, *Made in Detroit*, 142; May, *Most Unique Machine*, 123.

30. On the national open-shop drive, see David Brody, *Workers in Industrial America* (New York: Oxford University Press, 1980), 24–27; Montgomery, *Workers' Control*, 57–63. On the Detroit drive, see Nevins and Hill, *Ford*, 376–380, 512–521; Russell, "Coming of the Line," 30–31; Chalmers, "Labor in Autos," 188–193.

31. L. T. C. Rolt, *A Short History of Machine Tools* (Cambridge, Mass.: MIT Press, 1965), 148; Walter P. Chrysler, in collaboration with Boyden Sparkes, *Life of an American Workman* (New York: Dodd, Mead & Co., 1937), 68.

32. Marjorie T. Stanley, "The Interrelationships of Economic Forces and Labor Relations in the Automobile Industry" (Ph.D. diss., Indiana University, 1953), 16–18, 38; Nevins and Hill, *Ford*, 269–270, 380–383, 512–517.

CHAPTER 3

1. Glen A. Niemeyer, *The Automobile Career of Ransom E. Olds* (East Lansing: Michigan State University Business Studies, 1963), 29–51; Allan Nevins and Frank E. Hill, *Ford: The Times, the Man, the Company* (New York: Scribner's Sons, 1954), 220–221.

2. Nevins and Hill, *Ford*, 240–241, 260, 323–324.

3. Henry Ford, in collaboration with Samuel Crowther, *Moving Forward* (London: Heinemann, 1931), 151.

4. Oberlin Smith, "Modern Machine Shop Economies," *Cassier's Magazine* 17 (February 1900): 297–298; Robert S. Woodbury, *Studies in the History of Machine Tools* (Cambridge, Mass.: MIT Press, 1972).

5. Robert S. Woodbury, "History of the Grinding Machine," 98–108, in *Studies in the History of Machine Tools*.

6. Charles F. Kettering and Allen Orth, *The New Necessity* (Baltimore: Williams and Wilkins, 1932), 100.

7. Heald Machine Company advertisement, *The Automobile* 24 (March 1911): inside front cover. On the advantages to capitalists of interchangeable parts, see also Robert P. Thomas, *An Analysis of the Pattern of Growth of the Automobile Industry, 1895–1929* (New York: Arno Press, 1977), 120; Norman Beasley, *Knudsen: A Biography* (New York: Whittlesey House, 1947), 65; Overland advertising supplement to *The Automobile* 25 (August 1911): no page; "Growing Demand for Low-Priced Car," *Automotive Industries* 45 (November 1921): 1002; E. E. Thum, "Many Advantages Realized in Body of 5-Piece All-Steel Design," *Automotive Industries* 59 (September 1928): 370.

8. W. K. White, "What Some New England Makers Are Doing," *The Automobile* 20 (March 1909): 433–436; Harold Slauson, "Efficient System for the Rapid Assembly of Motor Cars," *Machinery* 16 (October 1909): 115; Keith Sward, *The Legend of Henry Ford* (New York: Rinehart, 1948), 32.

9. Sward, *Legend of Ford*, 32. See also "Duplication Methods Supreme," *The Automobile* 23 (October 1910): 650; C. B. Owen, "Organization and Equipment of an Automobile Factory," *Machinery* 15 (March 1909): 497.

10. Quoted in Jack Russell, "The Coming of the Line," *Radical America* 12 (May–June 1978): 33–34. On this assembly system at Ford, see also Hartley W. Barclay, *Ford Production Methods* (New York: Harper, 1936), 100; Fred H. Colvin, "Building an Automobile Every 40 Seconds," *American Machinist* 38 (May 1913): 761–762; Sward, *Legend of Ford*, 35; C. V. Avery, "How Mass Production Came Into Being," *Iron Age* 123 (June 1929): 1638.

11. Richard Muther, *Production-Line Technique* (New York: McGraw-Hill, 1944), 269; "Automobile Industry and Trade in Detroit," *The Automobile* 9 (December 1903): 612–613; "A Comparison of Methods of Automobile Manufacture," *Industrial Engineering and the Engineering Digest* 7 (February 1910): 89.

12. Quoted in Nevins and Hill, *Ford*, 326. See also Christy Borth, *Masters of Mass Production* (Indianapolis, Ind.: Bobbs-Merrill, 1945), 31.

13. "System Makes Car Building Profitable," *The Automobile* 26 (February 1912): 608. See also F. K. Hendrickson, "Automobile's Influence on Machine Tool Industry," *Automotive Industries* 45 (November 1921): 927; Horace L. Arnold and Fay L. Faurote, *Ford Methods and the Ford Shops* (New York: Arno Press, 1972), 247, 249; J. Edward Schipper, "Some Unique Facilities for Crankcase Production," *Automotive Industries* 45 (November 1921): 1020; John H. Van Deventer, "Ford Principles and Practices at River Rouge. IX—Machine Tool Arrangement and Parts Transportation," *Industrial Management* 65 (May 1923): 262.

14. "Automobile Industry and Trade," 611.

15. Henry Ford, *My Life and Work* (London: Heinemann, 1923), 90, 80. On the process of motor assembly at Ford, see also Arnold and Faurote, *Ford Methods*, 115, 118–127.

16. Ford, *My Life*, 87.

17. Arnold and Faurote, *Ford Methods*, 327–359, 129–131; Alain Touraine, *L'Evolution du travail ouvrier aux usines Renault* (Paris: Centre National de la Recherche Scientifique, 1955), 73–74.

18. Ford, *My Life*, 280.

19. Arnold and Faurote, *Ford Methods*, 275, 245.

20. White, "New England Makers," 434; Ford, *My Life*, 88–89; "Twenty Operations to Make Knight Sleeve," *The Automobile* 29 (October 1913): 649.

21. Quoted in Russell, "Coming of the Line," 35. On the independent discovery of time study in the auto industry, see also Nevins and Hill, *Ford*, 468–469; and Charles E. Sorenson, with Samuel T. Williamson, *My Forty Years with Ford* (New York: Collier, 1956), 46–47. For general treatments of Taylorism, see Harry Braverman, *Labor and Monopoly Capital* (New York: Monthly Review Press, 1974), 85–138; Dan Clawson, *Bureaucracy and the Labor Process* (New York: Monthly Review Press, 1980), 202–253.

22. "Scientific Management," *Industrial Worker* 3 (December 1911): 3.

23. Muther, *Production-Line Technique*, 239.

24. Van Deventer, "Ford Principles," 259.

25. Arnold and Faurote, *Ford Methods*, 41–42.

26. "Industrial Relationship," *Automotive Industries* 37 (November 1917): 887.

27. Ford, *My Life*, 209; Arnold and Faurote, *Ford Methods*, 41. On the general relationship between deskilling and the dilution of workers' market power, see Richard Edwards, *Contested Terrain* (New York: Basic Books, 1979), 126–127.

28. Paul U. Kellogg, "When Mass Production Stalls," *Survey* 59 (March 1928): 726.

29. For evidence of labor market manipulation, see Russell, "Coming of the Line," 30–31; Nevins and Hill, *Ford*, 517–518; William E. Chalmers, "Labor in the Automobile Industry" (Ph.D. diss., University of Wisconsin, 1932), 192, 200–201.

30. "The Manufacturer's Opportunity," *Automotive Industries* 43 (August 1920): 284.

31. "Labor Trouble Now Greatest Impediment to Reconversion," *Automo-*

tive Industries 93 (September 1945): 42. For Braverman's argument, see *Labor and Monopoly Capital*, 79–83. For a general argument about the capitalist focus on unit labor costs rather than wages, see Richard Edwards, "The Social Relations of Production at the Point of Production," *Insurgent Sociologist* 8 (Fall 1978): 110–111.

32. Adam Smith, *The Wealth of Nations* (Harmondsworth: Penguin Books, 1982), 112–113. See also Karl Marx, *Capital*, 3 vols. (New York: Vintage Books, 1977–1981), 1:458–461.

33. Ford, *My Life*, 103–105; Arnold and Faurote, *Ford Methods*, 245, 275. On the increased productivity of detail workers, see also Muther, *Production-Line Technique*, 23; Beasley, *Knudsen*, 61.

34. Ford, *My Life*, 77–78.

35. Muther, *Production-Line Technique*, 24.

36. Fred H. Colvin and Frank A. Stanley, *Running a Machine Shop* (New York: McGraw-Hill, 1948), 51. See also "Unusual Tool Grouping Lowers Costs of Nash Engine Production," *Automotive Industries* 50 (March 1924): 559–563.

37. Arnold and Faurote, *Ford Methods*, 6–8; Muther, *Production-Line Technique*, 23–24.

38. Mortier W. La Fever, "Workers, Machinery, and Production in the Automobile Industry," *Monthly Labor Review* 19 (October 1924): 17.

39. Chalmers, "Labor in Autos," 155–156.

40. Muther, *Production-Line Technique*, 233.

41. Arnold and Faurote, *Ford Methods*, 37–41; Barclay, *Ford Production Methods*, 115; Muther, *Production-Line Technique*, 22–23; Philip S. Hanna, "Hudson Prospering Through Efficiency," *Wall Street Journal*, October 8, 1926.

Chapter 4

1. For this conceptualization of mechanization, see Karl Marx, *Capital*, 3 vols. (New York: Vintage Books, 1977–81), 1:371–386; Harry Braverman, *Labor and Monopoly Capital* (New York: Monthly Review Press, 1974), 184–235.

2. See Alain Touraine, *L'Evolution du travail ouvrier aux usines Renault* (Paris: Centre National de la Recherche Scientifique, 1955), 24–29.

3. Both Marx and Adam Smith recognized this effect of the division of labor on tools and machinery. See Marx, *Capital*, 1:341–342; and Adam Smith, *The Wealth of Nations* (Harmondsworth: Penguin Books, 1982), 114–115. See also Roger Burlingame, *Backgrounds of Power* (New York: Scribner's Sons, (1949), 59.

4. Overland ad supplement to *The Automobile* 25 (August 1911): no page; Touraine, *L'Evolution du travail*, 74–75; Horace L. Arnold and Fay L. Faurote, *Ford Methods and the Ford Shops* (New York: Arno Press, 1972), 332–334, 341–344; Mortier W. La Fever, "Workers, Machinery, and Production in the Automobile Industry," *Monthly Labor Review* 19 (October 1924): 14.

5. On these steps in the mechanization of forging, see La Fever, "Workers, Machinery, and Production," 7–8; Thomas J. Fay, "Special Machinery Used in Making Automobiles," *The Automobile* 21 (October 1909): 596; J. Edward Schipper, "Automatic Control Employed in Spring Production," *Automotive Industries* 44 (March 1921): 506–509.

6. "Science in Spring Manufacture," *The Automobile* 32 (May 1915): 836.

7. Walter L. Carter, "Straight Line Production Attained in Wooden Body Building," *Automotive Industries* 53 (December 1925): 946–949, 982–985; Overland ad supp.; no page; "American Methods Count in Body Making," *The Automobile* 26 (February 1912): 560; J. Edward Schipper, "Quantity Production of Sheet Metal Bodies," *Automotive Industries* 38 (June 1918): 1183–1193; "Many Changes in Body Design," *The Automobile* 33 (December 1915): 1182–1184; La Fever, "Workers, Machinery, and Production," 8–9; "Intricate Welding Operations Vital Part of Ford Production," *Automotive Industries* 59 (July 1928): 86–89.

8. Norman Beasley, *Knudsen: A Biography* (New York: Whittlesey House, 1947), 50; Walter P. Chrysler, *Life of an American Workman* (New York: Dodd, Mead, & Co., 1937), 135–136; Arnold and Faurote, *Ford Methods*, 360–383; La Fever, "Workers, Machinery, and Production," 17–19; "Why the 1916 Cars Are Cheaper," *The Automobile* 33 (September 1915): 596.

9. On jigs and fixtures generally, see Fred H. Colvin, *60 Years with Men and Machines* (New York: McGraw-Hill, 1947), 51. For the use of these devices in the early auto industry, see "Automobile Industry and Trade in Detroit," *The Automobile* 9 (December 1903): 609–616; "The Manufacture of Automobiles," *Scientific American* 90 (January 1914): 29–30; Allan Nevins and Frank E. Hill, *Ford: The Times, the Man, the Company* (New York: Scribner's Sons, 1954), 224, 324–326.

10. David A. Hounshell, *From the American System to Mass Production, 1800–1932* (Baltimore: Johns Hopkins University Press, 1984), 288.

11. For a good overview of the use of compound machine tools in the early auto industry, see Thomas J. Fay, "Trend in Design and Fashion," *The Automobile* 21 (December 1909): 1141–1154.

12. L. T. C. Rolt, *A Short History of Machine Tools* (Cambridge, Mass.: MIT Press, 1965), 163–171; "Automobile Industry and Trade," 610–611; "Factory Miscellany," *The Automobile* 27 (August 1912): 459.

13. Thomas J. Fay, "Advanced Methods Obtained in the National Plant," *The Automobile* 22 (April 1910): 710–711; idem, "Trend in Design," 1142.

14. Fay, "Trend in Design," 1141–1144; "Efficiency in Milling and Boring," *The Automobile* 32 (February 1915): 377; "Factory Miscellany," *The Automobile* 27 (December 1912): 1240.

15. Nevins and Hill, *Ford*, 367–368; W. L. Carver, "When Should Old Machine Equipment Be Replaced?" *Automotive Industries* 50 (April 1924): 906.

16. Fay, "Special Machinery," 595. See also "How Production Problems Are Solved," *The Automobile* 22 (April 1910): 788–790.

17. Fay, "Trend in Design," 1145–1146. See also Touraine, *L'Evolution du travail*, 25.

18. On the Cadillac shops, see C. B. Owen, "Organization and Equip-

ment of an Automobile Factory," *Machinery* 15 (March 1909): 493–498. On truck and luxury car shops, see Joseph Geschelin, "GMC Truck Engines," *Automotive Industries* 75 (July 1936): 27; idem, "Cummins Diesel Production Carefully Planned," *Automotive Industries* 77 (July 1937): 21–26; idem, "Packard's 88 Acres of Production Efficiency," *Automotive Industries* 74 (May 1936): 628–637.

19. "How Production Problems Are Solved," 790; J. Edward Schipper, "Future Production Plans Will Require Special Machinery," *Automotive Industries* 40 (January 1919): 148.

20. "Science in Spring Manufacture," 839, emphasis added.

21. Arnold and Faurote, *Ford Methods*, 246.

22. Fay, "Special Machinery," 597.

23. H. E. Blank, "40 Years of Machine Tool Progress," *Automotive Industries* 81 (October 1939): 350–352; "Bores Eighty Cylinder Castings a Day," *The Automobile* 29 (November 1913): 906. Roger Burlingame similarly recognizes two distinct types of assumption of workers' skills by machines. In the first type, which corresponds to my repressive control, the machine assumes a skill that human workers are actually capable of performing. In the second, which corresponds to my nonrepressive control, the machine takes a skill of which human workers are not actually capable, but which exists only as an ideal in the mind. See Burlingame, *Backgrounds of Power*, 61.

24. On the wages of auto workers, see Paul F. Brissenden, *Earnings of Factory Workers, 1899 to 1927* (New York: Franklin, 1971), 124, 148; Paul H. Douglas, *Real Wages in the United States, 1890–1926* (New York: Kelley, 1966), 306–310; and U.S., Bureau of Labor Statistics Bulletin Nos. 348 (1922), 438 (1927), 502 (1930), 706 (1942), 1015 (1951) (Washington, D.C.: Government Printing Office).

25. Marx, *Capital*, 1:519–520.

26. La Fever, "Workers, Machinery, and Production," 1–27; "Factory Miscellany," *The Automobile* 27 (December 1912): 1190.

27. "How Production Problems Are Solved," 791; F. K. Hendrickson, "Automobile Influence on Machine Tool Industry," *Automotive Industries* 45 (November 1921): 927, emphasis added.

28. Beasley, *Knudsen*, 50–51.

29. Fred H. Colvin, "Forging and Machining Ford Front Axle," and "Special Machines for Making Pistons," *American Machinist* 30 (July–August 1913): 190, 350.

30. Although auto capitalists never admitted to such a logic, they clearly recognized that minutely divided labor was most economical only at lower levels of mechanization, while at higher levels, recombination of operations saved time. Thus, Henry Ford wrote: "In the early days of hand craftsmanship a single worker did all of a job; then came the cruder machinery and it was found most economical to split up the operations so that each machine and each man did just one small thing. Now we are heading back to the old days except that where then one man did the whole job, now a machine as far as possible does all of a job." *Moving Forward* (London: Heinemann, 1931), 129–130.

31. Fred H. Colvin, "Machining the Ford Cylinders—I," *American Machinist* 38 (May 1913): 842.

32. Ford, *Moving Forward*, 130–131.

33. "Factors in Production, Methods that Increase Manufacturing Efficiency," *The Automobile* 26 (May 1912): 1076.

34. Keith Sward, *The Legend of Henry Ford* (New York: Rinehart, 1948), 47.

35. Quoted in Nevins and Hill, *Ford*, 324.

36. For a similar conception of the twofold nature of machinery and technology, see Dan Clawson, *Bureaucracy and the Labor Process* (New York: Monthly Review Press, 1980), 191–194.

CHAPTER 5

1. Quoted in Allan Nevins and Frank E. Hill, *Ford: The Times, the Man, the Company* (New York: Scribner's Sons, 1954), 325. See also Keith Sward, *The Legend of Henry Ford* (New York: Rinehart, 1948), 34.

2. Horace L. Arnold and Fay L. Faurote, *Ford Methods and the Ford Shops* (New York: Arno Press, 1972), 105–110. See also Henry Ford, *My Life and Work* (London: Heinemann, 1923), 88–89.

3. Arnold and Faurote, *Ford Methods*, 277–281; John B. Rae, *American Automobile Manufacturers* (Philadelphia: Chilton, 1959), 130; "Factory Miscellany," *The Automobile* 28 (May 1913): 1000.

4. Arnold and Faurote, *Ford Methods*, 115–127.

5. Ibid., 327–359; Nevins and Hill, *Ford*, 471.

6. Arnold and Faurote, *Ford Methods*, 112–115; Ford, *My Life*, 81.

7. Charles Kettering and Allen Orth, *American Battle for Abundance* (Detroit: General Motors, 1947), 57; Glen A. Niemeyer, *The Automobile Career of Ransom E. Olds* (East Lansing: Michigan State University Business Studies, 1963), 48, 53; Duane Yarnell, *Auto Pioneering* (Lansing, Mich.: R. E. Olds, 1949), 83–85.

8. Charles Sorenson, *My Forty Years with Ford* (New York: Collier, 1956), 115; Arnold and Faurote, *Ford Methods*, 135–136.

9. Arnold and Faurote, *Ford Methods*, 135–139; Nevins and Hill, *Ford*, 473; Ford, *My Life*, 81–83; Sorensen, *My Forty Years*, 126–127; C. V. Avery, "How Mass Production Came Into Being," *Iron Age* 123 (June 1929): 1638.

10. Walter P. Chrysler, *Life of an American Workman* (New York: Dodd, Mead & Co., 1937), 134–136; L. V. Spencer, "Metamorphosis of the Motor Car," *Motor Age* 24 (March 1916): 5–11; idem, "Conveyor System Aids Big Production," *The Automobile* 35 (July 1916): 100–104; G. A. Gunther, "New Continuous Molding Reduces Studebaker Foundry Costs," *Automotive Industries* 59 (November 1928): 756.

11. Norman G. Shidle, "The True Function of an Employee's Lunch Room," *Automotive Industries* 44 (March 1921): 514.

12. Ford, *My Life*, 88–89; Arnold and Faurote, *Ford Methods*, 105–110; Philip S. Hanna, "Hudson Prospering Through Efficiency," *Wall Street Jour-*

nal, October 5, 1926; K. W. Stillman, "Fitting Material Handling Equipment to the Job," *Automotive Industries* 54 (September 1926): 563–564.

13. Stillman, "Material Handling Equipment," 563–564.

14. Hartley W. Barclay, *Ford Production Methods* (New York: Harper, 1936), 110, emphasis added.

15. Arnold and Faurote, *Ford Methods*, 279–280.

16. John A. Fitch, "Ford of Detroit and his Ten Million Dollar Profit Sharing Plan," *Survey* 31 (February 1914): 545; Ford foreman quoted in Jack Russell, "The Coming of the Line," *Radical America* 12 (May–June 1978): 39.

17. Ford, *My Life*, 81–83; Arnold and Faurote, *Ford Methods*, 135–139.

18. "Detroit's Automobile Factories Break Production Records," *The Automobile* 30 (May 1914): 1006, 1008–1009.

19. John H. Van Deventer, "Ford Principles and Practice at River Rouge. IX—Machine Tool Arrangement and Parts Transportation," *Industrial Management* 65 (May 1923): 259; Henry Ford, *Moving Forward* (London: Heinemann, 1931), 39.

20. Ralph C. Epstein, *The Automobile Industry* (New York: Arno Press, 1972), 33.

21. Richard Muther, *Production-Line Technique* (New York: McGraw-Hill, 1944), 70.

22. Arnold and Faurote, *Ford Methods*, 139, 151–153.

23. Philip S. Hanna, "Ingenious Tools Aid Motor Industry," *Wall Street Journal*, November 22, 1926.

24. Ibid.

25. Foreman quoted in Charles R. Walker, Robert H. Guest, and Arthur N. Turner, *The Foreman on the Assembly Line* (Cambridge, Mass.: Harvard University Press, 1956), 13.

26. Al Nash, "Job Satisfaction: A Critique," in *Auto Work and Its Discontents*, ed. B. J. Widick (Baltimore: Johns Hopkins University Press, 1976), 76–77.

27. On the effect of the moving line on worker-management conflict, see Richard Edwards, *Contented Terrain* (New York: Basic Books, 1979), 119–120; Charles R. Walker and Robert H. Guest, *The Man on the Assembly Line* (Cambridge, Mass.: Harvard University Press, 1952), 99; William Chalmers, "Labor in the Automobile Industry" (Ph.D. diss., University of Wisconsin, 1932), 160. On the number of Ford foremen, see Stephen Meyer III, *The Five Dollar Day* (Albany: State University of New York Press, 1981), 54–56.

28. James Bright, *Automation and Management* (Boston: Division of Research, Graduate School of Business Administration, Harvard University, 1958), 199; "Production Efficiency Offsets Rise in Wages and Material Prices," *Automotive Industries* 48 (May 1923): 1181–1182.

29. For years, the policy of the Ford Motor Company was to give workers a ten-minute "gift" for eating, during which they were not even allowed to leave their work stations. See Arnold and Faurote, *Ford Methods*, 60.

30. Jonathon N. Leonard, *The Tragedy of Henry Ford* (New York: Putnam's, 1932), 232; foreman quoted in Ely Chinoy, "Manning the Machines—The

Assembly Line Worker," in *The Human Shape of Work*, ed. Peter L. Berger (New York: Macmillan, 1964), 64; Lowell J. Carr and James E. Stremer, *Willow Run* (New York: Harper, 1952), 182.

31. On the general relationship between power and uncertainty in organizations, see Michel Crozier, *The Bureaucratic Phenomenon* (Chicago: University of Chicago Press, 1964), 145–174; Randall Collins, *Conflict Sociology* (New York: Academic Press, 1974), 286–347.

32. J. Edward Schipper, "Continuous Movement in the Essex Production Line," *Automotive Industries* 41 (August 1919): 416–421.

33. Norman G. Shidle, "Progressive Assembly System Increased Truck Production," *Automotive Industries* 43 (July 1920): 120–122; A. F. Denham, "New GMC Truck Plant Solves Problem of Diversified Production," *Automotive Industries* 58 (March 1928): 366–370.

34. See, e.g., J. Edward Schipper, "The Economical Employment of Gravity Conveyors," *Automotive Industries* 41 (September 1919): 467.

Chapter 6

1. "Automobile Industry and Trade in Detroit," *The Automobile* 9 (December 1903): 611; "Factory Miscellany," *The Automobile* 27 (November 1912): 1140.

2. "Factory Miscellany," *The Automobile* 27 (October 1912): 916.

3. Robert S. Woodbury, *Studies in the History of Machine Tools* (Cambridge, Mass.: MIT Press, 1972).

4. "Efficiency in Milling and Boring," *The Automobile* 32 (February 1915): 377; Horace L. Arnold and Fay L. Faurote, *Ford Methods and the Ford Shops* (New York: Arno Press, 1972), 73–75.

5. Robert S. Woodbury, "History of the Milling Machine," 89–90, in *Studies in the History of Machine Tools*. See also "Ohio Tilted Rotary," *Automotive Industries* 40 (May 1919): 1174–1176.

6. Philip S. Hanna, "Hudson Efficiency Seen in Machinery," *Wall Street Journal*, October 21, 1926.

7. Robert S. Woodbury, "History of the Grinding Machine," 151–161, in *Studies in the History of Machine Tools*; P. M. Heldt, "Machine Tool Men Discuss Production Problems at Annual Exhibit," *Automotive Industries* 53 (September 1925): 445–448.

8. K. W. Stillman, "Greater Production Economies Foreseen by Plant Executives," *Automotive Industries* 60 (May 1929): 72.

9. See the following articles in *Automotive Industries*: F. K. Hendrickson, "Automobile's Influence on Machine Tool Industry," 45 (November 1921): 927; "Bullard Designs a New Power-Operated Chuck," 52 (June 1925): 1056; "Automatic Holding Fixtures," 55 (December 1926): 1017.

10. See the following articles in *Automotive Industries*: "Full Automatic Grinder," 57 (September 1927): 342; "Screw Machine Feeder," 58 (April 1926): 634; Athel F. Denham, "Cost of Cylinder Block Machining Reduced

by Graham-Paige," and "Plymouth Speeds Materials Movement with Automatic Conveyor Handling," 60 (March–June 1929): 434–438, 940–942; Joseph Geschelin, "The New DeSoto Plant," 76 (February 1937): 187.

11. L. R. Smith quoted in Siegfried Giedion, *Mechanization Takes Command* (New York: Norton, 1969), 118. On the A. O. Smith factory, see also James Bright, *Automation and Management* (Boston: Division of Research, Graduate School of Business Administration, Harvard University, 1958), 14, 86, 95–97; Athel F. Denham, "Frames Produced Automatically in Two-Hour Cycle," *Automotive Industries* 58 (March 1928): 437–439; A. W. Redlin, "Handling of Materials and Frame Manufacturing Process are Automatic at Smith Plant," *Automotive Industries* 62 (March 1930): 466–468; John W. Anderson, "How I Became Part of the Labor Movement," in *Rank and File*, ed. Alice and Staughton Lynd (Boston: Beacon Press, 1973), 43.

12. Joseph Geschelin, "Production Lines," *Automotive Industries* 65 (October 1931): 543. See also "Seneca Falls Makes New Contribution to Fast Production," *Automotive Industries* 66 (June 1932): 876.

13. Natco advertisement, *Automotive Industries* 79 (November 1938): 13; "Ingenious Grouping of Machines," *Automotive Industries* 83 (December 1940): 489–498; Christy Borth, *Masters of Mass Production* (Indianapolis, Ind.: Bobbs-Merrill, 1945), 180–181; Joseph Geschelin, "Studebaker Know-How Speeds Flying Fortress Engine Output," *Automotive Industries* 88 (April 1943): 18–22, 70–74.

14. Joseph Geschelin, "Buick Cylinder Blocks Now Machined on First Unitized Transfer Line," *Automotive Industries* 96 (February 1947): 20–27; idem, "Independent Units Protect Automatic Transfer Lines," *Automotive Industries* 96 (October 1947): 30–34; Bright, *Automation and Management*, 59–64, 77–78.

15. Joseph Geschelin, "Advanced Tooling at Piston and Crankshaft Departments Reorganized by Ford," *Automotive Industries* 95 (October 1946): 18–23; idem, "Revolutionary Automation at Ford Operates with Iron Hand," *Automotive Industries* 99 (November 1948): 24–27; Bright, *Automation and Management*, 62.

16. See the following articles from *Automotive Industries*: Joseph Geschelin, "Knockout Attachment with Safety Guard Boosts Press Production," 64 (March 1931): 394–396; Birdsboro Hydraulic Presses advertisement, 90 February 1944): 130; C. A. Briggs, "Increasing Power Press Safety Without Reducing Production," 43 (September 1920): 614–616; "Intricate Welding Operations Vital Part of Ford Production," 59 (July 1928): 86–89; "Automatic Machines for Welding Increasing, Report Shows," 62 (March 1930): 406.

17. U.S., Employment Service, *Job Specifications for the Automobile Manufacturing Industry* (Washington, D.C.: Government Printing Office, 1935), 537–570; Joseph Geschelin, "Handling Mechanization Boosts Monroe Shock Absorber Output," *Automotive Industries* 96 (January 1947): 24–29, 84–86; idem, "Ultramodern Production Features at Chevrolet's New Flint Plant," *Automotive Industries* 94 (August 1947): 22–26.

18. "Marquette Die-Sinking Profiling Pantograph," *Automotive Industries*

73 (July 1935): 60; Pratt & Whitney advertisement for Keller Profiling Machine, *Automotive Industries* 87 (November 1942): 61; Edmund B. Neil and K. W. Stillman, "Machine Tools for Automotive Use Predominate at Cleveland Show," *Automotive Industries* 57 (October 1927): 496–497; David A. Hounshell, *From the American System to Mass Production, 1800–1932* (Baltimore: Johns Hopkins University Press, 1984), 285.

19. Joseph Geschelin, "Automatic Devices Reduce Inspection Costs," *Automotive Industries* 103 (November 1950): 32–33.

20. Henry Ford, *Moving Forward* (London: Heinemann, 1931), 40.

21. J. Edward Schipper, "Automatic Control Employed in Spring Production," *Automotive Industries* 44 (March 1921): 506.

22. Krueger quoted in Borth, *Masters of Mass Production*, 185; Cincinnati Milling Machine Company advertisement, *Automotive Industries* 88 (February 1943): 16; W. F. and John Barnes Company advertisement, *Automotive Industries* 84 (March 1941): 238.

23. Quoted in Bright, *Automation and Management*, 134.

24. Joseph Geschelin, "Higher Material Costs and Wages Put New Emphasis on Cost-Reducing Methods," *Automotive Industries* 69 (November 1933): 549–550.

25. George W. Hoehler, "More and Better Machines," *Automotive Industries* 97 (September 1947): 72. On the wages of auto workers, see note 24, chapter 4.

26. U.S., National Recovery Administration, Research and Planning Division, *Preliminary Report on Study of Regularization of Employment and Improvement of Labor Conditions in the Automobile Industry* (Washington, D.C.: National Recovery Administration, 1935), Exhibit 16, 11; "Special Equipment Cuts Machining Time," *Automotive Industries* 102 (January 1959): 52, 78.

27. W. L. Carver, "Production Progress in 1924," *Automotive Industries* 51 (October 1924): 750.

28. Victor Drilling Machine advertisement, *Automotive Industries* 52 (February 1925): 148; Heald Machine Company advertisement, *Automotive Industries* 94 (February 1946): inside cover.

29. Bullard advertisement, *Automotive Industries* 51 (July 1924): 107.

30. "Continuous Milling Machine with Fixed Production," *Automotive Industries* 43 (September 1920): 664, emphasis added.

31. Clayton W. Fountain, *Union Guy* (New York: Viking, 1949), 39–40.

32. Bright, *Automation and Management*, 59–60.

33. "New Norton Grinder Development Increased Production," *Automotive Industries* 53 (October 1925): 591.

34. Joseph Geschelin, "Increased Production and Reduced Cost of Grinding Achieved During Year," *Automotive Industries* 65 (October 1931): 655.

35. J. Edward Schipper, "Cutting Costs in the Manufacture of Small Units," *Automotive Industries* 44 (January 1921): 26.

36. For evidence of worker resistance during cyclical swings, see chapter 8.

37. Henry & Wright Manufacturing Company advertisement, *Automotive Industries* 50 (February 1924): 301.

38. W. F. and John Barnes Company advertisement, *Automotive Industries* 84 (March 1941): 238.

39. Gisholt Machine Company advertisement, *Automotive Industries* 91 (November 1944): 8.

40. J. Edward Schipper, "Better Cars at Lower Price—A Production Achievement," *Automotive Industries* 46 (June 1922): 1148.

41. "Growing Demand for Low Priced Closed Car," *Automotive Industries* 45 (November 1921): 1001–1003.

42. Charles Kettering and Allen Orth, *The New Necessity* (Baltimore: Williams and Wilkins, 1932), 87; idem, *American Battle for Abundance* (Detroit: General Motors, 1947), 72. A comparison of the passenger-car division of the industry with the truck and luxury-car divisions helps to substantiate this relationship between market demand, design, and production technology. The latter two divisions had much smaller markets for their products, which made sales a key problem. In order to ensure sales to the small market, product design had to be molded to the particular needs and desires of customers. Under these small-market conditions, design could not be totally subordinated to cost-cutting technology. It became an independent factor in production, often determining the type of technology used. For example, variable and custom designs militated against the use of specialized machinery in truck and luxury-car production. The more versatile universal machines were necessary. And these machines required skilled machinists, who exercised considerable skill and discretion in their work. As a result, workers in these divisions of the industry were able to exert greater control over their own work. See, e.g., K. W. Stillman, "Company Puts Production Control in Hands of Workmen," *Automotive Industries* 57 (August 1927): 272–273. When a large market for the product was absent, design became an independent variable in production and often prevented capital from adopting the type of technology that wrested control of the labor process from workers.

43. E. D. Kennedy, *The Automobile Industry* (New York: Reynal & Hitchcock, 1941), 138; Robert P. Thomas, *An Analysis of the Pattern of Growth of the Automobile Industry, 1855–1929* (New York: Arno Press, 1977), 203.

44. Emma Rothschild, *Paradise Lost: The Decline of the Auto-Industrial Age* (New York: Random House, 1973), 37–47; Alfred P. Sloan, *My Years With General Motors* (Garden City, N.Y.: Doubleday, 1964).

45. See the following articles from *Automotive Industries*: W. L. Carver, "High Production Jobs Handled on Standard Machines with Special Fixtures," 54 (May 1926): 770–771; K. W. Stillman, "Many Highly Specialized Jobs Now Being Performed with Standard Machine Tools," 59 (November 1928): 694–705; Joseph Geschelin, "Unit-Type Machines Fit the Program of Frequent Production Changes in Automotive Plants," 65 (August 1931): 194–198; H. E. Blank, Jr., "40 Years of Machine Tool Progress," 81 (October 1939): 345ff.

CHAPTER 7

1. The selection of one year as the amount of training and/or experience separating skilled from unskilled workers is not arbitrary, but rather it corresponds with a number of classification schemes devised by both scholars and manufacturers. See, for example, Henry Ford, *My Life and Work* (London: Heinemann, 1923), 110; Automobile Manufacturers Association data cited in William H. McPherson, *Labor Relations in the Automobile Industry* (Washington, D.C.: Brookings Institution, 1940), 8; U.S., Bureau of Labor Statistics, *Employment Outlook in the Automobile Industry*, Bulletin No. 1138 (Washington, D.C.: Government Printing Office, 1953), 12–14.

2. First Annual Report of the Michigan Department of Labor, cited in Allan Nevins and Frank E. Hill, *Ford: The Times, the Man, the Company* (New York: Scribner's Sons, 1954), 380; U.S., Bureau of the Census, *Thirteenth Census of the United States: 1910*, vol. 4, "Population, Occupational Statistics" (Washington, D.C.: Government Printing Office, 1914): 336–339; Stephen Meyer, III, *The Five Dollar Day* (Albany: State University of New York Press, 1981), 47–48.

3. O. J. Abell, "Labor Classified on a Skill-Wages Basis," *Iron Age* 93 (January 1914): 48; R. R. Lutz, *The Metal Trades* (Cleveland: Survey Committee of the Cleveland Foundation, 1916), 81.

4. James Bright, *Automation and Management* (Boston: Division of Research, Graduate School of Business Administration, Harvard University, 1958), 187–189.

5. Henry Ford, *Moving Forward* (London: Heinemann, 1931), 122. On the requirements of highly mechanized automobile jobs, see also Ely Chinoy, "Manning the Machines—the Assembly-Line Worker," in *The Human Shape of Work*, ed. Peter L. Berger (New York: Macmillan, 1964), 56–57; Charles Reitell, "Machinery and Its Effect upon the Workers in the Automobile Industry," *The Annals of the American Academy of Political and Social Science* 166 (November 1924): 38–39.

6. Reitell, "Machinery and Its Effects," 39.

7. Horace L. Arnold and Fay L. Faurote, *Ford Methods and the Ford Shops* (New York: Arno Press, 1972), 329.

8. Ford, *My Life*, 111.

9. Arnold and Faurote, *Ford Methods*, 42.

10. Bright, *Automation and Management*, 181; William Faunce, "Automation and the Automobile Worker," *Social Problems* 6 (Summer 1958): 69–70.

11. Alain Touraine, *L'Evolution du travail ouvrier aux usines Renault* (Paris: Centre National de la Recherche Scientifique, 1955), 115–123. James Bright also noted that automation in automobile plants required of workers greater "alertness, ability, and responsibility." But by "responsibility" he seemed to mean, like Touraine, simply a willingness to take orders and generally fit into the organization. See Bright *Automation and Management*, 181.

12. Many have challenged, however, the extent to which this shift consti-

tutes an upgrading of the work force. See, for example, Harry Braverman, *Labor and Monopoly Capital* (New York: Monthly Review Press, 1974), 424–447; Stanley Aronowitz, *False Promises* (New York: McGraw-Hill, 1973), 264–332.

13. On these changes in the tool shop, see Touraine, *L'Evolution du travail*, 125–136.

14. Ibid., 137–139; Bright, *Automation and Management*, 189–190; Faunce, "Automation," 70; Joseph Geschelin, "Observations," *Automotive Industries* 101 (September 1949): 58; "New Production and Plant Equipment," *Automotive Industries* 102 (June 1950): 52–53.

15. Robert W. Dunn, *Labor and Automobiles* (New York: International Publishers, 1929), 62–64.

16. *Thirteenth Census: 1910,* vol. 4, "Population, Occupational Statistics": 336; U.S., Bureau of the Census, *Fourteenth Census of the United States: 1920,* vol. 4, "Population, Occupations" (Washington, D.C.: Government Printing Office, 1923): 346–348; Lutz, *Metal Trades,* 81; Meyer, *Five Dollar Day,* 77.

17. *Thirteenth Census: 1910,* vol. 4, "Population, Occupational Statistics": 336; George E. Hayes, *Negro Newcomers in Detroit* (New York: Arno Press, 1969), 6–8; *Fourteenth Census: 1920,* vol. 4, "Population, Occupations": 347, 349; U.S., Bureau of the Census, *Fifteenth Census of the United States: 1930,* "Population, vol. 5, General Report on Occupations" (Washington, D.C.: Government Printing Office, 1933): 84; War Manpower Commission data cited in "Unauthorized Work Stoppages Continue in Many War Plants," *Automotive Industries* 88 (May 1943): 62; U.S., Bureau of the Census, *U.S. Census of Population: 1950,* vol. 4, "Special Reports, Part 1, Chapter D, Industrial Characteristics" (Washington, D.C.: Government Printing Office, 1955): 15.

18. Dunn, *Labor and Automobiles,* 63; William Chalmers, "Labor in the Automobile Industry" (Ph.D. diss., University of Wisconsin, 1932), 180–181, 229; Louis Adamic, "The Hill-Billies Come to Detroit," *Nation* 149 (February 1935): 177–178.

19. *Fourteenth Census: 1920,* vol. 10, "Manufacturers, 1919, Reports for Selected Industries" (1923): 868; U.S., Bureau of Labor Statistics, *Women in Factories* (Washington, D.C.: Government Printing Office, 1947), 6–7; *Census of Population: 1950,* vol. 4, "Special Reports, Part 1, Chapter D, Industrial Characteristics": 34.

20. These are officially called "man-hour productivity" indices. But I prefer to label this type of index "worker-hour output" for two reasons. First, the latter label is less sexist and better reflects the fact that women made up a growing minority of the auto labor force. Second, substituting "output" for "productivity" avoids confusion with the specific meaning of productivity that I have adopted from Marxist political economy. Conventional economic usage of "productivity" does not distinguish between increases in output resulting from greater quantities of labor expended in a given time (increased labor intensity), and those resulting from the same quantity of labor expended in a given time (increased labor productivity in the strict Marxist usage). These indices reflect the combined effects of increases in labor productivity and intensity. I use the term "output" to denote this.

21. On the interpretation of worker-hour output indices in the auto industry, see Marjorie Stanley, "The Interrelationships of Economic Forces and Labor Relations in the Automobile Industry" (Ph.D. diss., Indiana University, 1953), 48.

22. "Facts Challenge Conclusions in Henderson Report," *Automotive Industries* 72 (March 1935): 332; Henry Ford II, "Human Engineering Necessary for Further Mass Production Progress," *Automotive Industries* 94 (January 1946): 39; Andrew T. Court, "Measuring Labor Productivity," *Automotive Industries* 94 (March 1946): 44; U.S., Bureau of Labor Statistics, *Productivity Indexes for Selected Industries, 1978*, Bulletin no. 2002 (Washington, D.C.: Government Printing Office, 1978), 97.

23. Mortier W. La Fever, "Workers, Machinery, and Production in the Automobile Industry," *Monthly Labor Review* 19 (October 1924): 3–5.

24. Bright, *Automation and Management*, 59–60, 132–133.

25. Chalmers, "Labor in Autos," 168.

26. Stanley B. Mathewson, *Restriction of Output Among Unorganized Workers* (Carbondale, Ill.: Southern Illinois University Press, 1969), 135.

27. U.S., Bureau of Labor Statistics, *Productivity and Unit Labor Costs in Selected Manufacturing Industries, 1919–1940* (Washington, D.C.: Government Printing Office, 1942), 66; Spurgeon Bell, *Productivity, Wages, and National Income* (Washington, D.C.: Brookings Institution, 1940), 104–108.

Chapter 8

1. A more comprehensive treatment of worker resistance would of necessity include two important factors that I do not take into account here: American politics and culture. For treatments of working-class struggle that incorporate these broader concerns, see David Montgomery, *Workers' Control in America* (Cambridge: Cambridge University Press, 1979); Herbert Gutman, *Work, Culture, and Society in Industrializing America* (New York: Vintage Books, 1977); Stanley Aronowitz, *False Promises* (New York: McGraw-Hill, 1973); Jeremy Brecher, *Strike!* (San Francisco: Straight Arrow Books, 1972); Mike Davis, "Why the U.S. Working Class Is Different," *New Left Review* no. 123 (September–October, 1980): 3–44; idem, "The Barren Marriage of American Labour and the Democratic Party," *New Left Review* no. 124 (November–December, 1980): 43–84.

2. David Brody, *Workers in Industrial America* (New York: Oxford University Press, 1980), 14–21; Aronowitz, *False Promises*, 164–172; Montgomery, *Workers' Control*, 40–44; E. P. Thompson, "Time, Work-Discipline, and Industrial Capitalism, *Past and Present* 38 (1967): 56–97. For a treatment of worker resistance in the auto industry that is similar to mine, see Stephen Meyer III, *The Five Dollar Day* (Albany: State University of New York Press, 1981), 67–94. That these negative worker attitudes were not based simply upon the craft traditions of skilled workers or the preindustrial traditions of unskilled immigrants is demonstrated by data from later auto shops. Even auto workers thoroughly imbued with the culture and requirements of mass

production continued to hold negative attitudes toward their work. See, for example, Arthur Kornhauser, *Mental Health of the Industrial Worker* (New York: Wiley, 1965); Ely Chinoy, *Automobile Workers and the American Dream* (Boston: Beacon Press, 1955); Robert Blauner, *Alienation and Freedom* (Chicago: University of Chicago Press, 1964); Charles R. Walker and Robert H. Guest, *The Man on the Assembly Line* (Cambridge, Mass.: Harvard University Press, 1952).

3. Henry Ford, *My Life and Work* (London: Heinemann, 1923), 103. See also Henry Ford, *Today and Tomorrow* (London: Heinemann, 1926), 160; idem, *Moving Forward* (London: Heinemann, 1931), 121–122.

4. Ford, *My Life*, 43.

5. Ford, *Moving Forward*, 133.

6. Horace L. Arnold and Fay L. Faurote, *Ford Methods and the Ford Shops* (New York: Arno Press, 1972), 331.

7. Klann and Martin quoted in Jack Russell, "The Coming of the Line," *Radical America* 12 (May–June, 1978): 39–40.

8. Ford, *Moving Forward*, 39.

9. Harry Tipper, "The Need for a New Incentive for the Industrial Worker," *Automotive Industries* 39 (October 1918): 583.

10. Norman G. Shidle, "Practical Application of Education to Industry," *Automotive Industries* 42 (June 1920): 1413.

11. Samuel M. Levin, "Ford Profit Sharing, 1914–1920: I. The Growth of the Plan," *Personnel Journal* 6 (August 1927): 75–76.

12. Boyd Fisher, "How to Reduce Labor Turnover," *The Annals of the American Academy of Political and Social Science* 71 (May 1917): 14.

13. Boris Emmet, *Profit Sharing in the United States*, U.S. Bureau of Labor Statistics Bulletin no. 208 (Washington, D.C.: Government Printing Office, 1917), 115; John R. Lee, "The So-Called Profit Sharing System in the Ford Plant," *The Annals of the American Academy of Political and Social Science* 65 (May 1916): 308; Paul F. Brissenden and Emil Frankel, "Mobility of Labor in American Industry," *Monthly Labor Review* 10 (June 1920): 41–45.

14. Jonathon Leonard, *The Tragedy of Henry Ford* (New York: Putnam's, 1932), 25.

15. Quoted in Allan Nevins and Frank E. Hill, *Ford: The Times, the Man, the Company* (New York: Scribner's Sons, 1954), 520.

16. James O'Connor quoted in Russell, "Coming of the Line," 39; Keith Sward, *The Legend of Henry Ford* (New York: Rinehart, 1948), 48.

17. Meyer, *Five Dollar Day*, 82–83; Emmet, *Profit Sharing*, 117.

18. Fisher, "How to Reduce Labor Turnover," 10–11; Meyer, *Five Dollar Day*, 83–85; Russell, "Coming of the Line," 40; Arthur Pound, *The Iron Man in Industry* (Boston: Atlantic Monthly, 1922), 19.

19. Meyer, *Five Dollar Day*, 82–83; Ford, *My Life*, 111–112.

20. Reprinted with permission from Stanley B. Mathewson, *Restriction of Output Among Unorganized Workers* (Carbondale: Southern Illinois University Press), 127.

21. Frank Marquart, *An Auto Worker's Journal* (University Park: Pennsylvania State University Press, 1975), 11. For other examples of time-study ma-

nipulation by workers, see William Chalmers, "Labor in the Automobile Industry" (Ph.D. diss., University of Wisconsin, 1932), 121–122; Mathewson, *Restriction of Output*, 68–73.

22. Mathewson, *Restriction of Output*, 66. See also Chalmers, "Labor in Autos," 126–127. Auto capitalists themselves admitted that the practice of rate cutting was widespread. See, for example, Norman G. Shidle, "A Foreman's Thought on Piece-Rate Cutting," *Automotive Industries* 44 (June 1921): 1169; Harry Tipper, "How to Make Money by Being Honest," *Automotive Industries* 47 (August 1922): 332–333.

23. On banking, see Mathewson, *Restriction of Output*, 77–85; Walker and Guest, *Man on Assembly Line*, 146–147; Fred H. Colvin, *60 Years with Men and Machines* (New York: McGraw-Hill, 1947), 275.

24. John W. Anderson, "How I Became Part of the Labor Movement," in *Rank and File*, ed. Alice and Staughton Lynd (Boston: Beacon Press, 1973), 44. See also Joyce S. Peterson, "A Social History of Automobile Workers Before Unionization, 1900–1933" (Ph.D. diss., University of Wisconsin, 1976), 230–235.

25. Quoted in Studs Terkel, *Working* (New York: Avon, 1974), 235.

26. Chalmers, "Labor in Autos," 155; John Lippert, "Shopfloor Politics at Fleetwood," *Radical America* 12 (July–August 1978): 55–56.

27. Louis Adamic, "Sitdown: II," *Nation* 142 (December 1936): 703. For a contemporary example, see Aronowitz, *False Promises*, 36, 49.

28. Bill Watson, "Counter-planning on the Shop Floor," *Radical America* 5 (May–June 1971): 77–80.

29. Kornhauser, *Mental Health*, 170.

30. Meyer, *Five Dollar Day*, 92–93; Sidney Fine, *The Automobile Under the Blue Eagle* (Ann Arbor: University of Michigan Press, 1963), 22–23.

31. See, for example, the news columns of *Automotive Industries* 28 (January–March 1913); and Harry Tipper, "Countering the Propaganda of the Irreconcilables," *Automotive Industries* 40 (May 1919): 1071–1072.

32. Philip S. Foner, *History of the Labor Movement in the United States*, vol. 4, *The Industrial Workers of the World, 1905–1917* (New York: International Publishers, 1965), 383–390; Fine, *Auto Under Blue Eagle*, 24.

33. Fine, *Auto Under Blue Eagle*, 22–23; Meyer, *Five Dollar Day*, 171–172, 185–187; news columns of *Automotive Industries* 40 (May–June 1919).

34. Chalmers, "Labor in Autos," 208–238. On a similar interpretation of the labor struggles of this period, see Montgomery, *Workers' Control*, 91–112.

35. Ford, *My Life*, 257.

36. Charles E. Sorensen, *My Forty Years with Ford* (New York: Collier, 1956), 244.

37. Chalmers, "Labor in Autos," 207. See also Sidney Fine, *Sit-Down* (Ann Arbor: University of Michigan Press, 1969), 29; E. D. Kennedy, *The Automobile Industry* (New York: Reynal & Hitchcock, 1941), 252.

38. For a general treatment of the law of uneven development, see Ernest Mandel, *Marxist Economic Theory* (New York: Monthly Review Press, 1970), 91–92, 371–373; idem, *Late Capitalism* (London: Verso, 1978), esp. Chapters

2 and 3. On the persistence of small firms in the early period of the industry, see Robert P. Thomas, *An Analysis of the Pattern of Growth of the Automobile Industry, 1855–1929* (New York: Arno Press, 1972), 193–204.

39. On the relationship between worker resistance and uneven development, see Harry Braverman, *Labor and Monopoly Capital* (New York: Monthly Review Press, 1974), 146–149; Stanley Aronowitz, "Marx, Braverman, and the Logic of Capital," *Insurgent Sociologist* 8 (Fall 1978): 143–144.

40. Karl Marx, *Capital*, 3 vols. (New York: Vintage Books, 1977–81), 1: 621–628.

41. Thomas, *Pattern of Growth*; Epstein, *Automobile Industry*; John B. Rae, *American Automobile Manufacturers* (Philadelphia: Chilton, 1959).

42. On the general effect of the concentration and centralization of capital on the working class, see Karl Marx and Frederick Engels, "Manifesto of the Communist Party," in Marx and Engels, *Selected Works*, 3 vols. (Moscow: Progress Publishers, 1969), 1:115–116; Paul M. Sweezy, "Marx and the Proletariat," in *Modern Capitalism and other Essays* (New York: Monthly Review Press, 1972), 147–165.

43. Ford, *My Life*, 192.

44. Herbert Hasking, "Just Among Ourselves," *Automotive Industries* 77 (July 1937): 49; Norman G. Shidle, "Controlled Employment," *Automotive Industries* 68 (April 1933): 393. See also Norman G. Shidle, "The Small Town as a Manufacturing Center," *Automotive Industries* 43 (October 1920): 874–875.

45. Norman G. Shidle, "Keep the Lines Moving," *Automotive Industries* 68 (March 1933): 363.

46. On the capitalist strategy of decentralization, see the *Automotive Industries* articles cited in notes 44 and 45, as well as Sidney Fine, *Sit-Down*, 49; Joseph Geschelin, "Is Decentralization Industry's Next Step?" *Automotive Industries* 68 (May 1933): 584–585; "General Motors II: Chevrolet," *Fortune* 19 (January 1939): 109; Alfred J. Sloan, in collaboration with Boyden Sparkes, *Adventures of a White-Collar Man* (New York: Doubleday, Doran, 1941), 196.

47. "Government Analysis of Labor," *Automotive Industries* 38 (April 1918): 841; "Detroit Now Faces Labor Shortages," *Automotive Industries* 40 (May 1919): 1028.

48. Norman G. Shidle, "Labor Shortages Show Strikes Have Not Diminished," *Automotive Industries* 44 (February 1922): 424.

49. "Government Plan for Controlling Labor," *Automotive Industries* 38 (June 1918): 1238. See also "The Competition for Labor," *The Automobile* 36 (February 1917): 409. For more accurate estimates of increased labor turnover in this period, see Brissenden and Frankel, "Mobility of Labor in American Industry," 35–56.

50. Mrs. Wilfred C. Leland, *Master of Precision: Henry M. Leland* (Detroit: Wayne State University Press, 1966), 187. On increased struggles within the shops, see also Meyer, *Five Dollar Day*, 169–194; Allen Sinsheimer, "Health the Key to Better Industrial Relations," *The Automobile* 36 (February 1917):

426–431; "Industrial Relationship," *Automotive Industries* 37 (November 1917): 887.

51. On increased strikes and stoppages, see the following articles in *Monthly Labor Review*: "Strikes and Lockouts in the United States, 1916, 1917, and 1918," 8 (June 1919): 317; "Strikes and Lockouts in the United States, 1916, 1917, 1918, and 1919," 10 (June 1920): 210; "Strikes and Lockouts in the United States, 1916 to 1920," 12 (June 1921): 170. These statistics are for "automobile, carriage, and wagon workers," of which auto workers comprised the vast majority by this date.

52. U.S., Bureau of Labor Statistics, *Handbook of Labor Statistics, 1947*, Bulletin no. 916 (Washington, D.C.: Government Printing Office, 1948), 46; "Absenteeism Declining Slightly in Most War Production Plants," *Automotive Industries* 87 (December 1942): 50; Andrew T. Court, "Measuring Labor Productivity," *Automotive Industries* 94 (March 1946): 17, 43–44; Henry Ford II, "Human Engineering Necessary for Further Mass Production Progress," *Automotive Industries* (January 1935): 39, 74–76.

53. BLS, *Handbook of Labor Statistics, 1947*, 137; "Wildcat Strikes Slow War Production," *Automotive Industries* 87 (July 1942): 57–58; George Romney, "Why Manpower Limits the Automobile Industry's Output," *Automotive Industries* 92 (March 1945): 17, 74–78. Official BLS data probably underestimate the extent of stoppages because they exclude all those involving less than six workers and lasting less than one day. Industry data without such restrictions cited in the Romney article place the number of stoppages in five hundred auto plants in 1944 at one thousand forty-five.

54. For a general discussion of the homogenization of labor, see Marx and Engels, "Manifesto of the Communist Party," 116; Marx, *Capital*, 1:420; Paul M. Sweezy, "Marx and the Proletariat," 147–165; David Gordon, Richard Edwards, and Michael Reich, *Segmented Work, Divided Workers* (Cambridge: Cambridge University Press, 1982), 100–164.

55. On craft wages in the early auto industry, see Alain Touraine, *L'Evolution du travail ouvrier aux usines Renault* (Paris: Centre National de la Recherche Scientifique, 1955), 64–65.

56. R. R. Lutz, *The Metal Trades* (Cleveland: Committee of the Cleveland Foundation, 1916), 89. For estimates on the compression of the early wage structure of the industry, see Charles Reitell, "Machinery and Its Effects upon the Workers in the Automobile Industry," *The Annals of the American Academy of Political and Social Science* 116 (November 1924): 41; Robert M. Macdonald, *Collective Bargaining in the Automobile Industry* (New Haven, Conn.: Yale University Press, 1963), 83–88, 134–135.

57. See, for example, Walker and Guest, *Man on Assembly Line*, 84–85; Chinoy, *Auto Workers* 37–38. The greater variation in the wages of occupations in the auto parts division is probably due to the greater use of incentive wages, as well as the greater proportion of women workers in those occupations, whose wages were significantly lower than male workers.'

58. Chinoy, *Auto Workers*, 20, 64. On the collective nature of wage gains in the industry, see also Robert H. Guest, "Work Careers and Aspirations of

Automobile Workers," in *Labor and Trade Unionism*, ed. Walter Galenson and S. M. Lipset (New York: Wiley, 1960), 319–320.

59. Harry Tipper, "Standardization Without Understanding Is Harmful," *Automotive Industries* 44 (March 1921): 720; idem, "Paying the Worker a Fair Reward on His Just Worth," *Automotive Industries* 42 (May 1920): 1174–1175.

60. Richard Muther, *Production-Line Technique* (New York: McGraw-Hill, 1944), 223.

61. Irving Howe and B. J. Widick, *The UAW and Walter Reuther* (New York: Random House, 1949), 24. See also R. J. Thomas' testimony before the U.S., Congress, Senate, Temporary National Economic Committee, *Investigation of Concentration of Economic Power*, 76th Congress, 3rd session, Part 30: Technology and Concentration of Economic Power, Senate Library, vol. 656 (1940): 16376; Frank Marquart, "The Auto Worker," in *Voices of Dissent* (New York: Grove Press, 1958), 144–145; Lippert, "Shopfloor Politics," 55–56; Tom Cagle, *Life in an Auto Plant* (New York: Pathfinder, 1970), 4–6.

CHAPTER 9

1. The following discussion of industrial authority draws upon the general conceptions of Richard Edwards, *Contested Terrain* (New York: Basic Books, 1979), 11–22.

2. "The Winton Plant and its Product," *Cycle and Automotive Trade Journal* 8 (March 1904): 70.

3. Allan Nevins and Frank E. Hill, *Ford: The Times, the Man, the Company* (New York: Scribner's Sons, 1954), 270–271.

4. Duane Yarnell, *Auto Pioneering* (Lansing, Mich.: R. E. Olds, 1949), 41. For Max Weber's discussion of patrimonialism, see *Economy and Society* (New York: Bedminster Press, 1968), 1006–1012. My use of these Weberian terms is heavily influenced by their interpretation in Randall Collins, *Conflict Sociology* (New York: Academic Press, 1975), esp. 292–294.

5. John B. Rae, *American Automobile Manufacturers* (Philadelphia: Chilton, 1959), 203–204; Marjorie T. Stanley, "The Interrelationships of Economic Forces and Labor Relations in the Automobile Industry" (Ph.D. diss., Indiana University, 1953), 19. This discussion is based on the theoretical tenets about organizational control set forth in Collins, *Conflict Sociology*, 286–347. For a general discussion of this form of entrepreneurial control, see also Edwards, *Contested Terrain*, 25–27.

6. Nevins and Hill, *Ford*, 526.

7. Alain Touraine, *L'Evolution du travail ouvrier aux usines Renault* (Paris: Centre National de la Recherche Scientifique, 1955), 152.

8. Sumner H. Slichter, *Turnover of Factory Labor* (New York: Appleton, 1919), 281. On the general organizational control strategy of favoritism, see Collins, *Conflict Sociology*, 303–304.

9. On the generally lax atmosphere of shop supervision during this period, see Nevins and Hill, *Ford*, 381–383, 526.

10. Ibid., 383–384.

11. Samuel S. Marquis, *Henry Ford: An Interpretation* (Boston: Little, Brown, 1923), 141.

12. Clayton Fountain, *Union Guy* (New York: Viking, 1949), 142. On Sorensen, see also Keith Sward, *The Legend of Henry Ford* (New York: Rinehart, 1948), 181–182.

13. Nevins and Hill, *Ford*, 526; Robert Schrank, *Ten Thousand Working Days* (Cambridge, Mass.: MIT Press, 1978), 55; Norman Beasley, *Knudsen: A Biography* (New York: Whittlesey House, 1947), 30.

14. Touraine, *L'Evolution du travail*, 154–156; John H. Van Deventer, "Ford Principles and Practice at River Rouge. IX—Machine Tool Arrangement and Parts Transportation," *Industrial Management* 65 (May 1923): 262; Boyd Fisher, "Methods of Reducing Labor Turnover," in U.S., Bureau of Labor Statistics, *Proceedings of the Employment Managers' Conference*, Bulletin no. 196 (Washington, D.C.: Government Printing Office, 1916), 16–17.

15. John R. Lee, "The So-Called Profit Sharing System in the Ford Plant," *The Annals of the American Academy of Political and Social Science* 65 (May 1916): 298. For a good description of the organizational structure of large auto plants circa 1910, see Thomas J. Fay, "Distinguishing Features Found in 1910 Product," *The Automobile* 22 (January 1910): 28–30; and Nevins and Hill, *Ford*, 450–451.

16. "How System Rules One Factory," *The Automobile* 20 (April 1909): 719; Overland advertising supplement to *The Automobile* 25 (August 1911): no page; Horace L. Arnold and Fay L. Faurote, *Ford Methods and the Ford Shops* (New York: Arno Press, 1972), 97–101.

17. "System Makes Car Building Profitable," *The Automobile* 26 (February 1912): 606; Stephen Meyer III, *The Five Dollar Day* (Albany: State University of New York Press, 1981), 56–57; Arnold and Faurote, *Ford Methods*, 182–184. For a general discussion of the accounting system emerging in this period, see C. E. Knoepell, *Maximum Production in Machine Shop and Foundry* (New York: Engineering Magazine, 1911).

18. Julian K. Miller, "Quality Control Programs at Reo Reduces Costs," *Automotive Industries* 101 (September 1949): 32. On the obfuscation of authority, see also Edwards, *Contested Terrain*, 115–117.

19. Arnold and Faurote, *Ford Methods*, 42. On the relationship between bureaucracy and the requirement of predictability in enterprises with large amounts of fixed capital, see Max Weber, *Economy and Society*, 1091, 1095.

20. E. M. Hopkins, "Advantages of Centralized Employment," *The Annals of the American Academy of Political and Social Science* 71 (May 1917): 2.

21. Norman G. Shidle, "What Makes Labor Policy Successful?" *Automotive Industries* 43 (November 1920): 970. See also Allen Sinsheimer, "Keeping Men at Their Jobs," *The Automobile* 36 (March 1917): 524; Body Fisher, "Methods of Reducing Labor Turnover," 16–18.

22. William Chalmers, "Labor in the Automobile Industry" (Ph.D. diss., University of Wisconsin, 1932), 196; Sumner Slichter, *Turnover of Factory Labor*, 416.

23. This account of the early Ford Employment Department is drawn from the following sources: Arnold and Faurote, *Ford Methods*, 43–58; Lee,

"Profit Sharing," 300–301; O. J. Abell, "Labor Classified on a Skill-Wages Basis," *Iron Age* 93 (January 1914): 48–51; George Bundy, "Work of the Employment Department of the Ford Motor Company," in U.S., Bureau of Labor Statistics, *Proceedings of the Employment Managers' Conference*, Bulletin no. 196, 63–71; Henry Ford's testimony before the U.S., Congress, Senate, Commission on Industrial Relations, *Final Report and Testimony*, 64th Congress, 1st session, Senate Document no. 415, vol. 7 (Washington, D.C.: Government Printing Office, 1916): 7628–7631; H. Dubreuil, *Robots or Men?* (New York: Harper, 1930), 20–23.

24. Norman G. Shidle, "How an Effective Employment Department is Being Developed," *Automotive Industries* 43 (August 1920): 370–373; idem, "Effective Time Study Methods Increase Individual Production," *Automotive Industries* 43 (August 1920): 421–424; "Increasing the Rate of Pay," *Automotive Industries* 42 (March 1920): 725; Boyd Fisher, "How to Reduce Labor Turnover," *The Annals of the American Academy of Political and Social Science* 71 (May 1917): 12–13.

25. "Hiring and Separation Methods in American Factories," *Monthly Labor Review* 35 (November 1932): 1005–1017. For corroborating evidence, see Chalmers, "Labor in Autos," 194–198.

26. On the bureaucratization of worker discipline, see the following articles from *Automotive Industries*: Norman G. Shidle, "Reducing the Labor Turnover by Developing the Individual," 42 (April 1920): 1015–1017; Harry Tipper, "An Industrial Relations Policy that Makes Production Costs Less," 47 (September 1922): 473–476; "The Employment Department," 39 (September 1918): 469.

27. On the different authority structure of more skilled, varied work, see Touraine, *L'Evolution du travail*, 153; Ely Chinoy, *Automobile Workers and the American Dream* (Boston: Beacon Press, 1955), 72–73; Charles R. Walker, Robert H. Guest, and Arthur N. Turner, *The Foreman on the Assembly Line* (Cambridge, Mass.: Harvard University Press, 1956), 29–30, 74–75, 139–145.

28. Weber, *Economy and Society*, 987.

29. Allan Nevins and Frank E. Hill, *Ford: Expansion and Challenge, 1915–1933* (New York: Scribner's Sons, 1957), 514–524; Sward, *Legend of Ford*, 77–80; Marquis, *Henry Ford*, 139–145; "Efficiency Greater as Trade Slackens," *Automotive Industries* 43 (August 1920): 436.

30. Fountain, *Union Guy*, 41.

31. U.S., National Recovery Administration Research and Planing Division, *Preliminary Report on Study of Regularization of Employment and Improvement of Labor Conditions in the Automobile Industry* (Washington, D.C.: National Recovery Administration, 1935), Summary, 51. See also Claude E. Hoffman, *Sitdown in Anderson* (Detroit: Wayne State University Press, 1968), 18–21; Stanley, "Interrelationships," 160–161.

32. Allan Nevins and Frank E. Hill, *Ford: Decline and Rebirth, 1933–1962* (New York: Scribner's Sons, 1962), 47–48, 150–154, 230–239; Sward, *Legend of Ford*, 291–342; Carl Raushenbush, *Fordism* (New York: League for Industrial Democracy, 1937), 6–18; National Recovery Administration, *Preliminary*

Report on Auto Industry, Summary, 48–51, Exhibit 19, 9–11; James D. Hill, *A Brief History of the Labor Movement of Studebaker* (South Bend, Ind.: Studebaker Local No. 5, UAW-CIO, 1953), 11; Irving Howe and B. J. Widick, *The UAW and Walter Reuther* (New York: Random House, 1949), 29–31; John W. Anderson, "How I Became a Part of the Labor Movement," in *Rank and File*, ed. Alice and Staughton Lynd (Boston: Beacon Press, 1973), 47–54; Sidney Fine, *Sit-Down* (Ann Arbor: University of Michigan Press, 1969), 37–41; idem, *The Automobile Under the Blue Eagle* (Ann Arbor: University of Michigan Press, 1963), 152–154.

33. R. R. Lutz, *The Metal Trades* (Cleveland: Survey Committee of the Cleveland Foundation, 1916), 35–36.

34. National Labor Relations Board decision quoted in General Motors Corporation, *History of the Movement to Organize Foremen in the Automotive Industry, December 1938–May 1945* (Detroit: General Motors Corporation, 1945), 64–65.

35. Ibid.

36. Chalmers, "Labor in Autos," 160.

37. Walker and Guest, *Man on Assembly Line*, 99.

38. GMC, *History of the Movement*; Chrysler Corporation, *Pattern for Strikes* (Detroit: Chrysler Corporation, 1944).

39. GMC, *History of the Movement*, 23, 34–54; Chrysler Corp., *Pattern for Strikes*, 18–21.

40. GMC, *History of the Movement*, 82–92; Alfred P. Sloan, *My Years With General Motors* (Garden City, N.Y.: Doubleday, 1964), 391–392; Nevins and Hill, *Ford: Decline*, 337.

CHAPTER 10

1. This Marxist conceptualization of wages is based on the work of Ernest Mandel. See his Introduction to Karl Marx, *Capital*, vol. 1 (New York: Vintage Books, 1977), 66–73; *Marxist Economic Theory* (New York: Monthly Review Press, 1970), 143–148; *Late Capitalism* (London: Verso, 1978), 147–158.
The value of labor power is determined not only by the standard of living, but also by the value of the commodities making up the standard. Thus, even though the standard package of commodities remains the same, the value of labor power may rise and fall with the productivity of labor producing them.

2. On the rising tide of working-class social and political power during this period, see, for example, Richard Edwards, *Contested Terrain* (New York: Basic Books, 1979), 48–71.

3. Allan Nevins and Frank E. Hill, *Ford: The Times, the Man, the Company* (New York: Scribner's Sons, 1954), 528–532; Charles Sorensen, *My Forty Years with Ford* (New York: Collier, 1956), 133; Henry Ford, *My Life and Work* (London: Heinemann, 1923), 125; Samuel M. Levin, "Ford Profit Sharing, 1914–1920: I. The Growth of the Plan," *Personnel Journal* 6 (August 1927): 76.

4. Nevins and Hill, *Ford*, 532–534; Sorensen, *My Forty Years*, 131–136; Stephen Meyer III, *The Five Dollar Day* (Albany: State University of New York Press, 1981), 108–109.

5. Ford's statement in *New York Times*, January 9, 1914, quoted in Meyer, *Five Dollar Day*, 118; Ford pamphlet quoted in Meyer, *Five Dollar Day*, 118; Ford statement to editor of *Dearborn Independent* quoted in Levin, "Ford Profit Sharing," 77.

6. Henry Ford's testimony before the U.S., Congress, Commission on Industrial Relations, *Final Report and Testimony*, 64th Congress, 1st session, Senate Document no. 415, vol. 7 (Washington, D.C.: Government Printing Office, 1916): 7629.

7. Samuel Marquis, *Henry Ford: An Interpretation* (Boston: Little, Brown, 1923), 149–151.

8. John R. Lee, "The So-Called Profit Sharing System in the Ford Plant," *The Annals of the American Academy of Political and Social Science* 65 (May 1916): 302.

9. Ford, *My Life*, 128.

10. Antonio Gramsci, *Selections from the Prison Notebooks* (New York: International Publishers, 1971), 302.

11. Ibid., 303.

12. Ford, *Moving Forward* (London: Heinemann, 1931), 87.

13. Gramsci, *Prison Notebooks*, 304–305.

14. Nevins and Hill, *Ford*, 551–556; Allan Nevins and Frank E. Hill, *Ford: Expansion and Challenge, 1915–1933* (New York: Scribner's Sons, 1957), 332–338; Levin, "Ford Profit Sharing," 301–307; Keith Sward, *The Legend of Henry Ford* (New York: Rinehart, 1948), 59–60; Boris Emmet, *Profit Sharing in the United States*, U.S., Bureau of Labor Statistics Bulletin no. 208 (Washington, D.C.: Government Printing Office, 1917), 97–106; Meyer, *Five Dollar Day*, 123–147.

15. On working-class and immigrant cultures and their challenge to industrial capitalism, see E. P. Thompson, "Time, Work-Discipline, and Industiral Capitalism," *Past and Present* 38 (1967): 56–97; Meyer, *Five Dollar Day*, 67–94; Herbert Gutman, *Work, Culture, and Society in Industrializing America* (New York: Vintage Books, 1977); David Montgomery, *Workers' Control in America* (Cambridge: Cambridge University Press, 1979).

16. C. J. Shower, "Guiding the Workman's Personal Expenditures," *Automotive Industries* 38 (March 1918): 539.

17. Emmet, *Profit Sharing*, 115, 117; Ford's testimony, U.S., Commission on Industrial Relations, *Final Report and Testimony*, 7628; Ford, *My Life*, 129–130; Lee, "Profit Sharing," 308; "Bank Accounts of Ford Employees Gain 30% in 6½ Months," *Automotive Industries* 31 (October 1914): 683–685.

18. Nevins and Hill, *Ford*, 549. On the effects of the plan on worker morale, see also Nevins and Hill, *Ford: Expansion*, 335–336; Marquis, *Henry Ford*, 98; Sward, *Legend of Ford*, 60; Meyer, *Five Dollar Day*, 142–143.

19. Statistics on the effects of the plan are from Emmet, *Profit Sharing*, 117–119; moral effects of the plan come from Nevins and Hill, *Ford: Expansion*, 339.

20. Horace L. Arnold and Fay L. Faurote, *Ford Methods and the Ford Shops* (New York: Arno Press, 1972), 328.

21. Nevins and Hill, *Ford*, 542–544, 550–551.

22. Sward, *Legend of Ford*, 57.

23. "Bank Accounts of Ford Employees," 685; Ford's testimony, U.S., Commission on Industrial Relations, *Final Report and Testimony*, 7628; Emmet, *Profit Sharing*, 116.

24. Ford, *My Life*, 147. On the increased labor costs during 1914, see Nevins and Hill, *Ford*, 548.

25. "Production Incentives," *Automotive Industries* 53 (July 1925): 27. See also Harry Tipper, "Production Costs More Important Than Wage Rates," *Automotive Industries* 47 (October 1922): 782–783; idem, "The True Relation Between Wages and Unit Cost," *Automotive Industries* 45 (August 1921): 301–302.

26. Alfred P. Sloan, *Adventures of a White-Collar Man* (New York: Doubleday, Doran, 1941), 105.

27. Sidney Fine, *Sit-Down* (Ann Arbor: University of Michigan Press, 1969), 23. On these GM plans, see also Arthur Pound, *The Turning Wheel* (Garden City, N.Y.: Doubleday, Doran, 1934), 395–404.

28. J. Edward Schipper, "Willys Profit-Sharing Plan on 50–50 Basis," *Automotive Industries* 40 (May 1919): 944.

29. Albert R. Erskine, *History of the Studebaker Corporation* (South Bend, Ind.: Studebaker Corporation, 1924), 119–121.

30. William Chalmers, "Labor in the Automobile Industry" (Ph.D. diss., University of Wisconsin, 1932), 99–112; Joyce S. Peterson, "A Social History of Automobile Workers Before Unionization, 1900–1933" (Ph.D. diss., University of Wisconsin, 1976), 101; Emmet, *Profit Sharing*, 169.

31. Chalmers, "Labor in Autos," 100, 111–112; Spurgeon Bell, *Productivity, Wages, and National Income* (Washington, D.C.: Brookings Institution, 1940), 288–289; U.S., Bureau of Labor Statistics, *Productivity and Unit Labor Cost in Selected Manufacturing Industries, 1919–1940* (Washington, D.C.: Government Printing Office, 1942), 66.

32. Norman G. Shidle, "How the Industry Is Approaching the Wage Payment Problem," *Automotive Industries* 53 (September 1925): 496.

33. Harry Tipper, "Human Difficulties Predominate in Building Trade Wastes," *Automotive Industries* 45 (August 1921): 232.

34. Henry L. Gantt, *Gantt on Management* (New York: American Management Association, 1961), 97.

35. Robert Schrank, *Ten Thousand Working Days* (Cambridge, Mass.: MIT Press, 1978), 53–54.

36. Shidle, "How the Industry," 496–497.

37. Robert W. Dunn, *Labor and Automobiles* (New York: International Publishers, 1929), 129. On bonus systems, see also Norman G. Shidle, "Effective Time Study Methods Increase Individual Production," *Automotive Industries* 43 (August 1920): 421, 424; U.S., Bureau of Labor Statistics, *Wages and Hours of Labor in the the Motor Vehicle Industry: 1925*, Bulletin no. 438 (Washington, D.C.: Government Printing Office, 1927), 21–22; Shidle, "How the Industry," 496–497.

38. "Incentive Systems and Efficiency," *Automotive Industries* 55 (December 1926): 1017.

39. John Younger, "Production Progress—A Glimpse of the Future," *Automotive Industries* 57 (October 1927): 469; C. B. Gordy, "Measured Day Work Replaces Incentives in the Automobile Assembly Industry," *Society for the Advancement of Management Journal* 1 (November 1936): 162–163; U.S., Bureau of Labor Statistics, *Wages and Hours of Labor in the Motor-Vehicle Industry: 1928*, Bulletin no. 502 (Washington, D.C.: Government Printing Office, 1930), 16–21.

40. E. F. Roberts, "Departmental Bonus Systems Proves Successful Stimulate to Team Work," *Automotive Industries* 47 (July 1922): 187.

41. Philip S. Hanna, "Hudson Labor Plan Proves Profitable," *Wall Street Journal*, November 2, 1926. On group bonuses, see also Chalmers, "Labor in Autos," 124–125; Dunn, *Labor and Automobiles*, 130–132; Shidle, "How the Industry," 498; Ben Lifschitz, "Special Forms of Exploiting Workers," *Daily Worker*, August 22, 1928.

42. Athel F. Denham, "Day Rates Supplant Group Bonus," *Automotive Industries* 71 (December 1934): 702–703. See also C. B. Gordy, "Measured Day Work," 162–165; "Motor Industry Shifts Pay Plan," *Business Week* 67 (March 1935): 21; Joseph Geschelin, "Production Lines," *Automotive Industries* 71 (July 1934): 57.

43. U.S., Bureau of Labor Statistics, *Health and Recreation Activities in Industrial Establishments, 1926*, Bulletin no. 458 (Washington, D.C.: Government Printing Office, 1928), 68, 71. See also Robert M. Macdonald, *Collective Bargaining in the Automobile Industry* (New Haven, Conn.: Yale University Press, 1963), 58–59; Chalmers, "Labor in Autos," 96.

44. Boyd Fisher, "How to Reduce Labor Turnover," *The Annals of the American Academy of Political and Social Science* 71 (May 1917): 26; "General Electric Co. Creates Skilled Labor," *Automotive Industries* 37 (September 1917): 501. See also BLS, *Health and Recreation*, 18.

45. Harry Tipper, "Employee Stock Ownership Has Limited Value in Securing Labor Interest," *Automotive Industries* 46 (May 1922): 979.

46. Chalmers, "Labor in Autos," 92. See also Dunn, *Labor and Automobiles*, 149–157; Nevins and Hill, *Ford*, 347–349; Allen Sinsheimer, "A Family of 5000," *The Automobile* 36 (April 1917): 750.

47. O. J. Abell, "Labor Classified on a Skill-Wages Basis," *Iron Age* 93 (January 1914): 51.

48. "Debt and Efficiency," *The Automobile* 36 (May 1917): 862.

49. "Women in Industry," *Automotive Industries* 37 (September 1917): 554.

50. Allen Sinsheimer, "Benefits Count at Cadillac Factory," *The Automobile* 36 (March 1917): 653.

51. Forest E. Cardullo, "Industrial Betterment," *Machinery* 28 (November 1915): 171–201; BLS, *Health and Recreation*; "Drifting from Job to Job," *The Automobile* 36 (March 1917): 548.

52. C. J. Shower, "Reo's Clubhouse for Workers," *Automotive Industries* 38 (June 1918): 1136; "Athletics Increase Fisk Efficiency," *Automotive Industries* 37 (August 1917): 245.

53. Chalmers, "Labor in Autos," 95; U.S., Bureau of Labor Statistics, *Welfare Work for Employees in Industrial Establishments in the United States*, Bulletin no. 250 (Washington, D.C.: Government Printing Office, 1919), 82–89; idem, *Health and Recreation*, 39–50.

54. Dunn, *Labor and Automobiles*, 150.

55. Jean A. Flexner, "Selling the Company," *New Republic* 38 (April 1924): 174. On employee publications, see also Robert E. Park, "Make the House Organ a Human Interest Organ with a Punch," *Automotive Industries* 41 (September 1919): 572–574; Chalmers, "Labor in Autos," 97.

56. U.S., Bureau of Labor Statistics, *Characteristics of Company Unions, 1935*, Bulletin no. 634 (Washington, D.C.: Government Printing Office, 1938), 2.

57. Harry Tipper, "Experiments in Labor Organization Showing Results," *Automotive Industries* 46 (February 1922): 290; idem, "Co-ordination of Legislative and Operative Functions in Labor Essential to Success," *Automotive Industries* 39 (December 1918): 959.

58. Harry Tipper, "Social Surroundings Have Important Bearing on All Labor Questions," *Automotive Industries* 40 (February 1919): 367.

59. "Practical Welfare in Motor Factories," *The Automobile* 30 (May 1914): 959.

60. "Ford's Melting Pot," *The Automobile* 35 (October 1916): 611; Lee, "Profit Sharing," 305–306; Levin, "Ford Profit Sharing," 84–85; Nevins and Hill, *Ford*, 557–558; Meyer, *Five Dollar Day*, 156–162.

61. Fisher, "How to Reduce Labor Turnover," 15.

62. Dunn, *Labor and Automobiles*, 155; BLS, *Welfare Work*, 113. See also C. J. Shower, "Reo's Clubhouse," 136–138.

63. "Americanization from the Practical Point of View," *Automotive Industries* 39 (September 1918): 469.

64. Ibid.

65. Cardullo, "Industrial Betterment," 199; Fine, *Sit-Down*, 26–27; U.S., National Recovery Administration, Research and Planning Division, *Preliminary Report on Study of Regularization of Employment and Improvement of Labor Conditions in the Automobile Industry* (Washington, D.C.: National Recovery Administration, 1935), Exhibit 19, 15; Dunn, *Labor and Automobiles*, 153–154.

66. Erskine, *History of Studebaker*, 129.

67. BLS, *Welfare Work* 13, 119–121; idem, *Health and Recreation*, 86–87.

68. U.S., Bureau of Labor Statistics, *Wages and Hours of Labor in the Automobile Industry, 1922*, Bulletin no. 348 (Washington, D.C.: Government Printing Office, 1923), 10–12; Harry Tipper, "Fundamentals of Labor Question Ignored," *Automotive Industries* 46 (April 1922): 878. See also Tipper, "A Review of the Present Labor Situation," *Automotive Industries* 44 (January 1921): 182–183; idem, "What of the Safety and Personnel Departments?" *Automotive Industries* 44 (March 1921): 620–621; Chalmers, "Labor in Autos," 93–95.

69. "Industrial Plants Abandoning Many Personnel Activities," *Automotive Industries* 59 (August 1928): 163.

70. Harry Tipper, "Paying the Worker a Fair Reward on His Just Worth," *Automotive Industries* 42 (May 1920): 1175.

71. Ford's testimony, U.S., Commission of Industrial Relations, *Final Report and Testimony*, 7627; Emmet, *Profit Sharing*, 97.

72. On this last point, see Stuart D. Brandes, *American Welfare Capitalism, 1880–1940* (Chicago: University of Chicago Press, 1976), 81.

73. Edwards, *Contested Terrain*, 155–156; Sidney Fine, *The Automobile Under the Blue Eagle* (Ann Arbor: University of Michigan Press, 1963), 161.

CHAPTER 11

1. Harry Tipper, "Paying the Worker a Fair Reward on His Just Worth," *Automotive Industries* 42 (May 1920): 1174–1175.

2. Ibid.

3. O. J. Abell, "Labor Classified on a Skill-Wages Basis," *Iron Age* 93 (January 1914): 48–50; John R. Lee, "The So-Called Profit Sharing System in the Ford Plant," *The Annals of the American Academy of Political and Social Science* 65 (May 1916): 299–301; Boris Emmet, *Profit Sharing in the United States*, U.S., Bureau of Labor Statistics, Bulletin no. 208 (Washington, D.C.: Government Printing Office, 1917), 94–95; Allan Nevins and Frank E. Hill, *Ford: The Times, the Man, the Company* (New York: Scribner's Sons, 1954), 528–530.

4. Abell, "Labor Classified," 50.

5. Fred H. Colvin and Frank A. Stanley, *Running A Machine Shop* (New York: McGraw-Hill, 1948), 403.

6. Ibid., 407.

7. Abell, "Labor Classified," 50.

8. Samuel Levin, "The End of Ford Profit Sharing," *Personnel Journal* 6 (October 1927): 164–165.

9. Sumner H. Slichter, *The Turnover of Factory Labor* (New York: Appleton, 1919), 435–436.

10. Harry Tipper, "The Benefits of Details in Plant Management," *Automotive Industries* 42 (January 1920): 34–35.

11. Norman G. Shidle, "Reducing the Labor Turnover by Developing the Individual," *Automotive Industries* 42 (April 1920): 1017.

12. Ibid.

13. Ibid.

14. Norman G. Shidle, "Promoting from Within Organization Provides Incentive," *Automotive Industries* 43 (July 1920): 170; idem, "How an Effective Labor Policy Has Increased Production," *Automotive Industries* 45 (July 1921): 169.

15. "Promotion as an Incentive," *Automotive Industries* 47 (August 1922): 384; H. Dubreuil, *Robots or Men?* (New York: Harper, 1930), 171–173.

16. Fred A. Miller, "Aptitude Testing of Ford Workers," *Automotive Industries* 94 (May 1946): 28–29, 68.

17. Ibid. On latter efforts at divisive job structures, see also Joseph Ge-

schelin, "Production Lines," *Automotive Industries* 76 (April 1937): 598; E. L. Warner, "Training for National Defense," *Automotive Industries* 84 (March 1941): 319–322.

18. Robert M. Macdonald, *Collective Bargaining in the Automobile Industry* (New Haven, Conn.: Yale University Press, 1963), 108, 148, 195, 382; William McPherson, *Labor Relations in the Automobile Industry* (Washington, D.C.: Brookings Institution, 1940), 80.

19. For a general discussion of the determination of the occupational structure by class structure and class struggle, see Erik Olin Wright, "Class and Occupation," *Theory and Society* 9 (January 1980): 177–214. On early job classification systems, see Stephen Meyer III, *The Five Dollar Day* (Albany: State University of New York Press, 1981), 43–51.

20. David F. Noble, *American by Design* (New York: Knopf, 1977), 168–169, 180.

21. R. R. Lutz, *The Metal Trades* (Cleveland: Survey Committee of the Cleveland Foundation, 1916), 46; Daniel Nelson, *Managers and Workers* (Madison: University of Wisconsin Press, 1975), 95–98.

22. On the normative control of discretionary occupations and the function of education in furthering it, see Randall Collins, *The Credential Society* (New York: Academic Press, 1979), 22–32.

23. Mrs. Wilfred C. Leland, *Master of Precision: Henry L. Leland* (Detroit: Wayne State University Press, 1966), 124–125.

24. Edwin P. Norwood, *Ford Men and Methods* (Garden City, N.Y.: Doubleday, Doran, 1931), 185.

25. Ibid., 190. On the Henry Ford Trade School, see also Allan Nevins and Frank E. Hill, *Ford: Expansion and Challenge, 1915–1933* (New York: Scribner's Sons, 1957), 341–344.

26. Glen A. Niemeyer, *The Automobile Career of Ransom E. Olds* (East Lansing: Michigan State University Business Studies, 1963), 127–178; "Studebaker School for Employees," *The Automobile* 33 (September 1915): 581; Arthur Pound, *The Turning Wheel* (Garden City, N.Y.: Doubleday, Doran, 1934), 409–411.

27. On status groups, see Max Weber, *Economy and Society* (New York: Bedminster Press, 1968), 305–307, 932–938; Randall Collins, *Conflict Sociology* (New York: Academic Press, 1975), 38–39, 79–87.

28. Lutz, *Metal Trades*, 81, 95; U.S., Bureau of the Census, *Fourteenth Census of the United States: 1920*, vol. 4, "Population, Occupations" (Washington, D.C.: Government Printing Office, 1923): 346, 348; Nevins and Hill, *Ford*, 553; Irving Howe and B. J. Widick, *The UAW and Walter Reuther* (New York: Random House, 1949), 11–12.

29. Stanley Aronowitz, *False Promises* (New York: McGraw-Hill, 1973), 163–166; Nevins and Hill, *Ford*, 376; Roger Burlingame, *Backgrounds of Power* (New York: Scribner's Sons, 1949), 241–242; Peter Friedlander, *The Emergence of a UAW Local, 1936–1939* (Pittsburgh: University of Pittsburgh Press, 1975), 46.

30. Harry Tipper, "A Review of the Present Labor Situation," *Automotive Industries* 44 (January 1921): 182.

31. Herbert Hasking, "Just Among Ourselves," *Automotive Industries* 76 (January 1937): 77.

32. Friedlander, *Emergence of Local*, 15–16, 45–47, 66–69.

33. Quoted in Howe and Widick, *UAW and Reuther*, 209. On the distribution of blacks in the auto shops, see Lloyd H. Bailer, "The Negro Automobile Worker," *Journal of Political Economy* 51 (October 1943): 417–418; Herbert R. Northrup, *The Negro in the Automobile Industry* (Philadelphia: Industrial Research Unit, Wharton School of Finance and Commerce, University of Pennsylvania, 1968), 8–10; Robert W. Dunn, *Labor and Automobiles* (New York: International Publishers, 1929), 68–69.

34. U.S., Bureau of the Census, *Thirteenth Census of the United States: 1910*, vol. 4, "Population, Occupational Statistics" (Washington, D.C.: Government Printing Office, 1914): 338–339; idem, *Fourteenth Census: 1920*, vol. 4, "Population, Occupations": 346–349; idem, *Fifteenth Census of the United States: 1930*, Population, vol. 5, "General Report on Occupations" (Washington, D.C.: Government Printing Office, 1933): 468–471; Bailer, "Negro Auto Worker," 417.

35. Bailer, "Negro Auto Worker," 419–420.

36. Ibid., 418–419; Northrup, *Negro in Auto Industry*, 12–15.

37. See, e.g., Wyndham Mortimer, *Organize! My Life as a Union Man* (Boston: Beacon Press, 1971), 259n.

38. Quoted in August Meier and Elliot Rudwick, *Black Detroit and the Rise of the UAW* (New York: Oxford University Press, 1979), 36. On black responses to the unionization drive, see also Howe and Widick, *UAW and Reuther*, 209–211; Bailer, "Negro Auto Worker," 422; and Lloyd H. Bailer, "The Automobile Unions and Negro Labor," *Political Science Quarterly* 59 (December 1944): 550–555.

39. Bailer, "Auto Unions," 553–554; Meier and Rudwick, *Black Detroit*, 61–71; Howe and Widick, *UAW and Reuther*, 212–213; Frank Marquart, *An Auto Worker's Journal* (University Park: Pennsylvania State University Press, 1975), 89.

40. Meier and Rudwick, *Black Detroit*, 13–14.

41. Ibid., 9–22; Howe and Widick, *UAW and Reuther*, 215–219; Keith Sward, *The Legend of Henry Ford* (New York: Rinehart, 1948), 324–327.

42. Meier and Rudwick, *Black Detroit*, 80. On the handbills distributed by Ford, see Christopher C. Alston, *Henry Ford and the Negro People* (n.d., n.p., National Negro Congress and the Michigan Negro Congress), 15.

43. Meier and Rudwick, *Black Detroit*, 82–102; Sward, *Legend of Ford*, 410–414; Bailer, "Auto Unions," 554–555; Allan Nevins and Frank E. Hill, *Ford: Decline and Rebirth, 1933–1962* (New York: Scribner's Sons, 1962), 160–163. Probably the only reason that the other major manufacturer, General Motors, did not resort to similarly racist attempts to break the UAW strike against it was that very few blacks were employed in its plants.

44. U.S., Bureau of Labor Statistics, *Wages and Hours of Labor in the Automobile Industry, 1922*, Bulletin no. 348 (Washington, D.C.: Government Printing Office, 1923), 2–3; idem, *Wages and Hours of Labor in the Motor-Vehicle Industry: 1928*, Bulletin no. 502 (Washington, D.C.: Government Printing Office,

1930), 1; idem, *Wage Structure of the Motor-Vehicle Industry*, Bulletin no. 706 (Washington, D.C.: Government Printing Office, 1942), 23–25, 38–39.

45. BLS, *Wages and Hours in Auto Industry, 1922*, 23–24. For male-female wage differentials on the same jobs, see also Dunn, *Labor and Automobiles*, 74–76.

46. For employer justifications of sexual discrimination, see the following articles from *Automotive Industries*: H. W. Allingam, "Should Use More Female Labor," 35 (November 1916): 816; "Solving the Problems of Female Labor in a Car Making Plant," 39 (July 1918): 57; Allen Sinsheimer, "Female Labor's Place in Automotive Industry," 37 (September 1917): 531; "Some Problems of Female Labor," 38 (June 1918): 1119; "Selection, Training and Supervision of Women Workers," 39 (August 1918): 318–321. For the industry's experiences with female labor during the war, see these *Automotive Industries* articles: "Women in the Drafting Room," 37 (July 1917): 79; "Female Labor in Industries," 38 (May 1918): 1011; "Relative Efficiency of Male and Female Operatives," 39 (September 1918): 537–540; "Women in Factories Satisfactory," 38 (May 1918): 924.

47. "Relative Efficiency of Male and Female Operatives," 539.

48. "Female Labor in Industries," 1011.

49. "British Industry Better Equipped," *The Automobile* 34 (March 1916): 531.

50. Dunn, *Labor and Automobiles*, 76–77; U.S., National Recovery Administration, Research and Planning Division, *Preliminary Report on Study of Regularization of Employment and Improvement of Labor Conditions in the Automobile Industry* (Washington, D.C.: National Recovery Administration, 1935), Exhibit 19, 18–19; Sidney Fine, *The Automobile Under the Blue Eagle* (Ann Arbor: University of Michigan Press, 1963), 52, 242; "Absenteeism Declining Slightly in Most War Production Plants," *Automotive Industries* 87 (December 1942): 56; Sward, *Legend of Ford*, 425.

CHAPTER 12

1. U.S., National Recovery Administration, Research and Planning Division, *Preliminary Report on Study of Regularization of Employment and Improvement of Labor Conditions in the Automobile Industry* (Washington, D.C.: National Recovery Administration, 1935), Exhibit 19, 9. See also Walter Galenson, *The CIO Challenge to the AFL* (Cambridge, Mass.: Harvard University Press, 1960), 133–134.

2. Sidney Fine, *Sit-Down* (Ann Arbor: University of Michigan Press, 1969), 55–56.

3. National Recovery Administration, *Preliminary Report on Auto Industry*, Exhibit 19, 16–18; Galenson, *CIO Challenge*, 127–128, 134; Fine, *Sit-Down*, 61; Marjorie T. Stanley, "The Interrelationships of Economic Forces and Labor Relations in the Automobile Industry" (Ph.D. diss., Indiana University, 1953), 390, 394–395; Keith Sward, *The Legend of Henry Ford* (New York: Rinehart, 1948), 349–356.

4. Fine, *Sit-Down*, 140; Peter Friedlander, *The Emergence of a UAW Local, 1936–1939* (Pittsburgh: University of Pittsburgh Press, 1975), 26, 121. It should be noted that Friedlander explains the crucial role of these welders by their cultural rather than their occupational position.

5. For this interpretation of the union movement, see William H. McPherson and Anthony Luchek, "Automobiles," in *How Collective Bargaining Works*, Twentieth Century Fund (New York: Twentieth Century Fund, 1942), 572, 589–590; Stanley, "Interrelationships," 379–395. For a discussion of the general principles behind this particular analysis, see Albert O. Hirschman, *Exit, Voice, and Loyalty* (Cambridge, Mass.: Harvard University Press, 1970).

6. The UAW organizer quoted is Henry Kraus, *The Many and the Few* (Los Angeles: Platin Press, 1947), 78–79. On the ease of reaching workers concentrated in large factories, see Sward, *Legend of Ford*, 397–398; Kraus, *Many and Few*, 45..

7. Kraus, *Many and Few*, 214.

8. Frederick H. Harbison and Robert Dubin, *Patterns of Union-Management Relations* (Chicago: Science Research Associates, 1947), 23.

9. Frank Marquart, *An Auto Worker's Journal* (University Park: Pennsylvania State University Press, 1975), 94.

10. Dodge worker quoted in Marquart, *Auto Worker's Journal*, 78. On strikes and work stoppages during these early years, see Stanley, "Interrelationships," 237; George Romney, "Why Manpower Limits the Automotive Industry's Output," *Automotive Industries* 92 (March 1, 1945): 74.

11. Galenson, *CIO Challenge*, 175–176; Stanley, "Interrelationships," 249–255, 325–326; Frederick H. Harbison, "The General Motors-United Auto Workers Agreement of 1950," *Journal of Political Economy* 58 (October 1950): 399: R. J. Thomas' testimony before the U.S., Congress, Senate, Temporary National Economic Committee, *Investigation of Concentration of Economic Power*, 76th Congress, 3rd session, Part 30: Technology and Concentration of Economic Power, Senate Library, vol. 656 (1940): 16369; Harbison and Dubin, *Patterns of Union-Management Relations*, 141, 160–166.

12. Harbison and Dubin, *Patterns of Union-Management Relations*, 80–81; William H. McPherson, *Labor Relations in the Automobile Industry* (Washington, D.C.: Brookings Institution, 1940): 51–54, 121–123; Fine, *Sit-Down*, 323–324.

13. Reeves quoted in "Hits Worker Attitude," *Automotive Industries* 77 (November 1937): 639, 703. See also Romney, "Why Manpower Limits Output," 74; "Union's Usurpation of Management and Its Threat to the War Effort," *Automotive Industries* 92 (April 1945): 17–19, 54–58.

14. McPherson, *Labor Relations*, 81–82, 94–97; McPherson and Luchek, "Automobiles," 611–614; Robert M. Macdonald, *Collective Bargaining in the Automobile Industry* (New Haven, Conn.: Yale University Press, 1963), 92–98, 108–131, 145–158.

15. McPherson, *Labor Relations*, 117–127; Harbison and Dubin, *Patterns of Union-Management Relations*, 77, 169–173; "Seniority in the Automobile Industry," *Monthly Labor Review* 59 (September 1944): 463–474.

16. On the efforts of the UAW in the area of racial discrimination, see Au-

gust Meier and Elliot Rudwick, *Black Detroit and the Rise of the UAW* (New York: Oxford University Press, 1979), 117–174; Lloyd H. Bailer, "The Automobile Unions and Negro Labor," *Political Science Quarterly* 59 (December 1944): 566–577; Irving Howe and B. J. Widick, *The UAW and Walter Reuther* (New York: Random House, 1949), 219–234; Herbert R. Northrup, *The Negro in the Automobile Industry* (Philadelphia: Industrial Research Unit, Wharton School of Finance and Commerce, University of Pennsylvania, 1969), 16–22. On the UAW and sexual discrimination, see Patricia C. Sexton, "A Feminist Union Perspective," in *Auto Work and Its Discontents*, ed. B. J. Widick (Baltimore: Johns Hopkins University Press, 1976), 18–33.

17. Frank Cormier and William J. Eaton, *Reuther* (Englewood Cliffs, N.J.: Prentice-Hall, 1970), 185–230; Howe and Widick, *UAW and Reuther*, 108–148; "Union's Usurpation of Management," 19; Leonard Westrate, "With Collective Bargaining Established Union's Next Step is Management Control," *Automotive Industries* 93 (December 1945): 17.

18. Jack Stieber, *Governing the UAW* (New York: Wiley, 1962), 3–6.

19. Julian Chase, "Has Unionism Anything to Sell Us?" *Automotive Industries* 82 (January 1940): 47–58.

20. Quoted in William Serrin, *The Company and the Union* (New York: Knopf, 1973), 154.

21. Knudsen quoted in "Knudsen Reiterates GM Stand on UAW," *Automotive Industries* 77 (July 1937): 103.

22. For a history of this struggle over discipline, see the following *Automotive Industries* articles: "UAW Promises 'No Wildcat Strikes,'" 77 (August 1937): 169; "UAW Growing More Conciliatory," 78 (January 1938): 93–94, 101; "UAW Board Assumes Disciplinary Control over 'Wildcat' Strikes," 78 (May 1938): 649, 652–653. Note that Nelson Lichtenstein holds that the Executive Board did not assume full power over discipline of wildcat strikers until February 1944. See his *Labor's War at Home: The CIO in World War II* (Cambridge: Cambridge University Press, 1982), 190.

23. See the following articles in *Automotive Industries*: "UAW-CIO Seeks Corporation-Wide Stabilization Agreement," 89 (August 1953): 50; "Stepped Up Rate of Induction Causes New Manpower Problems," 90 (April 1944): 50; Leonard Westrate, "Let's Have Some Responsibility on the Union's Side," 94 (January 1946): 17, 96; "Reo and Murray Settlements Fix Union Responsibilities," 97 (September 1947): 23.

24. McPherson and Luchek, "Automobiles," 603–604; McPherson, *Labor Relations*, 48–50; "Ford's Partner," *Business Week* 79 (June 1941): 40.

25. Harbison and Dubin, *Patterns of Union-Management Relations*, 85; UAW steward quoted in Marquart, *Auto Worker's Journal*, 96. On the bureaucratization of the grievance procedure, see also Howe and Widick, *UAW and Reuther*, 238–243.

26. Harbison and Dubin, *Patterns of Union-Management Relations*, 41–44; Stieber, *Governing UAW*, 45–47, 98–101.

27. Stieber, *Governing UAW*, 21–36.

28. Henry Ford II, "Human Engineering Necessary for Further Mass Production Progress," *Automotive Industries* 94 (January 1946): 74.

29. "Ford's Partner," 42.

30. Ibid., 40–42.

31. McPherson, *Labor Relations*, 116.

32. McPherson and Luchek, "Automobiles," 596. For the National War Labor Board's ruling, see Nelson Lichtenstein, *Labor's War at Home*, 78–81.

33. Martin Glaberman, *Wartime Strikes* (Detroit: Bewick Editions, 1980), 1–15; Lichtenstein, *Labor's War at Home*, chapters 6 and 10. The emphasis on the structural constraint of union activity is drawn from Stanley Aronowitz, *False Promises* (New York: McGraw-Hill, 1973), 214–263.

34. Lichtenstein, *Labor's War at Home*, 178–202.

35. Harbison and Dubin, *Patterns of Union-Management Relations*, 113.

36. Macdonald, *Collective Bargaining*, 10–14, 347–355.

37. General Motors Corporation, *History of the Movement to Organize Foremen in the Automobile Industry, December 1938–May 1945* (Detroit: General Motors Corporation, 1945), 9. For similar clauses in other contracts, see Harvey Swados, "The UAW—Over the Top or Over the Hill," *Dissent* (Autumn 1963): 325.

38. 1950 GM-UAW contract quoted in "Treaty of Detroit," *Fortune* 42 (July 1950): 54.

39. Alfred P. Sloan, *My Years With General Motors* (Garden City, N.Y.: Doubleday, 1964), 402.

40. Maurice D. Kilbridge, "The Effort Bargain in Industrial Society," *Journal of Business* 33 (January 1960): 13; Harbison and Dubin, *Patterns of Union-Management Relations*, 135–136, 160–162; Stanley, "Interrelationships," 349–352; Thomas, TNEC Testimony, 16369; Local No. 2, UAW-CIO and the Murray Corporation of America, *Production Standards from Time Study Analysis* (Detroit: UAW-Murray, 1942), vii–viii; Frank Marquart, "The Auto Worker," *Voices of Dissent* (New York: Grove Press, 1958), 145.

41. Macdonald, *Collective Bargaining*, 90.

42. McPherson, *Labor Relations*, 81–82, 94–97; McPherson and Luchek, "Automobiles," 611–612; Macdonald, *Collective Bargaining*, 108–131.

43. McPherson, *Labor Relations*, 80–81.

44. Sloan, *My Years*, 400–401. See also Macdonald, *Collective Bargaining*, 159–180.

45. McPherson, *Labor Relations*, 125–127; Harbison and Dubin, *Patterns of Union-Management Relations*, 169–173; "Seniority in the Automobile Industry," 463–474.

46. Macdonald, *Collective Bargaining*, 204–205.

47. Ely Chinoy, *Automobile Workers and the American Dream* (Boston: Beacon Press, 1955), 39–40; McPherson, *Labor Relations*, 117–118; Harbison and Dubin, *Patterns of Union-Management Relations*, 77; "Seniority in the Automobile Industry," 464.

48. Chinoy, *Auto Workers*, 20.

49. Robert Guest, "Work Careers and Aspirations of Automobile Workers," in *Labor and Trade Unionism*, ed. Walter Galenson and S. M. Lipset (New York: Wiley, 1960), 320–322. See also Robert Blauner, *Alienation and Freedom* (Chicago: University of Chicago Press, 1964), 112–113; E. F. Shelley and Company, *Climbing the Job Ladder* (New York: E. F. Shelley and Company, 1970), 41–55.

50. McPherson, *Labor Relations*, 145.

51. Bailer, "Auto Unions," 563–565.

52. Meier and Rudwick, *Black Detroit*, 117–174; Bailer, "Auto Unions," 566–577; Howe and Widick, *UAW and Reuther*, 219–234; Northrup, *Negro in Auto Industry*, 16–22.

53. Meier and Rudick, *Black Detroit*, 165–172; B. J. Widick, *Detroit: City of Race and Class Violence* (Chicago: Quadrangle, 1972), 97–98; Howe and Widick, *UAW and Reuther*, 219–222.

54. Meier and Rudick, *Black Detroit*, 214–215; Northrup, *Negro in Auto Industry*, 31–39, 55; B. J. Widick, "Black Workers: Double Discontents," in *Auto Work and Its Discontents*, ed. B. J. Widick (Baltimore: Johns Hopkins University Press, 1976), 56–67.

55. Macdonald, *Collective Bargaining*, 108–109; R. J. Thomas, President, UAW-CIO, "Automobile Unionism, 1943," Report submitted to the 1943 Convention of the UAW-CIO (October 1943), 80, 92; Sexton, "A Feminist Union Perspective," 18–33.

56. "Union's Usurpation of Management," 19.

57. GM ad quoted in Howe and Widick, *UAW and Reuther*, 135.

58. Westrate, "With Collective Bargaining Established," 17.

59. Cormier and Eaton, *Reuther*, 185–230; Howe and Widick, *UAW and Reuther*, 108–148. For an account placing this struggle in the broader social and political context of postwar America, see Lichtenstein, *Labor's War at Home*, Chapter 11.

EPILOGUE

1. The philosphical basis of this discussion can be found in Karl Marx, "Economic and Philosophical Manuscripts," in *Karl Marx: Early Writings*, ed. Tom Bottomore (New York: McGraw-Hill, 1963), 63–219; idem, *Grundrisse* (New York: Vintage Books, 1973), 610–613, 704–712; Georg Lukács, *The Ontology of Social Being*, 3 vols. (London: Merlin Press, 1978–1980).

2. Daniel Zwerdling, *Workplace Democracy* (New York: Harper & Row, 1980), 19–29; David Noble, *Forces of Production* (New York: Knopf, 1984), 256–323. Some of these results of the GE Pilot Program are judgments made by Noble, since managers made few systematic attempts at evaluation. For a careful study of the effects of workers' control in a public industry, see Juan G. Espinosa and Andrew S. Zimbalist, *Economic Democracy: Workers' Participation in Chilean Industry, 1970–1973* (New York: Academic Press, 1978).

3. General Foods employee quoted in Zwerdling, *Workplace Democracy*, 28.

4. Noble, *Forces of Production*, 318.

Index

Index